Vajrakīlaya

Vajrakīlaya

A Complete Guide with Experiential Instructions

Practicing Deity Yoga in the Age of Strife

KYABJE GARCHEN RINPOCHE

Translated and compiled by Ari Kiev

SNOW LION

SNOW LION
An imprint of Shambhala Publications, Inc.
2129 13th Street
Boulder, Colorado 80302
www.shambhala.com

9 8 7 6 5 4 3 2

Printed in the United States of America

Shambhala Publications makes every effort to print on acid-free, recycled paper.

Snow Lion is distributed worldwide by
Penguin Random House, Inc., and its subsidiaries.

LIBRARY OF CONGRESS CATALOGING-IN-PUBLICATION DATA
Names: Rinpoche, Garchen, author. | Kiev, Ari, translator, editor.
Title: Vajrakīlaya: a complete guide with experiential instructions / Kyabje Garchen Rinpoche; translated and compiled by Ari Kiev.
Description: First edition. | Boulder, Colorado: Snow Lion, [2022] | Includes bibliographical references and index.
Identifiers: LCCN 2020027637 | ISBN 9781611809053 (trade paperback)
Subjects: LCSH: Vajrakīlaya (Buddhist deity) | Meditation—Buddhism. | Buddhist mantras.
Classification: LCC BQ4890.V33 R56 2021 | DDC 294.3/4435—dc23
LC record available at https://lccn.loc.gov/2020027637

Contents

Preface ix
Note to Practitioners xi
Translator's Introduction xiii
Text Conventions xix

PART ONE
Spiritual and Historical Context

1 Approaching These Teachings 3
The Deity 3
The Guru 11
My Personal Connection with the Practice 15
The Vajrakīla Lineage 17
The Vajrakīla Texts 20

2 Teachings Common to All Mantric Paths 29
Purpose 29
Worldly and Spiritual Systems 30
The Three Successive Paths 31
Autonomy 32
Gradual and Sudden Types 35
Ripening Empowerment 37
The Secrecy of Secret Mantra 39
Earlier and Latter Mantric Systems 43
Deity Yoga 45
Benefits of Mantra Recitation 74

PART TWO

Experiential Instructions on the Practice of Vajrakīla

3 Lineage Supplication Instructions 87
Introduction 87
Lineage Masters 88
View, Meditation, and Conduct 88
Mandala Deities 102
The Four Kīlas 103
The Four Māras 131
The Eight Qualities and Four Activities 140

4 Practice Manual Instructions 143
Refuge and Bodhicitta 143
Setting the Boundaries 157
The Disclosure 158
Consecrating the Offerings 161
Introduction to the Stages of Development 164
Visualizing the Immeasurable Palace 164
Visualizing the Deity 170
Invoking and Merging with the Wisdom Deities 205
Paying Homage 212
Making Offerings 213
Offering Praise 218
The Recitation of the Charm 219
Approach and Accomplishment 224
Offering the Charm 266
Subsequent Rites 268
Gathering In 271
Dedication 276
The Prayer of Auspiciousness 277
Summary of Deity Yoga 283

5 White Torma Offering Instructions 287

6 Kīla Consecration Instructions 291
The Implement, the Material Kīla 291
Aspects of the Implement According to the Tantras 295
Consecrating the Implement 296
Meaning of the Words of the Text 298

7 Bringing Down Blessings Instructions 309
The Material Mandala 310
Visualization and Meditation 312

8 Petition Instructions 319

9 Feast Offering, Restoration, and Repelling Instructions 323
Meaning and Purpose of the Gaṇacakra 323
Making Offerings 325
Ritual Practice of the Gaṇacakra 327
The Restoration 328
Drawing In 331
Liberation 332
Repelling 341
Gaṇacakra Offerings 342
The Gaṇacakra in Daily Activities 345

10 Taking Up Accomplishments Instructions 347

11 Practical Applications of the Instructions 355
Carrying Retreat Experience into Daily Life 355
Visualizing the Deity 358
Mantra Recitation 359
Antidoting Afflictions and Self-Grasping 362
The Guru 365
Maintaining the Samaya 366
Pure Perception 367
Benefiting Beings 369
Concluding Points 370
Dedication 372

PART THREE

Liturgical Source Texts

12 Lineage Supplication 377

13 Practice Manual 381

14 White Torma Offering 393

15 Kīla Consecration 395

16 Bringing Down Blessings 401

17 Petition 403

18 Feast Offering, Restoration, and Repelling 405

19 Taking Up Accomplishments 415

Notes 417
Quoted and Referenced Texts 427
Bibliography 429
Index 433
About the Author 479

Preface

For some years, I have been sharing at Dharma centers whatever knowledge I have about the practice of Vajrakīla. With rejoicing, I offer thanks to the Tara Foundation for having collected these instructions and provided for their assembly, allowing Ari-ma to translate and arrange them.

On account of my inferior intellect and meager study, I certainly lack the refined exposition capable of rousing delight in the learned. Even so, Vajrakumāra is the chief personal deity of my paternal ancestors. Likewise, since successive generations at Gar Monastery have practiced Vajrakumāra accomplishment retreats and since his routine *pūjas* came to be important there, I have relied on him as the destined deity with whom I have had an auspicious connection for lifetimes through karma and aspirations.

As I have had the good fortune to practice Vajrakumāra even from the time I was small, herein I have related whatever I could—with nothing but the intent to benefit others—based on the certainty associated with his felt blessing and on the slight experience I have gained. If masters of the learned who have a broad knowledge of sutra and tantra should opine on developing the good and rooting out the faults of these teachings, I will be most grateful.

With love and affection,
Könchog Gyaltsen, holder of the Garchen name
Translated by Ari Kiev

The Commitment Being, Vajrakīla

Note to Practitioners

It is taught that after cultivating precious *bodhicitta* and training in the progressive stages of the path, one can enter the door of the Secret Mantric Vajra Vehicle—first receiving empowerment, then transmission, and finally practice instructions. This mode of spiritual development is fundamentally relational in its approach; it depends on the human connection between guru and disciple. Indeed, this is how Garchen Rinpoche and countless other realized lineage masters were gradually initiated into the mantric path. Now, as ever, practitioners who aspire to become like them would do well to emulate their approach to the teachings.

Because Garchen Rinpoche's actions are shaped by both extreme love and extreme pragmatism, they can sometimes be unorthodox and difficult to fathom. Ever cognizant of how fleeting human life is and how rare the conditions are to meet with and receive the sublime Dharma, Rinpoche fulfills without delay the wishes of those who approach him with interest. He offers lovingly and in good faith that which he has received.

Rinpoche has often spoken of his firm commitment to not investigate disciples' good and bad qualities or spiritual histories. Only the buddhas can know an individual's karma and fitness to receive any teaching. In this regard, maintaining unwavering trust in the sources of refuge, Dharma guardians, and the workings of causality, Garchen Rinpoche considers a person's interest in and access to the Dharma sufficient indications of his or her karmic connection.

Because this manual includes secret teachings, I asked Rinpoche about the threshold for readership. He responded with the following words: "It is said that compassionately looking with a long-range view on the future time of dregs, the buddhas taught mantric sadhanas. Today that future has become manifest. Right now is the time of dregs, in which secret mantra teachings must be propagated. As Guru Padma prophesied, 'When the wicked era burns like fire, the potent force of secret mantra will blaze forth.'"[1]

Because of this and because it is far better to receive the buddhas' teachings than not, Rinpoche has offered the instructions herein without demanding prerequisites like empowerment. Maintaining pure perception without investigating or discriminating, he has given the Dharma with an open hand. This is one of the ways in which he upholds his *samaya*, or commitment, to beings and to the sources of refuge.

It is not Rinpoche's style to offer the Buddhadharma in a prescriptive way, establishing and policing rules of conduct. Instead, disciples must mature beyond outwardly imposed dictates, taking personal responsibility for our own actions, which are to be tempered by love and heedfulness of cause and effect. Thus, how we approach, receive, and integrate Rinpoche's instructions—how we uphold our own samaya—is a matter we must ultimately determine for ourselves.

Translator's Introduction

Although I had not fully understood it at the time, it seems the catastrophic terrorist attacks of September 2001 in New York City and Virginia became the final condition for the seeds of Kyabje Garchen Rinpoche's personal practice of enlightened body, Mañjuśrī Yamāntaka, and enlightened activity, Vajrakīla, to begin ripening in the New World. In February 2002, the Yamāntaka group accomplishment retreat, or *drubpa*, was established at Garchen Buddhist Institute (GBI) in Arizona. In the summer of that same year, even before a Vajrakīla retreat had begun at GBI, Rinpoche offered his first instructions in America on the practice of the *yidam*, or favored personal deity, of his current and former lives. It seems to me those instructions were bestowed with great aspirations for the practice yet to come, as Rinpoche repeatedly used phrases like "in the future when you actually practice Vajrakīla..." I came to regard those teachings as a sort of treasure, concealed in 2002 to be rediscovered after we as a sangha had collectively matured a bit.

The teachings gathered in this book were titled *Vajrakīlaya: Profound Points of Practice** by Rinpoche himself. They reflect an eighteen-year span of instructions to Western audiences, from the time Garchen Rinpoche was aged sixty-six through eighty-four. Although they utilized Vajrakīla texts as a basis, many of the pith

**Rdo rje phur pa'i nyams len gyi zab gnad.* Although Tibetan texts commonly use "Dorje Phurba" and "Vajrakīlaya" interchangeably when referring to the deity by name, throughout the present work the simple Sanskrit without any case markings, "Vajrakīla," has been adopted for use.

instructions contained herein are universally applicable to any deity yoga.

They were offered to different groups and individuals via different interpreters in different settings and times. They also include personal instructions Rinpoche gave in response to questions I had posed when translating and editing the practice texts on which this book is based. Since the guru's outer expressions of body and voice continually change to suit arising conditions, I hope this collection of teachings from diverse perspectives can provide readers a panoramic view of Vajra Youth (Vajrakumāra) beloved by Garchen Rinpoche.

As for the guru's mind, disciples often do not conceive of the master as a practitioner whose understanding of a text and relationship to the yidam and to sentient ones are in constant evolution. This is one of the many ways we dehumanize gurus through our idealized archetypal projections of them. In any case, looking at the arc of these teachings, I observed shifts in how Rinpoche presented them over time. I believe these shifts were conditioned by personal growth and by his interactions with us—students who were asking questions in our own process of understanding and relating to the deity.

Garchen Rinpoche once told me someone had said of him that he was outwardly a *sādhaka* of Ārya Tārā, inwardly a sādhaka of Vajrakīla, and secretly a sādhaka of Yamāntaka. Of course, people say many things about the guru. Since this statement was one Rinpoche himself chose to repeat and since he is not one to spread meaningless gossip, I asked him how he felt about it. He responded, "I don't know so much about that point. But I can say that the stupa [that was designed by Rinpoche at GBI] has the outer form of an eight-spoked wheel, or *cakra*, which is symbolic of Ārya Tārā, the Wish-Granting Cakra. Inside, the upper and lower steel beams of the roof and walls are like the conjoined domes of the sky-iron sphere [of Vajrakīla's outer mandala]. Secretly, the four sides where the eyes are painted symbolize the four immeasurables [the four cakras] of Yamāntaka. The top ornament of the jewel in the lotus symbolizes the essence, bodhicitta." I suppose this is as close to an acceptance of another's assessment of Rinpoche's main practices as he may ever come.

As for the teachings, Rinpoche has been unapologetic about the fact that he has not received the academic training of a *khenpo* and that his instructions are based on understanding revealed through direct experience. Thus, when giving teachings, Rinpoche has consistently emphasized the textual passages that have been meaningful to him as a meditator. Although anyone can complicate even the simplest of teachings, I have been struck by Garchen Rinpoche's ability to make the most profound Dharma accessible to beings of diverse faculties. Despite this, there are occasions on which he has chosen to touch on certain topics without clarification or elaboration.

After having reviewed and translated the audio recordings, I tried my best to elicit teachings from Rinpoche to fill in perceived gaps. Sometimes when I sought further clarification, the lama readily offered it; other times, he seemed vexed by my attention to passages whose meaning he deemed self-evident or not particularly profound. In the process, Rinpoche repeatedly admonished me against conceptual elaboration and dualistic grasping at conventional meaning.

In the end, I came to regard those junctures at which the guru chose not to elaborate as teachings in themselves. There is no instruction more profound than one whose meaning is revealed from within through reflection, practice, and—most importantly—through blessing. I hope that readers will regard whatever lacunae they may find in this book as points yet to be revealed through further study, contemplation, and actual practice.

I believe that in spite of its shortcomings by academic standards, this collection of teachings is endowed with singular beauty and meaning by the flawless motivation of Rinpoche's love for beings. That love has manifested as fearless generosity in sharing the fruits of a lifetime of yogic practice. While assembling these instructions, I often felt as though I were observing an intricate dissection—

watching Rinpoche wield a fine scalpel to cut away layers of diaphanous tissue to reveal progressively deeper layers of meaning. For me, the process had a quality of rawness and nakedness that turned the mind back on itself. I pray it can offer readers a similar experiential view.

Finally, I accept full karmic responsibility for any errors herein. Since Lama Garchen Rinpoche covered a broad range of mantric topics in these Vajrakīla instructions, if readers should find the content of some of them questionable or not credible, they may set doubtful points aside with neither acceptance nor rejection, supplicating the Three Jewels to reveal the meaning from within. Alternatively, they may seek clarifications from accomplished masters. Otherwise, please blame me—focusing on my lack of competence as a translator, my poor understanding of the Buddhadharma, my deliberate misrepresentation of the guru's sublime intent, or any other such narrative. One should strive to preserve one's connection with the authentic *vajra* master at all costs, since he or she is the source of every deity and every accomplishment. Now that humankind is fully entrenched in the age of the five dregs, it is essential that practitioners find a foothold for pure perception somewhere.

May all who have come into contact with Garchen Rinpoche, this text, or the waves that emanate therefrom swiftly accomplish existence-*vajrakīla*.

Acknowledgments

It is said that when enlightenment is attained, one awakens into the truth that everyone had been a buddha all along and that oneself alone had been the sole holdout—the last one to cross over. Reflecting on the gratitude I feel to friends who have generously shared their knowledge and skills to bring this created *nirmāṇakāya* into being, it makes sense to me that such a perception could someday dawn.

I offer sincere thanks to Kyabje Garchen Rinpoche for lovingly sharing the bounty of his experience and realization and to the senior disciple who conceived of and sought Rinpoche's approval for this project. In addition, I wish to acknowledge the spiritual centers that shared images and video and audio recordings of the teachings that make up this work: Garchen Dharma Institute in Taiwan, Drikung Kagyü Ratna Shri in Moscow, Drikung Treloknath Ling in Spain, Gar Drolma Buddhist Center in Ohio, Garchen Buddhist Institute in Arizona, and White Lotus Buddhist Center in New York.

Khenpo Yeshi in the United States and Khanpo Rigzin Wangyal in Ladakh have always supported my understanding through being generous with their knowledge. Frank Jen created the illustrations for the book—images that give form to his connection with the guru and deity. Piet Bernhard shared from the extensive collection of photographs he has taken of Garchen Rinpoche.

I am indebted to Michaela Perkounigg for refining the draft manuscript with care. Furthermore, I am most grateful to the staff at Shambhala Publications—to Casey Kemp and Anna Wolcott Johnson, who rectified my writing to the limit my stubbornness would allow, and to the design team who have created a work of beauty.

Finally, I wish to acknowledge the support of Tara Foundation, under whose auspices I was privileged to delve deeply into the guru's teachings.

To them and to all the other friends, artists, scholars, and practitioners who contributed to this work in ways great and small, I express my deepest appreciation. May their merits not be exhausted until samsara itself has collapsed.

Ari-ma

Prescott, Arizona
August 2020

Text Conventions

Throughout the commentary, Garchen Rinpoche quotes numerous other texts and pith instructions from great masters. Such quotations accord with the extensive memorization that was integral to the lama's education in childhood. Their inclusion is a living testament to the centuries-old oral tradition to which Garchen Rinpoche belongs. As the instructions herein are a work of blessing-transmission and not a work of scholarship, I have not sought out academic-style citations of the quotes given by the guru. Rather, I have transcribed the master's words as he spoke them and translated them to the best of my abilities. Transliterations of those Tibetan quotes may be found in the endnotes.

In addition, this book has been laid out according to the general structure of the practice manual and supplemental texts known as *An Unelaborate Liturgical Arrangement of the Method for Accomplishing Vajrakīla*, arranged by the 8th Garchen Trülku, Könchog Gyaltsen. All quotations from the main text are set in sans serif font and drawn from this sadhana, which is found in part 3 of this book.

Tibetan texts are rich in interlinear notes, which provide practice and recitation instructions, detail certain visualizations, and are used as headings, colophons, and the like. They are almost never meant for recitation. In this text, such notes are in italics.

Italics are also used to indicate all initial uses of non-English terminology incorporated into the translation (e.g., *khaṭvāṅga*). Foreign terms that have already been absorbed into the English lexicon (e.g., mantra) appear without diacritical marks and are not italicized. Mantras and seed syllables (e.g., HŪṂ̊) are rendered in small caps.

Since the liturgical texts were translated for English-language recitation with traditional melodies, they bear a unique feature. Specifically, ties appearing underneath letters (as in "Glorious") indicate that all the encompassed letters should be pronounced as one syllable rather than two.

When arranging the original Tibetan texts, Jamgön Kongtrül included only the practice manual, petition, and feast offering as a complete liturgy. In part three of this book, all material not present in these three source texts is indicated by a vertical khaṭvāṅga icon in the left margin. Such supplemental material has been included for one of two reasons: either because it is so commonly understood to be required recitation that it goes without stating among lamas or because it was added by Lama Garchen Rinpoche as a supplement for the purpose of the secret accomplishment retreat.

PART ONE

Spiritual and Historical Context

CHAPTER 1

Approaching These Teachings

The Deity

I remember when I was a child looking at a mind accomplishment sadhana that had been brought forth by the Drigung treasure revealer Lho Nüden Dorje. In the colophon of the text was a quote of Guru Rinpoche, which said that even though there were three thousand different mind accomplishment sadhanas in the land of Tibet, this one mind sadhana was the innermost quintessence in which all the others were subsumed. Thus, I felt extremely fortunate to have encountered the one practice that was the most profound of all.

Later, I saw another Guru Rinpoche mind accomplishment sadhana from one of the New Treasure (*tersar*) traditions. Imagine my dismay when I read therein that Guru Rinpoche had claimed it was the innermost quintessence of all mind accomplishment practices! At that juncture, I gave rise to some doubts, because it seemed as though Guru Rinpoche had lied. I thought, "This one says it is the innermost essence. That one says it is the innermost essence. What's up with this? Which one is the actual quintessence?" The more I studied, the more I began to see such claims everywhere. In the treasure, or *terma*, tradition, sadhanas of all deities say this sort of thing.

Gradually, as I gained experience, I came to understand my confusion as a sign of self-grasping. Those with dualistic grasping at self and other will think, "Since this sadhana and deity are the most profound, no other sadhana or deity can be equally profound."

However, the actual meaning of Guru Rinpoche's words is that even though there exist three thousand different mind accomplishment practices in Tibet, if a person engages this particular one—whichever one it may be—it is one and the same with all the others. No other practice is more powerful or efficacious. Thus, there is no deception in Guru Rinpoche's holy speech.

Similarly, when the qualities and history of a sadhana have been explained, someone with dualistic grasping will think, "Wow! If this deity is accomplished, these kinds of amazing signs and wonders arise! This yidam is really extraordinary!" However, those with experience will know that so many things—both accurate and inaccurate—are related in the explanatory tantras and historical narratives. It is best not to have a literal belief in all these things. It is said that deity accomplishment depends on one's manner of practicing, not on the deity him- or herself. The principal point is not the Dharma that is practiced; rather, it is the mode of practicing. The degree to which the deity can care for one through his or her potency, force, and attributes is determined by the degree to which one makes effort in cultivating the view, meditation, and conduct.

One who exerted unsurpassed efforts in practice was Lord Milarepa. In the story of his life and liberation, he promised that even when his body had passed away, he would not die. Rather, his mind would continue to abide within the five elements, which pervade the container and contents. As such, he would be present at all times for anyone who supplicated him anywhere. In this way, every buddha is all-pervasive. Despite this, ordinary beings like us remain unaware of their presence. In order to increase awareness, the enlightened ones have taught various sadhanas. The term *sadhana* means "method of accomplishment." No one other than *siddhas* and enlightened buddhas could give rise to such extraordinary methods, which are the basis of all the buddhas' attainments. Just as one must use a churn to extract butter from milk, so too must one utilize sadhana to extract the essence of the deities who naturally pervade the five elements.

In this regard, in the verse on deity yoga in his *Song on Realizing*

Fivefold Mahāmudrā, Protector Jigten Sumgön refers to the body as the "king of divine forms."[1] Since all sentient beings possess the mind of buddha nature—the very cause of the buddhas—they are like the buddhas' children. Among them, one who obtains a precious human body endowed with freedoms and connections is exceedingly rare. When such a person gives rise to love, compassion, and bodhicitta, it is like the coronation of a monarch. Whoever receives the bodhisattva's vow is like a king ascending the throne. Further, for practitioners of secret mantra, the pure deity with ornaments and implements is the natural physical expression of bodhicitta.

It is said that the deity one aspires to accomplish is endowed with four attributes: (1) knowing wisdom, (2) loving compassion, (3) the activities of enlightened action, and (4) the able force that grants protection.

Having first given rise to foremost bodhicitta, the deity has come to recognize the circumstantial and adventitious confusion of every sentient being of the six classes of wayfarers. He or she has realized our experiences of suffering—so acute and seemingly real—to be the illusory appearances of delusion. Thus, the first attribute of the deity to be accomplished is the knowing wisdom that recognizes all sentient ones' karma and propensities, which come from the confusion of grasping at that which is selfless as though it were a self.

Knowing the adventitious confusion that has arisen from self-cherishing and afflictions, the deity has succeeded in tearing down self-grasping through apprehending love and affection. Thus, his or her second attribute manifests as loving compassion. In this regard, in the Vajrakīla literature there is a very meaningful prayer of blessing that says, "All the buddhas regard beings with a mind of great love."[2] When its meaning has been understood, each word of this line has the power and ability to calm one's mind. The deity's heart essence is love and affection. The very nature of his or her past pledge to sentient ones is loving-kindness. Each time one gives rise to it—even if one is only focused on a tiny insect—it becomes a cause for accomplishing the supreme *siddhi*. When one repeatedly cultivates an actual feeling of love and affection, that itself is the deity's mind. That is the accomplishment of the yidam. On this basis, immeasurable great love can arise. This essential point must be understood.

For these reasons, the measure of one's capacity as a practitioner is the foundation that is bodhicitta—the altruistic intention to attain enlightenment for the benefit of beings. Regardless of whether or not the development-stage visualizations appear clearly, when one has the ground of bodhicitta, it will cause all of one's virtuous practices of body and speech to become like gold.

With practice, of course, signs of accomplishment will become manifest. One will come to see the deity as clearly as if he or she were physically present. One will naturally achieve common siddhis like clairvoyance, magical mantric powers, and the like. However, if one fails to retain the basis that is bodhicitta, rather than being golden, such accomplishments will be like brass, as there will be obstacles to the attainment of the ultimate ground. Many such faults are described in the scriptures. This is why I constantly teach about bodhicitta. If students can take to heart this one point, in the future, wisdom will increase and whatever is practiced will bear meaningful fruit.

It is said in the scriptures that Protector Jigten Sumgön obtained the assurance of bodhicitta. Because I was curious about this, long ago when I requested the bodhisattva's vow from Drubpön Chime Dorje, one of the masters from Gar Monastery, I asked him, "What does it mean to gain the assurance of bodhicitta?" He responded, "Those who wish to offer the bodhisattva's vow should consider: If having given the vow to someone, that person should later come threatening to take your life, what would you do? If you were to give rise to anger, the wish to retaliate, or even the intention to sever ties with that person, it would cause the vow to be lost. One who could fall under the power of anger in that circumstance has no basis for bestowing the vow."

The meaning of this is that no matter how much harm sentient beings may do, one must patiently guard the mind against anger and resentment, recognizing beings' harmful conduct to be reflections of their ignorance. For this purpose, one especially needs to be able to give rise to even greater love and compassion. As it says in *The Thirty-Seven Practices of Bodhisattvas*, "Even if a person I've dearly nurtured like my own child should view me as an enemy, to love him even more, as a mother does a child stricken with illness, is the bodhisattvas' practice."[3]

To have the assurance that you would give rise to compassion even for someone attempting to murder you is what is required to offer the bodhisattvas' vow. Thus, the vow is not easy to bestow. In order to grant it to others, one must truly possess it. One who lacks patience cannot bestow the vow on anyone, as he or she would only be mouthing empty words. It is important to consider this well. These words from *The Thirty-Seven Practices* are extremely important, as they signify the degree of patience that is required to bestow the vow. This is what it means to gain the assurance of bodhicitta on the conventional level. In addition, on the ultimate level, anyone who aspires to realize emptiness must be capable of maintaining it through compassion.

One may wish to obtain the fruition that is factual bodhicitta; however, if one fails to appropriately cultivate the conventional fictional bodhicitta that is love and compassion, one will only give rise to mere understanding of factual bodhicitta, lacking realization. If conventional fictional bodhicitta is not developed, even though one may comprehend emptiness or selflessness, the fruition will not be attained. The Tibetan term for an enlightened one is *sanggye*—*sang* meaning "cleared away" and *gye* meaning "expanded." So, although the self may be cleared away (*sang*), if one lacks bodhicitta, the fact of expansion (*gye*) will not become manifest. This is why the learned say, "Though selflessness may be realized, one is yet unenlightened."[4] Because of this, the most important point for practitioners is to accumulate conventional bodhicitta again and again.

Whichever deity one practices, his or her power derives exclusively from bodhicitta. So it is with the deity Vajrakīla. If one practices this yidam from among all the other yidams, one can attain buddhahood in a single lifetime. Those who wish to accomplish this deity must give rise to the mind set on supreme enlightenment and must sustain it until the rank of manifest, complete buddhahood has been attained.

The third attribute of the deity manifests as the activities of enlightened action. From among the buddhas' three *kāyas*, these activities come forth from the nirmāṇakāyas, who appear among sentient ones and pervade each of the six realms. They engage the activities that empty samsara from its depths, draining the vast ocean of suffering. In this way, the enlightened activities of the buddhas' emanations appear on the illusory, fictional level.

Finally, the fourth attribute is the able force that grants protection. The Three Jewels safeguard those who seek refuge and cultivate trust in Buddha, Dharma, and Sangha. From the moment one takes the vow of refuge and throughout all future lifetimes until enlightenment is attained, the Three Jewels will protect one. As a manifestation of the Three Jewels, the deity is endowed with the capability of protecting and caring for beings.

Although we often use the terms *deity* and *yidam* interchangeably, one should understand that the yidam is whichever deity to whom one has committed one's body, speech, and mind. That is to say, in the practice of deity yoga, one commits or binds (*dam*) one's mind (*yi*) to an ongoing cultivation of the practice. This term for "commitment" is etymologically related to the word *samaya* (*damtsig*).

There is also the yidam with whom one has been karmically connected in past lifetimes. For example, some people naturally gravitate toward a certain deity. Whenever they see his or her image, they feel interest and spontaneous joy. These are signs of karmic connection from former lives.

Each yidam has extensive and abbreviated tantras, sadhanas, and sets of activities. All yidams are endowed with equal blessing and potency. Even though there exist many thousands of deities, the heart—the very life force—of every one of them is the nondual unity of emptiness and compassion. Even if one meditates on one hundred thousand different deity forms, they all share this life force that is singular in nature. At the very basis, every deity is the same.

Thus, there is no point in creating a lot of distinctions, thinking, "My deity is most profound. Other deities cannot compare."

For example, in this world there are so many diverse people, each with different faces, bodies, and styles of clothing. But the buddha nature of their inner minds is singular. This nature, shared by buddhas and sentient beings alike, has but one basis. The only difference between buddhas and sentient ones is the scope of their love, compassion, and bodhicitta. This is the dividing line between buddhas and ordinary beings; however, there are no differences within the mind that is buddha nature.

Some practitioners, having become overwhelmed by the diversity of tantras and sadhanas, will ask, "Why can't there be just one deity and one mantra?" But this great diversity is necessary to meet the needs of various types of individuals with different dispositions. In general, although there are no superior or inferior deities, one will experience greater benefit from practicing the yidam deity of one's former lifetimes.

Regardless of which deity one practices, he or she is the essence that combines into one the mindstream of all the buddhas of the three times. Since sadhanas are the means whereby practitioners can accomplish deities, they present the overall qualities of the buddhas' mind. Even though there are different practice systems, they are all equally efficacious. Diverse abbreviated and extensive sadhanas are suited to different sorts of individuals with greater or lesser faculties. In the Vajrakīla literature, there are four different practice systems that suit four different types of people. There also exist various sadhanas of the four activities.

Depending on one's inclination, one may practice only one, any combination, or all four of them. Those who truly accomplish the deity become free of the ordinary concepts that label, categorize, or discriminate among divine beings. Thus, from the perspective of great accomplishment, there are no contradictions among whichever deities and sadhanas one practices.

Of course, there are differences in terms of deities' colors, ornaments, implements, and numbers of faces and limbs. When one is drawn to those outer appearances, it is simply a reflection of one's individual inclinations, interests, and past lives' connections. So, although practitioners have diverse individual preferences, there is no distinction whatsoever among different deities' power and force. The mind transmissions of all wisdom deities are the same.

Since this is so, those who claim there are differences among deities have made such judgments based on personal preferences. The reason they experience a particular deity as being more powerful is due to their karmic connection with that deity based on their training and meditation in former lives. So, for example, some will have great faith in and devotion to Guru Rinpoche, while others will say, "I have faith in Buddha Śākyamuni, but not in Guru Rinpoche." Such common appearances come from individuals' karmic imprints, but in actuality, the life force essence of Buddha Śākyamuni and Guru Rinpoche is one and the same. In fact, Guru Rinpoche was the emanation of the Bhagavan Buddha, having appeared for the difficult-to-subdue beings of this final time of dregs. He revealed the methods whereby afflictions need not be abandoned but rather could become the path itself. Thus, there is not the slightest difference between Buddha Śākyamuni and Guru Rinpoche. Not only that, but the mindstream of all the three times' buddhas is singular. Their bodhicitta is utterly immutable. Their aspiration that "every sentient one—mothers who equal space—have ease and ease's causes"[5] is unchanging.

Although every deity accomplishes all enlightened activities, it is good to consider a deity's primary activities. Some, like Vajrasattva, mainly display peaceful actions. Others, like Ratnasambhava, manifest enriching activity. According to the scriptures, Vajrakīla is principal among deities who dispel hindrances and obstructive forces. In particular, he is the great antidote to the afflictions of aversion and jealousy, the causes of all the sufferings of this worldly realm. Thus, although the mandala of Vajrakīla displays all the buddhas' activities, it particularly performs the destructive ones of suppression, burning, and casting. Those who do not understand this can become confused, thinking, "Yesterday, you prayed that all sentient ones have ease and happiness and be free of ill-being. Today, you engage practices to beat, cut, and slaughter them!" Even though ordinary beings give rise to such perceptions based on dualistic grasping, there is no need for doubt. Whatever actions one may engage through the four activities of pacification, enrichment, magnetization, and destruction, the bodhicitta underlying each of them is absolutely immutable.

It is said in the common development-stage texts that the root of both samsara and nirvana is the mind. If one recognizes the actual condition of the mind just as it is, whichever deity one practices, one will know that deity to be mind itself. The yidam is the guardian and protector of the mind. When one understands the qualities of the deity's knowledge, love, and capability, one will know him or her to be a changeless companion. It is through the yidam's steadfast friendship that one will become able to accomplish all the common and uncommon siddhis from now until the state of buddhahood is attained. Conversely, even though one may be diligent in deity yoga, if this point is not understood, one will end up practicing an independently existent, ordinary deity. This means that one will regard the deity as real and concrete, perceiving the yidam as no different from an ordinary being.

The Guru

Although there are many different lineages of empowerment, transmission, and sadhana, in the best case, a practitioner will recognize the mindstreams of every deity and the mind of the guru to be inseparable. Thus, if one wants to know the very root of secret mantra, it is, without a doubt, the guru. Although Lord Buddha appeared in the past, his current regent is truly the guru. It is the guru who bestows all the meaning of the buddhas' teachings. For this reason, one should place the guru at one's crown. His or her body is the Sangha; his or her speech, the Dharma; and his or her mind, the Buddha.

Furthermore, in the guru yoga of Jigten Sumgön, the root guru is said to be the embodiment of the Three Roots. That is the truth of the matter. The vajra master's body is the guru; his or her speech, the mandala of the yidam deity; and his or her mind, the *ḍākiṇī*, or skyfarer. The guru's speech is said to be the yidam, because it is through speech that one receives empowerment and transmission and is taught how to do a practice. That speech settles the point of many sutras and tantras through instructions about various deities, mantras, and development-stage yogas. Finally, the guru's mind is said to manifest as the Dharma guardians and the ḍākiṇī, or emptiness.

Here, it is important to note that for the sādhaka, the parallels to the Three Roots are different: the practitioner's body is the yidam; his or her speech is the ḍākiṇī and Dharma guardians; and his or her mind, the guru, the two types of bodhicitta. As for the speech aspect, it is through mantra recitation that the objectives of self and others are accomplished via the four activities and—in the context of Vajrakīla practice—the four *kīlas*. Each recited mantra transforms into the form of a deity. In this way, the recitation of mantra gives rise to ḍākiṇīs who stream forth and accomplish manifold activities. For example, if one recites a *māla* of *maṇi* mantra, one has sent forth a hundred divine forms who will work to bring about loving-kindness and compassion in the minds of sentient ones. Thus, the practitioner's speech is the ḍākiṇī. Finally, his or her mind is the guru, the view of actual truth that is nondual wisdom. In this way, the conception of the Three Roots is different in relation to the vajra master than in relation to the sādhaka.

The guru can also be understood in terms of the three kāyas. Ultimately, the guru's body is the nirmāṇakāya; his or her speech, the *saṁbhogakāya*; and mind, the *dharmakāya*. Thus, the guru is the one in whom the Three Jewels, Three Roots, and three kāyas are brought together. The guru who embodies such qualities is a suitable object of refuge. The one who goes for refuge, as well, is like a diamond in the rough, possessing the basis of all these same qualities. All sentient ones of the three spheres also share this same basis.

The embodied guru is the vajra master, the one who has accomplished the vajra of empty buddha nature. As such, he or she is able to reveal it to others. It is the vajra master who introduces the deity, the mantra, and the views of *mahāmudrā*, *dzogchen*, and the like by means of secret mantra empowerment. Thus, the precious vajra master teaches that which is adamantine. He or she introduces the vajra of mind.

It is said that the mind of the root guru is inseparable emptiness and compassion—the very life force of the deities. This is how the guru and yidam are related to the buddhas. If one can understand the play of the root guru's body, speech, mind, attributes, and activities, one will also understand a bit about the deity's identity.

Whenever one gains love, one gains a precious jewel. The Buddha is love. The guru is love. The Dharma is love. The yidam is love. If one relies on a guru, that reliance is based on one's mind. Gaining proximity to the guru's body is of no benefit, since it only brings many difficulties. The guru's speech is somewhat precious, as it is a vehicle through which meaning is understood. However, of chief importance is the guru's mind; that which must be attained by practitioners is the mind of the guru.

The Tibetan term for *guru* is *lama*. The scriptures say, "*La* stands for the soul (*la*) of all sentient ones. *Ma* stands for the mother (*ma*) of all sentient ones."[6] Here, the word *soul* means that the guru is an object of recollection and inspiration for beings. Because he or she loves sentient ones as a mother loves her child, beings are drawn to and inspired by the guru. For example, those who have discerning intelligence always bring to mind the Omniscient Victorious One—the Dalai Lama—and other realized gurus. It is because of such habits that fortunate ones are considered fortunate.

Even though sentient beings generally feel love for each other, because they are afflicted by self-grasping, their love is unstable. As soon as unfavorable conditions manifest, such love can vanish. Today, one has a close friend who is dear to one's heart. Tomorrow, if one argues with that person, he or she will become an enemy to whom one feels hostile. Not only that, but that being can remain an enemy even in future lifetimes if one's aversion and negativity are great.

In contrast, gurus are referred to as the "Noble Sangha" because they cultivate the altruistic mind based on impartial love for all sentient ones. By practicing patience, they respond to obstacles with equanimity, as is taught in *The Thirty-Seven Practices of Bodhisattvas*. Since bodhicitta is the basis for finally attaining the status of the buddhas, one must protect and preserve it at all costs.

In the context of both mahāmudrā and dzogchen, it is said that all attributes are brought together in the mind of the guru. Since there is no yidam without the guru, it is far more beneficial to practice guru yoga than to visualize the development stages of the deity. As it is said in many tantras, "Greater than visualizing ten million yidams' mandalas is to meditate once upon the guru."[7]

If this point is not well grasped, one can give rise to a perverted understanding, thinking, "It is so easy to recollect the guru. I always think of the guru, because I stay near him and can speak to him directly." But this is a mistaken notion. The outer guru is only the metaphorical guru. He or she is a nirmāṇakāya—an embodied emanation whose body, speech, and mind are manifestations of the Sangha, the true Dharma, and the Buddha. In actual fact, to meditate on the guru is to recollect the guru's mind, not his or her form. Thus, the thing to be revealed is the inner, ultimate, actual guru, who is one's own mind. The essence of one's mind is buddha nature. Whenever it is seen, one has seen the inner guru.

In this regard, in his instructions on four-kāya guru yoga known as *Devotion, the Life Force Yantra*, Protector Jigten Sumgön taught that when meditating on the guru as the nirmāṇakāya, one should imagine the guru in his or her embodied form. When meditating on the saṁbhogakāya, one should visualize the guru as the yidam. Then, when meditating on the dharmakāya, one should visualize the guru as the HŪṂ syllable. This extremely profound instruction illustrates that the inner guru, the dharmakāya, is inseparable from the HŪṂ syllable.

If this key point of the guru as the mind's nature is not habituated by meditating again and again, even though one may visualize many deities, they will be lifeless. Every deity's life force is the nondual union that is emptiness-compassion.

My Personal Connection with the Practice

In my case, through the power of karma and aspirations, I have been connected with Vajrakīla for lifetimes. As the personal deity of my paternal ancestors in this life, Vajrakīla was my first yidam. When I was between the ages of eleven and thirteen, my father and guru, Mase Sengge, introduced me to the approach mantra from the secret accomplishment retreat. This group retreat is referred to as *sangdrub* in Tibetan.

I have received the empowerment of Vajrakīla from the treasure of Ratna Lingpa several times. First, when I was very young, I received it, along with the oral transmission, from the Drigung Kagyü lama Könchog Tengye. He had been a disciple of the former Garchen Rinpoche, Trinle Yongkhyab, and had spent many years in retreat. As a child, I was required to recite the approach mantra one million times. During that period, I memorized *The Necklace of Sapphires*, the extensive sadhana text. Later, I received empowerment again from Siddha Chime Dorje, who bestowed the great empowerment of the Eight Sadhana Teachings following a monthlong great accomplishment retreat of the same. I also received Vajrakīla empowerment from a few other lamas such as Mahāsiddha Arig Tengye and Lama Sanggye Tendzin. Those are the lines of transmission through which I offer these teachings.

Garchen Monastery also has a great historical connection with this deity. One of the holy caves where Yeshe Tsogyal practiced Vajrakīla is located there. From early times until the present, the monastery has maintained the continuity of the great accomplishment retreats (*drubchen*) of the Eight Sadhana Teachings, which include Vajrakīla.

As a child, I found that the solitary practice of unfamiliar liturgies was entirely devoid of feeling. I only gave rise to great faith in the deity as the result of doing group accomplishment retreats. In this way, I came to appreciate the resplendent blessings of such retreats. So, in my thinking, it is good for sādhakas to participate in accomplishment retreats early in their training. Then, once one has done so, the understanding and experience gained in group retreats can be carried into one's personal practice.

From my childhood until now—first in Tibet and later in exile—I have continued to practice this deity. Even after 1958, when outer spiritual practices were disrupted, I consistently cultivated the practice in secrecy. Since I have maintained the approach and accomplishment of Vajrakīla and Yamāntaka ever since I was a child, I became habituated to them and understood their efficacy at an early age. Thus, I feel a great connection to them. Even though I have not had the opportunity to do extensive practices in this life, I have direct feeling and personal experience of the heart-potency and precious blessings of the practice lineage. As a result, I have gained the path of emancipation for this and future lifetimes. Thus, I have been fed and nourished by this lineage.

It is on this basis that I teach the practices of these deities to others. Due to my own experience with them and my students' love for me, my students have also grown fond of and drawn close to them. In this way, just as my gurus bestowed on me the transmission of the blessing-practice lineage, I have also offered it to my followers.

In this lifetime, I have not received much in the way of commentary or instructions on Vajrakīla. Instead, my understanding of the inner meaning has been gained through repeated experience of group secret accomplishment retreats. As I'm a bit of a fool, without any learning, I don't know how to explain this practice as other great masters can. However, like a patient who has experienced healing from taking medicine, I can now recommend that medicine to others who are sick. Thus, based on the bit of Vajrakīla practice I have done, I can offer some introduction that comes from knowledge gained through inner experience. In order to further your understanding of the practice, it is good if you can also receive instruction from other masters and study commentaries written by learned khenpos and lamas. Beyond that, in order to gain experience and realization, consistent practice is indispensable.

What is important is that one maintain the practice of a deity. Having done so, one can bestow upon others—based on one's own experience of the deity's blessing—whichever deity one has accomplished. This is the meaning of the blessing-practice lineage. For this reason, it is essential to draw near to the deity, gaining direct, personal experience for the benefit of self and others.

Some years ago, I was involved in a serious car accident when traveling to participate in an accomplishment retreat in Tibet. After that, I received a phone call from a government official saying that since I could die at any time when traveling here and there, I must name a regent. In response, I told him that although I have been given an important name, in truth, I am just traveling around eating up the offerings of food given by faithful ones. Therefore, there is no need for me to have a successor. Since I have done what I could to benefit beings, I will have no regrets whenever I die. These words come from true confidence and conviction. Even though I have named no successor or spiritual heir, disciples should have no doubt about the continuity of the transmission after my passing. My mind will always be present for those who have faith and love. Anyone who accomplishes the Dharma I have taught will become my heart child. This is the nature of the lineage of practice and blessing.

In this regard, the practice of accomplishment retreats is now continuing in the West, where the conditions are very different than in their place of origin. Even so, since these retreats are of such great benefit, practitioners are truly fortunate to be able to participate in them. Thus, one should give rise to a similar conviction that even if one were to die during the retreat, one would be free of regret.

The Vajrakīla Lineage

This Vajrakīla transmission has appeared in the present through a few different routes. The transmission was first bestowed in the land of Akaniṣṭha by Great Glorious Vajrakumāra to a circle of the buddhas of the four family lines by means of the self-resounding *dharmatā*. Vajrakīla's method of accomplishment is one of the Eight Sadhana Teachings that were practiced by the eight great knowledge holders (*vidyādharas*) of India.

In general, there are four types of transmission lineages. The first of these, the mind lineage of the victorious ones, refers to teachings that were directly transmitted from one enlightened mind to another, without the need of speech. The second, the sign lineage of knowledge holders, refers to the teachings that were transmitted in their entirety through mere gestures and signals. Third, the hearing lineage of individuals was transmitted by one master speaking words that were heard by disciples. Some traditions, like the Sakya, have had an unbroken transmission of this hearing lineage from the time of Guru Rinpoche until the present. Finally, the aspirational lineage of treasure teachings originated with Guru Rinpoche and Yeshe Tsogyal. In order that their blessing-transmission not decline, Guru Rinpoche spoke the words of the teachings to Yeshe Tsogyal, who transcribed them and concealed the written works as treasures to be revealed in the future by destined ones.

How did Guru Rinpoche himself obtain the Vajrakīla transmission? After having received from Buddhaguhya monastic ordination and the name Śākyamitra, he requested the empowerment of Vajrakīla from Khenpo Prabhahasti of Zahor. Even though Guru Rinpoche was an emanation of Lord Buddha, his request was denied by Master Prabhahasti, who said, "You lack the fortune for me to bestow the empowerment on you. You should ask the ḍākiṇī Sukhacakra in Sosaling Charnel Ground."

When Guru Rinpoche went to Sosaling in India and requested empowerment, through her miraculous powers, Sukhacakra transformed him into a HŪṂ syllable and swallowed him. Then, over a period of days, she completely bestowed upon him the four empowerments from within her four places—crown, throat, heart, and secret center. Having received the empowerment of the four activities within her womb, he exited her body via her secret sign, becoming her son. In this way, the *bhikṣu* Śākyamitra came to be known as Padmasambhava, the Lotus-Born One. With these four miraculous empowerments from Sukhacakra, the entirety of lineage transmissions and pith instructions of the Vajrakīla tantras was granted to him.

Through emerging from the ḍākiṇī's *bhaga*, Guru Rinpoche gained the ultimate, precious life empowerment. How is it possible for a monk, a holder of the *vinaya*, to receive such empowerment? From the perspective of ultimate factual truth, the secret mantra samaya is indistinguishable from the great vinaya. As for the bhikṣu's ordination, there is ultimately no vow to hold, nor is there anyone who holds the vow. When those who have been introduced to *rigpa* engage the actual practice, it is as Jigme Lingpa said: "As long as aware knowing does not lose its autonomy, nothing more than this is needed."[8] When aware knowing is in possession of its autonomy, afflictions dawn as primordial awareness. Thus, the vow to be held is the liberation of afflictions. The holder of the vow is discerning intelligence.

In this way, not only is the outer discipline of the bhikṣu's vows of individual liberation maintained, but the inner commitments of the Bodhisattva and Secret Mantric Vehicles are simultaneously preserved. This is mahāmudrā—"the single key point of the three vows, the conduct" taught by Protector Jigten Sumgön. Therein, the three successive paths are combined into one. The objective that is the life empowerment is an extraordinary key point of secret mantra. This is how the outer mantric sign empowerment that was bestowed on the Lotus-Born should be understood.

For the purpose of giving introduction, the guru can expediently regard the disciple who receives empowerment as being like his or her child. Since the guru ultimately understands his or her own mind, the disciple's mind, and the buddhas' mind to be one and the same, this perception is not tainted by dualistic grasping. In this way, the fourth empowerment, the precious word empowerment, is bestowed.

There are many historical accounts of how the inconceivably great master Guru Rinpoche accomplished the four types of siddhi: (1)

the siddhi of a knowledge holder with mastery of life, (2) the siddhi of the four activities, (3) the siddhi of the underground treasure, and (4) the supreme siddhi of mahāmudrā. This final attainment occurred at Yangleshö in Nepal, where he practiced Vajrakīla in retreat, becoming utterly victorious over obstacles and fully accomplishing the yidam deity.

Thereafter, he demonstrated the deity's activities by dispelling obstacles, gathering disciples, and performing vast enlightened actions. After Guru Padmasambhava introduced the Eight Sadhana Teachings to Tibet, Tibetan knowledge holders accomplished the great purposes, qualities, and abilities of the eight *herukas* through practicing his instructions. In this way, the eight great knowledge holders of Tibet manifested and became transmitters of their respective practice lineages.

Among them, Yeshe Tsogyal attained the common and supreme siddhis and became the principal transmitter of the Vajrakīla tantras and sadhanas. Her liberation story documents numerous miracles attributed to her, such as reviving the corpse of a young man and having a spring emerge from the spot where she had thrust her kīla (*phurba*) into stone. Such demonstrations are examples of the common siddhis—the peaceful, enriching, magnetizing, and destructive displays that accomplish the benefit of self and others. Finally, Lady Tsogyal achieved the uncommon siddhi—the royal seat of dharmakaya, the status of the buddhas, which is inseparable from the realization of mahāmudrā. Those who really want to engage this practice of Vajrakīla must study the accounts of her life and liberation.

The Vajrakīla Texts

It is said that when Guru Rinpoche left India for Tibet, two men were needed to bear the load of the palm-leaf volumes of Vajrakīla literature alone. Those writings came to symbolize Guru Rinpoche's subjugation of all obstructive forces. The Vajrakīla literature is like the wish-granting tree, as it allows one to accomplish the common and supreme—whatever one could desire. Guru Rinpoche himself arranged in Tibetan language each of the Vajrakīla sections of tantra—thirty-six different subdivisions in all. Fully complete and lacking nothing, this literature is likened to a vast tree. It includes four rootlike tantra sections, eight trunk-like sections, and ten branch-like smaller tantras. Further, there are three leaflike tantra sections, four beautifying flowerlike sections, four tantra sections like ripened fruits, and three tantras that complete anything missing.

How do such manifold, great qualities as these emerge? The *tathāgatagarbha*, the essence of those arrived at suchness, is like a diamond. The all-encompassing activities of pacification, enrichment, magnetization, and destruction spontaneously emerge from the buddha nature, just like the many rainbow reflections that spring forth from a diamond in a ray of sunlight. This buddha nature—the kīla of primordial awareness-rigpa—is the root from which this vast collection of teachings has come forth.

This particular sadhana is said to be the heart quintessence of Vajrakīla. This means it is like the pure portion of Vajrakīla's heart-mind, without any extraneous taint. Nowadays, people compose written works based on the knowledge they have gained from study. The Vajrakīla literature is nothing at all like that. Rather, it has come into being through sādhakas' personal experience of the deity from their practice, accomplishment of siddhis, and nurturing a mind of affection for sentient ones. For those followers who would come in the future, Guru Rinpoche and Yeshe Tsogyal gave rise to a mind like that of a mother for her only child. The texts were composed with the intent to give sentient ones the means of accomplishing the fruition—siddhis like their own. Marking the texts with terma signs, they sealed them with their intent, definitively resolving the matter.

Guru Rinpoche taught that the treasures were not to be propagated during his era, but that they would come forth in the future, at times of great hardship. Thus, Yeshe Tsogyal was entrusted with the responsibility of concealing them for later discovery. Why would he give them to her? Due to her vast altruistic intent toward all beings, Yeshe Tsogyal was the destined guardian of the teachings of future generations. On the basis of her unparalleled commitment to benefit others, Guru Rinpoche gave her the entrustment. In the future, when beings would have coarse afflictions and the legions of *māras* would do extreme harm to all sentient ones, the treasures would be revealed. Thus, Lady Tsogyal concealed these Vajrakīla texts in the rocky crags of Kongpo.

Later, the great emanated treasure revealer Sanggye Lingpa invited these teachings out of their place of concealment. Because they came from underground, they were referred to as "earth treasures." They then passed through many spiritual generations—from treasure revealer to treasure disciples, to their disciples, and so on in an unbroken lineage. Those who practiced the teachings gained wondrous signs of accomplishment. There have been many keepers of these Vajrakīla treasures. For example, the text we are practicing is an amalgamation of the works of Sanggye Lingpa with a treasure revealed later by Ratna Lingpa.

Regarding these termas, Guru Rinpoche clearly apprehended the names, birthplaces and conditions, and specific attributes of those who would reveal each of his treasures in the future. These precise details are recorded in his prophecies. The destined beings named and described by him would naturally and spontaneously meet with these treasures. One should understand that such miracles occurred through the force of aspirations. Nowadays, we make short-term wishful prayers and then have a lot of doubts about whether or not they will actually be accomplished. However, there is no need for doubt. The aspirations of all the buddhas are without limit. They will not be exhausted until samsara has been emptied of sentient ones. If such vast and far-reaching aspirations as Guru Rinpoche's have been accomplished, one can believe that the aspirations one makes based on accumulated roots of virtue will also be fulfilled.

Precious treasures such as the Vajrakīla texts have come to be through aspirations. In their era, Guru Rinpoche and Yeshe Tsogyal concealed them as termas within rock. How is it even imaginable that they could have known the exact names and circumstances of treasure revealers who would appear so many generations in the future? If one really considers this, one cannot help but wonder at the extraordinarily amazing power of aspirations! Such is the lineage of blessing and practice to which we are heirs! The resplendent blessings of this transmission, which have been subsumed within one lineage holder after the next, rely first on empowerment, oral transmission, and experiential instructions and then on actual meditation practice.

As for instructions, the Vajrakīla teachings compiled here are based on the texts I assembled for students' practice and titled *An Unelaborate Liturgical Arrangement of the Method for Accomplishing Vajrakīla.*[9] Therein, the main text is the Ratna Lingpa practice manual. Although there exist oceans of brief and extensive Vajrakīla sadhanas, in my experience, most of the brief ones are not very clear or present only a small fraction of the vast scope of Vajrakīla practice. Even though the practice manual of Ratna Lingpa is only one among countless others, it has the good qualities of being clear, concise, and yet complete.

Reasons These Texts Were Selected

As I have benefited so much from secret accomplishment retreats in this life, I wished for my students to experience their blessing as well. However, in order to engage such retreats, it is necessary to complete a number of different activities, not all of which are included in Ratna Lingpa's concise practice manual alone. Since my students have great, devoted interest in secret mantra, I was obliged to provide them with the complete texts required for the secret accomplishment retreat in a concise form easy to recite. For this purpose and because it had been requested by a faithful student, I chose to supplement the original practice manual with a few additional texts. With a beneficial intent, I selected particularly meaningful texts that would support those who actually do the practice.*

*The concise practice manual used for the secret accomplishment retreat assumes readers are familiar with the extensive sadhana. Also, since Garchen Rinpoche's practice manual has been supplemented with some texts from the extensive sadhana,

Authorship, Origins, and Dates

The Ratna Lingpa practice manual came into being over many generations. The extensive Vajrakīla sadhana was composed by Sanggye Lingpa (1340–1396). Later, Ratna Lingpa (1403–1478) revealed the root terma text. Chagme Rāga Asya (1613–1678) then condensed Sanggye Lingpa's verses on the stages of development, composing an extremely abbreviated practice manual.

In arranging the practice manual we are using today, Jamgön Kongtrül Lodrö Thaye (a.k.a. Pema Garwang Tsal, a.k.a. Yönten Gyamtso, 1813–1899) combined the root terma text of Ratna Lingpa with the brief sadhana by Chagme Rāga Asya. An early English translation of this text was made by the Palyül lineage and titled *The Daily Practice of the Secret Attainment of the Unsurpassed Extremely Secret Vajrakīlaya Called "The Essence of the Play of Concerned Activity."* It was this translation that my students practiced before a versified translation became available.

As for the supplemental texts in the versified translation titled *An Unelaborate Liturgical Arrangement of the Method for Accomplishing Vajrakīla*, at the beginning I included a lineage supplication, composed by the Kagyü lama Jamgön Kongtrül. Seeing this, some may think, "Oh! Garchen Rinpoche must have replaced the lineage supplication from the Palyül text with this one because he's Kagyüpa!" There actually are people who are saying such things. But they are mistaken.

Each sadhana and ritual practice has its own uncommon enlightened intent, all of which can be subsumed within bodhicitta. For example, the practice of Mañjuśrī Yamāntaka has the extraordi-

---

the style of practice is inevitably an amalgamation of the two. When sādhakas understand the distinction between these two modes of practice, they can recite the concise sādhana alone or in conjunction with the supplemental practices as they wish. Likewise, they can visualize according to the methods of the practice manual or they can visualize the elaborate mandala while reading the words of the concise text. In order to distinguish between the two, all the supplemental material in part three of this book appears with a vertical khaṭvāṅga icon in the left margin.

nary intent that is the four cakras, which must be introduced to Yamāntaka practitioners. Vajrakīla, on the other hand, has the four kīlas. Not only that, but the entire Earlier System (Nyingma) has view, meditation, and conduct, which are expressed in the Vajrakīla lineage supplication as the fortress, the abyss, and the life force, respectively. Since the lineage supplication includes these and other aspects of enlightened intent particular to Vajrakīla, one who has understood its meaning will be able to comprehend the meanings of all the myriad Vajrakīla rituals and practices. It is for this reason that I chose to supplement the practice manual with this particular lineage supplication.

Jamgön Kongtrül also composed *The Consecration of the Material Kīla Mandala: The Development Stages of the Foremost Prince* and *The Māra-Subduing Secret Mantra Sanctuary*. Although the authorship of the other supplemental texts is uncertain, they have all been drawn from *The Great Treasury of Precious Termas*,[10] a compilation of Earlier System treasures and commentaries collected and assembled by Jamgön Kongtrül. Each of the supplemental texts was added because it offers a deeper understanding of the full scope of Vajrakīla practice. To deeply contemplate the meaning of these texts will be very efficacious for meditators.

English Verse Translations

Now, the buddhas' teachings have been flourishing in Western countries for many years. Due to merit and intelligence, fortunate Westerners have understood the qualities of the Buddhadharma and wish to practice it. In my thinking, the method or the approach to practice is extremely important, since it can nurture or hinder personal experience. It is only through actually engaging the practice that one can know firsthand the qualities of different methods.

According to my own experience, versified texts that conjoin words, meaning, melody, and music are very precious, since they cause the lineage blessing to enter one's mindstream. For this reason and because my students have extremely great faith, I have established the recitation of English verse translations in which the words and meaning are unified.

Now, many students have become well accustomed to the group accomplishment retreats of Kīla and Yamāntaka. Every secret mantra sadhana is a method of accomplishment whereby the deity becomes actually manifest in one's mindstream. One becomes matured, or ripened, through the deity's blessing reaching one's mind. Thus, the lineage supplication refers to the māra of the aggregates being liberated into the form of the ripened deity:

> The aggregates' māra, conquered, is
> freed into the ripened deity.

If one merely considers this sentence alone, the entire meaning will be understood. Through reciting the English verses again and again, the words, meaning, and melodies will become unified in one's mind. This is an important point.

In the West, the majority of sādhakas practice using only transliterated Tibetan. They say it is possible to read the prose translation silently while simultaneously verbalizing the transliteration. However, most people probably cannot do this. Because it is devoid of meaning, if one relies on transliteration alone, it will be difficult to attain the fruition during this human life. Indeed, one is unlikely to experience any benefit at all for many lifetimes into the future.

For example, if one reads a sadhana in transliterated Tibetan, it is like being fed a meal of grain alone. Of course, it is food. But what sort of sensation and nutrition does it give? If one practices using the meaning translation in prose, the meal becomes a bit more flavorful. But when the practice presents the meaning in verse and employs melodies, musical instruments, and so forth, it is like mixing grains with vegetables, oils, and seasonings prepared in different ways so that the meal becomes truly delicious and nourishing.

People may say that there are special blessings to be had from the recitation of Tibetan syllables. But the reality is that when the Tibetan lamas and monks pass away, it will make no sense for Western disciples to continue practicing in the Tibetan language without comprehension.

By using chantable English texts, disciples will be able to maintain this practice without outside support. When people can chant the words of the verse translation and simultaneously grasp the meaning in a language they understand, wisdom arises. Whatever secret mantra practice one does, the important point is to fathom its meaning. This is why we have undertaken the difficulties of translating the texts into English verse, learning the rituals, melodic chant, musical instruments, and the like.

Transmission

Before starting this practice, it is good to receive the reading transmission. While doing so, one should listen intently, neither reading nor taking notes. Keeping the mind in one-pointed meditation, one can look at a *thangka* or other image of the deity from time to time. Then, closing one's eyes, one should cause the deity's form to appear in the mind. After having received the transmission, it is good to read the translated text once with an open and relaxed mind, focusing on the inner meaning.

Although in Tibet reading transmissions are given in Tibetan, elsewhere it is suitable for them to be offered in other languages, such as English. Thus, one should request transmission from senior students who have already received transmission themselves.

CHAPTER 2

Teachings Common to All Mantric Paths

Purpose

Although the present purpose is to engage the practice of Vajrakīla, in general, whether one trains according to the Individual Liberation, Bodhisattva, or Mantric Vehicles, the aim of every Buddhist practice is to cultivate the two types of bodhicitta. The ultimate fruition is just this and nothing else: to give rise to conventional bodhicitta—the four immeasurables—in one's mindstream and, having done so, to realize ultimate bodhicitta, the actual condition of the mind, the nondual wisdom in which self and other are inseparable. All Buddhist practices are simply methods to introduce these two and to cause the yogin to realize them.

Ultimate factual bodhicitta is the basis of buddhahood itself; however, it is not subject to cultivation through effort. Therefore, the principal point of the entire spiritual heap of the eighty-four thousand Dharmas boils down to the cultivation of conventional, or fictional, bodhicitta. One's mind is already the nature of emptiness; what is lacking is compassion. When one generates loving-kindness and compassion, all the qualities of the Dharma will be realized from within the mind that is the inseparable union of compassion and emptiness.*

*Although fictional bodhicitta is an inconceivably great virtue, since it is rooted in dualistic grasping, it manifests on the level of deluded truth. Hence, this false reality is called "completely fictional" (*kündzob*). In contrast, so-called ultimate bodhicitta is

As it is said in *The Sutra on Emancipation*, "Just as the ocean is an exemplar of the Great Vehicle, the water in a cow's hoofprint exemplifies the Smaller Vehicle."[1] The mind of the Great Vehicle individual is vast like the infinite ocean. His or her immeasurable loving-kindness makes no distinction between those who are close and distant. In contrast, with only a narrow focus on oneself, one's kith, and kin, a Small Vehicle individual cannot give rise to vast love and compassion.

When this main point has been understood, every practice one does will have the same meaning and purpose. All spiritual practices come down to this essential point. For one who maintains this understanding, it will be easy to achieve the fruition.

Worldly and Spiritual Systems

Those who obtain a precious human body will meet with both worldly and spiritual systems on this earthly plane. These systems attempt to establish sentient beings in happiness free of suffering. The worldly systems of human beings are focused on obtaining happiness and freedom from suffering for the present life alone. Although they seek to block the sufferings beings experience as results of their actions, they are never completely successful. This is because they cannot uproot the underlying causes of suffering.

On the other hand, authentic spiritual systems establish beings in happiness free of suffering for both present and future lifetimes. By putting a stop to the very causes of suffering, spiritual methods invariably end the results as well. Thus, if one wishes to put a final end to suffering, it is necessary to utilize spiritual methods, no matter how skilled one may be in worldly ones. The myriad sufferings of this world come from the fault of not understanding the methods of authentic spiritual systems for stopping the causes of suffering.

---

nondual awareness, the superior fact rooted in unobscured truth. Thus, it is referred to as "factual" or "superfactual" (*döndam*).

The Three Successive Paths

People can put an end to such causes using both shortcuts and longer paths. In the context of Buddhist teachings, we speak of the three successive paths. As is said in the *Hevajra Root Tantra*, "Sentient ones are the very nature of buddhas. Even so, they are veiled by adventitious stains. When those stains are cleared away, beings are the very essence of buddhas."[2] Thus, the three successive paths of individual liberation, bodhisattvas, and secret mantra are for the purpose of clearing away sentient ones' defilements.

The first two of these are longer paths. In order to practice them, one should act according to the text *The Thirty-Seven Practices of Bodhisattvas*, cultivate precious bodhicitta, and engage the conduct of the six transcendent perfections. Those six are (1) generosity, (2) ethical discipline, (3) patience, (4) diligence, (5) meditative absorption, and (6) discerning intelligence. Practicing in this way over the course of many lifetimes, one will finally attain buddhahood, the state of having fully transcended misery.

In this regard, it is important that practitioners distinguish between virtues accumulated with and without bodhicitta. When any virtuous action is sealed with bodhicitta, there will always be a twofold positive result. For example, even the smallest act of generosity sealed with bodhicitta will finally result in enlightenment. In addition, one will achieve the precious human form, good companions, wealth, prosperity, and the like in the three higher realms along the way. As a result of the altruistic motivation, one's virtuous accumulations will never be exhausted. Such merits continue to increase until enlightenment is attained.

Sakya Paṇḍita taught that merit accumulated through bodhicitta is like the sun—continually shining forth naturally and without effort. On the other hand, merit accumulated with a selfish motivation is like the oil in a butter lamp: once it has burned away, the light dies out. Therefore, it is said that when the time of death comes, the only precious thing one can keep is bodhicitta.

The short path is the Secret Mantric Vajra Vehicle, which is distinguished from the paths of individual liberation and the Bodhisattva Vehicle by empowerment. According to Protector Jigten Sumgön, secret mantra empowerment is the dividing line between sutra and tantra. An individual who has trained in bodhicitta in former lives and who is endowed with great intelligence is one who can, in accord with his or her faculties, become a buddha by traversing the short path. Receiving empowerment is the gateway to such practice. Having done so, one can travel the short path by maintaining the mind of secret mantra certainty. This is the unwavering belief that every sentient being is a buddha at the very basis. Such certainty is the foundation on which secret mantra practitioners can attain buddhahood in a single lifetime and in a single body.

Although it is generally taught that these three paths are suited to different individuals' faculties and intelligence, it is not as though one is fixed in one category or another for the duration of one's life. For example, someone who has great perseverance can become a practitioner of highest faculties even if he or she lacks great discriminating intelligence. In addition, one can understand the three successive paths to manifest within the arc of a single practitioner's lifetime. When one first enters the door of Buddhist practice, the path of individual liberation is appropriate. Later, one progresses gradually into the paths of bodhisattvas and mantrins. Likewise, the three successive paths can be said to converge in even a single ritual practice.

Autonomy

In order to understand empowerment, one should first understand the notion of autonomy.* In general, from the perspective of worldly

*The Tibetan term for "empowerment" is *wang*, which simply means "power." The term for "autonomy" is *rangwang*, which literally means "self-power." The term for "dependence" is *zhenwang*, or "other-power." In this regard, secret mantra empowerment becomes a means whereby one attains independence, autonomy, or self-control, with the enlightened mind having fully mastered body and speech rather than mind being under the sway of self-grasping.

systems, those who live in free, democratic societies have great independence. However, such places are free only in terms of the provisional, outer perspective. In such lands, the majority of people dwell in ease and happiness, but a minority helplessly experience poverty, hunger, instability, and the like, which they cannot get rid of. Thus, those individuals have no autonomy despite living in free societies. Even those beings who do not experience social and economic perils still face the hardships of aging, illness, death, and being driven uncontrollably to various births in cyclic existence. This is because no matter how many pleasures one may enjoy, until one has obtained autonomy at the very root, one is powerless to not experience sufferings. As such, one is said to be dependent.

From the perspective of the authentic spiritual system that is the Buddhadharma, autonomy consists in having the freedom to achieve happiness. One accomplishes this by attaining births in the three higher realms of humans, demigods, and gods along the way and, ultimately, by attaining the status of the buddhas.

This occurs first through having self-control—that is, control over one's own mind. Under the influence of self-grasping, all samsaric sentient beings fall under the power of afflictions. In this way, they uncontrollably accumulate karma, which results in all the diverse sufferings that arise while they continually wander in cyclic existence. Thus, the afflictions of passion, aversion, delusion, and the like should be understood as dependencies. Bound by cherishing an illusory self, beings are dependent on, or under the power of, another. It is not as though anyone else imposes suffering on one; it is simply that under the influence of self-grasping, one cannot avoid afflictions and the sufferings that result from them.

In this regard, Ngülchu Thogme Zangpo says in *The Thirty-Seven Practices of Bodhisattvas*, "All ill-being without exception has come from wanting my own welfare."[3] So, all suffering manifests from grasping at the notion of a self. From self-grasping arise passion, aversion, and delusion, through which one accumulates the causes of birth in the three lower realms.

On the other hand, *The Thirty-Seven Practices* says, "The complete buddhas have been born from the altruistic mind."[4] This means that all the buddhas attained the independence of compassion and bodhicitta by having first liberated themselves from self-grasping. On this basis, they have seen factual, true reality, recognizing the five afflictive poisons—(1) passion, (2) aversion, (3) delusion, (4) pride, and (5) jealousy—to be by nature the five wisdoms.

With the intention of achieving that same kind of autonomy, Dharma practitioners cultivate the altruistic mind. Whenever one has the intention to benefit others, one will naturally guard ethical discipline, which is the cause of attaining human births. Whenever the altruistic mind is present, one will practice generosity, which becomes the cause of attaining wealth and resources. When one has the altruistic mind, one will spontaneously cultivate patience, which frees one from hunger, poverty, and the like. Thus, the first three of the six transcendent perfections—generosity, ethical discipline, and patience—are the natural qualities of loving-kindness. They are spontaneously present with a mind of love. They bring about the autonomy that allows one to take births in the three higher realms of gods and humans along the way.

In addition, when one cultivates calm abiding conjoined with love and compassion, one becomes free of self-grasping. This calm abiding is parallel to the fifth transcendent perfection, that of meditative absorption. Then, through the view of special insight, which is the nature of the sixth perfection, discerning intelligence, one will finally attain the status of the buddhas. In order to achieve calm abiding and special insight, one must have diligence, the fourth perfection, which is said to be like a companion to the other five. Although one may study a lot of Dharma, without diligence, one will be unable to obtain any fruition. Thus, it is through these six transcendent perfections that practitioners of the Bodhisattva Vehicle will attain emancipation gradually, over the course of many lifetimes.

As for the quick path, a distinctive feature of secret mantra is that it enables one to attain autonomy of mind through bodhicitta, which is the direct antidote to self-grasping. This autonomy is of three kinds: outer, inner, and secret.

The form of the principal deity, the retinue, and the mandala are the natural way of abiding of the buddhas' kāyas and pure fields. Thus, the outer autonomy, or empowerment, occurs when these are introduced as bases for stabilizing meditation.

Next, when one emerges victorious over self-grasping through cultivating the altruistic intent, one will attain the autonomy of bodhicitta. This is the inner autonomy, or empowerment.

On that basis, one realizes the aggregates (*skandhas*), elements (*dhātus*), and sense fields (*āyatanas*) of the body-mind continuum to have been pure from the very beginning. This attainment of secret mantra pure perception is the secret autonomy, or empowerment.

After having received empowerment, since those who cultivate bodhicitta still have propensities on the inner levels of body and speech and on the outer levels of forms and sounds, deity yoga is taught as the antidote to such imprints. Thus, self-control of the body is achieved through cultivating the development stages of the yidam deity, verbal self-control through the mantra recitation with its radiating out and gathering in of light rays, and mental self-control through bodhicitta. By these means, one's own three doors of body, speech, and mind will be realized as being inseparable from the pure deity's enlightened body, speech, and mind.

In this way, one achieves happiness and freedom from suffering not only for oneself. Rather, having become equal to the enlightened ones, the meditator will display the miraculous manifestations of the buddhas' three kāyas until samsara itself has been emptied out. This fulfillment of one's own and others' purpose is what it means to accomplish the fruition of buddhahood in a single lifetime. The autonomy of bodhicitta, which is gained through secret mantra empowerment, is just that profound and meaningful.

Gradual and Sudden Types

As for accomplishment of the fruition, tantric texts distinguish between gradual and sudden types. It is said that some individuals attain liberation gradually through great effort, while others do so all at once, seemingly without needing to progress in stages. This latter type is said to recognize the nature of mind effortlessly in a single instant. However, Protector Jigten Sumgön disputed this, teaching that in actuality, there is no such thing as a sudden type. This is because even those beings of highest faculties who appear to attain liberation all at once by means of the secret mantra are merely demonstrating the effects of having purified the mind's obscurations in former lives through the paths of individual liberation and the Bodhisattva Vehicle. In this way, everyone can be considered a gradual type.

For example, when children are born, some fortunate ones are joyous and open with smiling faces. Their behavior is naturally loving and generous. Others are ill-tempered or fearful, having thick, afflictive obscurations from the start. The different qualities of their dispositions are obvious in infancy and are signs of their karmic imprints from former lives.

Such differences can also be observed among Dharma practitioners, who are characterized as being of high, middling, or lesser faculties. Some people, even though they listen to secret mantra teachings with interest, cannot understand them. However, if they can realize this lack of comprehension to be the result of not having accumulated sufficient virtue in past lifetimes, they will be inspired to cultivate virtuous activities in the present. By doing so, they can continue to progress on the path in stages.

The greatest fortune someone can have is to be endowed with compassion, faith in the Three Jewels, and the wish to enter the door of secret mantra. The desire and intention to enter the Vajra Vehicle—the result of having cultivated the altruistic mind to some degree throughout past lifetimes—is a sign of extreme good fortune and is exceedingly precious. Through making effort in accord with that intention and through cultivating the altruistic motivation that is bodhicitta, in the best case, one will attain the state of buddhahood. In the middling case, one will temporarily attain birth in the three higher realms, in which the good fortunes of gods and humans are enjoyed. Thus, everyone can, sooner or later, attain the state of buddhahood. In this regard, all beings are the same. All those who have faith eventually become suitable vessels for the secret mantra teachings.

Ripening Empowerment

Regardless of the vast or small scope of one's virtuous activities, one's motivation is of primary importance. Pure roots of virtue will come forth from reciting even a single maṇi mantra as long as one's motivation is pure. Motivation is of two types. The first, the one I am constantly repeating in your ears, is bodhicitta. One should never be parted from the thought, "Sentient ones extend as far as the limits of space. In order to liberate them all from confused and dreamlike sufferings, I must establish them on the ground of Vajradhara, the essence of mind—the great self-knowing primordial awareness." All those who have obtained the precious human body have the causal basis for attaining buddhahood. However, this knowledge must be introduced to those who have not yet received introduction. In the context of secret mantra, this introduction is done by means of empowerment, which is said to mature the immature. Thus, when receiving empowerment, one must give rise to a vast motivation, thinking, "Having introduced every sentient one to ultimate bodhicitta, I will lead them to the state of the buddhas. For this purpose, I shall enter the mandala of the deity." This is the motivation that is bodhicitta.

The second motivation is to become a suitable vessel for the teachings of the Secret Mantric Vajra Vehicle. This requires great intelligence and pure perception. The precious human body is possessed of the six constituents of earth, water, fire, wind, space, and consciousness, together with the singular basis that is mind. That mind is shared by buddhas and sentient ones alike. In order to understand secret mantra empowerment, one should consider the example of a flower that has a seed, a bud, and a blossom. The deity whose empowerment is to be conferred is like the seed of the flower. The master who confers the empowerment is like the blossom. The disciple on whom empowerment is conferred is like the bud of the flower, which is caused to open by the strength of bodhicitta. Through this example, one can understand the ripening empowerment as the means whereby the seed takes root in the mind of an immature sentient being, to mature gradually into a fully blossomed flower.

In general, this secret mantra perspective is the actual, true condition of the mind. Every sentient one possesses the essence of the buddhas. This was taught by the Bhagavan Buddha, who said, "Sentient ones are the very nature of buddhas."[5] If one has a mind, one has the cause of buddhahood. It is through the mind that the buddhas come into being.

In this way, every wayfaring being of the six classes possesses the cause of buddhahood. However, since they are under the influence of self-grasping, the result is a bit distant for them. For example, among many seeds, only a few will meet with good soil, warmth, and moisture—all the favorable conditions necessary to sprout. Because of this, few seeds will grow while many will go to waste. Similarly, most sentient beings take birth in the three bad migrations of animals, *pretas*, and hell denizens. This is because, circumstantially, they do not yet have the fortune to obtain a precious human body, the only birth in which one may encounter and utilize the secret mantra teachings.

On the other hand, those fortunate ones who obtain a human body endowed with the freedoms and connections can enter the path of secret mantra and attain the spiritual eye. With it, they will cease to perceive this world, the outer container, as ordinary. Since this world is comprised of the five elements, in actuality it is the nature of the great mother-consorts of the five buddhas. As such, the physical container is entirely comprised of nirmāṇakāyas of the buddhas. Likewise, the inner contents, confused sentient ones, have buddha nature at the very basis. Thus, it is only due to the temporary condition of ignorance that sentient ones experience dreamlike confusion, circumstantially wandering in samsara. At the very ground, all beings' afflictions are the nature of the five wisdoms. Thus, since both the container and contents are fundamentally the very nature of purity, confused appearances arise only temporarily. To overcome such circumstantial appearances, one must cultivate the mindful awareness that spontaneously transforms the five afflictions into the five wisdoms. This awareness is the root of all autonomy. Whenever an empowerment ritual includes five separate empowerments, they create auspicious interdependent connections for such awareness to emerge.

In brief, the master who bestows empowerment is the actually manifest body of the yidam. That is to say, the wisdom deity himself or herself—the saṁbhogakāya—is the one who confers empowerment. That deity arises from bodhicitta, which comes from the buddhas. The buddhas, in turn, appear from among sentient ones. The ordinary body, speech, and mind of anyone who gives rise to the altruistic motivation and receives ripening empowerment will transform into the mature state of the pure deity's body, speech, and mind. First, it is necessary to mature the mind. Then, secondarily, one must mature the speech and body in stages. Whichever sadhanas one practices, at the start, when taking refuge, one must cultivate bodhicitta. In actuality, the cultivation of bodhicitta even precedes refuge. Bodhicitta is that which ripens the mind. Through it, one will attain enlightenment, the royal seat of the buddhas' three kāyas. Having thus freed oneself from suffering, one will become able to show others the means of liberation.

As for those who request empowerment, the aggregates, elements, and sense fields of all samsaric sentient ones are pure at the basis. Therefore, anything that appears to be impure is like a dream or an illusion. Receiving secret mantra empowerment enables one to settle the point that phenomena are fundamentally pure and give rise to certainty about that purity. Then, on the basis of empowerment, practitioners must receive "liberating instructions," the point-by-point guidance that explains the correct means of practice.

The Secrecy of Secret Mantra

The quick path—the Secret Mantric Vajra Vehicle—is referred to as secret not because it is something to be concealed or covered up but because its meaning cannot be fathomed. This is the case for ordinary beings of the six classes, who experience the sufferings of the three lower realms due to the afflictions of the three poisons. This is like when water, which is inherently crystal clear, accidentally becomes tainted by impure substances. However, when the water is purified and returned to its natural state, it is suitable for drinking and bathing. Similarly, the fundamental buddha nature is pure at the very basis. This quality of the mind is referred to in the dzogchen tradition as "pure from the beginning." In the context of mahāmudrā, it is called "primordial purity." These two terms have the same meaning. Whenever the afflictive poisons meet with bodhicitta, they are transformed into the five wisdoms, just as wood changes into flame when fuel meets with fire. In this way, sentient ones can transform into buddhas. The fact that suffering beings can attain the status of the buddhas is not something that needs to be kept hidden; it simply is not readily understandable.

In this regard, the Bhagavan Buddha said, "Sentient ones are the very nature of buddhas. Even so, they are veiled by adventitious stains."[6] Such adventitious defilements are easy to understand. Sentient beings are merely temporarily obscured by self-grasping and afflictions. If the mind were impure from the beginning, then it couldn't be purified through practice. When this is understood, it causes one to take courage and think, "Oh! All my impurities are merely extrinsic and transient!"

What are the adventitious defilements of the mind? They are the ongoing ignorance that is referred to in *The Aspiration of Samantabhadra* with the following words: "Co-emergent ignorance is a distracted, unaware consciousness. Thoroughly conceptualizing ignorance is to grasp at self and other as two."[7]

Co-emergent ignorance is one's failure to examine the mind with the mind. It manifests concurrently with the notion of an "I." People think, "As long as things are all right with me, then everything is fine. If things are not going well for me, nothing is fine." This mindset, in which the self is of primary importance, is co-emergent ignorance.

Then, as for the mind of thoroughly conceptualizing ignorance, when various outwardly appearing forms arise, one has the notion, "That is other; this is me." By failing to examine the inner mind, one falls into dualistic perceptions of self and other. From the start, this manifests as the distinction between male and female, which is observed among all humans, animals, and flora throughout this worldly realm. When pure, this distinction is the nature of method and wisdom. When impure, it gives rise to manifold dualistic perceptions. By recognizing this habit in one's own mind, one can understand the dualistic grasping in the minds of all sentient beings of the three realms.

It is said that these two kinds of ignorance have been present throughout beginingless samsara. Thus, it is impossible to say when they began. But, in actual fact, ignorance is not continuous. When the phenomena of one lifetime have been exhausted and a person falls unconscious at death, the moment he or she awakens from that unconsciousness, that individual arrives in the first bardo, or intermediate state, experiencing the dharmakāya. This interruption in the continuity of ignorance happens for every sentient being and is the sign that all beings possess buddha nature. If one recognizes the dharmakāya at that juncture, the recognition itself is the very attainment of the status of buddhahood in the first bardo.

Thus, if one understands every sentient being to be a buddha at the basis, the various belief systems, distinctions, and biases found in this worldly realm—such as the idea, "I am Buddhist; he is not"—become meaningless. By knowing the mind itself to be the causal basis of buddhahood, one's mind becomes open and spacious. One experiences deliverance merely through hearing this. One feels joy just knowing this fundamental truth, which is the basis for the pure perception of the Vajra Vehicle.

Since the power of the development stages lies in the purification of perceived impurity, the final fruition of their practice is the attainment of pure perception. This does not mean that one should project a notion of purity onto phenomena that are tainted. Rather, from the perspective of the Vajra Vehicle, primordial purity is the recognition of things as they truly are. In the song titled *Lotus Melody of Eighteen Perfections*, Drigung Dharmarāja said, "Understanding appearance-existence to be the deities' forms is the perfection of secret mantra's development stages."[8]

Whoever has such an outlook of perceiving all sentient beings as pure at the very basis will attain the deity's attributes. The greater one's pure perception, the more it is to one's own advantage. Someone who truly has pure outlook will see all things as pure—including those things that are impure. Conversely, like a jaundiced person who sees a conch as being yellow in color, someone with an impure perception conditioned by self-grasping will perceive everything as corrupted—even that which is pure.[9] The distinction between these two views lies in the greater or lesser scope of one's wisdom. It is in this context of secret mantra pure perception that one can begin to understand the practice of Vajrakīla.

There are those who say secret mantra teachings should not be propagated but should be kept hidden. In one sense, this accords with the intent of Guru Rinpoche, who concealed his tantric teachings as treasures, commanding that they not be propagated during his era. On the other hand, Guru Rinpoche specified that the occasion of their propagation would be the time of dregs, when humanity would face great tribulation. He clearly prophesied that at such a time, when the blessing of other Buddhist spiritual practices will have declined due to not having been well maintained, the blessing power of his treasures would remain undiminished.

For this reason, beings of this present time of dregs should utilize the secret mantra teachings and practices of the Earlier System. Their accomplishment is within reach; it is attainable. Now is the time for methods of accomplishment such as Vajrakīla and Yamāntaka to be put to use.

Even so, it is said that there are two types of beings to whom it is unsuitable to reveal the teachings of the Secret Mantric Vajra Vehicle. The first type of unfit vessels for the teachings are those who cannot give rise to bodhicitta. This is because those who lack bodhicitta will be completely unable to comprehend the secret mantra. Therefore, it is essential to train in conventional bodhicitta from the beginning. This is done by means of the preliminary practices, which include the four mind-changing contemplations:

(1) the difficult-to-obtain precious human body, (2) death and impermanence, (3) karmic causes and effects, and (4) the faults of cyclic existence. It is taught that through training the mind in these ways and through practicing the uncommon preliminaries of refuge and so forth, one will become able to comprehend the profound meaning of secret mantra teachings.

The second type of unfit vessels are those who lack great discriminating intelligence. Although they may be very learned, such people still give rise to perverted views of secret mantra. In this regard, Rāga Asya's *Aspiration for the Pure Field of Great Bliss* says, "A greater misdeed than killing the three realms' sentient ones is to denigrate bodhisattvas."[10]

It is said that perverted views of gurus and virtuous friends send one to the hell realms. What does this mean? Perverted concepts are the nature of hostility. The afflictions of hostility, animosity, and hatred are the root causes of hell-realm phenomena. For this reason, it is taught that to reveal the secret mantra teachings to those who hold perverted views is unacceptable.

Among Buddhist practitioners, perverted views can also manifest as sectarian bias. Even though one may be very devoted to one's own lineage, it is important to train in cultivating an impartial, pure perception of all traditions. Otherwise, if one holds the view "only my tradition is right; others have it wrong," such thinking shows one does not know how to practice Dharma. Although one may engage spiritual practices, if they are done based on such concepts of attachment and aversion, one's "Dharma" will become a cause of falling to the lower realms. To maintain perverted views will corrupt the mind no matter how pure one's spiritual lineage may be. For this reason, true practitioners will always respect different lineages, thinking, "Other traditions are as good as mine. The inner meaning is the same!"

Earlier and Latter Mantric Systems

The entirety of the four great Indian Buddhist philosophical tenet systems can be subsumed within the single point that is practice.

The Bhagavan Buddha taught the two paths of the causal Vehicle of Characteristics and the resultant Vajra Vehicle as the practical methods for liberation from samsaric sufferings. In the Causal Vehicle, it is taught that one cannot attain buddhahood without having gathered the accumulations of merit and wisdom for three limitless *kalpas*. This is because one's accumulation of karma and afflictions since time without beginning is so profound and because the ignorance underlying it naturally lacks existence and cannot be seen.

For countless lifetimes, one has had no opportunity to encounter the buddhas, to listen to their Dharma, or to practice it. Because of this, one continually accumulates a mixture of virtue and misdeeds. It is only due to one's virtuous habits throughout this limitless stretch of time that some degree of wisdom-intelligence and compassion arise, bringing one into contact with the buddhas and their teachings. Through their kind influence, one can encounter the Fruition Vehicle of Secret Mantra, whereby the attainment of buddhahood becomes possible in a single lifetime. Such accomplishment is based on the buddha nature that is inherent in the mind of every sentient being.

As for this resultant Vajra Vehicle, there are two traditions of secret mantra in Tibet.[11] Although the fruitions of their practices are the same, there is some difference in their modes of practice. Specifically, the Latter Systems, or Sarma, embrace the four classes of tantra, which are elaborate and extensive and suit those individuals of highest faculties. On the other hand, the Earlier System of secret mantra, or Nyingma, is the blessing-practice lineage of Guru Rinpoche, who taught the four branches of approach and accomplishment based on direct experience. The sadhanas of the Earlier System are very abridged. They are the methods whereby one can easily yet effectively practice the branches of approach and accomplishment simultaneously in a single liturgy. As this present text is a treasure, or terma, of the Earlier System, its practitioners should have some understanding of the four branches of approach and accomplishment, which will be presented in the teachings on mantra recitation.

This method of accomplishing Vajrakīla is derived from the Eight Sadhana Teachings, which were first practiced by the eight great knowledge holders of India. These teachings were collectively entrusted to Guru Rinpoche as the *Tantra of the Gathering of Sugatas of the Eight Sadhana Teachings*.[12] Guru Rinpoche, who was also the principal holder of the Vajrakīla transmission, established the Eight Sadhana Teachings in Tibet, where they became the basis of the *mahāyoga* transmissions of the nine successive vehicles of the Earlier System.

Among the Eight Sadhana Teachings, there are nine sadhana sections with nine different mandalas. Since all of them are complete within any single one, through entering just one mandala, one enters them all. Among the nine, the mandala of Kīla Activity is located in the northern direction. As Vajrakīla is the embodiment of all the buddhas' activities, his is called "the mandala of enlightened activities."

Deity Yoga

Because the development-stage yogas are extremely profound and difficult to comprehend, one may think there is no benefit in practicing them unless their complete meaning has been understood. However, this is not at all the case. Even when one does not have a great understanding of the words of a teaching, if one simply tries to put into practice whatever has been understood as it is being taught, the mind will naturally become relaxed, open, and clear. Even when one's comprehension is not good, since the qualities of Dharma are already naturally present in the mind, the meaning will eventually dawn from within. For this reason, it is very effective to meditate as one is receiving the teachings. When the mind becomes open and relaxed, one reaches a sort of spontaneous understanding in which it is not necessary for the meaning to be explained by anyone else. This is particularly so in the context of group accomplishment retreats. Since the deities actually assemble in the practice mandala, practitioners' minds naturally become open and clear. Thus, regardless of whether one is a being of high, middling, or lesser faculties, practicing deity yoga brings great benefit.

Words from Guru Rinpoche on Deity Yoga

The following words of Guru Rinpoche from the tantra known as *The Union of Sun and Moon* summarize the intent of deity yoga. It would be good to write them down and to remind oneself of them every time one meditates on the deity.

> First, one familiarizes the deity's aspects. When those aspects arise in the mind, ordinary thoughts are destroyed. In between, one familiarizes divine pride. When that pride has become stable, one attains autonomy. Finally, one familiarizes the deity's blessings. Through the potency of those blessings, others' appearances are transformed.[13]

Each of us has a little bit of discriminating intelligence and compassion at the basis. If, on top of that, one meditates on the appearance of the deity—his or her aspects—one will forget the ordinary body. Even when the visualization is not clear, it is said that merely to recollect the deity is of great benefit. In this regard, the realization narrative of Avalokita known as *The Lotus King Tantra* says, "The body of Guardian Avalokita is that in whom every buddha is gathered. By one's visualizing or just recalling him, the immediate misdeeds are cleansed."[14] In this regard, to see in the mind a mere picture of the yidam is not of much benefit; the point of visualizing the form of the deity is to recall and come to embody his or her attributes.

In *The Precious Treasure of Sakya Paṇḍita's Fine Explanations*, the body is referred to as "a container for the ocean of sufferings."[15] One should consider that all the activities of this lifetime are dedicated to nothing other than looking after the body's needs—feeding, clothing, housing, and caring for it. Since body and mind are conjoined, whenever some harm befalls the body, the mind experiences ill-being. This suffering arises due to the mind's cherishing of the body. If one is pricked with a needle, one experiences pain. Even though it is the body that gets pricked, the pricking sensation occurs in the mind. Similarly, it is by means of the body that the mind experiences heat, cold, hunger, thirst, and the like.

Because one believes the body to be real, one has great attachment to it. This attachment engenders physical propensities in the mind. As a result of such attachment and propensities, one continues to experience physical sufferings even in the bardo, the intermediate state between death in one life and birth in the next. If one looks within and reflects on how physical pain and suffering can be experienced even after the body has been cast off, one will see that the body and mind are conjoined. Since one can experience either bondage or liberation on the basis of the body, the precious human form is extremely powerful. If one's practice becomes separated from bodhicitta, the body becomes like a demon to the yogin. However, if one can practice secret mantra methods conjoined with bodhicitta, one can attain buddhahood in a single lifetime and in a single body. If, in this way, the body manifests as a deity, it is extremely beneficial for the practitioner. Thus, whether the body becomes a hindrance or a benefit depends on the presence or absence of bodhicitta.

One's present body of flesh and blood has been created by past karmic imprints. Whenever one cultivates great love for the deity, a habit of the deity is imprinted on the mind. When the deity's form manifests, it appears within the mind itself. That mind abides like a mirror that continuously reflects the positive or negative karmic habits one has established. When the imprint of the deity is stable in one's mind, it becomes a cause to arise in the deity's form in the bardo.

Although one cannot see one's karmic propensities at present, tomorrow when one's consciousness enters the bardo, they will become manifest. For this reason, one should in this lifetime establish positive karmic imprints of oneself as the deity, clearly and one-pointedly habituating to the deity's form. This can be accomplished by looking at paintings or statues and then causing the deity's image to arise in the mind's eye, recalling him or her with love and affection. As one trains in this way, sometimes the deity will arise on its own in various forms, large and small. As one again and again cultivates the visualization, it will gradually become clear. It is fitting that just as the deity's form can suddenly manifest clearly, sometimes it just as suddenly vanishes like a rainbow.

If one accumulates mantra recitations with a mind of great love for the deity, one will eventually reach a state in which one never forgets the yidam, even when one is not actively visualizing his or her form. Then, whenever one sees an image of the deity, love will spontaneously arise and one will feel great delight. Even though the image is not the actual deity, one will regard the representation of the yidam's form as something precious and will want to offer it great respect. This is a sign of having forged a connection with the deity.

Then, whenever one experiences some difficulty or fear, the first thought will be of the deity. For example, at the first sign of peril we Tibetans often call out, "Venerable Tārā!" or the name of any other deity or guru in whom we have faith. This is an exceedingly good habit. By one's recollecting the deity or the guru and calling him or her by name, blessings will immediately enter one's mind and will most definitely provide protection. The point is that with or without visualization, mere recollection of the deity is sufficient. The most important thing is to bring the deity to mind again and again. This will cause ordinary concepts to disintegrate and ordinary physical propensities to be forgotten. Always recalling the deity, one will come to realize that one's mind and the deity's mind are nondual.

Later, if the stages of development should really arise with vivid, rainbowlike clarity, one will understand that they have come about through nothing other than mind. When one investigates minutely, although the mind itself is free of form, shape, or color, it is like a mirror in which the deity is being reflected. If, in this way, one recalls the deity at all times, he or she will truly become stable. This can reverse all the habits and conditioning related to the body. When ordinary concepts are torn down, one forgets the body. Once the body has been forgotten, every physical propensity is cast off like ragged clothing. In this way, the mind is purified.

I myself have some experience of this. Since I had never done any development-stage training at all when I was a small child, if I needed to visualize the form of the deity on a large scale, I would imagine it filling the building I was in, such that the deity's head would reach the ceiling. If I had to visualize many deities at once, I felt ill at ease because they would not all fit comfortably in the limited space.

However, after I had visualized the deity and mantra strand again and again and had gained a bit of familiarity, sometimes the deity would suddenly appear without my being aware of the building at all. That is to say, once some of my inner grasping at the body had been purified, outer grasping at the building and the like had also fallen away and become absent. Then, when I would close my eyes, there would be no thought of the building being present or absent.

This illustrates how the development-stage practices can gradually purify all grasping. To feel uncomfortable when visualizing a large deity because it does not fit inside the building is a sign of impurity. It indicates that the mind is unaccustomed to the stages of development. After becoming habituated, if one closes one's eyes, then whatever one thinks of can more or less be seen without manipulation or doubt. Sometimes the appearance arises. Even when it does not, one need only have love for the deity.

The point is that even if one has no time to practice rituals, one should still train in the development stages by closing one's eyes and again and again recalling with affection the deity's form. If one does that, sometimes the body of the deity will arise easily like a rainbow. This appearance is the natural expression of one's own mind. Sometimes the deity's form will just as suddenly disappear. This is the union of development and completion. Understanding this, one will be devoid of grasping at perceived objects and their characteristics. That is to say, when there is no grasping at the appearances of divine forms, there will be no disappointment at their disappearance. Such are the benefits that can be experienced through training in the development stages—the methods for transforming ordinary concepts.

In addition to reflecting on the benefits, one should also consider the faults of not refining away propensities through these means. If, for example, one dies while experiencing this sort of grasping at an outer structure, such a mental imprint could condition rebirth as a mollusk that carries the house of a shell wherever it goes. In this way, one should understand Guru Rinpoche's words about destroying ordinary thoughts through familiarizing the deity's aspects.

In order to support such training, it is good to study texts about the recollection of purity. Praising the signs of the deity, such texts focus on the symbolic meaning of the deity's physical appearance, ornaments, and implements, which symbolize the ten transcendent perfections and the like. It is good for sādhakas to have some understanding of this.

There are manifest benefits that emerge from familiarizing the stages of development. For example, if one experiences a lot of pain and physical illness, in the best case, one's disease will be cleared away. If not, at least the symptoms will be minimized. Although I have many sicknesses, I do not seek much medical intervention. This is due to the qualities of the development-stage yogas, which disrupt the habit of identifying with the gross body of flesh and blood.

In the future, physical obscurations will become purified through these means. Now, although one has outer physical illnesses, if one grasps at them, those outer illnesses will be conjoined with inner suffering, making the hardship even greater. Because deity yoga diminishes grasping, it brings manifest benefit to those who practice it.

Next, Guru Rinpoche's statement continues with the words, "In between, one familiarizes divine pride. When that pride has become stable, one attains autonomy."

With regard to deity yoga, many people give rise to doubts, thinking, "If I meditate on the deity, am I *actually* the deity? Since the deity is not really me, it must be something false." These sorts of apprehensions are completely mistaken. Others think they must be convinced that "I *am* the deity!" This is also not right, since there will be no benefit from a deity practice rooted in grasping at an "I."

In order to avoid these extremes, one should first investigate whether or not the deity is really oneself. This question is definitively resolved by buddha nature. In this regard, the words of the disclosure in the subsequent rites of the Vajrakīla text read, "From the start we've been inseparable..." What this means is that since time without beginning, the cause—one's mind that is the buddha nature—has been the same as the mind of Vajrakumāra. Even so, that mind is veiled by adventitious stains. Those stains are only self-grasping and afflictions. Apart from them, the basis that is the mind of oneself and the deity is one.

This mind that is buddha nature is singular. Due to the fault of self-grasping, the yidam's qualities have not yet become manifest. However, the moment one gives rise to bodhicitta, the altruistic motivation, that is the actual mind of the deity. Thus, one can resolve for oneself the question of whether or not one is truly the deity. Since the yidam's mind is the unification of emptiness and compassion, if one gives rise to an instant of altruistic intent, one possesses the yidam's mind in that instant. Even though one may have no understanding of the development-stage yogas, one still becomes the actual deity. It is necessary to generate belief in that. In order to believe in the buddha nature—the buddhas' command—one must truly have faith in bodhicitta. This is the best sort of divine pride, whereby autonomy will truly be attained.

The issue of autonomy, or self-control, can also be understood in the following way: When one is never separated from love and compassion, one will not fall under the power of afflictions. Being no longer controlled by afflictions, one will not accumulate karma. The very nature of love and compassion is generosity, ethical discipline, and patience. On the basis of these three, one will circumstantially attain births in the three higher realms. Then, through concentration and discerning intelligence, one will ultimately attain the status of the buddhas. In order to cultivate each of these perfections, diligence is required.

This is the meaning of the words of the refuge vow ceremony, whose text states that as a result of having taken the vow, one will ultimately attain the status of the buddhas and will experience the ease and happiness of the three higher realms along the way. The causes of these attainments are loving-kindness and compassion. Even if one had all the wealth and enjoyments in the world, tomorrow at the moment of death, they would be of no benefit and, in fact, would only be harmful. Conversely, when the buddha nature that is one's mind becomes conjoined with love and compassion, one will truly attain great autonomy. The central autonomy is not to fall under the sway of afflictions.

For example, if one gets angry at a friend and then recalls the fault of anger, one will give rise to patience and, by doing so, avoid accumulating karma. Conversely, if one falls under the power of anger, then one's practice is lost, resulting in negative karmic accumulation. Therefore, one should understand that to generate altruistic intent liberates self-grasping. When self-grasping is liberated, the six afflictions are invariably liberated.

Guru Rinpoche's quote concludes with the words, "Finally, one familiarizes the deity's blessings. Through the potency of those blessings, others' appearances are transformed."

How should one understand the deity's blessings? Yeshe Tsogyal once asked Guru Rinpoche, "There are so many deities. From whence have they come?" Since they have arisen from bodhicitta, Guru Rinpoche replied, "That which is called the 'deity' is bodhicitta."[16] This means that the altruistic intent is the very life force of the yidam. It is only through bodhicitta that one transforms into the deity. The dividing line between samsara and nirvana is bodhicitta.

Thus, when one makes the aspiration, "May all men attain the status of Avalokita; may all women attain the status of Ārya Tārā," the focus is not on people's outer bodies. Rather, one is praying that the qualities of the deities' bodhicitta be developed in the inner minds of beings. If one has powerful love and compassion, it will accomplish one's own purpose—the status of buddhahood—and will also accomplish the purpose of others, bringing benefit to sentient ones. For example, if a guru—a virtuous friend—has qualities, he or she will possess loving-kindness and compassion for disciples. If the guru lacks these, though he or she may have a connection with disciples, those disciples will not experience benefit from that connection. Only one who has love and compassion will bring about delight in the minds of humans and nonhumans.

To give another example, dogs and cats always follow those who care for them with love. Since this is the case on a small scale, if one can cultivate love and compassion for all sentient beings, it will make offerings to all the buddhas and will simultaneously purify all beings' obscurations. Therefore, one should reflect on the great power of loving-kindness and compassion—the deity's blessings—to transform others' appearances.

The King of Aspirations for the Conduct of Samantabhadra refers to "the force of all-pervading love."[17] Anyone who aspires to pervade all the buddhas and all sentient ones must have love and compassion. Since one's present qualities of love are too weak, they must be strengthened and increased. One must practice the methods whereby precious, supreme bodhicitta can arise where it has not yet arisen, can be protected from decline where it has arisen, and can further and further increase. These three refer to the progressive stages of the paths of individual liberation, the Bodhisattva Vehicle, and the Secret Mantric Vehicle. By teaching the methods of emancipation from the sufferings of the three lower realms, the path of individual liberation causes bodhicitta to emerge where it has not yet arisen. Through the bodhisattvas' conduct of the six transcendent perfections and the repeated cultivation of bodhicitta, that which has arisen does not decline. Finally, through pure perception, practitioners of the secret mantra cause bodhicitta to increase ever further.

Sometimes practitioners become discouraged, thinking sentient beings are so numerous, they are inexhaustible and cannot all be freed. Whenever this occurs, one should recall that all beings have buddha nature. However great their confusion, it is merely an adventitious defilement; it is not ultimately real. This is the meaning of the words, "there's no real object of compassionate aid" in the generation of bodhicitta from the Yamāntaka practice manual.[18] When this point has been well understood, the bodhisattva will give rise to a heroic and greatly courageous mind.

Purifying Propensities through Deity Yoga

It is only on the basis of this heroic mind that a practice of deity yoga can flourish. Through meditating on the deity, one purifies the inner physical propensities accumulated since time without beginning. As a result, imprints regarding outer forms will be cleansed. Through mantra recitation, one purifies the inner propensities of speech. As a result, imprints related to outer sounds will be cleansed. Finally, through continually cultivating bodhicitta, one purifies self-grasping. In this way, even an hour of sadhana practice clears away obscurations of body, speech, and mind. In addition, by remaining inseparable from the clear appearance of the yidam, one becomes impervious to harm from any demonic forces, spells, or obstructors.

On the other hand, those who lack this sort of method of accomplishment reinforce propensities of samsaric activities day and night without interruption. On the basis of material forms, sounds, and mental afflictions, beings continually accumulate karmic imprints. Reflecting on this, one should develop an appreciation for the development stages, which are of benefit in this life, in the bardo, and in future lives.

For those who cherish such practices, group accomplishment retreats offer opportunities to engage sadhanas intensively for a period of time. With regard to their benefits, *The Thirty-Seven Practices of Bodhisattvas* states,

> When one has abandoned evil lands, afflictions gradually wane.
> When one is without distraction, virtuous practice waxes on its

> own. When one is clear-sighted, certainty in Dharma is born.
> Keeping to solitude is the bodhisattva's practice.[19]

The benefit of remaining in solitude is that one becomes clear-sighted. Thus, as the text says, "certainty in Dharma is born." It is for the purpose of becoming clear-sighted that people remain physically and mentally isolated in retreat.

Some will think a group practice like the Vajrakīla secret accomplishment is not an actual retreat because instead of being alone, one is in a gathering of many people. Although this is a different sort of retreat, it is still a retreat. In spite of the size of the gathering, one's body is isolated from frivolity because one has temporarily renounced ordinary beings' worldly activities, which are focused on the concerns of this life. As one diligently pursues mantra recitation alone, one's speech is isolated. Not following after thoughts of past, present, or future but remaining with awareness single-pointedly focused on the deity and mantra, one's mind is isolated. In this way, the three isolations are complete within the group accomplishment retreat. The benefit of this is that the mind becomes clear.

It is good to investigate the difference between clarity and the lack thereof. When one is preoccupied with worldly samsaric pursuits—continually following past thoughts and anticipating the future—countless thoughts and emotions come to mind. These are mere concepts rooted in confusion. They are the strong views arisen from grasping at perceived objects and their defining characteristics. As an antidote to these, one visualizes appearing forms as the deity, transforms sounds into mantra, and turns the mind to love and compassion. Every view arisen from grasping at perceived objects and their characteristics should be cleared away. In order to achieve this, the core point is to purify self-grasping through love and compassion.

Grasping at physical propensities is refined away through the clear appearance of the deity. Grasping at sounds is purified by the recited mantra. Because it is extremely effective to practice in this way, the benefits of deity yoga have been elaborated in the tantras.

It is said that by meditating again and again on the shape or aspects of the deity, one refines away grasping at the ordinary body of flesh and blood. Thus, the gross physical form is forgotten.

When actually engaging the practice, some students have become fearful, thinking they will lose their bodies or speech if they cultivate the stages of development. But to lose the body is the best sensation! One *should* lose the body! All the propensities of samsara without beginning have arisen from body-based self-grasping. When the body is lost, the imprints of the deities' kāyas and pure fields will spontaneously appear. These are signs of the destruction of ordinary concepts—the maturation of that which was immature. If one practices, signs such as these will arise. Merely to meditate on the deity's aspects has this sort of power.

Everything I have just explained is based on a single line from *The Thirty-Seven Practices of Bodhisattvas*: "When one is clear-sighted, certainty in Dharma is born."[20] Every Dharma teaching without exception is subsumed within this line.

This last point about the benefits of the deity and mantra can be found in the texts known as *The Exposition on the Great Accomplishment of Vajrakīla from a Thousand Perspectives*,[21] which is the speech of Guru Rinpoche, and *The Thorough Explanation of the Eight Sadhana Teachings*.[22] In brief, the meaning is that by repeatedly meditating on the deity, one will forget body-based propensities.

Attainment of Buddhahood through Deity Yoga

People generally think buddhahood is something far distant. But this is not so. All the buddhas emerge from sentient beings. For example, Buddha Śākyamuni was once the son of Śuddhodana; Ārya Tārā was once a princess. As mentioned previously, the Tibetan term for *buddha* is *sanggye*—*sang* meaning "cleared away" and *gye* meaning "expanded." That is, when dualistic grasping has been cleared away, the mind expands, merging into the space of the dharmakāya. Some may wonder what happens or where one goes when enlightenment is attained. The answer is that one's mind, free of any reference point, utterly pervades the sphere of phenomena.

Through cultivating the stages of development and completion, those of highest faculties will, like Milarepa, become buddhas in their very lifetimes, manifesting the dharmakāya in the first bardo. If one is unable to attain buddhahood at that first juncture, then it is possible to do so in the second bardo. At the moment of waking from sleep, one generally has disordered thoughts such as "Where am I? Who am I?" So, from the first moment of conscious awareness, there is a sense of self. However, through training in the development-stage yogas, one continually recalls the deity with a mind of great love, reciting his or her mantra and seeing an approximation of his or her form in the mind. As a result, at the moment of waking, one will recall and transform into the deity and the mantra, purifying the propensities of body and speech.

By having trained in this way, those of middling faculties will be liberated into the saṁbhogakāya in the second bardo. That is to say, as soon as one thinks, "Now I have died," through the power of love, the thought of the deity will immediately arise in one's mind. Thus, the mind will transform into whichever deity one has practiced. In that very instant, the mind will have been subdued by the deity. This is because the mirrorlike mind becomes free of self-grasping the moment one recalls the deity. Thus, the inherent qualities of the buddha nature are made manifest in that moment. The individual who is free of dualistic grasping himself or herself will transform into the deity. Even a person with dualistic grasping will become like a small child seated on the lap of his or her parent, the yidam deity. Such are the benefits of meditating again and again on the deity's form and mantra.

Even those of lesser faculties who are not liberated into the dharmakāya or saṁbhogakāya must in any case become buddhas as nirmāṇakāyas in the third bardo due to having obtained empowerment in the Secret Mantric Vajra Vehicle. These are some of the ways in which buddhas actually manifest from among sentient beings.

Finally, even for those who do not have such accomplishment at the time of death, there is still great blessing from having made a connection with these practices. For example, it is said that if one receives a tantric empowerment yet does not practice at all in that life, one will again receive empowerment after seven lifetimes and will then become able to engage the practice.

Introduction to Visualizing the Deity

Those who aspire to accomplish the transformation of ordinary body, speech, and mind should first learn about the practice of deity yoga. By studying and understanding secret mantra development and completion, one will establish a basis for practicing them. In this regard, it is not necessary to limit one's study to texts specific to Vajrakīla. Instead, it is sufficient to focus on any text that explains deity yoga. Since all deities are the same in essence, if one understands development and completion for one deity, one will understand them for all. Nevertheless, if one is particularly interested in Vajrakīla practice, one should focus on texts of the Earlier System—rather than the Latter—as there are some differences in the methods of meditation.

Each sadhana can have different descriptions of a single deity's appearance, ornaments, implements, and the like. Thus, one should visualize according to whatever is written in the particular text one is practicing. Since there are many different treasure revealers who have taught many different practices of even the same deity, if one relies on thangkas and other images, one should make certain that they accurately depict the deity described in one's own sadhana.

It is said that the form of the deity is the union of clarity and emptiness, as is the immeasurable palace. The more one trains in the development stages, the clearer the forms of the deity, retinue, and mandala become. That clarity is empty in essence, like a rainbow with no material substance at which to grasp. These insubstantial forms of the mandala and deities parallel this world and the beings therein. Hearing this, some give rise to doubts, thinking, "Both the container and contents are real—solid and unyielding. They seem to me to have the nature of stability and permanence."

However, in actuality, the entire container and everything therein are an aggregated mass of atomic particles. Every single day, the component parts of this mass erode, being subject to dispersion. This is well understood by scientists. Suspended in empty space, this earthly realm can be struck by an asteroid and smashed to bits in a single instant. It can be destroyed at any moment due to myriad conditions. In actual fact, container and contents lack inherent existence, just as Lord Buddha taught. They are adventitious, illusory phenomena.

In order to introduce this truth, it is taught in the development-stage yogas that meditators should first imagine empty space. Therein, all the phenomena of samsara and nirvana are transient, fleeting, and illusory. Like rainbows, they suddenly appear and—just as suddenly—disappear. The outer worldly container is an example of this. As for the inner sentient contents, their bodies are simply microcosms of the container. That is to say, the entire world is mirrored in a single individual's body.

When learning to visualize oneself as the deity, one will encounter conditioned physical imprints. Ordinarily, one thinks that this body of flesh and blood is one's own. However, this is not the case. The body is merely like a temporary dwelling. Thus, it is said in *The Thirty-Seven Practices of Bodhisattvas*, "Consciousness, the guest, will cast aside the guesthouse of the body."[23] So, the body does not belong to oneself; it is like a worn-out costume that must be discarded at the time of death. Since the body is not one's own, the mind is of principal importance. When the deity emerges in the mind, one understands the mind to be the creator of the deity. This is the first experience of the development stages' effectiveness.

Since there are so many different sorts of individuals with different dispositions, some types are better suited to the practice of the development-stage yogas. In particular, those with untamed, restless thoughts and clinging to concrete experiences of embodiment absolutely require the stages of development.

In the past, when my root gurus would offer instructions on deity yoga, they taught that practitioners should first investigate the degree of grasping at their own bodies. People who have great clinging to the body of flesh, blood, and bones and who strongly identify with their bodies as being very substantial—as though they were truly existent—should particularly engage the development-stage practices. Those with rigid, unyielding concepts about the gross physical form will especially benefit from the progressive trainings of deity yoga. This will allow such types to gradually realize the aggregates, elements, and sense fields as being divine in nature.

Others, through habits established in former lives, do not really think much about their bodies as being existent or nonexistent. When I was a small child first receiving instruction in deity yoga, my guru asked me, "How do you conceive of your body?" I answered, "I don't really think about it. It's not as though I have a body, and it's not as though I don't." He told me this is the best sort of view of embodiment. An individual with this kind of experience should give rise to the complete form of the deity all of a sudden, without thinking that the gross body is existent or not. Because such types have good habits from the past, they should emphasize the completion-stage yogas, focusing principally on the concentration being, who will be described later.

It is common for those who are unaccustomed to visualization to have difficulty imagining the deity's body. In order to train in the development stages, one should set up an image of the deity and study it while giving rise to a mind of great faith. Merely to look at an image and recognize the deity to be Vajrakumāra by his color, ornaments, and implements is an inconceivably great merit. Repeatedly viewing the deity's image will cause his form to appear in the mind's eye, just like a picture one is drawing. The mind is like an empty mirror; the deity image is like a reflection in that mirror. Since the self is a mere construct, when one continually thinks of the deity—the naturally manifest shape of bodhicitta—one's mind will emerge as the deity.

One should trace the body of the deity from the crown protuberance down to the lotus beneath his feet, visualizing the crown ornament, the dress, and accoutrements one by one. This should be done repeatedly. When one closes one's eyes, these images will arise vaguely in short glimpses. When they first appear, it will seem like they are facing oneself—as though one's own body were separate from the deity.

But where do they actually abide? If one can forget the material body, it becomes like an empty vase, inside which the deity is produced by the mind. Gradually, one will come to recognize that the image is actually oneself. One will know that one's mind inhabits the visualized form of the deity. In this way, the body of flesh and blood is forgotten. Once this has been established, one can train by imagining the form of the deity becoming as large as Mount Meru, filling the billionfold universe, or becoming as tiny as a mustard seed. Since the mind alone is the creator of these phenomena, such development-stage trainings are easy to accomplish.

As long as one has a body, one is subject to self-grasping. In other words, clinging to the "I" is an inherent feature of embodiment. Whenever there is self-grasping, there are propensities. Even so, if one does not part from the clear appearance of the deity while in one's embodied state, one will become able to recall the deity and instantaneously to receive his or her blessing in the bardo of dharmatā. Since only a mental body appears in the bardo, one can easily manifest as the deity, whose form vividly arises the moment it is brought to mind. The instant that resplendent blessing is received, there will be neither self-grasping nor propensities.

This distinction between the embodied state and the unembodied state, especially, should be clearly understood through individually discriminating intelligence. When the mind is unencumbered by physical form, it easily emerges in the shape of whatever is imagined. Thus, the moment one visualizes the deity, the mind will transform into the deity. Such ability comes from having trained in the stages of development. If one contemplates this, one will understand the benefit and power of deity yoga. Regardless of one's current level of proficiency in visualization, one should have confidence that even an unclear, momentary glimpse brings about benefits that cannot be conceived.

General Introduction to the Stages of Development

Since we human beings are subject to birth and death, the development-stage yogas are for the purpose of mastering the birth phase of becoming, while the completion stage is related to the death phase of becoming.

Although there are many different types of development-stage yogas, it is not necessary to consider each of them as being distinct. The four main types are taught in accord with the four modes of birth within the six classes of beings: womb birth, egg birth, birth from warmth and moisture, and miraculous birth. These are also related to the four classes of tantra: action, conduct, yoga, and unsurpassed yoga tantra, respectively.

The more extensive development-stage yogas are referred to as "the five-step development of manifest enlightenment" and are said to purify womb births. The four-step vajra development purifies egg births. The three-step *samādhi*, or concentration, development purifies births through warmth and moisture, such as insect births. Finally, the fourth mode involves a single step and is known as "the development through instantaneous surge." It purifies miraculous births, such as those of gods born from flowers, as well as of demons, *rākṣasas*, pretas, and hell beings. Therefore, the four types of development-stage yogas block rebirths via the four modes.

A yogin should first become familiar with the five-step mode of development. By doing so, he or she becomes capable of blocking the doors to inferior types of birth in the six realms. Having trained in the pure perception of container and contents, one will perceive one's future parents as yidam deities. Thus, free of ordinary appearances, the sādhaka will perceive him- or herself as the HŪṂ syllable and so forth. Through mere recollection, transformation is achieved. With such pure perception, consciousness transforms into the deity; oneself and one's parents actually become pure deities capable of acting for the welfare of sentient ones. In this way, even though, according to outer appearances, one may take rebirth in the worldly realm of human beings under the influence of karma, one will obtain a precious human body of pleasing form in a noble family line.

After one has a general understanding and experience of the most elaborate stages of development, one can then gradually simplify the style of practice, engaging four and then three steps of development stages. Finally, one will become very familiar with the deity, the sadhana recitation will be committed to memory, and one will know by heart the accompanying melodies. At that juncture, in accord with miraculous birth, the deity will spontaneously appear in the mind as soon as one gives rise to the notion "I must benefit sentient ones." His or her body can easily be imagined so large that it fills all of space or as tiny as the minutest conceivable form. This sort of mental agility is endowed with great potency. Thus, when one has become habituated to the causes that are the development stages of secret mantra, one will finally attain, in an instant, the result—miraculous birth in accord with unsurpassed yoga tantra.

With regard to profound, miraculous birth that occurs in an instant, it is said in the supplemental verses to *Gongchig: The Single Intent, the Sacred Dharma*, "The sudden approach to the deity is a profound key point."[24] This refers to realization manifesting in the instant of recollection. Although this method of knowing things to be as they truly are is taught in accord with unsurpassed yoga tantra for those of highest faculties, it is also easy for beginners. In order to practice it, one must first arouse compassion for sentient ones, then cause the deity's complete form to appear suddenly in the mind. On the basis of that clear appearance, one should give rise to faith and love. When I was small, I also trained in this method, which is well suited to novices. This means of instantaneous engagement is the union of development and completion in which one realizes the beginningless inseparability of oneself and the deity.

It is also on this basis that the practitioner can realize the saṁbhogakāya in the bardo. When one dies and falls into unconsciousness, the mind separates from the body. If one immediately recalls the deity the moment one reemerges into awareness—even if the visualization is unclear—the mind will merge into the heart of the actual yidam in a single instant. This occurs due to the sādhaka's great love for the yidam deity.

Otherwise, if even the slightest other concept arises between unconsciousness and the recollection of the deity, the innate mind becomes obscured, giving rise to the imprints of one's previous embodied life. Lacking autonomy, one will thus follow whichever karma and habits are most prominent and will encounter difficulties. Under the influence of delusive karma and propensities, one misperceives negative births as good circumstances, conditioning rebirth in the bad migrations of animals or other inferior life forms.

For these reasons, it is taught that in order to gauge one's ability to attain enlightenment in the second bardo, one should look at what happens at the moment of waking from sleep. If one can immediately recall the deity at the moment of waking, one can determine that one will be able to attain enlightenment in the second bardo. Thus, it is extremely important to become habituated to this recollection.

In order to understand the meaning of the development stages, one must know that all visualized phenomena are present as adventitious, transient events. In the completion stage, these phenomena disintegrate. Beings habitually grasp at the outer container that is this world and its inner sentient contents as being real and inherently existent. However, if one practices this union of development and completion again and again, such grasping will also fall apart.

When it does fall apart, what sort of felt experience arises? When the generated immeasurable palace and so forth are deconstructed in the completion stage, how does it feel? For example, if one thinks of this building and then closes one's eyes, it can feel as though the building is no longer present.

How is it if one does not train in this way? As I described before, when one sits inside a room and visualizes the deity, if the visualized form becomes too large, one will have the perception that the deity's crown has reached the ceiling. This is a sign that one continues to grasp at appearances as being real. In this way, training in the development stages is extremely beneficial for destroying the mind's grasping.

If one can clearly visualize the stages of development in the mind, it will benefit one's activities and support the accomplishment of the common siddhis along the way. However, even without siddhis, it is important to practice until such clear appearance is finally achieved. The development-stage visualizations transform the mind's various gross and subtle thoughts. In this regard, the Tibetan king Songtsen Gampo said in the *Maṇi Kabum*, "The transformation of ordinary thoughts is named 'the stages of development.'"[25] These words are very meaningful. By recalling the pure, clear appearance of the deity and the emanating out and gathering back of light rays, one transforms the impure into the pure. At that juncture, it will be easy to transform the pure into the view that is emptiness, wherein propensities cannot be established. Finally, the mind's grasping at phenomena as being real and true will be destroyed. This destruction of all grasping is the point of the uncommon siddhi. These are the ways in which the development stages purify the mind's obscurations.

Whenever one has a perception of something as being true, one should train first by giving rise to doubt about whether or not it is actually true. From that, one should think that one's grasping at that phenomenon as real is itself incorrect. In this way, by continually disrupting one's belief in the validity of one's own perceptions, one becomes familiarized with the illusory nature of appearances. Although one can carry on daily activities while abiding in this awareness, it becomes no longer possible to interact with worldly phenomena in the same ways as ordinary beings.

One should contemplate well and then train in these different methods of engaging the development stages during meditation sessions and also during daily activities.

General Introduction to the Completion Stage

In the contexts of action and conduct tantra, both development and completion are a bit extensive. In the contexts of yoga tantra and the unsurpassed yoga tantra class to which Vajrakīla belongs, once one has become habituated to the more elaborate development and completion, it is suitable to begin practicing them with less and less elaboration.

While one is asleep, the earthly container and contents perceived in dreams are entirely fabricated by the mind. Appearing like a movie on a screen, the dream space one inhabits is a creation of collective karma and imprints. Once one has a conceptual understanding of the composite, impermanent nature of phenomena, then one engages the development-stage yogas in order to realize the ultimate meaning. One should meditate on this planet Earth as being the complete and pure mandala of the deity, even if the visualization is merely approximate. Insubstantial like cumulus clouds, the visualization is the illusory union of clarity and emptiness.

Then, when one trains in the completion stage, all outer appearances dissolve gradually, like clouds vanishing or fog dispersing. The entire mandala is gathered into the father-mother consorts in union. The mother consort then dissolves into the heruka,* who is gathered into the seed syllable at the heart, which also disappears. In this way, one slowly gathers the visualization together in progressive stages like the petals of a flower closing. Finally, having dissolved into the dharmakāya, one abides in empty awareness.

For the Vajrakīla practitioner who understands the actual condition of the mind, there is an abbreviated completion stage: the visualized, rainbowlike mandala of the deity suddenly dissolves without a trace as one places the mind in the view. These examples illustrate the variability of the methods for practicing the completion stage depending on one's degree of habituation to the nature of mind. The final point of the completion stage is to arrive at the view, the fact of emptiness, the inseparability of self and other. Since it will be impossible to cultivate the completion stage while being unacquainted with the view, it is important to familiarize it.

*The Sanskrit term *heruka* is translated into Tibetan as *trakthung* and means "blood drinker." It refers to any wrathful male yidam who bears the charnel-ground attire. In the present text, it most often pertains to the deity Vajrakīla.

In this regard, *The Sutra on Emancipation* says, “More meaningful than to revive all sentient ones who fill the three realms is to enter absorption one time.”[26] Such are the benefits of cultivating meditative states according to the Greater and Smaller Vehicles.

When one has become habituated to this practice, even though the appearances of the worldly container and sentient contents are outwardly visible, whenever one leaves them aside and closes one’s eyes, since the mind has become free of grasping, one cannot tell whether one is indoors or out. During a group retreat, the notion of individual sādhakas in the assembly breaks down and all merge into nondual wisdom-awareness. By training in the rainbowlike development stages and the gathering-in of completion, even though the entire world remains manifestly present, the moment one merely closes one’s eyes, it is as though nothing at all exists. This is a sign that clinging to things as real is being reversed. On this basis, the sādhaka may begin training in the gathering-in of the principal and mandala in a single instant.

Practitioners must understand that these outer phases of completion-stage meditation have a great connection to the inner dissolution of the physical elements at the time of death. This is the import of the completion stage’s gathering phase, which parallels the death phase of becoming. At the time of death, there are three junctures. These are the junctures of (1) the luminosity of deep sleep, (2) equilibrium, and (3) death. Since the mind itself is deathless, it continues beyond these junctures.

Because sleep and death are parallel experiences, one dies a small death every night. By training in dream yoga, one will come to understand the stages of dying precisely. As one falls asleep, the dissolutions of earth, water, fire, and wind are experienced, each one being consumed by the next. Finally, falling unconscious into the deep sleep state, one experiences the unconsciousness of dying. If one really wishes to train in the completion stage, one should train in dream yoga.

When one’s karmically destined life span is exhausted, this same process will be experienced in dying. However, unlike sleep, one will not reemerge from this dissolution. The outer five elements will each dissolve—earth into water, water into fire, and fire into wind. As wind dissolves into space-consciousness, the body will become devoid of warmth like a lamp that has run out of oil. Then, one will fall unconscious. Finally, the consciousness will transfer from the body. Even though the corpse is left behind like a withered flower, it is no longer sustained by the five elements, whose inner essences have gathered into one another. Finally, the essences themselves are exhausted.

After the consciousness has left the body, it follows the course of karmic winds. For those who have cultivated bodhicitta, it is driven by the winds of bodhicitta, causing the forms and spheres of pure buddha realms to appear. For those whose karma is rooted in dualistic grasping at self and others, thoughts of desire and aversion will drive the karmic winds, causing rebirth among the six classes of wayfarers. In this way, the winds of autonomy are known as "wisdom winds" and those of dependency are called "afflictive winds." These different manifestations of wind energies can be understood as follows: Those who know how to practice are able to recognize strong thoughts and afflictions as they arise. Because their discriminating intelligence perceives thoughts as thoughts, they disintegrate like waves merging back into the ocean. This state of autonomy causes the wisdom winds to guide the bardo consciousness to the pure buddha realms or to a birth in the human realm in which one can act for the welfare of others. This is how nirmāṇakāya emanations manifest.

Conversely, when one habitually falls under the influence of arising afflictions, one accumulates karma of body and speech, which drives karmic winds. As a result, many hardships and sufferings are experienced throughout one's life. These are exceeded only by the sufferings that come after death. In this way, sādhakas should understand the distinction between wisdom winds and karmic winds.

In general, the completion stage is spoken of in terms of knowing the actual condition of the mind. Even so, some people give rise to doubts, thinking that no matter how much one cultivates the completion stage, this planet Earth still remains. Such doubts are utterly mistaken. Like a bubble on the surface of water, this earthly realm is continually subject to destruction. There are tens of thousands of planets—as many as the stars in space. Each night, countless numbers of them along with all the life forms that dwell thereon are smashed to dust and carried away by winds. If one contemplates this, one will understand how impermanent this world—suspended in empty space—actually is. The inner body is similarly impermanent. And since the body is host to hundreds of thousands of microorganisms, the body isn't just oneself alone. This is why it is called an aggregate; it is a composite phenomenon. As long as something is composite, it is impermanent.

Tomorrow, when one's body has died, one's consciousness will not even perceive planet Earth. Driven by karmic winds, consciousness will have departed into empty space like an airplane from which the land is no longer visible. Thus, consciousness will wander throughout the three planes. As for the aggregates, even though there will no longer be any form, one will still have sensation, cognition, formatives, and consciousness. Since these will be present, one will continue to experience sufferings like those of one's embodied life. Such is the state of dependency of beings in the bardo.

There are those who receive these instructions on development and completion and think that they apply only to meditation sessions—that they are not for continuous use. Such thinking is mistaken. As development and completion are directly related to the stages of conception, birth, and dying, they should be practiced each morning as one wakes and each night as one falls asleep. In the best case, they will eventually become integrated into each moment of one's daily experience.

When waking in the morning, one awakens into the daytime stages of development. It is said that all daytime appearances are like dreams. In order to stabilize this understanding, one should think in the following way: "When I was conceived into my mother's womb, it was as though I fell into a dream that lasted until I took birth in this worldly realm. Similarly, all my present experiences of this life are the illusory, dreamlike phenomena of one single day. Tomorrow, after I have died, this entire life will seem to have been a dream. I will think, 'Yesterday I arrived in the human realm. Today I have reached the bardo.'"

By training in this way, one will become truly able to perceive this life as a dream. This is the purpose of dream yoga and of the yogas of development and completion—to experience each of these junctures as the illusory phenomena of a single day.

Group Accomplishment Retreats

At this point, disciples have generally received many diverse practice instructions from various teachers in different places. This is like having gone to market and bought a lot of food. In order to be nourished, though, one must actually prepare and eat the food. Otherwise, it becomes rotten and goes to waste, and on top of that, one still feels hungry! Similarly, the instructions one has received must be put into practice in order to obtain the results. To participate in an accomplishment retreat is like actually eating the food and tasting its flavor.

One can give rise to some degree of conceptual understanding when language is used to explain the teachings, but if one fails to apply the methods through continual practice, mere knowledge will not bring much benefit. In this regard, we speak of the triad of understanding, experience, and realization. First, one must comprehend the meaning of the teachings. Then, one must gain experience of them by cultivating meditation again and again. Finally, with realization emerges profound belief.

For example, it is taught that afflictions are primordial awareness. Once this has been understood, one cultivates the mindful awareness that recognizes thoughts as they arise. Meditating with each new thought, one can experience directly how thoughts arise and disappear one after the next. Through habituating to this experience, one gains realization, knowing with confidence that afflictions are empty. Since thoughts and emotions are immediately neutralized by awareness, they cannot have any effect. In this way, all the teachings must be integrated through these three stages of understanding, experience, and realization. The secret accomplishment retreat is a very powerful means of doing so.

Because one's normal day-to-day life is quite comfortable and, by contrast, retreats are inconvenient, sometimes students perceive retreat to be a hardship. However, the comforts one experiences in this life are only the fleeting results of virtuous karma gathered in former lifetimes. When the pleasures of this life result in distraction from Dharma practice, it is a manifestation of the māra of the son of the gods. That is to say, within this human realm, some experience comforts like those of the gods. This is something practitioners must be heedful of. By considering the causes that have given rise to one's present comfort and by contemplating its temporary nature, one will be inspired to persevere in practice.

Due to distraction, it is difficult to perceive one's thoughts and afflictions. Through practice in retreat, the mind settles down and one can begin to see those afflictions that were not seen before. So, when beginning serious Dharma practice, one is confronted with the difficulty of seeing one's own faults. At this juncture, since one feels worse and more afflicted, insight can seem to be a greater hardship than the ignorance of not seeing. However, as one becomes habituated to the practice, one finds there is no happiness without it. In this way, one's habits gradually change.

Sometimes practitioners also experience illness in retreat. By understanding illness and pain as opportunities to purify latencies that have always been present, one comes to appreciate the ripening power of practice. Considering this, one will feel motivated to persevere with diligence.

Sādhakas should also reflect on how—during the course of a human life—so much time is wasted in sleep, which is the nature of ignorance. The night sessions during the secret accomplishment retreat help to purify the obscurations of such laziness. For this reason, it is very important that practitioners maintain the night sessions. Whenever a dull mind of drowsiness manifests, one can dispel it by developing anger at sleepiness and contemplating all the useless hours one has wasted in sleep. In addition, one can expel the breath strongly, remove a layer of clothing to keep the body cool, or circumambulate the mandala. By sleeping less and less each night, eventually the body will require only five or six hours per night. Otherwise, if one places no limits on sleep, the body will demand more and more of it. Some people sleep day in and day out like animals. Once such habits are established, it becomes very difficult to reverse them later in life.

Even in Tibet, where the conditions are much harsher than those in the West, I found that I never became the least bit fatigued during great accomplishment retreats. There, the weather is unimaginably cold and uncomfortable, with no conveniences like indoor heating. Since the monks and I did such retreats a number of times under harsh conditions, we were accustomed to it. Now, having come to the West, we have grown used to comforts such as air conditioning and heating. The memories of what it was like in Tibet have faded, so now we feel tired even doing a single retreat under the best conditions!

Whenever sādhakas feel discouraged by the hardships of practice, it is good to take a long view, thinking, "Now is my opportunity to practice. If I fail to do so today, what will I do later when I encounter difficulties? What will I do at the time of death?" When experiencing the slight privations of the present, one should place those difficulties within the larger context of past and future experiences. One should reflect on how important it is to practice now for the sake of future lifetimes, since the conditions one will face later in this life and in subsequent lives are uncertain.

As the main focus of the accomplishment retreat is the practice of deity yoga, one should understand that however many instructions one receives, however many different practices one does, all deities are of a singular nature. All wisdom deities are subsumed within whichever deity one practices. All deity yogas lead to a single fruition, which is the purification of physical, verbal, and mental obscurations. One is thus ripened into the pure body, speech, and mind of the deity. When one continually visualizes the present, impure aggregate of flesh and blood—this composite phenomenon—as being like a rainbow, it ripens into the yidam deity, the saṁbhogakāya. Diverse nirmāṇakāyas who can act for the sake of sentient ones emerge from that. Since the group accomplishment retreat leads to this sort of fruition, it is extremely worthwhile.

In fact, Guru Rinpoche taught that to take part in such a retreat for seven days is of greater benefit than seven years of solitary practice. How is this so? In a group accomplishment retreat, there are gathered many people of diverse high, middling, and lesser faculties. Since the ground of their mind is singular and since the physical aggregates, elements, and sense fields of beings are also the same, if practitioners assemble and cultivate bodhicitta, connect with the yidam, and recite mantra together, their merits are multiplied exponentially. When an assembly includes individuals who are well habituated to approach and accomplishment, each member of the group receives the same force of blessing as do those experienced meditators. If there is even one person in the assembly who has great qualities, everyone present will reap the benefit of that person's meditation. Furthermore, if one hundred people gather together in an accomplishment retreat, each individual participant accumulates the merit of the virtuous physical and verbal conduct of all one hundred. This is due to the qualities of bodhicitta. Therefore, one need not think, "Since I am only a new practitioner, I cannot really participate in accomplishment retreats."

Another reason why such group retreats are so efficacious is that if sādhakas come together in a retreat for a short period of time, they support one another in exerting themselves and maintaining single-pointed focus free of distraction. Conversely, when one is in long-term solitary retreat, there is a great risk of becoming distracted, sleeping a lot, and taking it easy.

After having gained the experience of the accomplishment retreat, at night when one lies down to sleep, in the best case, one should play a recording of the mantra and fall asleep recalling the retreat experience. Then, hearing the sound of the mantra in one's dream state, one will awaken into the appearance of the accomplishment retreat. This is a sign that one's propensities are being reversed. When the appearances of the deity and mantra arise in the mind, one will become manifestly able to accomplish them within the pure fields.

In order to engage this training, one should wake up naturally, without the aid of an alarm. When falling asleep with the intention to wake at a certain hour, one will usually wake within a minute or two of the designated time.

If through the power of the mantra's sound, one can recall the deity at the moment of waking from sleep, it is certain that one will attain buddhahood into the saṁbhogakāya in the second bardo. This was taught by my own guru, Khenpo Münsel.

Similarly, if one again and again gives rise to the mirrorlike mind of rigpa, it will be accomplished. One will attain mastery over whichever created habits one trains in. In this regard, one should look at the propensity that first arises at the moment of waking from sleep. If the thought of "I" appears, that self-grasping will obscure the mind. On the other hand, if the appearance of the deity arises based on the sound of the mantra, one need not have any doubt. The most important fruition of the accomplishment retreat is the destruction of self-grasping that occurs through visualizing the deity and reciting his or her mantra. It is of vital importance to practice these points and to carry forward the positive habits laid down during the accomplishment retreat.

Benefits of Mantra Recitation

As a support to the practice of deity yoga, practitioners should understand the nine benefits of mantra recitation that were explained by Guru Rinpoche.

The first benefit—the perception of mantra as the actual deity—is the principal one. It can be understood in a number of ways. Since the mantra is the name of the deity, with each recitation, one calls out to him or to her. Thus, the recitation is like calling a companion on the phone, creating a connection between the deity and the sādhaka. In this way, mantra is a means of meeting and becoming acquainted with the deity. Through meeting repeatedly, a bond of love and compassion is cultivated and a friendship stabilized. By remaining close for a lifetime, the sādhaka and yidam mingle and become one in mind and activities.

In addition, some ritual texts of the Latter System refer to the different sorts of ḍākiṇīs: mantra-born and field-born. That is to say, some are manifestly born within this human realm, while others spontaneously arise from mantra itself. From each mantra that is recited with the force of bodhicitta, one illusory, rainbowlike saṁbhogakāya form manifests. From each one of those deities emanate ten more wisdom deities, and from each of those emanate ten more, making a hundred, and so on. In this way, one should visualize that millions of primary, secondary, and tertiary emanations stream forth by means of the recitation.

For example, in the mantra OṀ MAṆI PADME HŪṂ, each syllable is a seed syllable representing one of the teachers of the six classes of beings. Thus, the divine, illusory forms of those guides manifest with each recitation, pervading the six realms. The scope of their emanations, capabilities, and activities is directly related to the sādhaka's motivation—to the vastness of his or her development of bodhicitta.

When one has the wish to benefit every sentient being of the three realms, a single mantra can instantaneously pervade the pure buddha-fields as well as the suffering hearts of all beings. This occurs on the level of the ultimate factual truth that is dharmatā. Of course, on the conventional fictional level of dualistic views, there exist innumerable buddhas and innumerable sentient ones. However, on the ultimate level, in which both self and other lack inherent existence, all these manifold appearances are but miraculous displays of the mind. One should understand mantra as deity in these ways.

The second benefit is the perception of mantra as offering. Generally, people continually think, "I need this. I want that." However, by cultivating faith, love, and the wish to benefit others, one can antidote such habits of desire, avarice, and greed through the practice of offering.

With each mantra recitation, one makes offering to all the buddhas. A person who has given rise to bodhicitta as well as trusting, lucid, and aspiring faith will naturally want to practice generosity, thinking, "How wonderful it would be if I could make offerings to the pure buddha-fields!" Likewise, one will wish to make offerings to lamas and monasteries and to support pūjas and the like. Even though he or she may not be endowed with great material resources, a person who has such wishes will eventually become able to make actual offerings to the buddha-fields through imagining vast offerings. In the future, having purified the mind's obscurations and the propensities of avarice and greed through this merit, one will experience results that resemble the cause—perfect wealth and common accomplishments.

Even though one may think, "I have no wealth or resources at all," one can still supplicate to become able to make offerings. The nature of bodhicitta is such that when one supplicates in this way, one's own aspiration will enter the mindstreams of various kinds of sentient ones, so that those who do have such resources will be inspired to practice generosity and to make offerings. This is because the basis that is bodhicitta is singular; the mind of all beings has but one basis. So, even if one cannot personally practice vast generosity, such results can still occur. This is how all the pure buddha-fields have come into existence—through the qualities of aspiration, love, and bodhicitta. One who understands the unified basis of bodhicitta will be able to see this at work.

In order to become generous, one should think about the obstacles to generosity. One way in which people's miserliness manifests is in the reluctance to pay taxes. This is something practitioners should consider. If a dollar is paid in taxes, the government uses that money to improve the conditions in the country. For as long as beings are enriched by those improvements, one will continue to reap the benefit of one's generosity. When this is understood, there is no need to have an attitude of stinginess. If, say, one aspired to do something that could benefit the entire country, one could not find a suitable means of reaching everyone. However, merely paying taxes allows one to act in the service of the entire nation and everyone therein! Not only that, one serves all those around the world who receive aid from one's country.

In this way, practitioners should consider every expenditure to be the practice of generosity. For example, when someone who has the Buddhist view stays in a hotel, that person can reflect with gratitude on having a place to stay and can pay the bill with the aspiration that the hotel will flourish through his or her generosity. With this sort of good motivation, every expenditure becomes virtue.

Even when one loses wealth and possessions to others, one can be grateful, thinking that karmic debts are being exhausted through the retribution. By understanding the mindset of offering and generosity, one can practice the skillful means that dispel all suffering of loss.

Someone who doesn't understand this point encounters a double loss: Since one must pay the bill anyway, one loses their precious wealth in the moment. Then, in the long run, one accumulates only stinginess, having lost out on the opportunity to gain merit through practicing generosity with joy.

Thus, in order to purify bad rebirths in disadvantaged conditions due to the karmic accumulation of avarice and greed, one must make offerings to the Three Jewels above and practice generosity for the impoverished below. When meditating on the emanating out and gathering-back of light rays during the mantra recitation, one should imagine that the revolving mantra strand radiates rays of light. At the tip of each light ray is an offering goddess. Each of them further emanates ten goddesses, who each emanate ten more, and so on until space is filled with elaborate offerings to the innumerable pure buddha-fields of the materials found in this world. By conjoining recitation with the force that is bodhicitta, one can accomplish actual vast offerings to the buddhas.

This is not a mere fabrication; the space constituent is naturally pervaded by the force of the five elements' richness. However, those who lack merit cannot access this wealth. For example, when people are enjoying a delicious picnic, all around there are countless insects on the verge of starvation who have no power to receive the bounty of the food that is right there! This is solely due to the faults of avarice and greed, which come from self-grasping. Considering this, one can see that the fully ripened effect of actions is truly inconceivable. Though coexisting in the same space and time, some experience the delights of the higher realms while others experience the torture of the pretas' realm. Since there is not the slightest difference between the minds of those insects and our own minds, it is appropriate to give rise to trepidation about one's own karmic accumulation. These are some of the points sādhakas should consider regarding the perception of mantra as offering.

The third benefit is the perception of mantra as dispelling obscurations. Whenever one recites mantra with compassion for all sentient beings of the six classes, light rays and emanations that are the nature of compassion spontaneously radiate outward. These rays of love and compassion touch all sentient ones, purifying their obscurations, karmic habits, sufferings, and the self-grasping that is their cause—melting them like the sun's rays on fallen snow. To whatever degree one has compassion, one will possess a corresponding power to benefit beings.

This is how even the deities, who are the nondual union of emptiness and compassion, come into being. They are the physical expressions of love and compassion for all sentient ones of the six classes—for example, pretas, who endure hunger and thirst, and hell beings, who suffer extremes of pain, heat, cold, and the like. So, if one wishes to cultivate deity yoga, the important point is to give rise to love and compassion for suffering sentient ones. The root of their suffering is self-grasping, through which they give rise to afflictions and engage actions, which create imprints in the mind. Such imprints are continually reflected back to them as their inner experiences of suffering. For example, the natural reflection of aversion is the projection of the hell realms. Thus, self-appearances are all reflections of the phenomena of one's own mind.

For one who has not yet realized the actual natural state of the mind—one who cannot see phenomena as they truly are—even if that person were to travel to the pure buddha-fields, he or she would perceive them as hell realms. Conversely, for one who has the mindset of perceiving things as they truly are—one who understands the natural expressions of bodhicitta—even the hells will appear as pure fields. This illustrates how self-appearances are mere reflections of one's own phenomena.

From the ultimate perspective, if one cultivates the mind wishing to benefit others, it tears down one's own and others' self-grasping. When through the mantra recitation, sentient ones are pervaded by bodhicitta, they will all transform into the deity.

From the conventional perspective, the rainfall, sun, moon, flora, and fauna—all of these are truly the spontaneous manifestations of buddhas and bodhisattvas that have come into existence through aspirations and through the force of love. Everything that brings benefit to beings has its root in bodhicitta. For someone who knows how to view these things, they are unmistaken divine manifestations in this worldly realm—nirmāṇakāyas that bring actual benefit. They appear for the purpose of increasing beings' gratitude and trust. Thus, the dispelling of obscurations should be understood as the ability to benefit mothers—sentient ones of the six classes—in ways great and small.

The fourth benefit is the perception of mantra as siddhis, or actual accomplishments. During every empowerment, sādhakas supplicate the vajra master to bestow accomplishments, such as the eight great common siddhis and the supreme siddhi. What does this mean? By meditating again and again on the mantra strand, one gives rise to an abiding love for the deity. Due to the power of love, the practitioner becomes free of the ego. Freedom from self is the nature of bliss. In this way, when one can no longer forget the deity, one experiences the bliss of selflessness. Siddhis should be understood, then, as the emergence of selflessness in the mind.

On the basis of selflessness, one receives the deity's blessings in the form of light rays that bestow the buddhas' enlightened body, speech, and mind. Since they are the nature of the five elements, the light rays also grant the accomplishment of longevity. Because the mind is the basis of the actual accomplishment of the deity, one first realizes the deity's appearance. Then, in the bardo, one will attain the deity's complete attributes, thus accomplishing all of his or her abilities.

Having actually experienced the potent capacity of those blessings, one will become able to transmit them to others. Then, whenever the pure deity's form arises in one's mind, there will be direct benefit to beings. In this regard, the scriptures say, "Finally, one familiarizes the deity's blessings. Through the potency of those blessings, others' appearances are transformed."[27] Mantra as siddhis should be understood in this way.

Some people think that the actual accomplishment of the deity will result in his or her outward physical manifestation. This is a greatly mistaken idea. Rather, when one closes one's eyes and suddenly thinks of the deity, he or she can appear in great and small forms—momentarily arising and just as suddenly disappearing. This is a sign of the siddhi of the deity. Likewise, when one's love for all other sentient beings is stable and one's patience can withstand any degree of harm by them, these are the true signs of accomplishment.

Fifth is the perception of mantra as blessing. In terms of the visualization that accompanies the approach mantra, this is described with the words, "Every blessing of body, speech, and mind comes like rainfall as white OṀ, red ĀḤ, and blue HŪṂ̐, merging ceaselessly into my three places." But the actual blessing is this: By focusing on the revolving mantra conjoined with samādhi, the mind becomes devoid of self-grasping. Thus, the deity's bodhicitta and one's own mindstream inseparably mingle, like milk poured into tea. The deity's love reaches one's mind, increasing one's capacity for love and compassion. This, in turn, enriches discriminating intelligence, which enables one to abandon harming others and to give rise to the mind wishing to accomplish beings' benefit. Because mantra carries the blessings of the deity's mindstream, one should understand mantra as blessing.

The sixth benefit is the perception of mantra as the mandala. A sādhaka trains in the daily ritual practice of the deity, beginning with refuge and bodhicitta and going step by step through the development and completion stages of the sadhana. Later, through continued practice, the union of development and completion is habituated. Finally, one will reach the point at which one can suddenly give rise to the entire deity and mandala in an instant of recollection. The mandala and the deity will have become indistinguishable like the sun and its rays. At that juncture, it is not necessary to recite the liturgy, since to chant the mantra even once will invoke the complete mandala of deities.

Thus, the outer container will be perceived as the nature of the deity's mandala; the inner sentient contents will be recognized in their pure aspect at the very basis. In this way, the intent of great accomplishment will be realized. Such spontaneous manifestation of pure appearance is the meaning of mantra as the mandala.

Closely related to this is that mantra can function as *homa*, or the fire pūja. In this context, the outer container is to the body as the inner contents are to the mind. Since many hundreds of thousands of microorganisms dwell in and on the human body, one should think that the macrocosm of the container and contents is complete within the microcosm of one's own body-mind continuum. Thus, when the digestive fire extracts nutrition from the food one has consumed, it becomes a fire pūja, whereby one makes offering to the mandala of deities. This accords with Lord Milarepa's instruction on food and drink as being the *gaṇacakra*.

Seventh is the perception of mantra as enlightened activities, which have both common and supreme aspects. The common siddhis manifest as the ability to benefit self and others through the recitation of mantra and the ability to accomplish whichever of the four activities—pacifying, enriching, magnetizing, or destructive—one may practice. If, for example, one meditates on the revolving mantra while experiencing physical pain, the pain can be pacified. One can visualize that the light rays arisen from the mantra manifest in the aspect of flames at the place of pain or illness. Meditating on selflessness by imagining that the entire body has become a heap of flames brings actual benefit for all physical illnesses. Even if one has a karmic malady that must be experienced, although it may not be completely healed by this method, at least one's pain will be greatly diminished. In this way, obscurations will also be purified. Conversely, if one grasps at the thought of illness, one can worsen whatever physical problems are present and can even give rise to sickness where none exists. When the mind is focused on pain, the wind energies gather in that place of pain. Wherever the wind energies gather, the blood pools, creating stagnation and giving rise to disorders.

Because of this, skillful ones have compassionately taught the methods of meditating on the deity, the mantra, and the mind-wind energies that pervade the body. For example, I have a friend, a lama, who can recite mantra over metal or stone for a few minutes and have it become as hot as a branding iron, which can then be used to heal people.[28] In the past, he has helped me greatly by touching such consecrated implements to my body. Mantra-born accomplishments such as this, clairvoyance, and various other miracles are examples of the common siddhis of enlightened activities.

Eighth is the perception of mantra as dharmatā. First, practitioners must train in recognizing the innate purity of all impure perceptions. When there is no longer any such thing as impure appearance, the union of appearance-emptiness is realized. Just like rainbows in space, phenomena appear in spite of their emptiness and are empty in spite of their appearances. As it says in the *Heart Sutra*, "Form is empty; emptiness is yet form."[29] This awareness is utterly free of dualistic grasping. Although diverse appearances manifest, they utterly lack a separate, independent existence.

Audible sounds should be understood in a similar way. Ordinary sounds produce grasping thoughts of attachment and aversion; however, because mantra is the nature of sound-emptiness, it scatters diverse thoughts, sufferings, and afflictions. When one recites the mantra while meditating free of thought, the empty nature of mind is revealed. Since the mantra can suspend thoughts and introduce the nature of mind as dharmatā, the mantra itself is considered to be dharmatā. These qualities are known through actually engaging the practice.

Finally, because mantra recitation brings about whatever siddhis and activities one could want and because it is capable of accomplishing the purposes of self and others, the ninth benefit is the perception of mantra as a wish-fulfilling jewel. Especially, as mentioned before, one should have the perception of mantra as siddhis. In order to attain the status of the buddhas, it is necessary to accomplish the deity. To do this, one should visualize only the deity's form and recite the mantra again and again. One must mingle one's mind with the deity via the first three branches of approach and accomplishment. Then, having become inseparable from the deity by meditating on the mantra strand, one can engage whatever activities are necessary. This nonduality of the sādhaka and deity in the context of great accomplishment is the supreme siddhi, the attainment of the Buddha's state. The all-knowing Longchen Rabjam taught that if one becomes inseparable from the deity through approach and accomplishment, all activities will naturally and spontaneously follow.

In addition, among the representations of the wish-granting enlightened body, speech, and mind, those of the buddhas' speech are of principal importance. As was prophesied by Lord Buddha, "In the future dregs of time, I shall come in written shapes."[30] Thus, since letters are the actual buddha, it is taught that they are very precious.

In this regard, it is said that a prayer wheel is the mantra strand made materially manifest. All virtues of body, speech, and mind are made complete in the prayer wheel. To turn the wheel with the hand is a substitute for offering prostration and circumambulation of holy sites. It is also a substitute for the verbal recitation of mantra. If, for example, a prayer wheel contains one hundred million mantras, with each revolution of the wheel, one hundred million emanated mantra-born deities stream forth like rainfall, pervading everywhere. As for the mind, it is necessary to have vigilant mindful awareness to maintain the constant revolving of the wheel. Since the prayer wheel stabilizes concentration, its benefits are exactly the same as those of the mantra strand.

Thus, Guru Rinpoche taught that to whatever extent one turns the prayer wheel, the three incessant things are present: "Ceaseless offerings are made to all the buddhas. Sentient ones' obscurations are ceaselessly purified. Actual accomplishments for oneself are without cease."[31]

These three come about through the power of samādhi. Since all the buddhas' blessings are like a continual rainfall, simultaneously dissolving into oneself and others, the two objectives are spontaneously accomplished. With regard to incessant actual accomplishments, to whatever degree one generates faith, love, and compassion, one experiences a corresponding purification of the obscuration of self-grasping. This is the actual accomplishment of the deity. While provisionally one attains the common accomplishments of births in the higher realms and so forth, ultimately one will attain the status of the buddhas, the supreme accomplishment. Such siddhis are the direct and actual benefits of the mantra wheel.

As an incentive to practice and as an encouragement to faith, when going about, sitting, or waking from sleep, one should recall these nine benefits of mantra, which are the sublime speech of Guru Rinpoche.

PART TWO

Experiential Instructions on the Practice of Vajrakīla

CHAPTER 3

Lineage Supplication Instructions

Having established some context and background for these teachings, we can now turn our attention to the practice text itself, which begins with a supplication to the masters of the lineage. It is titled *Melodious, Māra-Destroying Vajra Song: The Lineage Supplication That Encompasses the Buddha-Word and Treasure Transmissions of Vajrakīla.**

Within secret mantra mahāyoga, there can be found the subdivisions of tantra and sadhana. The sadhana class is further subdivided into the section of the buddha-word (*kama*) and the section of treasures (*terma*). In the beginning, there was the lineage of the buddha-words. It came in successive stages from Buddha Vajradhara, through Vajrapāṇi, Master of the Secrets, to Tilopa, Nāropa, Marpa, Milarepa, Gampopa, and so on. This is the secret mantra tradition of the Latter System. Later, in Tibet, Guru Rinpoche concealed the Dharma teachings as treasures to be brought forth by treasure revealers of future generations. Thus, from his era onward, there appeared the treasure tradition of the Earlier System. The Vajrakīla lineage supplication is addressed to the masters of both the buddha-word and treasure lineages.

It is an extremely meaningful Kagyü text that was composed by Jamgön Kongtrül. From the lineage supplication alone the totally

*Henceforth, Lama Garchen Rinpoche quotes extensively from the practice manual and supplemental texts, which he has assembled into the work titled *An Unelaborate Liturgical Arrangement of the Method for Accomplishing Vajrakīla*. The complete translation of these texts is found in part 3 of this book.

complete, sublime intent of all Vajrakīla practice can be understood. However, its import is not limited to the deity Vajrakīla, as it presents the entire path of Buddhist practice.

Lineage Masters

First, when supplicating the lineage masters to receive their blessings, it is good for practitioners to have some understanding of the origins of this transmission lineage, which were described previously.

Although the life stories of the lineage masters are beyond the scope of the present work, it is worth noting that Prabhahasti and Vimalamitra were among the eight Indian knowledge holders. Prabhahasti, who had received the transmission of Kīla Activity, was one of the teachers of Vajra Thötreng Tsal (a.k.a. Guru Rinpoche). Vimalamitra and Śīlamañju were contemporaries of Guru Rinpoche. Together, these three *ācāryas* helped to codify the Vajrakīla practices and their commentaries. Further, "Queen of Great Bliss" referred to in the text is Yeshe Tsogyal. She is also "the māra-subduing queen" whose speech is praised in the colophon of the practice manual.

Since the accounts of the lives of great siddhas are so inspiring, I encourage students to read the liberation stories of the Vajrakīla masters named in the lineage supplication and empowerment text.

View, Meditation, and Conduct

The buddhas' blessings are ever present. Even so, the practitioner must express his or her wish to receive them. Through making sincere requests, one engages one's connection with the Three Jewels and Three Roots, opening the door for them to bestow the bounty of their blessings. Thus, through supplicating the lineage masters, one expresses one's aspiration to do as they have done by attaining the fortress of the view, crossing the abyss of meditation, and seizing the life force that is conduct. From the perspective of the Earlier System, this triad of view, meditation, and conduct is of essential importance.

There are countless commentaries that clarify many different aspects of the view, meditation, and conduct according to the needs of those of high, middling, and lesser faculties. For those who want to understand the inner meaning of the lineage supplication, what is important is not so much the words but, rather, the key points to be meditated upon. Therefore, I would like to offer a bit of explanation of the stages of the grounds and paths from the perspective of practice using my own personal experience as a reference.

The Fortress of the View

In the first verse, one calls by name some of the masters of the buddha-word lineage—the lineage of the profound view—and supplicates them as follows:

> To the buddha-word lineage I pray:
> primal Küntuzangpo-Dorje Chang,
> five families' blood-drinking herukas,
> great Lekyi Wangmo, Prabhahasti,
> Vajra Thötreng Tsal, Vimamitra,
> Queen of Great Bliss, māras' subduer,
> Śīlamañju, worship's great object,
> lord and subjects, you the twenty-five,
> in particular, Nanam and Chim,
> Shübu, Rongzom, and the clan of Khön—
> may I gain the fortress of the view!

In brief, "the fortress of the view" is the buddhas' teachings, namely, the scripture and reasoning of Madhyamaka, the mahāmudrā of the Latter System of secret mantra, and the dzogchen of the Earlier System. If these three are summarized, they are the exclusively clean, actual condition of the mind itself. To whatever degree one is able to realize the mind's nature, there will be a corresponding degree of confidence and freedom from doubt.

How does this lack of doubt arise? Some meditators gain confidence through tenacity of mind, experiencing the hardships of intensive practice, as did Milarepa. However, most give rise to freedom from doubt through the interaction of the guru's blessing with their devotion.

Practitioners can ascertain for themselves whether they are free from doubt. If one continually looks outward in search of answers to questions, it is difficult to arrive at such freedom. On the other hand, when one meditates on the mind itself, one understands, "This is it; there is no doubt." In this way, when one determines for oneself that the buddha nature is the causal basis of buddhahood, the fortress of the view is gained.

Until that fortress has been attained, one must cultivate assurance in conventional bodhicitta—that is, love and compassion for all who have not yet realized the mind's nature. Precious bodhicitta protects the mind from afflictions. When one is never parted from the thought "I want to become able to benefit sentient ones day and night without interruption," assurance in the view is close at hand.

One should begin to nurture conventional bodhicitta first by contemplating the kindness of loved ones, then by cultivating patience for those enemies who despise one. By one's practicing in this way, conventional bodhicitta free of bias will gradually become stabilized. This conventional, or fictional, bodhicitta leads to the realization of ultimate, or truly factual, bodhicitta, "the fortress of the view." Once the two types of bodhicitta have become stable, one will not give rise to anger even if someone takes one's life.

In addition, attaining the fortress of the view can be understood in three stages that accord with the paths of individual liberation, bodhisattvas, and secret mantra. From the perspective of individual liberation, when one engenders great belief in the undeceiving and incontrovertible nature of karma, the fortress of the view has been gained.

For someone engaging in the practice of conventional bodhicitta, the fortress of the view should be understood as follows: When one has absolute certainty in the notion that every sentient being without exception has been one's parent and that the mind set on benefiting others is the cause of buddhahood, one will cherish that mindset like one's own life force. This is the incontrovertibility of cause and effect on the inner level. Through it, one attains the fortress of the fictional view that is conventional bodhicitta.

Once this fortress of the conventional view has been gained, when one sees the actual condition of the mind, one engenders trust in the view that is the nonduality of self and other. This is the fortress of the ultimate, or truly factual, view. Because these sorts of understandings arise naturally during practice, there is no need to regard the view as something distant.

In the context of secret mantra, when one comprehends this fortress of the truly factual view, every outer object that appears is like an illusion, not existing as a separate entity. Together with this freedom from dualistic grasping comes the arising of pure perception, in which self and other become divinely manifest, appearing like deities with rainbow forms, like the reflections that appear from a faceted crystal. Such experience is the attainment of the fortress of the view from a secret mantra perspective.

The term *fortress* refers to a great conviction free from any doubt about the preciousness of bodhicitta. It is a confidence beyond change or transition. Regardless of what others may say or what conditions may occur, from one's own side, no uncertainty can arise. When one has such freedom from doubt about the view, the fortress has been attained. At the outset, it is all right if one only gives rise to this sort of confidence provisionally based on circumstances. Eventually, it will become stable and unconditional.

The Abyss of Meditation

When the fortress of the view is attained, self and other, samsara and nirvana, love and compassion are all seen as circumstantial and illusory. At this juncture, the perilous abyss of meditation is encountered. The path of meditation is perilous because when difficulties arise in practice, the meditator can give rise to sudden, unmitigated afflictions.[1] Thus, in the second verse, one supplicates the masters of the lineage of treasures—the blessing-practice lineage—with these words:

> To the treasure lineage I pray:
> Chökyi Wangchug, plumed Rigdzin Gödem,
> Sanggye Lingpa, Drime Dorje, and
> Rinchen Palzang, self-freed Padma Ling,
> Düdül Nüden, Dzamling Dorje Tsal,
> Ratön, Choggyur Lingpa, and the rest—
> may I cross meditation's abyss!

This treasure lineage has manifested on the basis of the Bodhisattva Vehicle and the Secret Mantric Vehicle, with its emphasis on deity visualization and mantra recitation. In this context, if one wishes to stabilize the view, it is important to do so not only under good conditions, such as during meditation sessions, but also when one meets with great obstacles and negative circumstances, which are referred to as "the abyss of meditation." Thus, in all daily activities, no matter what one is engaged in, one should seek to cultivate mindful awareness and the clear appearance of the deity. Once these become stable, whatever one encounters can be brought onto the path without one falling under the power of adverse conditions.

Each individual can check the degree of his or her own realization by looking at how he or she responds to negative circumstances. When meeting with unfavorable conditions, one perceives the limit of what has been accomplished through spiritual practice. Once one has reached a certain level of the view, one no longer falls under the power of pleasure, pain, or any other such experience. One is fit to cross the abyss of meditation when mindful awareness cannot be influenced by outer circumstances and when knowing is self-sustaining.

The abyss of meditation can also be understood in different ways according to the three vehicles. From the perspective of individual liberation, the abyss is faced when one separates from heedful, mindful awareness—specifically, mindfulness of the incontrovertibility of cause and effect mentioned earlier. As a result, there will occur faults, such as vinaya defeats and downfalls, in one's actions of body, speech, and mind.

From the causal Great Vehicle perspective, four root downfalls to the bodhisattva's vow are taught. These downfalls are (1) praising oneself and disparaging others with attachment to gain or respect, (2) failing to help someone who is suffering when one is able to do so, (3) failing to forgive someone who has apologized, and (4) making false claims about one's own attainments. In brief, these four are subsumed within the root downfall of forsaking sentient ones, which can be understood in the following way:

During daily activities, passion, aversion, ignorance, and the like sometimes arise between friends or between guru and disciple. For example, when someone returns one's generosity with harm, one tends to become resentful, thinking, "Even though I have treated him well, he is mistreating me." Such a juncture is the meditational abyss to conventional bodhicitta. Since the root downfall of forsaking sentient ones can occur if one falls under the power of these afflictions, the bodhisattva must guard his or her mind. In order not to be influenced by self-grasping, one should recall the instructions from *The Thirty-Seven Practices of Bodhisattvas*, taking care not to allow one's bodhicitta and altruism to be wasted.

Even if sometimes one's altruistic intent is involuntarily lost, one should recognize that one has become angry, thinking, "This is not right! I have really lost bodhicitta!" In this way, by acknowledging and laying aside such faults day and night without interruption, one can restore conventional bodhicitta. Thus, it is said that conventional bodhicitta is like a gold chain: although it is easily damaged or broken, it is also easily repaired.

In other systems, such as that of individual liberation, if one's vows become corrupted, whether or not they can be restored depends on the presence or absence of self-grasping. Since all beings are afflicted by self-grasping, the vows of individual liberation are not subject to restoration—either they are preserved or they decline.

Thus, the potential for easy restoration is a special quality of the bodhisattva's vow. By practicing as described, understanding one's own anger from the perspective of love and bodhicitta, one will immediately be able to acknowledge faults and afflictions, apologize, and lay them aside. In this way, confident in the fortress of the view, one can continually restore the vow day and night whenever one encounters the abyss of meditation and falls under the power of obstacles.

From the perspective of the fruition Great Vehicle, Vajrakīla practice is the beneficial antidote to the three types of obstacles—outer, inner, and secret. Outer obstacles take the form of natural disasters like earthquakes, floods, fires, or tornadoes, which occur through imbalances of the four elements. Outer obstacles also manifest as accidents like airplane crashes. Some examples of inner obstacles are imbalances of the channels and wind energies—which can emerge when engaging yogic practices—as well as different kinds of illnesses. Finally, the secret obstacles of confused thoughts are the various afflictions and delusions that arise in the practice of mahāmudrā—confusions that are difficult to clear away with other antidotes.

In order to understand outer obstacles from the perspective of secret mantra, one should consider the following: The outer five elements that make up the container and contents are all divine in nature. Similarly, sentient beings are truly endowed with the buddha nature at the very basis. Thus, all outer objects are inherently pure. When sentient ones, earth, water, rocks, trees, and the like are perceived as ordinary, a root downfall to the secret mantra vows occurs. Such impure appearances manifest only due to the power of one's own afflictions. Thus, a practitioner of the Secret Mantric Vajra Vehicle encounters the abyss of meditation when perceiving impure appearances. By maintaining mindful awareness, one should recognize and lay aside the obstacles of impure perceptions.

After entering the path of Dharma and practicing for many years, some people fall under the power of inner obstacles and adverse conditions. Sometimes their relationship with a spiritual master deteriorates when they perceive faults and contradictions in that virtuous friend's conduct. In addition, sometimes they experience various physical illnesses and the like.

Such problems in one's relationship with the guru arise from not having maintained well the samaya with virtuous friends in former lives. Even so, these kinds of adverse conditions can become goads to spiritual accomplishments. It is said that however profound one's practice is, there will be correspondingly great obstacles on the path. Through sustaining the view, it is possible to become victorious over such obstacles, transforming them into siddhis. When one maintains this view, whatever great or small obstacles arise, one will be heedful not to fall under the power of even the slightest thought or affliction. In this way, all outer and inner obstacles will be rendered harmless.

Thus, the principal issue is the secret obstacle of confused thoughts. In this regard, Milarepa sang, "Among evil forces, thoughts are the greatest."[2] All harmful forces emerge from thoughts alone. For example, if one has a bad dream due to karma and imprints, one can give rise to a lot of superstitious thoughts about it, seeking out divinations and grasping at the possible meanings in such a way that the problem becomes bigger and bigger. In this way, something that was actually nothing to begin with becomes an obstacle capable of causing actual harm. This is a fault of being unable to subdue thoughts.

It is said that when one has a good dream that indicates accomplishments, it is best not to tell others about it. If it is disclosed, the accomplishments can disappear. Conversely, when one has a nightmare, one should recognize it as confused thinking and simply abandon it. In this way, practitioners should place in equanimity all judgments of good and bad. The best way to reverse any ill effects of dreams and bad omens is to recite the approach mantra of Tārā or other deities. If one sets aside all concepts about one's dreams, not disclosing them to others, they will be unable to do any harm at all. Through bringing down the secret obstacles of confused thinking in this way, there is no question that outer and inner obstacles will also be dispelled.

In his *Treasury of Experiential Pith Instructions*, the all-knowing Longchen Rabjam points to another way in which the abyss manifests, with the words "Just before siddhis are attained, all kinds of obstacles arise."[3] This occurs through the stirring-up, or provocation, of latencies. Throughout this and former lives, one has accumulated negative actions that have not yet ripened into suffering. Such negative imprints abide in the *ālaya*, or underlying consciousness, as latencies. For example, if one has an underlying biliary disease, it may not actually manifest until one consumes fatty foods.

Although such latencies tend to be suppressed in the context of individual liberation, their provocation is a necessary part of secret mantra practice. It is not as though some guru or master steps forward with the intention of provoking a practitioner. Rather, such provocation occurs as a natural consequence of one's own practice. Through blessings, hidden, latent illnesses or afflictions are stirred up. As they rise to the surface, they can be cut off, or liberated.

When one fails to take advantage of the opportunities presented by these junctures of provocation, one falls under the power of afflictions and they become obstacles. For this reason, practitioners should continually cultivate the heedful, aware mind that recognizes such secret obstacles to be signs of accomplishment. The supreme method of maintaining this recognition is the first of the four kīlas, that of primordial awareness-rigpa. Although these four will be explained in detail a bit later in the lineage supplication, for now, it is sufficient to know that the kīla of primordial awareness-rigpa is the view of mahāmudrā.

In this regard, in *The Supplication in Seven Chapters*, the Lotus-Born Guru who was victorious over all obstacles describes his own experience when practicing in the Yangleshö cave: "Hindrances and obstructive forces were liberated by Vajrakīla; mahāmudrā siddhi was attained in that holy place."[4] Through accomplishing mahāmudrā, foremost among all attainments, one will accomplish the two objectives. This means that by attaining the dharmakāya, one's own purpose will be fulfilled. Then, from the dharmakāya there will spontaneously emerge the form kāyas (*rūpakāya*)—that is, the saṁbhogakāyas and nirmāṇakāyas. Through these outer manifestations of enlightened speech and form, the purposes of others will be fulfilled.

If one can bring illness, affliction, and other obstacles onto the path through recognizing provocation and liberating it in the moment, one will attain a great, high ground. This is the occasion at which the abyss of meditation and the life force, conduct, come together.

The Life Force That Is Conduct

The third verse is addressed to some of the other great masters of the Vajrakīla transmission lineage, the lineage of vast conduct. In brief, the entirety of conduct can be subsumed within the instruction to "abandon harm to others and its cause, accomplish help to others and its cause, and become adept at the pure perception of the vessel and contents."[5] With the following words, practitioners supplicate for blessings to sustain the conduct:

> To the Dharma keepers, transmitters, I pray:
> Ma, Nyag, and the eight named Glorious,
> Nub, So, Zur, Odren, Lang, Venerable
> Ācārya Nuru, Langlab Jangdor,
> four supreme and honored disciples,
> Darchar, Rinzang, Rogchal, Terdag Ling,
> Venerable Chagme, and all the rest—
> may I seize the conduct, the life force!

Here, I should mention that the words of this verse appear differently in different editions of the Tibetan text. Sometimes the text reads, "May I seize the system (*söl*) that is conduct!" This notion of conduct being a system, or a custom, accords with the conventional meaning. It refers to the proper ritual engagement of various physical and verbal activities, such as playing musical instruments, chanting, and practicing *mudrās*, or hand gestures, and dance. The desire to practice well such outer ritual trainings with body, speech, and mind is a means of gathering vast accumulations of merit that will bear fruit for lifetimes. To practice in this way is an inconceivably great result that resembles the cause. If one performs the ritual practices properly, one seizes the system that is conduct. Conversely, if one performs them carelessly or incorrectly, the system is not retained. This conventional outer-level reading of these words is of primary importance for beginners.

Other editions read, "May I seize the life force (*sog*) that is conduct!" The notion of conduct being one's very life force accords with the ultimate meaning. This reading is of principal significance for a disciple who has seen the ultimate truth and holds the view.

Since both readings are acceptable, one can understand this line in two different ways. One should consider one's own experience and determine based on individually discriminating awareness which reading is more suitable.

With regard to the latter reading, conduct is the means whereby one maintains the two types of bodhicitta under all conditions, even at the cost of life. In the best case, having understood factual truth, one will experience phenomena as follows: All sights will dawn as the deity, appearance-emptiness. All sounds will be heard as mantra, sound-emptiness. All thoughts will be known as the play of primordial wisdom, awareness-emptiness. When sights, sounds, and thoughts manifest purely, the life force is truly being retained.

Having comprehended the view and traversed the abyss of meditation, one seizes the life force, conduct. That is to say, as one cultivates the view, one encounters the abyss yet does not fall under the power of conditions and obstacles, which invariably arise during the conduct of daily activities.

Such conduct is conditioned by two types of thoughts: virtuous or unvirtuous. In other traditions, it is said that there exist indeterminate thoughts, which are neither virtuous nor unvirtuous. However, if one really investigates, that which is called "indeterminate" is merely very subtle happiness or very subtle suffering. Thus, Dharmarāja Jigten Sumgön taught that there is no such thing as indeterminate thoughts. Since they are the nature of ignorance and delusion, they are nonvirtue. To maintain a view that is not overpowered either by happiness or by suffering and that transcends the duality of virtue and nonvirtue is conduct.

In this regard, it is said in *The Ganges: An Experiential Pith Instruction on Mahāmudrā*, "Your own mind, beyond color or form, is untainted by the black and white phenomena of evil and virtue."[6] Here, the word *black* refers to the suffering and ill-being caused by nonvirtue. *White* refers to ease, happiness, and all that is virtuous. The moment one gives rise to clinging to pleasure, the mind becomes obscured.

Sometimes, even when a practitioner is aware of the dividing line between virtue and nonvirtue, he or she consciously chooses to abandon virtuous conduct in the moment in order to indulge in what appears to be pleasure. For example, while enjoying heedless banter among friends, one may experience a moment of awareness—realizing that one has been engaging in divisive speech, harsh words, or gossip. Even though one knows better, one decides to suppress the wisdom of the inner guru in order to continue frivolous misconduct. Despite having had the extraordinary advantage of hearing and contemplating the teachings, by clinging to the deceptive pleasure of distraction, one throws away meditation in the moment. One willfully disregards the Dharma that has been taught by the guru.

This active ignoring is a misdeed graver than misconduct arisen from mere ignorance. Since karmic causality is incontrovertible, such choices that obscure the mind invariably ripen into suffering. A further downfall occurs when one abandons conventional bodhicitta, ignoring the effects one's actions of body and speech have on others, especially those who are vulnerable or of lesser faculties.

Thus, even though one may realize an exceedingly profound view, the conduct must not be lost in the view. It is for this reason that

Guru Rinpoche instructed practitioners of secret mantra, "The view is even loftier than the sky, yet karmic causality is even finer than flour."[7] Understanding this, meditators must unify the view and the conduct. This is accomplished outwardly by maintaining the conduct of individual liberation—preserving personal discipline and refraining from any action that would harm others. Inwardly, one upholds the bodhisattva's vow by never separating from love and compassion. Secretly, one maintains the mantric commitments by realizing the nonduality of self and other. In this way, having renounced gross misconduct, true practitioners should identify and then abandon ever subtler deviations from the conscience that is a manifestation of the inner guru.

In brief, clinging binds one to samsara. The person who becomes fettered by pleasure will definitely be bound by suffering. Conversely, the individual who is not bound by happiness cannot be bound by hardship. Some of the qualities of the mind not fettered by ill-being are expressed in *The Thirty-Seven Practices of Bodhisattvas*:

> Though I may lack sustenance, be constantly abused, stricken by grave illness and evil spirits, in return to be undaunted and to take upon myself all wayfarers' misdeeds and ill-being is the bodhisattvas' practice.[8]

Thus, whether one is experiencing pleasure or pain, if one does not part from the truly factual view, one recognizes both happiness and suffering to be concepts. When a concept is recognized through the view, regardless of whether it is pleasant or unpleasant, it is liberated. In this way, to bring afflictions, suffering, and illness—as well as bliss and happiness—onto the path is to retain the life force, conduct.

In order to accomplish this, one must have a view that is self-sustaining—that is able to hold its own. Never parting from mindful awareness throughout all one's activities, one avoids falling into dependency. In this regard, Jigme Lingpa said, "As long as aware knowing does not lose its autonomy, nothing more than this is needed."[9] This is simple to understand. The view, meditation, and conduct—the fortress, the abyss, and the life force—are complete within not allowing autonomous knowing-awareness to lapse.

Stated another way, if the fortress of the view has truly been gained, the life force, conduct, is retained and the abyss of meditation traversed. Both meditation and conduct are integrated within the single method that is assurance in the view. This is an absolutely essential point.

From a yogic perspective, one maintains the conduct by stabilizing mindful awareness together with the clear appearance of the deity. Never parting from vigilant mindful awareness, one identifies the coarse and subtle thoughts that arise when sitting or going about—during all one's activities throughout the three periods of the day.

Likewise, throughout the night, one recognizes the dream state and apprehends the luminosity of deep sleep. When day and night become indistinguishable and the mind remains uninterruptedly free of distraction throughout every action, one will have perfected the activities of body, speech, and mind. Whatever one does will spontaneously accomplish the benefit of others, all activities will become merit, the dream state will manifest as luminosity, and so forth. In this way, one will retain the life force that is conduct.

In brief, all the dualistic distinctions of conventional truth fall away within the actual condition of the mind itself. In this context of nondual awareness, Lord Milarepa expressed the ultimate qualities of the view, meditation, and conduct:

> The view is free of scripture and reasoning.
> Meditation is free of experience.
> Conduct is free of time.
> The guru is free of compassion, and
> the disciple free of devotion.[10]

Mandala Deities

The fourth verse elaborates the deities who make up the mandala of Vajrakīla with the following lines:

> To Kīla's divine mandala hosts I pray:
> Vajrasattva, who's comprised of peaceful and
> wrathful families' illusory displays,
> Dharmevajra, Master of the Secrets, and
> Dorje Namjom who cuts out confusion's root.

In general, all the Vajra-family deities are combined within Vajrakumāra. In particular, Vajrakumāra is the extremely wrathful great personage in whom are gathered together peaceful Vajrasattva, wrathful Vajrapāṇi (the "Master of the Secrets," also named Dharmevajra), who appears in both the Earlier and Latter Tantric Systems, and the one who is known in the Sutra System as Vajravidarana (Dorje Namjom). Indeed, the five families of the victorious ones—all the buddhas of the ten directions and three times—are subsumed within Vajrakumāra, who is described next:

> Dharmasphere-born body of compassionate wrath,
> actor of a hundred moods, the blazing, great
> māra tamer, god who's perfected as one
> the activities that suitably tame beings,
> Glorious Great Vajrakumāra, most supreme,
> space and wisdom's union, Khorlo Gyedebma,
> ten strengths and perfections, ten wrathful pairs' mode,
> falcon hosts, gate guards, almighties, and oath-bounds—
> may I conquer māras completely!

All demonic forces are subsumed within the four māras, which are elaborated in subsequent verses. As the essence of the body, speech, mind, attributes, and activities of all the three times' buddhas, Vajrakīla is completely victorious over the māra of the aggregates, the māra of afflictions, the māra of the lord of death, and the māra of the son of the gods. Understanding this, one can truly supplicate him with the words, "May I conquer māras completely!"

The Four Kīlas

These four māras are associated with the four kīlas. That is to say, the utterly secret kīla of unfurled and pervasive primordial awareness, the inner kīla of immeasurable compassion, the secret kīla of bodhicitta, and the outer material kīla of signs are the means of prevailing over the four māras. All the characteristics and inner meaning of the yidam Vajrakīla are subsumed within the four kīlas. Furthermore, since all the practices of the Bodhisattva Vehicle and the Secret Mantric Vehicle are complete within these four, they are of extreme importance.

The Kīla of Pervasive Wisdom

The principal among them is the first one, the kīla of unfurled and pervasive primordial awareness. This is also referred to as the kīla of primordial awareness-rigpa or, less commonly, as the symbolic kīla of blessing. In the context of mahāmudrā, the view is often termed *primordial awareness*. In a dzogchen context, it is called *rigpa*. However, the essential meaning is the same. It is the ultimate factual bodhicitta referred to in the following verse:

> Self-arisen rigpa's mastery—the
> blue-black weapon—shines forth in place of
> life force as primordial wisdom-wrath.
> When the dharmasphere is planted with
> all-pervasive wisdom's kīla, may
> all dualistic concepts be cut off!

This kīla of unfurled and all-pervasive wisdom is connected with the fortress of the view that was explained earlier. There is but one primordial awareness-wisdom, the singular mind of all the buddhas' omniscience. Rigpa is seeing the mind itself, the actual condition that is mahāmudrā. It is knowing the union of clarity and emptiness to be nondual. This kīla has the quality of transparency. That is, since it represents the scattering of all thoughts and emotions through mindful awareness, it renders every apparently substantial thing unobstructive. By abiding within this nature of mind, one is able to liberate afflictions spontaneously. In this way, whatever negative conditions one meets are brought onto the path instead of becoming impediments.

This kīla of primordial awareness-rigpa has three aspects. The first is the kīla of the expanse. The empty expanse is like the outer sky, which is a metaphor for the inner mind. The second aspect is the kīla of wisdom—the view of mahāmudrā, which scatters all thoughts and afflictions. Finally, when meditating on the nature of mind that is mahāmudrā, one's mind merges with the outer sky. Thus, one realizes that rigpa—the basis of mind—and the expanse are singular in essence. This unified expanse-rigpa is the third aspect, the kīla of nonduality, the supreme among all kīlas.

Since no new teaching is being presented here, it is important that practitioners not become overwhelmed by terminology. What is being explained are things one regularly practices already. For example, when meditating, one experiences nondual clarity and emptiness, through which one understands that there is no difference between the outer sky and one's inner mind.

When a thought or emotion arises from within that state, the mindful awareness that recognizes it is the kīla of primordial awareness-rigpa. The moment the thought has been recognized, it is liberated in its own place, like a bubble on the surface of water that appears for a moment and then bursts. In this way, the thought has been struck by the kīla of primordial awareness-rigpa. Whatever may arise—a thought, an affliction, grasping at things as real—when it is liberated in its own place, it is the dharmakāya into which it has been liberated. This scattering of thoughts through mindful awareness is what is to be practiced continually. It is nothing other than the basic meaning of mahāmudrā and dzogchen. For those who have already been introduced to this view, it is not necessary to say much.

Those who have not should consider well these words:

> Self-arisen rigpa's mastery—the
> blue-black weapon—shines forth in place of
> life force as primordial wisdom-wrath.

In order to understand their meaning, first it is necessary to distinguish clearly what rigpa is. When one looks at the mind with the mind and recognizes that a thought has arisen, one must discriminate between the thought and that which recognizes the thought. Rigpa is not the thought itself; rather, it is the knowing aspect that is capable of apprehending the thought. It is that which recognizes whatever appears in the mind. It immediately knows whenever an affliction has arisen. It is the vigilant mindful awareness referred to in *The Thirty-Seven Practices of Bodhisattvas*:

> In brief, whatever course of action one takes, one should ask, "What is the state of my mind?" Accomplishing others' purpose through continually being mindful and vigilant is the bodhisattvas' practice.[11]

If one looks directly at that knowing awareness, inquiring into what it is or where it is, it immediately vanishes, having become like space. When one turns the mind back upon itself, there is no mind to be seen. Although it pervades everything, it is not an object of investigation.

If I were to ask who among you recognizes rigpa, some would respond, "I don't recognize it." Yet rigpa itself is the very one that gave rise to the thought "I don't recognize it." It is the knower of one's own nonrecognition. The moment one tries to identify that knower, it disappears. Since that knowing awareness is the nature of emptiness, it is invisible. Not even the buddhas can see it. In this way, one should understand the mind to be the union of clarity and emptiness. Clarity is the knowing awareness that recognizes whether or not thoughts or emotions are arising. Emptiness is the transparency of that awareness. It is all-pervading, like space. If one asks how rigpa has manifested, it is spontaneously arisen—not created by anyone or anything at all. Thus, the text refers to it as "self-arisen."

Since it is the dividing line between samsara and nirvana, the difference between mastery and nonmastery of self-arisen rigpa should be understood.* This can be clarified by distinguishing between consciousness (*namshe*) and primordial awareness (*yeshe*), each of which has a knowing, cognizant quality (*she*). The consciousness is that which knows how to do various activities. It also distinguishes among the superficial appearances of outer objects. In the state of non-mastery, when one does not perceive the actual condition, the mind manifests as consciousness—the ordinary life force. All sentient beings—those with and without forms—have this consciousness that is conjoined with self-grasping in its impure state. Lacking self-recognition, consciousness manifests as the notion of an "I," the cause of all the innumerable sufferings of birth and death in cyclic existence.

Conversely, when the knowing aspect of consciousness is used to look at its own face, then that knowing aspect becomes like space, the nondual union of clarity and emptiness—the actual condition of the mind that is mahāmudrā. In this way, when cognizance is turned back on itself and recognizes itself, it becomes primordial awareness, the causal basis of the buddhas. In the scriptures, it is said, "Since it has been present from the beginning, it is called 'primordial.' Since it is all-knowing, it is called 'awareness.'"[12]

*What is translated here as "mastery" is *tsaldzog* in Tibetan. The term *tsal* means "liveliness" or "expressivity" and is synonymous with another term, *nüpa*, which means "potential." Thus, it is the natural potential of self-knowing—the capacity of the mind to give rise to myriad thoughts and emotions and to be aware of them. Every gross or subtle thought or emotion that arises is merely the expressivity of rigpa. The second syllable, *dzog*, means "complete." So, the term "mastery" refers to having brought to completion this lively, self-aware expressivity of rigpa.

This is the wisdom of individual reflexive rigpa referred to in the prajñāpāramitā literature. When one has understood the actual condition of the mind, the entire container and contents—samsara and nirvana—are known as the nature of wisdom, the domain and the play of primordial awareness. They are all-encompassing purity without the slightest taint.

By seeing this, one knows one's own mind to be buddha. Thus, one will know every sentient being to be a buddha at the fundamental ground. Once this has been understood, one has seen the singular basis, the underlying life force of every phenomenon of samsara and nirvana. Such experience becomes a cause for developing belief. From the perspective of autonomy, which was explained earlier, the root of all empowerment and independence is to give rise to adamantine reflexive awareness.

It is said in *The Aspiration of Samantabhadra*, "If just that is known, such is buddha; if not, such is a sentient one drifting through samsara."[13] Similarly, Milarepa said, "When this is not comprehended, it is ignorance. When it is comprehended, it is self-knowing primordial awareness."[14] This is the meaning of the first kīla. In the beginning, one must understand rigpa. Having understood it, one will know everything. This is the meaning of the phrase "Everything becomes liberated through knowing the one."[15] From this—the actual condition of the mind—every other quality arises. Compassion spontaneously increases and one becomes able to eliminate afflictions. This is what is meant by self-arisen rigpa's mastery.

The method of entry into this practice was explained by the wisdom ḍākiṇī Niguma to Nāropa as follows: "As long as the spark of wisdom is weak, one must time and again feed the flame of mindfulness."[16] This means that when one first glimpses the nature of mind, it is like a weak spark. When the strength of awareness is feeble, thoughts and afflictions can overpower it, just as a log can snuff out a small flame. Since it can be easily extinguished at that stage, vigilant mindful awareness and afflictions appear to be two different things. Therefore, in order to eliminate afflictions, one needs constant diligence in meditation. The method to strengthen the flame of awareness is compassion conjoined with wisdom. As one continually cultivates it, the spark becomes a flame, which increases in strength by burning each arising thought as fuel. Eventually, rigpa becomes like a powerful fire that consumes without discrimination whatever it touches, liberating every thought—great and small—into primordial awareness-wisdom. Finally, one sees that awareness and afflictions are not two. This is what Lord Milarepa meant when he sang, "When afflictions and primordial awareness are no different, one has mastered the full measure of realization."[17]

The afflictions themselves are the nature of emptiness; they themselves are wisdom. Through mindful awareness alone, all the five afflictions are dominated. Even though one may feed five different sorts of kindling to a fire, they are all equally and without distinction transformed into flame. Aversion is nothing other than mirrorlike wisdom; lust is individually discriminating wisdom. In this way, afflictions and wisdom are not separate.

For example, if one recognizes that one has suddenly become very angry, the knowing aspect of the mind that gives rise to the recognition is rigpa itself. If that rigpa maintains its autonomy, one will not follow the affliction of anger or its associated thoughts and emotions. There will be no need to argue or fight. In this way, the fuel of afflictions is consumed by the fire of rigpa; one becomes free of the affliction merely by abiding within rigpa.

Mastery, then, is the capacity of the knower to recognize the mind's diverse expressions without wavering. Since, through recognition, thoughts are liberated on arising, there is no need to fear afflictions or to think they are bad. Such fears and doubts arise only due to nonmastery.

In the development stages of Vajrakīla, this quality of mastery takes a form. It appears as the blue-black-hued weapon referred to in the text. The weapon is a metaphor for the visualized HŪṂ̊, the seed syllable of every deity. Those who have not yet understood rigpa can naturally experience selflessness through cultivating ongoing awareness of the HŪṂ̊ syllable, which scatters self-grasping and causes one to forget the body. As the HŪṂ̊ is the nature of empty awareness in the aspect of a flame, it burns away the "I," giving rise to the experience of selflessness. The moment one thinks of the seed syllable HŪM̐, all other thoughts and emotions temporarily cease. Although some cannot yet feel this, they will eventually be able to experience it through cultivating the visualization.

At present, one should utilize this method of the seed syllable. As long as one remains in the state of nonmastery, meditating on or verbalizing the HŪM̐ syllable can cut off and destroy whatever thoughts or emotions arise.

In connection with these lines from the lineage supplication, there is a special secret mantra method for accomplishing mastery. It is described in the extensive Vajrakīla practice manual with these words:

> HŪM̐! The wrathful vajra cuts off aggression.
> In the depths of space there dawns a dot,
> a great and blazing blue-black weapon
> shining forth in place of life force.
> Visualize it in the core of your heart.[18]

It is said that one should engage this visualization to scatter or destroy self-grasping and accomplish the kīla of unfurled and pervasive wisdom. While one imagines the HŪM̐ syllable in one's heart center, there clearly appears in the depths of space a blue-black HŪM̐ or a blue-black vajra like the dawning of a bright star. From it appears a sudden bolt of lightning. The instant its brilliant light shines forth, it strikes the mirrored HŪM̐ or vajra at one's heart, igniting it like explosives that blow one's body to particles. This completely destroys dualistic consciousness and clearly distinguishes mind from body. The mind that grasps at a self is destroyed together with the body. What remains is luminosity, the indestructible mind that is the buddha nature, abiding like space. Empty and cleared out yet brightly vivid, it is totally unfurled, pervading everywhere. It is said that those of highest faculties should meditate in this way.

Another method that uses the HŪM̐ syllable to scatter thoughts and emotions is as follows: First, one should cause the HŪM̌ to appear clearly in the mind. Then, when intense bliss or a forceful affliction such as great suffering arises, if one shouts "HŪM̌!" the wind energies will conjoin at the navel, causing them to enter the central channel. This is similar to exclaiming the syllable "PHAṬ!" in dzogchen practice.

Having experienced how shouting "HŪM̌!" causes thoughts and emotions to scatter, one will search for the next thought to disrupt. By dispersing thoughts again and again, finally one will recognize and abide within the post-attainment that is rigpa. Generally, one distinguishes between the "equipoise" of formal meditation sessions and the "post-attainment" that is every other post-meditative experience. However, liberation on arising occurs when rigpa has seized and is holding its own place. This is the post-attainment that is rigpa—a state in which equipoise and post-attainment are indistinguishable. One should try this method for oneself, meditating and investigating whether a powerful thought or emotion can be dispersed through exclaiming "HŪM̌!" Then one will understand the potency of the HŪM̌ syllable.

Wherever one goes in the world, one can witness people's bodies being destroyed by violence, accidents, disease, and famine. However, in all those cases their self-grasping minds remain unharmed. In order to accomplish the destruction of self-grasping, one must destroy thoughts and emotions, since it is those very thoughts and emotions that created the body in the first place. One who becomes skilled at scattering thoughts now will become able to destroy self-grasping in the future.

The blue-black weapon that is the seed syllable is extremely powerful. Since it is the union of emptiness and compassion, it destroys the self-grasping that causes beings to wander the six realms. It demolishes karmic habits, leaving clear rigpa in its wake. Even though a bomb can wreak terrible destruction and a few together could wipe out the entire planet, they could never destroy self-grasping or karmic habits. It is only by means of the weapon of bodhicitta taught by the buddhas that this can occur. Thus, the seed syllable is even more powerful than an atomic bomb. For these reasons, it is referred to as a "great weapon" in the extensive Vajrakīla sadhana. This ability of the seed syllable to scatter all thoughts and dualistic view is the quality of rigpa. This is what is meant by "the kīla of unfurled and pervasive primordial awareness." That kīla is none other than Vajrakumāra himself.

Referring to the mastery of self-arisen rigpa, the text says,

> ... blue-black weapon—shines forth in place of
> life force as primordial wisdom-wrath.

Here, the term *life force* is not the "life force, conduct" explained earlier. The life force mentioned here is the notion of an "I," the doer who engages in worldly, samsaric activities. It is the aforementioned consciousness. For example, when one experiences hunger, pain, or peril in a dream, even though the body is lying comfortably in bed, the mind's experience of hunger or peril is exactly the same as in the waking state. It is due to the imprints of self-grasping that such dramas are played out in the dream state. That self-grasping consciousness is the life force referred to here. If one investigates whether or not a self is truly present in these dreaming and waking experiences, one finds that there is none. There really is no "I."

However, if one cannot scatter these experiences of self-grasping during the waking and dreams of this lifetime, the sufferings experienced in the bardo will be far more intense than those of this life. Lacking any physical form, one will manifestly endure the sights, sounds, smells, and sensations of the three lower realms as though one had a body.

Understanding this, it is wise to investigate how the self came into being. It is something all sentient ones have entirely fabricated. If one thinks there is an "I"—a self—then that self is one's own creation. If one leaves it in its own place without attaching a name to it, then it can neither be said to exist nor to not exist. When one believes there is an "I," then it is present. When one does not, it is absent. The entire six realms have come about through beings' belief in a self. It is only due to the imprints of karmic habit that one reconstructs a self after every death. Within the mind's pure nature, there is no self or other to be found. While abiding in that nature, one loses the "I." As soon as one emerges from that, the "I" is reassembled. So, one is recreating it moment by moment.

Due to grasping at a self, all beings fear death. But the body is not the self. One day the body will disintegrate. When it dies, does the mind also die? No, the mind is deathless. So, for the practitioner, once the body has been destroyed, the HŪṀ syllable arises in place of self-grasping consciousness—the ordinary life force. In this way, the kīla of unfurled and pervasive wisdom liberates the māra of the lord of death by seizing the ordinary life force of sentient ones. The only thing that remains, then, is wisdom—the space-like clarity-emptiness that has the same essence as the dharmakāya. Thus, one arrives at the post-attainment that is rigpa. This primordial awareness-wisdom is the buddha nature itself. It is Vajrakumāra.

This wisdom that destroys thoughts and afflictions has a fierce quality, which spontaneously manifests as the flame heaps that surround wrathful deities or as the flaming sword of Mañjuśrī. The symbolic meaning is that when one has realized the essence that is rigpa, whatever thought or affliction arises is immediately burnt away or cut off, leaving pristine mind in its wake. This is how the five afflictions are transformed into the five wisdoms on arising. The purpose of practicing wrathful deities, then, is to realize mahāmudrā. Vajrakīla and Yamāntaka are extraordinary methods for realizing the view. In this way, one should understand the "primordial wisdom-wrath" that emerges to replace life force to be none other than Vajrakumāra himself.

The words of the lineage supplication continue,

> When the dharmasphere is planted with
> all-pervasive wisdom's kīla, may
> all dualistic concepts be cut off!

In this regard, Milarepa said, "The learned who understand do not see consciousness; they see primordial awareness."[19] This primordial awareness-wisdom is like space in that it suffuses everything, even apparently solid material forms. For this reason, the kīla of unfurled, pervasive primordial awareness is referred to as "pervasive." Lacking any obstruction or hindrance, it is completely dispersed, without any substance to be grasped at. This is what is meant by the term *unfurled*. For example, the bodies of all sentient beings are pervaded by mind. If not, the body is a corpse. Yet, if one tries to pinpoint where the mind is located, one cannot identify any single object, as mind is invisible and spread out everywhere. Thus, the terms *pervasive* and *unfurled* should be understood in this way.

This kīla of unfurled, pervasive primordial awareness is the view of mahāmudrā, of dzogchen, as well as of the scripture and reasoning of Madhyamaka. Although it goes by many names, it has but one meaning—the actual condition of the mind in which there is no distinction between mind and the space of the dharmasphere. By abiding therein, one transcends dualism.

For example, if one observes the mind closely when meditating on the HŪṂ syllable, there is no dualistic grasping. Thus, that which is called "primordial awareness" is nonduality. When one has been introduced to the actual condition of mind—when one comprehends the rigpa that is like space without center or limits and abides therein—one understands the nonduality of self and other. This is also referred to as the view of inseparable samsara and nirvana, the view of the single taste.

In general, when one speaks about the nonduality of self and other, it is possible to understand it clearly from a conceptual perspective. Yet it is only by engaging the actual practice that one can have a direct experience of the real condition that is the sky-like mind. Through such experience, self-grasping and ego boundaries dissolve, eliminating the separation between self and other. In this way, the kīla of primordial awareness-rigpa shuts down dualistic concepts. Through continually engaging the practice, one can habituate a direct experience of the view. Once one has finally attained mastery, thoughts and emotions will no longer do any harm. One will no longer need to apply any antidote, as the mind will naturally abide clear and empty like the sky. When every thought that arises is understood to be rigpa, all thoughts become empty. In this way, the kīla of unfurled and pervasive wisdom is planted into the sphere of phenomena.

Although many words are used to explain this kīla of pervasive wisdom, in the end understanding does not come from concepts. It arises only through turning the mind inward on itself. By doing so, one will penetrate the meaning. In this regard, Milarepa said, "Do not try to resolve phenomena; resolve the mind."[20] Since investigation of the outer phenomena of samsara and nirvana is without end, a lot of talk and conceptualization bring only limited benefit. In brief, the fruit of having mastered rigpa is that all dualistic concepts will be cut off.

Rigpa is not something exotic. It is already present as the knower of whatever happiness, suffering, and afflictions are arising in one's own mind. In the state of nonmastery, even though one may recognize the afflictions in one's mind, one cannot liberate them. Thus, they condition karmic accumulations that result in suffering. However, once one has attained mastery of rigpa, one becomes able not only to recognize afflictions but also to render them impotent and eliminate them. In this way, as one abides in ultimate factual bodhicitta, every thought and emotion of duality and separation will be cut off.

The Kīla of Immeasurable Compassion

Second is the kīla of immeasurable compassion, which is nothing other than conventional fictional bodhicitta in its immaterial aspect. The verse on the second kīla begins as follows:

> Skandhas, dhātus, [āyatanas]—the
> three seats—pack the vajra channel wheels.[21]

There is much that is taught about the three seats—the aggregates (*skandhas*), elements (*dhātus*), and sense fields (*āyatanas*). Even so, it is possible to understand them simply by apprehending a single point. In general, people vaguely conceive of the self as a complete whole that includes the body and mind. For example, one can consider an automobile, which can be thought of as a single thing. However, when just one small electrical circuit in the car is not functioning, the entire vehicle can be rendered useless. Similarly, practitioners should conceive of the body as a composite that has come about due to numerous causes and conditions. If one slight cause or condition is removed, the body as we know it ceases to be. When the compounded phenomenon of the body is understood in this way, it deconstructs one's grasping at embodied forms. This is how to understand the basic meaning of the aggregates.

The subtle body is one aspect of the entire body-mind continuum. It includes the cakras, which are comprised of the channels. Although sentient ones' aggregates, elements, and sense fields are pure at the very basis, that purity is not realized by ordinary beings. Thus, they perceive the composite body of flesh and blood in its unripe, impure state. When the mind of the perceiver is impure, the aggregates, elements, and sense fields of the body-mind continuum appear ordinary. One cannot attain liberation through the methods of secret mantra without comprehending the fundamental purity of the container and contents.

Since the mind is the buddha nature and the three seats are fundamentally pure, every impure appearance is merely a temporary circumstance along the way. When one cultivates great love and compassion, they become conditions for recognizing the basic purity of the gross and subtle bodies. Just as wood turns into fire when it meets with a flame, so too the bodies and speech of sentient ones transform into pure deities and mantra when the mind meets with bodhicitta. Similarly, through the mind's contact with bodhicitta, thoughts and afflictions are transformed into primordial awareness. Thus, that which is called "purity" is emptiness—the realization that all perceived things and their defining characteristics ultimately lack any true existence.

One should understand the elements to be outer manifestations, the aggregates to be inner manifestations, and the sense fields to be secret ones. The five aggregates are (1) form, (2) sensation, (3) cognition, (4) formatives, and (5) consciousness. Functioning on the level of mind, they parallel the five afflictions—(1) passion, (2) aversion, (3) ignorance, (4) pride, and (5) jealousy—which are by nature the *tathāgatas* of the five families when perception is pure. Likewise, the elements function on the level of the body, which is comprised of the five elements of (1) earth, (2) water, (3) fire, (4) wind, and (5) space. Thus, the heap of elements is by nature the mother-consorts of the five tathāgatas. The sense fields are the interaction of the six sense faculties—the (1) eye, (2) ear, (3) nose, (4) tongue, (5) body, and (6) mind—with the six outer objects of the senses. These outer objects are (1) forms, (2) sounds, (3) smells, (4) tastes, (5) tactile objects, and (6) phenomena. In this way, the entire outer container and inner contents are nothing other than the naturally pure buddha couples of the five families, who are spontaneously present in the cakras of the subtle body.

These pure channel wheels are dependent arisings. They are referred to in the text as being vajra, or "adamantine." Here, the term *vajra* points to their empty nature. In this regard, although the mind is empty, it is endowed with clarity. Thus, it is not a mere nothing. Just as saṁbhogakāya manifestations arise from out of the dharmakāya, so too the empty channel wheels that are packed with deities emerge from the mind that is the union of emptiness and clarity.

The text says that the vajra channel wheels are filled to capacity with the "three seats." The aggregates, elements, and sense fields—naturally complete within the body-mind continuum—abide as the three seats, which are the nature of the holy hundred families of peaceful and wrathful deities. In brief, these three are the seat of the buddhas and bodhisattvas, the seat of the female knowledge-consorts and goddesses, and the seat of male and female wrathful ones. Simply put, since innumerable divine hosts ceaselessly come forth like particles in a dust storm or like snowflakes in whirling flurries, they need a place to dwell. Surrounded by light rays, they densely pack one's aggregates, elements, and sense fields. Since these are the natural dwelling places of the deities, their innate purity is introduced when one receives secret mantra empowerment.

This primordial purity is also explained in *The Aspiration of Samantabhadra*, in which it is taught how the five wisdoms dawned from the singular essence of mind itself and how all the other buddhas came forth from those five wisdoms:

> Rigpa's unencumbered clarity aspect has one essence with five wisdoms. From their maturation, the primal buddha's five families emerged. As the wisdoms further expanded, the forty-two buddhas arose. As the five wisdoms' dynamism dawned, the sixty blood drinkers emerged.[22]

This arising in stages of diverse enlightened manifestations from the single point of awareness itself is described in texts that elaborate the benefits of receiving empowerment into the one hundred families of the holy peaceful and wrathful deities. I would encourage those who have access to such texts to study this point in greater detail.

One will not reach a clear understanding of the above through a lot of talk. Rather, one should develop confidence in the main point, which is expressed in the next lines of the lineage supplication:

> Unelaborated consciousness
> is fulfilled as the vajra, great bliss.

What this means is that the bodies of oneself and others—all sentient ones—are pure at the very basis. Likewise, the ordinary consciousnesses of beings, when free of elaboration, are fundamentally the buddha nature. This "unelaborated consciousness" is great, nondual bliss beyond transition or change. "The vajra, great bliss" is the dharmakāya. All impurities are merely adventitious, transient events, arisen through self-grasping like water in which ice floes have temporarily appeared. Thus, one recognizes that the false perception of impurity has arisen from fleeting self-grasping alone. Although that self-grasping causes beings inconceivable sufferings, those sufferings are illusory in nature. Once sentient beings have become separated from their self-grasping, they will attain the status of the buddhas.

When this vast understanding dawns, one takes ultimate refuge. On the conventional level, one spontaneously gives rise to love and compassion, thinking, "It is only due to transient circumstances that beings have become crazed." Such compassion brings manifest benefit to sentient ones. Through it, one becomes able to free self and others from ill-being. In this way, one sees that the connection between buddhas and sentient ones is forged on the basis of love and compassion. Thus, the verse on the kīla of immeasurable compassion concludes,

> When the six wayfarers are struck by
> measureless compassion's kīla, may
> they possess compassion's great lifeline!

In general, practitioners can experience a little bit of compassion when encountering someone who is suffering. But when one actually considers the four mind-changing contemplations, again and again reflecting on the sufferings of the six classes of wayfarers, one sees that not a single being escapes samsaric pain. Because of this, it becomes impossible to have bias—feeling compassion for this one, but not for that one. Wherever there is space, sentient beings can be found. As it says in *The King of Aspirations for the Conduct of Samantabhadra*,

> The extent of sentient ones
> is the limit of space itself;
> so too do my aspirations
> reach as far as their karma and afflictions.[23]

Since beings are coextensive with space, one must again and again contemplate the four immeasurables, cultivating compassion for all beings without exception. Within this contemplation, sometimes it becomes unnecessary to cultivate anything. This is because the instant one sees the mind's nature, that mind pervades everywhere through its own natural force. Then, although one may encounter someone who is suffering greatly, it may seem surprising how unnecessary it is to generate any special compassion for that individual. In this regard, the liturgy of Mañjuśrī Yamāntaka says,

> Self from others can't be cleft; thus, there's
> no real object of compassionate aid.[24]

At this juncture, even though one does not actively cultivate compassion, compassion is also not lost.

It is just this sort of boundless compassion that arises for sentient beings when one experiences the all-pervasive mind, the nondual union of emptiness and compassion. That is to say, as soon as one gets a glimpse of the mind's nature, one recognizes self and other to be fundamentally one. Likewise, one understands that all the suffering of sentient beings is merely the delusion of not perceiving the mind one has just seen. As a result, immeasurable compassion spontaneously arises. Thus, Milarepa said in his *Hundred Thousand Songs*,

> When one has understood emptiness, compassion arises.
> When compassion has arisen, there is no self or other.
> When self and other are absent, others' purpose is
> accomplished.[25]

One should never part from this kind of immeasurable compassion for all sentient ones. This is what it means to plant the kīla of measureless compassion into wayfarers. It is this kīla that binds sentient ones to the buddhas. In this regard, the power of one's love can pervade only as far as the scope of beings one is able to fathom.

When planting the kīla of measureless compassion into the six classes of wayfarers, although the liberation itself is instantaneous, on the level of conventional fictional appearances, each sentient one will be freed from samsara gradually and in stages according to his or her individual karma and fortunes. For example, since they are free of the bonds of karma, all the buddhas are like a vast ocean of free-flowing water. Conversely, the collective karmic accumulation of sentient beings—oneself and others—is like a great snowfall. When the sun shines, although the finest snowflakes and the thinner accumulations will melt first, the thicker patches of snow and ice will eventually melt away as well. Similarly, each time one gives rise to the sunlight of immeasurable compassion for sentient ones, it benefits the collective, gradually melting away beings' total karmic accumulation. The thicker patches are merely grosser accumulations. In the end, they will all be melted by the same sunlight, becoming fluid again. Since compassion is the warmth that brings about this change, even when buddhahood has been attained, one must continue to cultivate it.

Since all buddhas and all sentient beings share the singular basis that is buddha nature, one has an innate connection with all beings. That connection is strengthened through the cultivation of love and compassion, which are able to clear away the adventitious defilement, the fault of self-grasping. Thus, "compassion's great lifeline," referred to in the text, is like the cord that binds together the beads of a māla. The mind of anyone for whom one feels compassion will become the same as the mind of the one cultivating compassion. It is through giving rise to great compassion for the six classes of beings that one will become able to melt the ice of self-grasping, thus establishing beings on the ground of the buddhas. By understanding how the connections among beings are strengthened through affection, one will become confident of one's ability to bring manifest benefit to others.

The important point is that one actually generates love for sentient ones. When meeting someone I have never met before, I cultivate love, recalling that even though we may not have met in this life, at some time in the past this person has been a kind parent to me. By practicing in this way, one can truly learn the meaning of the oft-recited words "every sentient one—mothers who equal space."[26] By considering this well, one can cause one's love to pervade all beings everywhere.

It is said that before appearing as Prince Siddhartha, Lord Buddha took five hundred pure and five hundred impure births. The purpose of those births was to accumulate love through acting in accord with the six transcendent perfections. It was on the basis of this accumulation of immeasurable love for all beings that he finally attained the state of buddhahood. Once one has understood the qualities of the buddhas' love, one will know it to be the supreme means of benefiting sentient ones.

The antidote to beings' suffering is the four immeasurables—measureless (1) loving-kindness, (2) joy, (3) compassion, and (4) equanimity. These four are subsumed within the kīla of immeasurable compassion. The actual condition of the mind itself is inseparable from great love and compassion. It enables one to provide sentient beings with the lifeline that will draw them out of samsaric suffering. One who gives rise to great compassion for all those who grasp at a self will become able to set them on the path of emancipation. By doing so, one will attain the status of a buddha for oneself while simultaneously fulfilling the aims of others.

This second kīla has a great connection with the practice of the sadhana, in which one visualizes the deity and recites his mantras. One should give rise to certainty that through engaging the four branches of approach and accomplishment, one can liberate innumerable sentient ones. In this way, one should understand how beneficial the kīla of immeasurable compassion is.

Thus far, I have explained the first two kīlas, which parallel the two truths. The kīla of primordial awareness-rigpa is ultimate truth and the kīla of immeasurable compassion is conventional truth. By understanding these two, one will understand all dharmas.

The Kīla of Bodhicitta

The third of the four stakes is the kīla of bodhicitta. It is cultivated based on the four immeasurables. It refers to conventional bodhicitta, the red and white constituents that abide within the physical body. Since it is the substantial cause of samsara, this seed essence is often regarded as a fault. However, because it is the basis for realizing the nondual wisdom of bliss and emptiness, it is also the substantial cause of nirvana. Thus, for the yogin who mixes lust with primordial awareness through the practices of the channels and wind energies, it is the city of the vajra body, the deity mandala in which all the channels are ḍākiṇīs and all the seed essences are *vīras*, or heroes.

What is the relationship between the seed that abides in the body and bodhicitta? Delight, bliss, love, and compassion for others are the nature of bodhicitta and also the nature of the physical seed essence. These two are completely intertwined. When the seed essence degenerates, it leads to inconceivable faults, such as illness and a decline in life span and personal magnetism.

Conversely, if it is not allowed to degenerate, it gives rise to physical bliss and emotional love and happiness. In this way, discriminating wisdom and longevity increase. For yogic practitioners, these constituents become the cause of realizing the rainbow body, through which the progressive stages of the four yogas of mahāmudrā can be instantaneously realized.

The seeds of a buddha's three kāyas are innately present in each of us. The subtle channels are the seed of the nirmāṇakāya; the wind energies, the seed of the saṁbhogakāya; and the seed essences, the seed of the dharmakāya. Because these seeds abide within the precious human body, they are the physical bases for engaging the trainings of the channels and wind energies. By training in these yogas according to the stages of development and completion, the yogin can attain the status of the buddhas' three kāyas. Such results are supported by yogic practices—like those taught in the Six Yogas of Nāropa—that rely on the body of a partner. In the context of secret mantra empowerment, disciples are introduced to some of these teachings, which Lord Milarepa referred to as the "oral instructions of the hearing lineage."

When the impure aggregate—this immature compounded body—

matures, it will ripen into the pure illusory body, which is uncompounded like a rainbow. From that will arise the buddhas' perfectly complete knowledge and love. For those who understand the meaning of the indwelling channels and constituents in the context of the development stages, oneself and one's partner are not ordinary but are the clear appearance of the father-mother consorts. Their union symbolizes the ultimate great pleasure of inseparable emptiness and compassion. When practitioners unite sexually, maintaining sacred outlook and liberating inner afflictions through mindfulness, impure channels and winds are transformed into pure primordial awareness. By sealing the kīla of bodhicitta with the kīla of primordial awareness-rigpa, such yogic practice can ripen into the result—the attainment of rainbow body or the accomplishment of the saṁbhogakāya in the bardo. Such maturation is a bliss beyond change or transition. Through it, innumerable saṁbhogakāya and nirmāṇakāya emanations who act for the sake of sentient ones spontaneously manifest. Thus, the lineage supplication reads,

> [Symbols,] meanings, signs[27]—the union of
> wisdoms with the kāyas—radiate and
> gather dreadful, blazing wrathful ones.

Every aspect of a deity's appearance can be understood on the three levels of symbol, meaning, and sign, which function on the secret, inner, and outer levels, respectively. If, for example, the deity carries a khaṭvāṅga, the implement itself is the outer sign. The severing of the three poisons by its three prongs is the inner meaning. The realization of tathāgatagarbha, the buddha nature, by one who has overcome affliction in this way is the secret level of symbolic meaning.

Similarly, the sexual union of the father and mother deities is the outer sign. Their mutual experience of great bliss is the inner meaning. Inseparable, nondual bliss beyond transition or change is the secret symbol.

Thus, every ornament, implement, and expression of the deity is endowed with these three aspects, which represent the qualities of his inner mindstream—facets of body, speech, mind, attributes, and activities. No matter how numerous they may be, they are all subsumed within the union of kāyas and wisdoms, the nondual unity of clarity and emptiness. The outer bodies of the deities are empty by nature. The natural expressions of primordial awareness, they are the manifest physical signs of the mind's inner accomplishment.

As for the three kāyas, the word "wisdoms" refers to the dharmakāya; "kāyas," to the saṁbhogakāyas; and the "dreadful, blazing wrathful ones," to the nirmāṇakāyas. The last two of these comprise the rūpakāyas—the form bodies who make themselves known on the levels of body and speech. All the myriad divine assemblies within the mandala of Vajrakumāra have come into being through the bodhicitta of the buddhas. The father and mother Vajrakumāra are the physical manifestations of the two types of bodhicitta—all the buddhas' compassion and emptiness. Through the union of these two emanate their innumerable children, the saṁbhogakāyas and the blazing wrathful nirmāṇakāyas.

In addition, the term *kāyas* refers to the outer stages of development, and *wisdoms* to the inner samādhi of the completion stage. In this union of development and completion, countless tiny wrathful ones simultaneously radiate out and gather back. Thus, the text continues,

> When the mother's sky is planted with
> bodhicitta's kīla, may clouds of
> emanations, foremost heirs, stream forth!

On the outer level of signs, the father and mother consorts appear as two. Thus, ordinary beings project their sexualized desires onto the deities in union. However, on the inner level of meaning, the couple are the nondual union of emptiness and compassion-bliss. Thus, on the basis of the consorts' relationship, nondual wisdom can be realized. Finally, on the symbolic, secret level, there manifests the union of appearance and emptiness. That is to say, once the inseparable union of emptiness-compassion has been realized, from that union will spontaneously appear innumerable rūpakāya emanations who pervade the vast expanse, acting for the welfare of all sentient ones.

One should understand how this relates to the accomplishment of each of the three kāyas. Through visualizing the divine father-mother couple replete with signs according to the development-stage yogas, one will conquer the māra of the aggregates and will realize one's own body as nirmāṇakāya. By engaging the inner yogic practices of the channels, wind energies, and seed essences on the basis of the development stages, one brings the afflictions—chief among which is lust—onto the path. Finally, when one has cultivated the stages of development in conjunction with bodhicitta and pure perception, they will ripen into the saṁbhogakāya in the bardo. Thus, innumerable nirmāṇakāya emanations will be sent forth for beings' benefit. Such rūpakāyas emerge through the force of interdependent arising. This is the meaning of the words "may clouds of emanations, foremost heirs, stream forth!"

Finally, afflictions arise due to the psychophysical aggregates. That is to say, out of the māra of the aggregates manifests the māra of afflictions. When, through the view, afflictions are transformed into the five wisdoms, the māra of afflictions will be conquered and the dharmakāya realized.

Stated differently, by realizing unelaborated consciousness—the buddha nature—and by cultivating the stages of development, one liberates one's own mind and body. Then, one becomes capable of liberating others through whichever means are appropriate for them. This brings us to the discussion of the fourth kīla.

The Material Kīla of Signs

Having realized the previously described view that is the union of emptiness and compassion, one can then engage all-encompassing enlightened activities by means of the material kīla of signs. Thus, the text reads,

Sentient contents of existence grasp
at three poisons and appearances;
yet as vajra wrathfuls they're complete.
When harmdoers are pinned by material
kīlas of signs that won't let them go,
may the pangs endured be finalized!

At the very basis, all sentient ones are established "as vajra wrathfuls." This is a sign that all beings are endowed with buddha nature. The entire outer container of this universe and all its inner contents, sentient ones, are innately pure. However, under the influence of circumstantial karmic winds and confused propensities, all the appearances of samsara arise and beings cannot free themselves from suffering. Thus, the text says they "grasp at three poisons and appearances."

The words "material kīlas of signs that won't let them go" refer to the sādhaka not forsaking sentient ones. Through compassion, one holds on to those beings who suffer from the three afflictive poisons, not releasing them. The water dragon (*makara*) on the material kīla is symbolic of this. It is said that once the water dragon locks its jaws onto its prey, it cannot open them again. This is an example of how the bodhisattva holds with compassion all sentient ones who are subject to karma, the three poisons' afflictions, and their attendant sufferings without releasing them from his or her love until they have been liberated from samsara.

The point is that every sentient one must be freed from the three poisons. In order to accomplish this, there exist both peaceful and wrathful methods. Peaceful methods are like using water and detergent to wash dirty clothes or like administering medicine to cure an illness.

Beings who cannot be liberated through such peaceful means require something like invasive medical interventions that accord with magnetizing and destructive activities. Thus, it is said that one must have the kīla of wisdom-rigpa for one's own sake and have the material kīla of signs for others' sake.

Outwardly, this material kīla—which has been taught through interdependence—refers to the different types of stakes fashioned in various shapes from different materials. Since the material kīla has the form of a peg or a stake, it can be used symbolically to strike or to pin down vital points in those to be subdued. The word "signs" denotes the ornamentation on the physical kīla. Inwardly, the four kinds of material kīlas accord with the four activities—pacifying, enriching, magnetizing, and, like the one mentioned in this verse, destructive. As for materials, silver is related to pacification, gold to enrichment, copper to magnetization, and iron to the destructive activities of suppression, incinerating, and casting weaponized *torma*.

In brief, these four activities are methods of liberating sentient ones. Just as medical treatments can be mild, average, or intense depending on the severity of the illness, so too enlightened activities are appropriate to the corresponding affliction. Planting the material kīla of signs into harmdoers through destructive activity is like an invasive surgery that is necessary to treat a severe illness. It is taught that the compassion required for wrathful, destructive activities is even greater than that required for peaceful ones.

Such obstructors and harmdoers have exceedingly dense obscurations and perverted aspirations. Even though they possess the buddha nature, it is only through violence that they can be separated from their afflictions. For such arrogant ones, it is unbearable to be forcibly drawn into the triangular incarceration pit and liberated from self-grasping through the blissful dance of the father and mother in union. Here, it is important to note that sādhakas should not think they are liberating only the afflictions of harmdoers and oath transgressors. Rather, they should recognize their own afflictions, looking at the jealousy, aversion, and so forth in their own minds, since these are indistinguishable from outer harmdoers and oath transgressors. This collective mass of one's own and others' afflictions is then drawn in and liberated on the basis of the material kīla.

After delusion (flesh), lust (blood), and aversion (bones) have been offered as a gaṇacakra to the mandala of deities, harmdoers have finally been freed of self-grasping, emerging as divine children of father and mother Great Glorious Vajrakumāra. In this way, one should eliminate afflictions and purify obscurations, establishing harmdoers in the pure buddha-fields. This so-called liberation offering is one of the various methods of liberation to be found among destructive activities.

What is the purpose of liberation through destructive activity using the material kīla of signs? It is to emancipate the unfree, leading sentient beings out of the three lower realms and into the three higher ones, where they are then guided to some degree of renunciation, virtue, and an understanding of cause and effect. In this way, they can give rise to the mindset of individual liberation. Those who have trained within that path are then led to generate bodhicitta. Having cultivated the outlook of the causal Great Vehicle, they can gradually engage the resultant practices of secret mantra. In this way, sentient ones of the six classes are guided step by step to higher states of being. Thus, the realms of hell denizens, pretas, and animals are gradually emptied out and all those beings take birth as humans who can listen to the Dharma. These are the methods whereby beings can attain emancipation in stages.

Ways of Understanding the Four Kīlas

In summary, the four kīlas are related to the view, meditation, conduct, and activities in the following ways: First, the kīla of primordial awareness-rigpa signifies the view. It is said that every mandala is naturally established through assurance in the view. Second, having established the mandala of samādhi through the kīla of immeasurable compassion, one engages the actual practice of meditation. Third, the kīla of bodhicitta establishes the mandala through the wisdom of nondual bliss-emptiness. Since one must train in the yogas of the channels and wind energies when manifestly cultivating the kīla of bodhicitta, one should understand this kīla to be conduct. Finally, having established the compounded, material kīla as the reflected mandala of the deity, activities are made totally complete.

The four kīlas can also be understood in terms of the different types of beings who are best suited to accomplish them. Since practitioners are referred to as vessels of the teachings, among Vajrakīla sādhakas, there are different types of vessels who are better suited to accomplish one or another of the four kīlas according to their different dispositions. While receiving this teaching, one should consider which sort of individual one is. This is something one must recognize for oneself; it is not for anyone else to determine.

First, the kīla of primordial awareness-rigpa is to be accomplished by the sky-like individual. Superior and magnanimous, this sort of person has a very intelligent mind and sharp faculties. When such a person is introduced to rigpa's liveliness by means of empowerment, the moment he or she recognizes the essence that is the kīla of reflexive primordial awareness, that kīla has been planted. Whoever has seen reflexive wisdom has planted the kīla of primordial awareness-rigpa into the ground of the dharmasphere, severing all dualistic grasping.

Second, the kīla of immeasurable compassion is accomplished by the person who is stable and unwavering like a mountain, has faith and great compassion, and delights in accomplishing others' purpose. Having trained in the four immeasurables for the sake of self and others, this individual generates and upholds the commitment of unsurpassed bodhicitta. Once such a disciple has received secret mantra empowerment, then it is suitable to bestow on him or her the foremost pith instruction of activities. Through planting the kīla of compassionate emanation into the ground that is sentient ones, this type of sādhaka brings the purposes of self and others to their end point.

Another text mentions the existence-kīla of the development stages in relation to the kīla of immeasurable compassion. The type who accomplishes it is quite proud and has a stable mind. It is said that this mountain-like individual attains the supreme and common siddhis through practicing the stages of development.

So, the second kīla has two categories. The first is the person who attains realization through great compassion alone. The second is the individual who attains realization based on the development stages unified with compassion.

Next is the kīla of bodhicitta. It is to be accomplished by the person who is very diligent and has great lust like the *kalantaka* bird. Being introduced to great bliss by means of the third empowerment, this individual cultivates the yogas of the channels and wind energies, relying on a consort endowed with auspicious marks. Recognizing desire as inseparable great bliss-wisdom, this practitioner brings ultimate truth to its final point by planting the kīla of bodhicitta into the ground that is the lotus. Thus, this kīla of bodhicitta is the means of bringing desire onto the path through yogic practice.

Finally, the individual who is like a sandalwood tree will eradicate all faults through the fourth kīla, the material kīla of signs. This sort of person maintains resolute discipline, has a vast intent to guard and benefit the buddhas' teachings, and is good-hearted. When, having received empowerment, such an individual practices the deity's approach, accomplishment, and activity engagement, he or she will give rise to certainty about the entire container and contents being the mandala of Vajrakīla—the certainty of knowing things as they truly are. Together with this realization, such types will be able to accomplish whatever activities they set their minds to—particularly, destructive activities—by planting the material kīla of signs into the ground that is enemies and obstructors. Thus, the material kīla of signs is the means of bringing aversion onto the path.

Here, it is important to note that the only possible danger in practicing wrathful sadhanas is for those people who are already of an angry disposition. One must understand that the wrath of the wrathful deity is one of love and compassion and not confuse this with the wrath of aggression.

The scriptures explain four different types of substances for accomplishing the four kīlas. First, for the kīla of primordial awareness-rigpa, one should practice using the divine kīlas, a rock crystal, a mirror, or other similar things as supports. Here, the term *divine kīlas* refers to all the material kīlas set out within the material mandala. Second, the kīla of immeasurable compassion is accomplished through the development stages' deity visualization, mantra recitation, and samādhi, using sentient ones as the object of meditation. Its accomplishment substances are the material kīlas of the four activities, which are included within the divine kīlas and are the physical manifestations of immeasurable compassion. Third, the kīla of bodhicitta is accomplished through the emanating out and gathering back of light rays. As supports, one should use a *kapāla*, or skull cup, with auspicious marks for the accomplishment container as well as a vajra and lotus. Finally, the accomplishment substances of the material kīla are twofold. During approach, the implement of a material kīla and mustard seeds are required. During accomplishment, an effigy *yantra* becomes the receptacle of an obstructor's life force and serves as the support. Such yantras—also called *liṅga*—are diagrams, which can include the targeted individual's name and likeness. They are sometimes very elaborately drawn and are used for destructive activities.

The Four Māras

When engaging the practice of the yidam Vajrakumāra, who is all the buddhas of the ten directions and three times gathered together, one supplicates that complete victory over māras, or demons, be attained. The final fruition of the view, meditation, and conduct will be the total conquest of the four māras. Although these four can be explained in two different ways according to the vinaya or according to the *chö* practice of the Latter System, the meaning in the lineage supplication accords with the vinaya and with the words of Lord Buddha. These four māras are (1) the māra of the aggregates, (2) the māra of afflictions, (3) the māra of the lord of death, and (4) the māra of the son of the gods. Because these māras cause all the three realms' sentient ones to wander in the vast ocean of samsaric sufferings, it is important to understand their meaning. In brief, since they rob sentient ones of happiness, all sufferings are māras.

The first of them, the māra of the aggregates, leads to the second. That is, by grasping at the psychophysical aggregate, one gives rise to the māra of afflictions, the second of the four. Then, having accumulated karma through afflictions, one experiences great suffering at the time of death. This is the third māra, that of the lord of death. Finally, for the duration of one's embodied life, one grasps at life's pleasures. Having become distracted by such grasping, one finds no leisure to engage that which is truly meaningful—the practice of the authentic Dharma. This is the māra of the son of the gods.

Ultimately, there is no māra to be found. All outer demons, obstructors, and those who lead astray arise from the self-grasping and three poisons in the mindstreams of sentient ones. Thus, the actual māra is nothing other than inner thoughts and afflictions. It is important to understand that whatever hardship or suffering one is experiencing at the moment, it is the result of negativities one has accumulated in the past, not something caused by others. All afflictions are completely conquered by discerning intelligence—the nature of Vajrakumāra's heart-mind—which manifests as the ability to recognize afflictions as faults. Each of us has in his or her mind a bit of the aware intelligence of Vajrakumāra. Using that awareness to turn away from negative actions of body, speech, and mind is the means for attaining future ease and happiness.

In *The Thirty-Seven Practices of Bodhisattvas*, it is taught that all maras arise from self-grasping. That is to say, on the basis of grasping at an "I," one gives rise to afflictions, karma, and their subsequent sufferings. The sole antidote to this is the cultivation of bodhicitta. Conventional bodhicitta is the mind wishing to accomplish others' benefit, and ultimate bodhicitta is meditation. So, by cultivating love, compassion, and awareness, one creates the causes of future happiness. There will be no error when practicing in this way.

The Māra of the Aggregates

The first māra is that of the aggregates. As previously described, the aggregates are the heap of psychophysical components that constitute a sentient being. Since this single māra amounts to cherishing the body, it is the source of the entire world's suffering. People toil day and night without respite in order to accumulate millions, yet, in the end, all that work is only for the purpose of keeping the body comfortable with food, clothing, lodging, and the like. In brief, the māra of the aggregates is all the considerations for this life alone. This māra gives rise to the suffering of being continually without leisure.

Furthermore, while one is embodied, one experiences illness, physical pain, and so forth. These experiences create imprints in the mind—imprints one carries even beyond death, after the consciousness has separated from the body. So, even when there is no longer any physical basis for pain, due to the power of self-cherishing imprints, one continues to experience pain, illness, hunger, and the like as though one had a body. Indeed, sufferings are experienced even more acutely through the mental body of the bardo than through embodied form.

When one considers the dream state, in which one inhabits a body conditioned by self-grasping, such imprints become obvious. The method of conquering this mental body is to practice the development-stage yogas, visualizing the illusory form of the deity, which is like a rainbow. Through such practice, one forgets the gross body of flesh and blood, together with its karma and imprints. As soon as the ordinary body has been forgotten, the mind itself spontaneously manifests as the deity. If, in this very moment, the clear appearance of the deity is visualized, the body is immediately transformed into the deity. The accomplishment of the deity will happen for anyone who dispenses with the gross body. Since this can be easily achieved by means of the material kīla of signs, it is said to liberate the māra of the aggregates.

Through stabilizing awareness of the deity, one begins to reverse ordinary propensities of embodiment, the māra of the aggregates. When the deity always remains in one's awareness—when one never forgets the deity—karma and physical propensities will be entirely purified. This is what is meant by these lines:

The aggregates' māra, conquered, is
freed into the ripened deity.

When the mind is liberated from the imprints of embodiment, that which is called the "aggregate" spontaneously manifests as the deity's clear appearance. This creates the conditions to become a buddha in the saṁbhogakāya during the bardo and brings about the transformation of afflictions into discerning intelligence.

For example, when my companions and I were in prison, we all experienced inconceivable hardships. As the sufferings were often unbearable, many people committed suicide. The Communist guards used to taunt us, saying, "You lamas are supposed to be a refuge for others, but you can't even protect yourselves!"

However, in spite of the hardships, the virtuous friends among us—like Khenpo Münsel—were immeasurably happy. In their inner experience, they were joyous regardless of outer conditions. This is because they had reached a state free of self-grasping—a state in which appearances had become like dreams. To whatever degree cherishing of the body is cleared away, one will regard phenomena as correspondingly illusory. In this way, on the outer, inner, and secret levels, our gurus manifestly attained liberation from suffering.

Although we were required to do hard labor every day for twenty years, Khenpo Münsel didn't experience a single day of work. Naturally and without effort, he obtained this sort of independence, which enabled him to spend his days in practice. He and his cellmates recited the *Seven-Line Supplication* one hundred thousand times. He even held gaṇacakra offerings. The Chinese guards treated him well and were known to beat those who criticized him. When people denounced him, in the end the negativity would turn back upon the denouncers themselves.

Because Khenpo Rinpoche was crippled by leg problems, for twenty years we always had to carry him to the toilet. However, once we were released from prison, miraculously, he could walk without any trouble at all. He had no further problems with his legs.

In this way, Khenpo Münsel had liberated the māra of the aggregates through the clear appearance of the deity. One can gain similar accomplishments by means of deity yoga. However, if the māra of the aggregates is not conquered in this lifetime, much suffering will be experienced in the bardo. When this is understood, one will comprehend the potency of the development stages.

The Māra of Afflictions

The māra of afflictions is closely related to the māra of the aggregates. This was discussed previously in the commentary on the kīla of bodhicitta. Through the stages of development, the bondage of the body is liberated. Then, through the experience of bliss-emptiness, the bondage of afflictions is liberated. Thus, the text says,

> The afflictions' māra, conquered, is
> marked with the seal of bliss-emptiness.

Every sort of affliction can be subsumed within passion and aversion. It is said that although it is relatively easy to liberate aversion, it is difficult to liberate passion. This is because aversion—and every other affliction—is complete within desire. Pleasure is the object of beings' desire. By habitually grasping at contaminated, exhaustible bliss, ordinary beings give rise to myriad sufferings.

However, the māra of afflictions is liberated through the kīla of immeasurable compassion, which itself is inseparable from the experience of uncontaminated bliss. That is to say, when the view is introduced, if it is truly recognized, one understands that bliss itself is the fundamental disposition of the mind. When, having understood this, one again and again habituates to the nonduality of self and other, it gives rise to the experience of changeless great bliss. Then, the pure portion does not degenerate; oneself and one's partner are mutually free of clinging. This is what it means to be "marked with the seal of bliss-emptiness." Having understood the nature of bliss to be empty, one is free of self-grasping. When there is no grasping at a self, there is neither grasping nor clinging to one's partner. This realization of the view transforms not only grasping but every sort of affliction into primordial awareness-wisdom. The factor that brings about this transformation is mindfulness-rigpa. One who has understood the kīla of primordial awareness-rigpa can master strong afflictions by recognizing them on arising. In this way, rigpa is like fire and afflictions are like fuel.

By understanding the true nature, one experiences an uncontaminated, inexhaustible great bliss, which is beyond transition or change. When the mind is completely free of grasping, such bliss spontaneously manifests. It is Samantabhadra, the Ever-Excellent One, the completely changeless, blissful nature of the mind itself. It continuously and spontaneously abides in the mind. Whenever it is seen, the mind is entirely without grasping. Thus, there is no space in which negative emotions can arise. Such is the true nature of unconditioned bliss, which conquers the māra of afflictions.

The Māra of the Lord of Death

The third of the māras is that of the lord of death. As all sentient beings experience birth, aging, illness, and death, all are subject to the perils of dying. The fear of being separated from life force arises on the basis of self-grasping and can be observed even in small insects. As Milarepa taught, when there is self-grasping, there is death. As long as one remains unfree of self-grasping, one will not be free of the composite aggregate that is the body. Being unfree of the body, one will experience death again and again within the bardo. For example, one can consider the hell denizens who experience the sufferings of death many hundreds of times each day.

However, if one is without self-grasping, there is no grasping at the body. The rainbowlike form that emerges in place of the physical body is not subject to death. Thus, through realizing the actual condition of the mind, the buddha nature, one comprehends the fact that it is beyond birth and death. From the perspective of tathāgatagarbha, birth and death are known to be mere concepts conditioned by karma. Thus, the māra of the lord of death is conquered by the kīla of primordial awareness-rigpa. If this one kīla is seized, one will naturally master the other three kīlas. Similarly, if one conquers the māra of the lord of death, the other three māras will simultaneously be defeated. As Lord Tilopa said in *The Ganges: An Experiential Pith Instruction on Mahāmudrā*, "If the root of a tree with lush branches, leaves, and petals is cut, its ten thousand branches and hundred thousand leaves wither."[28] This point is expressed in the following lines:

> The lord of death's māra, conquered, finds
> the empowerment of immortal life.

Having cultivated the development stages during one's lifetime, one will arise in the bardo as the rainbowlike form of the deity with ornaments. Thus, even though the gross physical body is subject to destruction, since the pure mind of rigpa is unborn, it cannot die. Understanding that the body is like old clothing that must be discarded, one becomes free of fear and of the suffering of death. This realization of the indestructible nature is itself the conquest of the māra of the lord of death, the empowerment of immortality.

The Māra of the Son of the Gods

The fourth of the four māras, the son of the gods, manifests as being greatly distracted by the delights and comforts of this life. In general, beings have extreme clinging to pleasure, longing for the five desirables, which appear as diverse (1) forms, (2) sounds, (3) smells, (4) tastes, and (5) tactile objects. For gurus and virtuous friends like me, this māra also arises when we become distracted by fame and renown. Grasping at an "I," we become carried away by the māra of the son of the gods. You guys give a lot of nice food and money, and this is the result! Since the actual Vajrakīla is mindful awareness, he helps one to recall, "I mustn't become distracted! I need to recognize that the māra of the son of the gods has arrived!" Thinking in this way, one will remember that such attachment and clinging create imprints of the pretas' mental outlook, causing suffering. Thus, one will give rise to an appropriate fear.

Since whatever ease and comfort one experiences at present are due to one's past loving actions of body and speech, they are composite phenomena, which are the nature of impermanence. Sentient beings' enjoyment of pleasures involves a wavering of the mind from the natural state. Because of that wavering, awareness is unable to hold its own seat. This state is characterized by outflows or leakage (*zagche*) of mind and wind energies. It is said that every bliss with outflows is a cause of suffering. This means that clinging to desirables starts out as pleasure but invariably ends up becoming pain.

In spite of this, accomplishment is possible in the future, since the kīla of bodhicitta conquers the māra of the son of the gods. As the pure buddha-fields are the spontaneously present nature of bodhicitta, they are devoid of grasping or clinging. The "primordial purity" that is referred to in dzogchen is rigpa. When one has realized the fact—the actual condition of the mind that is buddha nature—all the qualities of the kāyas and pure fields come into existence of their own accord, like the rainbow reflections that appear when a ray of sunlight strikes a crystal. The spontaneously present nature of great bliss, their perfectly complete qualities of happiness and ease are inherent, appearing through neither effort nor exertion. Thus, the text reads,

> May the gods' son's māra, conquered, yield
> spontaneous attainment of the grounds!

By abiding in the actual condition of the mind, one becomes free of attachment to the five desirables. The mind's fundamental disposition, the dharmakāya, is changeless great bliss without transition. If one wants to understand this in detail, one should read Gampopa's *Precious Garland of the Supreme Path*, in which the ten characteristics of spontaneously produced great bliss are elaborated.

Although there is much that is taught on this topic, ultimately, when the disposition of the mind has been understood, all thoughts and emotions come to destruction. Then, one is without any suffering at all, as one knows bliss to be a concept and suffering also to be a concept. Within the fundamental disposition that is rigpa, there is neither happiness nor suffering. Thus, "spontaneous attainment" means that on the basis of having realized ultimate truth, one finally accomplishes a bliss beyond transition or change. This is the spontaneously present great bliss of Samantabhadra.

When, in this way, one has put a stop to grasping at illusory pleasures, the bodhisattva grounds will be naturally accomplished. Having attained buddhahood within the dharmakāya, one will circumstantially have dominion over all the vast and encompassing saṁbhogakāya buddha-fields, which are the spontaneously present nature of great bliss. Such bliss is unfabricated and beyond mundane constructs. As all the pure fields are nothing other than one's own perceptions, one will become able to enjoy and make use of them. This enjoyment is an aspect of the mind without limits and is the circumstantial meaning of "spontaneous attainment."

Likewise, diverse nirmāṇakāyas who engage activities benefiting beings will manifest. Thus, the purpose of others will naturally be fulfilled through the accomplishment of one's own purpose. In this way, the māra of the son of the gods is conquered, giving rise to spontaneously present great delight free of effort, as is described in *The Aspiration for the Pure Field of Great Bliss.*

In this context, Earlier System practitioners speak of the four types of knowledge holders. Since the teachings on the four types of knowledge holders elucidate the grounds and paths, I would encourage you to study them in various texts.

Summary of the Four Māras

In brief, this lineage supplication alone elucidates the main points of Vajrakīla practice, together with their fruitions. Through the stages of development, the body is ripened into the deity, thus conquering the māra of the aggregates. Tasting the unconditioned bliss of the divine couple, one gains experience of bliss-emptiness wisdom, whereby afflictions are transformed into primordial awareness. Thus, the māra of the afflictions is conquered. By being introduced to the nature of mind, one realizes the fact of the view that transcends birth and death, thus conquering the māra of the lord of death. Then, abandoning grasping at the pleasures of this life, one gains mastery of the grounds and pure fields, accomplishing one's own and others' purpose. Thus, the māra of the son of the gods is conquered. This conquest of the four māras is the result of Vajrakīla practice.

The Eight Qualities and Four Activities

The lineage supplication closes with the following verse:

> Swiftly may I manifest the eight
> qualities and four activities!
> Specially, having burnt the noxious hearts
> of hinderers, foes, and obstructors with
> fierce mantras—direct acts' fiery point—
> may I gain Glorious Heruka's state!

Through engaging the practice of Vajrakumāra, one will naturally and spontaneously accomplish the eight qualities and all the enlightened activities of the buddhas. These eight qualities are the eight kinds of powers referred to as "common siddhis." They include clairvoyance, sorcery, miracles, the mythical eye potion, swift-footedness, and the like. The four enlightened actions are the four activities carried out by the beings in the mandala: pacifying, enriching, magnetizing, and destructive.

In particular, the "fierce mantras—direct acts' fiery point" signifies destructive activities—the methods for subduing harmdoers. The noxious heart of every hinderer, enemy, and obstructor is nothing other than the ignorance that is self-grasping and its attendant afflictions. As such, the afflictions of enemies and obstructors are the same as one's own. Through overcoming one's inner aggression and aversion, the outer aversion of every enemy will simultaneously be overcome. Thus, these lines refer to the burning away of self-grasping by the sharp kīla tip of discerning intelligence and compassion, which can cut through anything. The final fruition of this will be the attainment of buddhahood—the supreme status of Great Glorious Heruka.

Finally, within this lineage supplication, the meaning of all Vajrakīla tantras is combined and both the buddha-word and treasure transmission lineages are drawn together. Therefore, I encourage you to study it in detail and also to ask other spiritual guides the questions you might have about it.

CHAPTER 4

Practice Manual Instructions

The lineage supplication is followed by the practice manual, which is titled *Essence of Display: A Regular Secret Accomplishment Liturgy of the Unsurpassed, Most Secret Vajrakīla*. It presents in concise form the stages of development and completion.

Refuge and Bodhicitta

All presentations of the successive paths are basically the same. The foundation of every practice is the taking of refuge and the generation of bodhicitta. Whatever extensive or abbreviated practice one does, its root is refuge and bodhicitta. Although this text has just two short verses devoted to these prayers, whether one's practice bears fruit will ultimately depend upon the quality of one's refuge and bodhicitta. Even before going for refuge, one should always give rise to the altruistic mind, thinking, "Every sentient one in the three realms must be liberated from suffering by means of the three successive paths!"

Then, at the start of the practice, it is good to imagine all the objects of refuge gathered in space before all sentient ones. Although a clear visualization of the field of accumulation is not present in this text, one can be found in the extensive practice manual of Vajrakīla:

> As rays of light shine forth from the HŪṂ at my heart, the gurus, knowledge holders, and divine assemblies of the mandala of Great Glorious Vajrakumāra are awakened into the cakra that pervades space.[1]

Thus, one should imagine that the divine beings—with the principal deity Vajrakumāra in the center—come, gathering like cumulus clouds filling the entire sky. In this way, one should go for refuge. This refuge is the path whereby all sentient ones wandering in samsara can seek protection from their limitless sufferings. The Three Jewels of Buddha, Dharma, and Sangha are the ground. The Three Roots of guru, yidam, and ḍākiṇī are the path. The three kāyas are the fruition. Thus, the verse of refuge reads,

> NAMO! Sentient ones, wayfaring beings and I,
> with respectful three doors, take refuge
> in the guru, yidam, and Three Jewels
> with the victors' oceanic hosts.

Since refuge in the Three Jewels is common to all paths, the words "Three Jewels" refer to the foundational path of individual liberation, which was revealed by the Bhagavan Buddha. Even though the Sangha has come from the Dharma and the Dharma has come from the Buddha—if there were no manifestation of the Sangha as the virtuous friend, one would have no chance at all for understanding any Dharma. It is through the spoken words of the Sangha that one can first hear, then contemplate, and finally meditate on the teachings. This allows beings to understand how to follow in the footsteps of past masters. For this reason, it is said that among all the Three Jewels, the Sangha of gurus and virtuous friends is the ultimate and final refuge. If one can give rise to faith and trust in all virtuous friends as being very precious, one will understand the final point of refuge at its very root.

According to the Sutra System, the guru is the embodiment of the Three Jewels. The form of a single guru—one virtuous friend—is the Sangha. His or her speech is the Dharma and his or her mind the Buddha. Since some are unable to give rise to faith in the guru as the Buddha, they will say that the guru is not the actual Buddha. In order to resolve this issue, practitioners should understand that that which is called "Buddha" is the empty mind endowed with love and compassion. Regardless of a guru's faults, there is no such thing as a virtuous friend who is entirely lacking in compassion. To search for the Buddha by looking at a master's outer attributes is a manifestation of delusion. Rather, one should look inward at the buddha nature, which of course is present in every being. If one maintains the pure perception of a master's mind as the actual Buddha, only good qualities will follow.

For the beings of this present era, the Bhagavan Buddha emanated in the form of Guru Padmasambhava. They two are one and the same, without any distinction. In this time of dregs, when all sentient ones' afflictions and sufferings are coarse, it is difficult for beings to abandon gross affliction and to enter the path of monastic virtue. As there was no other way to tame the beings of this age, there emerged the teachings of the Secret Mantric Vajra Vehicle, whereby afflictions are liberated in their own place without one needing to abandon them.

As one engages the inner practices of secret mantra, one relies on the Three Roots, which are alluded to in the text with the words "guru, yidam." In this context, the virtuous friend is precious in the following ways: the master's body manifests as the guru, his or her speech as the yidam, and his or her mind as the ḍākiṇī. All three of these are aspects of one's own mind. Likewise, the speech aspect of the yidam and the true Dharma are one. This is because the guru uses speech to teach the development and completion of the yidam, through which one can become habituated to deity yoga and can accomplish the saṁbhogakāya in the second bardo. The mind aspect that is the ḍākiṇī is the sign of emptiness, nondual wisdom. This empty mind should be understood as the buddha nature. Thus, in the context of secret mantra practice, the guru is the actual embodiment of the Three Roots.

As for the fruition, the guru's body is the nirmāṇakāya, his or her speech the saṁbhogakāya, and mind the dharmakāya. As such, the root guru embodies every object of refuge. Although there exist diverse methods of understanding and practice, one should know the Three Jewels, Three Roots, and three kāyas to be singular in nature. In addition, "the victors' oceanic hosts" refers to all the buddhas of the three times. Having appeared throughout innumerable kalpas, they are as numerous as the grains of sand in the Ganges.

As one visualizes the holy objects of refuge, one should imagine oneself—together with all sentient beings—taking refuge before this vast field of accumulation. This is the meaning of the words "Sentient ones, wayfaring beings and I."

The Three Types of Faith

The text continues, "with respectful three doors, take refuge." In general, whenever one engages body, speech, and mind in virtuous activities, one is showing respect to the Three Jewels. Since true respect for the Three Jewels and Three Roots requires having the three types of faith, one must investigate one's own mind to see whether or not they are present. These three are (1) lucid, (2) aspiring, and (3) trusting faith.

First, when one understands the attributes of the Three Jewels' and Three Roots' omniscience, love, and capabilities, one will know them to be inconceivable. It is only through their blessing that one comes to follow the path of liberation. When one considers well their qualities, faith in those qualities and in the word of the buddhas spontaneously dawns. Thus, one will regard them as an incontrovertible refuge. Because it arises on the basis of understanding the attributes of the objects of refuge, lucid faith is a belief that is well informed. In order to develop it, one should contemplate that all the infinite qualities of the deities and their pure realms have manifested from the buddhas, who have arisen from among sentient ones. In this regard, when prostrating before the Jowo statue in Lhasa, Drugpa Künleg said,

> At first, we two were similar. You became a manifest buddha through great perseverance; I have wandered in samsara through great laziness. I, the lazy Drugpa Künleg, pay homage to you, diligent Śākyamuni![2]

Buddhahood is attained through the diligence that comes from having trained in the two types of bodhicitta. In contrast, having not yet abandoned self-grasping, lazy sentient ones wander in samsara. However, any individual who practices can attain enlightenment.

To understand this, one should consider the elements—the sun, wind, earth, and water. Each of these has innate power that when harnessed can generate electricity. Wherever in the world it is found, electricity is of the same nature. It can dispel darkness and can power machines to accomplish whatever is desired. Even though the power of the elements is always present, unless their natural force is harnessed or gathered together, there is no way to utilize it.

So it is with discriminating intelligence. Although intelligence itself is of a singular nature, it manifests in myriad mundane and spiritual ways. While mundane discriminating intelligence leads to endless wandering in cyclic existence, transmundane intelligence results in emancipation from samsara.

When the ground of the buddhas is attained, the qualities of the buddhas' three kāyas arise effortlessly to spontaneously accomplish the two objectives—of self and others. This is like a diamond in a ray of sunlight; the qualities of its rainbow reflections are inherent in the jewel itself. Regardless of which deity one practices, all wisdom deities have but one life force, which manifests in various ways.

Similarly, although we speak of the five wisdoms for didactic purposes, ultimately, there is only one wisdom with diverse manifestations. The buddhas' omniscient wisdom is that which is aware of all sentient ones' individual sufferings, causes, results, fully ripened karma, and the like. This mind of empty awareness, the sky-like dharmakāya, also appears as (1) mirrorlike wisdom, which simply reflects whatever appears without any grasping; (2) the wisdom of equality, which is free of scrutinizing anything that appears; (3) individually discriminating wisdom, which is the unobscured knowledge of karmic causes and results of happiness and suffering down to the subtlest levels; (4) activity-accomplishing wisdom, which is the buddhas' effortless achievement of sentient ones' ease and benefit; and (5) dharmasphere wisdom. This final wisdom is like a diamond in which rainbow reflections of five colors are innately present, since within the buddhas' omniscient wisdom alone the nature of all the others is complete. Thus, one should understand these five manifestations of the buddhas' wisdom, which were taught in *The Aspiration of Samantabhadra*. As for the buddhas' form kāyas, until samsara itself has been emptied out, the saṁbhogakāyas and nirmāṇakāyas—extending as far as the limits of space—will appear and engage activities. Such is the force of the buddhas' knowing wisdom. By reflecting in this way on the Three Jewels' qualities, one will give rise to lucid faith, which is based on clear understanding and is utterly unlike blind faith.

The second type of faith is aspiring faith. If one were completely free of suffering, there would be no basis at all for understanding it. One would merely abide comfortably among the six classes of wayfaring beings. Within those six classes, the best circumstances are found in the human realm, which is like a nirmāṇakāya pure field. In spite of this, we know the sufferings found in this realm of Jambudvīpa to be inconceivable. What is the method for becoming free from such sufferings? It is to go for refuge in the Three Jewels. Thus, in the best case, one will give rise to the motivation to free oneself and all others from samsaric sufferings through great compassion. Such a wish is aspiring faith.

Once one has recognized self-grasping to be the cause of suffering, whatever one does becomes focused principally on the aspiration to benefit others. In this way, one's own purpose is naturally accomplished. Understanding this, people temporarily give rise to an artificial sort of bodhicitta. That is, they arouse altruism with the motivation to accomplish their own objectives. Ordinary people like us think, "Since it will benefit me, I will cultivate bodhicitta." This is referred to as "fabricated bodhicitta" and is the starting point for the arising of unfabricated bodhicitta. Although some may disparage such contrived bodhicitta, it is exceedingly rare to find a bodhisattva who can give rise to altruism based solely on his or her accumulation of merit in former lives.

Later, once one has given rise to actual bodhicitta, even if one wanted to mentally grasp at one's own objective, there would be nothing to hold on to. One will have become incapable of sustaining such a wish. Just like every buddha, one will have the ability to give away one's own body and life force to fulfill the needs of others. It is truly possible to achieve this sort of fruition. So, one should understand aspiring faith, in its fabricated and unfabricated manifestations, as the mind wishing to free every sentient being from suffering.

In this worldly realm, parents, national leaders, educators, and the like all serve as guardians. However, even in a country that has great wealth, power, freedom, and opportunities, people are still helpless against the experiences of suffering. Although worldly methods attempt to shelter beings from hardship, the only protection they can offer is provisional protection from results that manifest outwardly. They cannot provide true protection from the inner causes that abide in the mind. For example, when the weather is hot, we turn on the air conditioning. When it's cold, we turn on the heating. Because such means focus on results, they are unable to sever the root causes of suffering. It is only through giving rise to belief in karma, cause and effect, that beings can find ultimate protection from causes.

Thus, the actual protection provided by the Three Jewels comes from revealing the path. One should consider whether or not the Three Jewels have the power to grant the protection that is refuge. If one really reflects, there will be no doubt whatsoever that even though others are incapable of protecting one, the Three Jewels are an immutable refuge.

Of course, even the Three Jewels are limited in their ability to give protection to faithless ones who lack bodhicitta. If one accumulates many refuge recitations without faith, although some benefit will come, one cannot experience the actual fruition. Conversely, even if one is unable to do any other spiritual practice, one should have confidence that the Three Jewels have the ability to protect those who understand cause and effect and who generate some degree of bodhicitta. As long as a faithful one has a mind free of doubt, even if he or she cannot recite the refuge prayers many times, the benefits of refuge will be obtained. As it is said in *The Supplication to Guru Rinpoche That Spontaneously Fulfills All Wishes*, "With neither ambiguity nor doubt, we pray. . . ."[3] This sort of assurance is trusting faith, the third type of faith, which is rooted in the teachings on cause and effect.

Lord Buddha taught that causality is incontrovertible. Since its manifestations are infinite, some might assume causality itself to be something complex. In fact, it is not; it comes down to only two things. The first point is that the sole cause of all the sufferings of all sentient ones is self-cherishing—the habit of continually thinking of the "I." The heap of eighty-four thousand afflictions comes from just this. Thus, self-grasping is the root cause of all samsaric wandering. When one prays that sentient beings be parted from ill-being and its causes, one is actually praying that they be free from the afflictions, which are rooted in grasping at a self.

The second point is that the cause of all happiness is the altruistic mind. There is no method to destroy self-cherishing except to cultivate conventional bodhicitta—the mind set on benefiting others. This is the skillful means taught by the compassionate buddhas. By praying that sentient beings have ease and ease's causes, one is giving rise to discriminating intelligence and loving compassion, from which all the attributes of the complete buddhas emerge. Those who wish for freedom from suffering must train in this altruistic mind.

Just as all the statues in a dark temple become visible when a single lamp has been lit, so too when one understands these two points of self-cherishing versus altruism, the entirety of karmic causality has been understood. This trust in cause and effect describes trusting faith. It emerges when one settles the point that love and affection are the only causes of happiness.

As soon as one gives rise to these three types of faith, whatever activities are undertaken will be fruitful. In brief, lucid faith comes from understanding good qualities. By again and again recalling the Three Jewels' attributes, the mind becomes infused with lucid faith. It becomes free of taint by self-cherishing or by the passion, aversion, and ignorance that give rise to all beings' heedless conduct of body, speech, and mind.

Since actual refuge is the generation of bodhicitta, refuge is naturally accomplished by maintaining the wish to benefit others and by being focused on virtue. In brief, when one's intent is nothing but to liberate the sentient from sufferings through body and speech, then the only thoughts in the mind are the ways of accomplishing that benefit. Through such aspiring faith, one's words and actions toward others become gentle.

Having this kind of altruistic mind as the basis, one shows respect by means of the three doors. Through respectful body, one visualizes the deity's form and folds one's hands in homage. Through respectful speech, one recites the prayer of refuge or engages the mantra recitation. The moment one feels in one's heart true caring for beings or recognition of the Three Jewels' inconceivable qualities, the mind becomes respectful. The instant bodhicitta arises, there dawns true respect for buddhas and sentient ones. In this way, through bodhicitta, body, speech, and mind become united in engaging virtue. This is the meaning of taking refuge with "respectful three doors."

Although the outer Three Jewels are the Buddha, Dharma, and Sangha, the inner Three Jewels arise from one's own side. In this regard, the Buddha is one's vigilant mindful awareness—the innate tathāgatagarbha. The Dharma is the cultivation of loving-kindness and compassion. The Sangha is the confidence that even though others may be motivated by self-cherishing, one has become exalted through maintaining a commitment to love, patience, and altruism.

Thus, when mindful awareness does not part from the Dharma that is compassion, the Three Jewels' protection will be present in fact. Discerning intelligence itself gives protection. However, when we speak of refuge, we do not mean protection from death! Once one has taken birth into a body of composites, death will follow, right? But, since the continuum of lifetimes is like the beads of a māla strung together by a single strand, the Three Jewels' protection extends from one lifetime to the next, bringing benefit and ease. Thus, it will not be necessary to take so many more births before attaining buddhahood. When reciting the refuge prayer, one should give rise to certainty in the Three Jewels' protection, thinking, "Of course it is so!" Otherwise, there is no way to truly take refuge while harboring doubts in the mind. One should take this to heart.

If one goes for refuge for oneself alone, there will be no benefit. Thus, one must cultivate bodhicitta. In order to do so, one needs to give rise to compassion in the mind. The karmic habits laid down throughout beginningless samsara are due to nothing other than self-grasping. It is only through cultivating compassion that they can be torn down. Even if one were to go for refuge for a hundred eons, if compassion were lacking, emancipation would not be attained. Thus, the cultivation of bodhicitta is indispensable.

This should not be done on a small scale. In the Drigung Kagyü tradition, we pray,

> Placing foremost all impediments to omniscience and release, enemies averse to me and obstructors who harm, I'll cause every sentient one—mothers who equal space—to have ease, be free of ill-being, and swiftly gain truly complete, precious, unsurpassed enlightenment.[4]

If one can give rise to compassion for enemies, only then will one truly have compassion. I mean, who doesn't have love and compassion for friends? Even so, the sort of compassion one has for those who are near and dear is unreliable, because if they turn against you tomorrow, they will become enemies. Thus, impartial love and compassion are extremely important for the development of bodhicitta, which is expressed in the text with these words:

> Alas! For me to release all wayfarers
> by upending samsara into
> the mandala of Karmakīla,
> I'll rouse mind—the four immeasurables.

One who goes for refuge in the Three Jewels without giving rise to bodhicitta will not achieve emancipation from the ocean of samsaric pain. Thus, if one really wishes to liberate oneself from samsara, such individual liberation can only be accomplished through the intent to benefit others. Those who think that individual liberation equals freedom for oneself alone will not achieve the emancipation they so desire. Why? Because the very thing from which one needs to be liberated is the mind of self-cherishing. Whenever one catches oneself thinking, "I need protection," one should immediately apply this thought to all others as well. The motivation to benefit others protects both self and others, thus accomplishing the two objectives. For this reason, the verse on generation of bodhicitta begins, "Alas! For me to release all wayfarers...."

If one needs to free every sentient being from the ocean of samsara, it will be necessary to shake up samsara from its very depths. In order to accomplish this, one should understand that that which is called "samsara" appears only from the frozen, conventional perspective that is total fiction. That is to say, the illusory appearances of samsara arise circumstantially under the influence of adventitious self-grasping, which leads to the accumulation of karma and imprints. Although such appearances can manifest like a solid and intractable block of ice, the moment one's mind becomes conjoined with bodhicitta, they melt away. Thus, from the perspective of actual fact, the entirety of samsara is illusion-like and devoid of inherent existence. The ice and the water are inseparable. When the sun of bodhicitta rises, sending warmth in all directions, there is no such thing as samsara. When this point has been realized, samsara is stirred from the depths—emptied out into the mandala of the deity.

That deity is Karmakīla in father-mother aspect, the great sovereign of the activities of all the buddhas. In this regard, Vajrakīla is praised in the extensive practice manual with the words "You arise in the destructive form that has drawn into one the activities of all the ten directions' and three times' buddhas."[5] This is why Ratna Lingpa placed Amoghasiddhi, lord of the Karma family—among all the five families—as the chief of this mandala. Among body, speech, mind, attributes, and activities, the accomplishment of enlightened activities is the Karma heruka's principal purpose.

The Four Immeasurables

The last line of the bodhicitta prayer reads, "I'll rouse mind—the four immeasurables." With these words, one cultivates the preliminaries. Thinking that the preliminary practices are for beginners and that they are not particularly meaningful, some set them aside or do them carelessly. They regard the so-called actual practice of the deity's development stages as being of primary importance. In this regard, Protector Jigten Sumgön said, "Those things not profound to others are profound here."[6]

It is true that the development stages are the basis on which one attains the deity's body. If one merely wishes to attain the form of the deity, one should meditate on the development stages alone. Sādhakas should consider whether they hope to accomplish a deity who is dead or alive. Since a corpse can achieve nothing, those who want to realize a living deity must have the life force that is love and compassion.

Thus, the preliminaries—known as *ngöndro* in Tibetan—are not different from refuge and bodhicitta. In actual fact, the preliminary practices of refuge, Vajrasattva, and the like, in which practitioners gather hundreds of thousands of accumulations, are for the sole purpose of stabilizing the mind of refuge and bodhicitta.

If one practices without cultivating bodhicitta, one will only accomplish partial virtues of body, speech, and mind, thus creating the causes to achieve the circumstantial, happy result of births in the three higher realms. However, in order to achieve the ultimate result of buddhahood, one must clear away self-grasping and expand the wisdom realizing the nonduality of self and others. Bodhicitta is profound because it can accomplish this final fruition. Even if one were illiterate, knowing nothing at all about visualization or mantra recitation, as long as one had love and compassion, one would hold the deity precious and would have faith in him or her. The moment one gives rise to compassion, one has attained the mind of the deity—the mind of enlightenment. If day and night without interruption, one's only thought were how to benefit sentient beings, the siddhis of the deity would be actually, manifestly close at hand. The true deity is accomplished on this basis.

In order to generate bodhicitta, one must engage the four trainings known as the four immeasurables. First, immeasurable loving-kindness is the most important point. If it is well cultivated in one's mindstream such that it becomes pervasive, immeasurable compassion will spontaneously arise. In general, since whatever slight compassion we ordinary beings have is rooted in attachment, it is directed only at those few who are near and dear to us. In order to overcome this fault, practitioners should think in the following way: "Throughout my countless births in cyclic existence, every sentient being has, at one time or another, been my kind parent. All those beings on whom I have relied must now become the objects of my compassion."

For example, in this assembly, there are many people. Some are familiar; some are unfamiliar. Even so, one should have the same impartial affection for strangers as for old friends. By maintaining this view, one will have a sense of great familiarity with and goodwill for even those one is meeting for the first time. Such is the power of loving-kindness.

Lord Buddha taught that loving-kindness is even more precious than the sun. How is this so? When someone is suffering, he or she cannot be relieved merely by taking a sunbath, since the sun can only warm someone's body. However, if that same person receives a phone call from a loved one, that simple conversation can give a great feeling of relief. Even a small gesture of love has great power to alleviate suffering. If the love of one individual is so powerful, how is it possible to fathom the power of the buddhas' love, which reaches all sentient ones impartially?

By considering this well, one can develop faith and devotion, which will inspire the cultivation of loving-kindness. When one has love for others, it is easy to be patient. With patience, meditation comes easily. Otherwise, if one merely recites refuge and bodhicitta prayers while feeling aversion to the person sitting nearby, there is a contradiction between word and deed. Such faults in practice can become causes to take birth in the lower realms. Thus, in order for love and compassion to develop fully, one must learn to rejoice in others' good fortune. One's love should be free of partiality or bias toward beings. If one can abide in the absorption of impartial loving-kindness until tears fall from one's eyes, then one can begin to give rise to genuine compassion.

In general, compassion is of two types. The first type is an unbearable, self-justifying compassion, which can be experienced, for example, when one contemplates with dualistic grasping the pain and suffering of another. It can be seen in some religious traditions in which practitioners sometimes become deranged by generating compassion based on grasping at perceived objects as being real and true. This contrasts with the second type of compassion— that is, the compassion of the four immeasurables. For practitioners of the Buddhadharma, the actual aim is an inconceivably vast compassion unified with emptiness, in which one realizes that all beings—as well as their innumerable sufferings—lack inherent existence.

Next, since every sentient being is endowed with buddha nature at the very basis, each one can attain the status of the buddhas. Thus, no matter how great the delusion and sufferings of beings may be, every sentient one without exception innately possesses the cause of buddhahood. Merely understanding this gives rise to immeasurable joy, the third of the four immeasurables.

Finally, in general, equanimity is described as an impartial mind that neither cherishes some nor holds others distant. Although this is a clear explanation, the actual meaning of immeasurable great equanimity comes from the understanding that ultimately buddhas and sentient beings are not separate. This is actual equanimity from the profound perspective of secret mantra, which is rooted in the nonduality of samsara and nirvana. When it is understood, it brings forth the deeply joyful mind of immeasurable equanimity.

The cultivation of these four immeasurables is the generation of precious bodhicitta, which is a necessity for all paths. The sole cause of every suffering is self-grasping, whose only antidote is the intent to benefit others. When properly practiced, such altruism fulfills Lord Buddha's instruction to "thoroughly subdue your mind."[7]

In order to guard the bodhicitta that has been generated, virtuous friends of the past have taught that there are two things practitioners should avoid investigating, as they cause separation between self and others to increase. First, one must not examine one's own qualities, since it is a cause for pride. Second, one must not scrutinize others' faults, as this leads to aversion and blame. The mind of blaming others amounts to an ethical defeat. On the other hand, whenever one has respect for others, the respect itself gives rise to excellent qualities, like the dog's tooth that manifested precious relics as a result of the old woman's faith.[8]

Setting the Boundaries

After bodhicitta has been generated, the boundaries are set with the following verse:

> HŪṂ. In the measureless, spontaneously
> present nature, even labels like
> "hindrance" and "misguider" don't exist.
> That's been clearly known primordially;
> thus, the boundaried mandala has been
> naturally, spontaneously produced.

With the setting of the boundaries, the intended meaning of unsurpassed yoga tantra is presented. "The measureless, spontaneously present nature" refers to the basic purity of this worldly container and its inner contents, which are primally composed of the elements of earth, water, fire, wind, and space. As is explained in the secret mantra teachings, these elements are, in nature, the mother-consorts of the five families' buddhas. When one maintains this awareness, the immeasurable palace is comprised of rainbow-colored light, which is the nature of the four activities. In this way, the outer worldly container is established. As for the aggregates, elements, and sense fields of sentient ones—the inner contents—they are pure from the very beginning.

Because of the strong dualistic habits of beginners who distinguish between self and other, happiness and suffering, gods and demons, and the like, other rituals expel obstructive forces when establishing the boundaries. However, from the ultimate nondual perspective, obstructors lack any inherent existence. That which one labels "obstructor" is nothing other than an idea, a concept. Obstructive forces are merely the confused appearances of dualistic grasping—attachment and aversion, likes and dislikes, and so forth. Such manifestations of dualistic thoughts can be transformed into the dharmakāya. From this perspective of liberation on arising, there is no such thing as forces that hinder or lead astray.

Within the view of inseparable samsara and nirvana, dualistic grasping does not exist. The text refers to the realization of this truth with the words "That's been clearly known primordially." As one abides within the view totally free of distraction from this awareness, "the boundaried mandala has been naturally, spontaneously produced."

Thus, the protective sphere of the boundary is set. When this has been understood, the entirety of appearance-existence becomes the inherently established immeasurable palace of this world together with its inner, divine sentient contents—naturally pure from the beginning. It is only due to adventitious defilements that one experiences the apparent duality of self and other and the arising of obstructive forces. So, the ultimate nonexistence of any obstructive force is itself the yantra, or protective circle.

The Disclosure

In my thinking, since the words of each section of this factual practice manual are based on ultimate truth, the text is extremely profound and meaningful. In this regard, the verse of disclosure begins as follows:

> OṀ. Features of disclosure and disclosed
> come undone in their own place within
> the authentic, spontaneous expanse
> of primordial purity unfurled.

In general, when grasping arises, one accumulates karma and then needs to disclose or confess it. However, a person who comprehends the view and who is habituating to it through meditation knows appearance-existence to be the dharmakāya at the basis. The view is pervasive. Wherever space pervades, the dharmakāya pervades there, too. When one abides without distraction from this pervasive mind that is rigpa, the notion that there is anything to be disclosed is itself a concept. When concepts are liberated in their own place and transformed into primordial awareness-wisdom on arising, the one who discloses, that which is to be disclosed, and the objects to whom one discloses are indistinguishable. In this way, the disclosure is naturally self-existent, without need of fabrication. Thus, the text says, "Features of disclosure and disclosed come undone in their own place." This is the ultimate factual disclosure from "the authentic, spontaneous expanse of primordial purity unfurled." In this regard, Ārya Nāgārjuna said, "Herein, there is nothing at all to be dispelled nor is there anything whatever to posit. One really and truly looks at that which is truly so. To see it is complete liberation."[9] Thus, the king of all disclosures is the view of mahāmudrā. I suppose this must be what the words of the text mean.

Stated another way, that which is to be disclosed are afflictions. The root of all afflictions is ignorance. When ignorance is present, there is a distinction between grasping mind and grasped-at objects. From that dualistic distinction emerge attachment and aversion. However, when afflictions are understood through the kīla of primordial awareness-rigpa, they are torn down by wisdom. Delusive thoughts and their associated feelings are immediately destroyed.

In this context, the affliction to be confessed and the one who confesses, as an antidote, become indistinguishable. Both of them are the empty mind that is rigpa itself. Thus, there are no separate, distinguishing features of disclosure and disclosed. If arising afflictions do not overpower the view, then it is like that. The afflictions and the view are not separate.

However, when the view is overwhelmed, one falls under the power of ignorance, heedlessness, and unmitigated afflictions. Through ignorance—the nonrecognition of the mind's actual condition—dualistic grasping arises, conditioning thoughts based on attachment and aversion. One should disclose whatever adventitious grasping at concepts has arisen but not been eliminated through primordial awareness-rigpa. Thus, the disclosure continues:

> Yet, should there be the delusions of
> ignorant, dualistic grasping, they've
> been disclosed before you naturally
> emanated hosts of deities. SAMAYA A ĀḤ.

The "naturally emanated hosts of deities" and one's own mind are indistinguishable, like the sun and its rays. In the presence of the deities, who are the essence that is awareness-wisdom, one lays bare all delusions, leaving them in rigpa. In this way, disclosure is made. When heedful awareness-rigpa has seized all afflictions, this is the disclosure of the view—the great, principal means of disclosure.

But you should really read the commentaries given by other masters. And those of you who are knowledgeable should teach one another. I can only give rough explanations. Maybe these instructions are OK; maybe they're not. Self-absorbed and arrogant, I say whatever I please, disregarding correctness. Lacking regret for my own misdeeds, having no sense of whether or not I myself have attained liberation, I shamelessly advocate disclosure from the lofty perspective of the ultimate view. If you see that I don't know what I'm talking about, then come back tomorrow and tell me, "You got this wrong; you got that wrong." Please come back and let me know.

Consecrating the Offerings

Next, the offerings that have been laid out are consecrated with these words:

> Primally self-born, pure *amṛita*,
> great redness, six causes freed into
> the expanse, and *mahābaliṅta*,
> appearance-existence structured in
> basic ground—these three great essences
> cannot be exhausted! OṀ ĀḤ HŪṀ.
> OṀ VAJRA PUṢPE, DHŪPE, ĀLOKE, GANDHE, NAIVEDYE, ŚABDA ĀḤ HŪṀ.

These inner offerings of amṛita, *rakta*, and torma are characteristic of the practices of highest yoga tantra. In order to understand their meaning, one should first understand that the entire outer worldly container and inner sentient contents have naturally come into being based on sentient ones' afflictions of lust, aversion, and delusion. All beings grasp at and cling to these afflictive mental states and to the substantial matter of container and contents as being real and true. The substances of amṛita, rakta, and torma are themselves comprised of the naturally pure five elements. Amṛita symbolizes all sentient ones' aversion. Rakta symbolizes lust and torma, delusion. When these three are gathered and consecrated by sādhakas, the material substances themselves are rendered insubstantial and devoid of inherent existence. In this way, the three afflictive poisons in the mindstreams of all the three realms' sentient ones are refined away, transforming them into the pure essence of offering substances. As they are offered, the mandala deities consume them out of great compassion, thus destroying sentient ones' afflictions and suffering.

There are many different sorts of outer and inner, self-arisen, utterly pure amṛita. The Sanskrit word *amṛita* is *dütsi* in Tibetan. The syllable *dü* means "māra" and refers to the dualistic grasping that ripens into afflictions. The syllable *tsi* means "elixir" or "extract." The elixir that is wisdom renders the mind free of thought. When the māra of afflictions becomes wisdom, it is like an alchemy that transforms poison into medicine.

When dualistic grasping is present, all experience is divided into attachment and aversion. On the one side, one grasps at outer desirables and enjoyments. On the other, one avoids that which appears unpleasant. In actuality, phenomena are neither clean nor unclean, neither pure nor impure. When the mind is free of dualistic grasping, everything is the nature of purity. As mentioned previously, the aggregates, elements, and sense fields are pure from the beginning. The self-arisen constituents of sentient ones are the very nature of the method aspect that is amṛita. This offering elixir is comprised of the eight substances and the five elements—earth, water, fire, wind, and space—which are the natural manifestations of the five buddhas' consorts. Thus, the "primally self-born, pure amṛita" mentioned in the text should be understood in this way.

The next offering is rakta, the wisdom aspect. It is referred to in the text as "great redness, six causes freed into the expanse." The six causes are the six afflictions: (1) aversion, (2) avarice, (3) ignorance, (4) desire, (5) jealousy, and (6) pride. These are the causes that give rise to the six classes of wayfaring beings within the desire realm: (1) hell denizens, (2) pretas, (3) animals, (4) humans, (5) demigods, and (6) gods, respectively.

Since blood, or "great redness," is equivalent to the lust in which all the other afflictions are subsumed, under the influence of ignorant, dualistic grasping, it becomes a cause for all the manifold confused appearances of samsara's six realms. These appearances are said to be "conditional" because the phenomena of the hell realms appear based on the condition of aversion, preta-realm phenomena appear through the condition of avarice, and so forth.

Although the affliction of desire is present in the blood, when it is fully liberated, it manifests as the wisdom that liberates every other affliction. This is why rakta is required as an offering substance. Recognizing the power of blood, some religious systems call for offerings of blood sacrifices. Due to this greatly mistaken view, they cause unbearable suffering.

In our system, that which manifests as desire under the influence of dualistic grasping is, in its nondual essence, the nature of great bliss. By means of bliss, lust can be transformed into primordial awareness-wisdom. Since the wisdom deities never waver from the view, they consume this offering substance as a means of freeing samsaric sentient ones from lust.

Finally, the word "mahābaliṅta" in the text refers to the offerings of the great torma. It is said in the scriptures, "Within appearance—the container-world that is the torma vessel—existence, contained sentient ones, is refined as the torma."[10]

The physical aggregates of sentient ones have been created by self-grasping, the source of which is delusion. The essence of the torma is sentient ones' grasping at the entire container and contents as being real. As such, the torma itself signifies the delusion of sentient beings. Because of this, one should imagine the substance of the torma to be as vast as Mount Meru.

When one performs the liberation in the *gaṇapūja*, the consciousnesses of obstructive forces are transferred to the dharmasphere and their aggregates are given over to the gaṇacakra. In this way, one makes offerings. The torma offering has basically the same meaning as the liberation. The offering of the torma is "appearance-existence structured in basic ground." This appearance-existence is the worldly container and its sentient contents.

These material offering substances—like the five elements and the mother-consorts of the five families dwelling in the expanse of the five wisdoms—are inexhaustible essences that will abide until samsara itself has been emptied out. Offering the three substances, one should mentally gather up the totality of beings' three poisonous afflictions, which have given rise to all the six realms. With the syllables OṀ ĀḤ HŪṀ, they are sealed with the three vajras—consecrated by the buddhas' enlightened body, speech, and mind. OṀ is the syllable of form, appearance-emptiness. ĀḤ is the syllable of speech, all sounds that are without essence and are empty like echoes. HŪṂ is the nature of all thoughts, emptiness-rigpa. The offerings are then devoured by Vajrakīla's manifestation as Vajrarākṣasa, or Adamantine Carnivore. In this way, through meditating on the act of offering, the one who offers, and the recipients of the offering as being nondual, one consecrates the inner offerings.

Introduction to the Stages of Development

It is taught that the form of the deity emerges out of emptiness and is developed in stages. Before engaging the development stages, though, one should understand and have confidence that all phenomenal appearances are devoid of inherent existence and are selfless by nature. This is why development-stage visualizations so often begin with the words OṂ SVABHĀVA ŚUDDHĀḤ SARVA DHARMĀḤ SVABHĀVA ŚUDDHO HAṂ, which point to purity as the fundamental nature of all phenomena, including one's body. This is the nonreferential, threefold perceptual sphere, in which there is no grasping at phenomena, self, or other as having any reality at all. It is the fortress of the view.

Since the mind is like an empty mirror, which reflects whatever is placed before it, the moment one thinks about the deity abiding in space, that deity's form is reflected in the mirror of the mind. Further, when one merely recalls the deity, his or her love enters one's mindstream. In this way, the mind becomes free of self-grasping. Since there is no thought of the gross physical body when the mind is free of self-grasping, one need not dissolve the body in order to give rise to the deity.

Visualizing the Immeasurable Palace

The development stages begin with the visualization of the immeasurable palace, which is introduced by the following words:

> HŪṂ. The immeasurable and manifold
> palace is the object that appears.

Every constituent of the outer container that is this world appears only circumstantially. In the end, it lacks existence at the very basis. Every aspect of the concrete existence perceived by beings has come about according to individuals' karmic imprints. These circumstantial, fleeting phenomena are composites; they are the nature of great emptiness. Thus, Protector Jigten Sumgön said, "The stages of development are thoroughly established from the very beginning."[11] So, although Jambudvīpa is comprised of the composite and impermanent five elements, those five elements have come into being under the influence of the continuity of mind—the union of clarity and emptiness.

In actuality, the five elements that make up this worldly realm are divine. Through their rainbowlike nature, the entire outer container manifests. One should roughly or approximately imagine this. Since the object that appears is clarity-emptiness—like a rainbow—it is sufficient to regard it as being devoid of inherent existence and not truly established.

Just as rainbows appear only circumstantially through the interaction of sunlight with water droplets, so too does this entire universe come into being. Because of this, it has no ultimate, concrete existence. If one who understands this fact meditates again and again on the rainbowlike immeasurable palace of the deity, one's grasping at the outer worldly container as real will be torn down. Eventually, having become free of grasping at things as real and true, one will perceive this world as indistinguishable from the rainbowlike saṁbhogakāya pure realms. This is the reason one must visualize the immeasurable palace as being comprised of rainbow-colored lights. Once one has purified grasping at substantial appearances, the saṁbhogakāya pure realms are spontaneously present.

The immeasurable palace manifests in various ways. From the perspective of outer practice, its perceivable qualities of the lotus seat and so forth are of principal importance. As for the inner and secret practices, when one perceives this world that is the container as appearing yet insubstantial, like a rainbow, the immeasurable palace is naturally, spontaneously produced. In this case, one need not pay great attention to generating every visualized detail of the palace.

The next line of the text indicates the sphere, or the field, in which the palace appears:

> A fiery, blue three-point mandala...

Even though the words indicate a triangular shape, one should understand the mandala to be three-dimensional, appearing as an inconceivably vast, blue-black tetrahedron. It is a metaphor for the element of unelaborated space, the outer sky, the source of phenomena. Its dark blue color represents the changeless essence that is the empty dharmasphere, which is unaffected by the mistaken views of eternalism and nihilism. For example, wrathful tormas have a similar shape, which gives them stability. Since they cannot stand on the tip, they must be set on their base; there is only one way to place them. Thus, nothing can alter the stability of the torma's base.

The triangular shape also symbolizes the three kāyas. To understand this, one should look inward at one's own mind. The fundamental natures of the outer sky and of inner rigpa—the tathāgatagarbha itself—are of one and the same essence. Thus, one angle of the triangle is the dharmakāya—the empty, sky-like essence. It is not, however, a mere nothing, as its nature is clarity—a vivid brilliance conjoined with cognizance of emptiness. This is the angle of the saṁbhogakāya nature. Further, a great compassion without reference point naturally emerges for every sentient one who has not yet recognized this union of clarity and emptiness. This all-pervasive, compassionate activity is the angle of the nirmāṇakāya. In this way, one should understand the triangular mandala as a symbol of the three kāyas' attributes.

Inside that mandala, one visualizes the environs of the immeasurable palace. If one wishes to learn about the palace in detail, the Latter-System Vajrakīla texts of the Sakya tradition include an extensive mandala visualization. It is related to the following lines of text, which present only a glimpse of the elaborate visualization:

> ...wherein the eight charnel grounds surround
> an expanse that flares with wisdom flames...

Temporarily and circumstantially, the pure dharmasphere carries the impure appearances of samsara. Although the outer container that is this world is vast, it is simply a macrocosm of one's own body, which is dependent on the eightfold group of consciousness. That eightfold group is the consciousnesses of the (1) eye, (2) ear, (3) nose, (4) tongue, (5) body, (6) mind, (7) afflicted mind, and (8) ālaya. When the nature of this eightfold group is obscured, it manifests as attachment and clinging to the five desirables and the like. Whenever there is attachment, there is also aversion. Thus, all perceived impure samsaric appearances arise from the eight consciousnesses, which are symbolized by the eight charnel grounds.

However, since the mind is empty in nature, it is innately pure. When one recognizes the innate purity of the eightfold group, one understands all that past attachment and aversion to have been confusion. For example, when a person dies, the corpse is thrown into the charnel ground or into the funerary pyre. Similarly, when one understands the eightfold group of consciousnesses to be confusion, like a corpse without an owner, it spontaneously manifests in its purity as the eight male and female bodhisattvas. In this regard, the eight consciousnesses of oneself and all beings of the six realms are the same in nature. The eightfold group of consciousnesses, which is symbolized by the eight charnel grounds located on the outer fringes of the mandala, should be understood in this way.

Although it is not mentioned in this concise practice manual, in the midst of this blazing triangular blue-black sky with charnel grounds and heaps of wisdom flames, one generates step by step the four elements that make up the outer container that is this world: wind, fire, water, and earth. The space element, which contains and pervades them, has already been visualized with the triangular blue mandala. It is not as though these four elements have been primordially present; rather, they are adventitious, transient events. They are compounded phenomena that are the nature of impermanence and ultimately subject to destruction. During the completion stage, they vanish in an instant like rainbows. Thus, the elements that compose the outer palace are no different from those that make up one's own body.

As for the stages of development that have already been visualized, the blazing blue tetrahedron symbolizes ultimate factual truth. The eight charnel grounds represent conventional fictional truth. The heaps of wisdom flames signify ultimate wisdom, the deities' nature. Next, the union of ultimate and conventional manifests as the outer protective sphere, which is indistinguishable from self-appearances.

One should imagine the outer mandala as two iron wheels, each with eight arc-shaped spokes. These wheels are like two ribbed domes conjoined to make a sphere. This protective sphere of the surrounding mandala is the actual dwelling place of the deities, with one wrathful couple in each of the four cardinal directions, four intermediate directions, zenith, and nadir—ten directions in total. In this way, eight wrathful couples appear in the eight cardinal and intermediate directions, with an additional couple above and another below. As will be described later, mandalas of these ten great wrathful ones are mirrored like crystalline rainbow reflections in the principal's heart, in his body mandala, in the inner mandala inside the immeasurable palace, and in the handle of the material kīla.[12]

This protective sphere encompasses the entire support to be meditated upon—the immeasurable palace as an extremely vast mansion. In order to understand the immeasurable palace, one can consider the example of planet Earth, which is like a mansion suspended in empty space. When engaging the development-stage visualizations, one should transform every material thing that appears into the contents of the immeasurable palace. The outer surroundings of the deity are completely contained within the eight-spoked protective sphere. The text reads,

> ... is where there appears the measureless
> palace through wisdom projections formed.

The mandala of the immeasurable palace is symbolic of the inner mind. Just like the reflections that arise from a crystal, the pure immeasurable palace that appears in the mind is established through wisdom projections. Whatever self-appearances manifest outwardly, they arise within space and are pervaded by space. Thus, the entirety of appearance-existence is inseparable from mind. Appearances and mind are one. Perceived things and their defining characteristics are the inherently established, rainbowlike immeasurable palace. It is said to be cubical in shape, with a door on each side. The point here is that there is no contradiction between diverse self-appearances and emptiness. Just as with the dark blue triangular mandala that symbolizes the three kāyas, these appearances are naturally complete in the inherently existent empty mind. Since these wisdom projections appear from the perspective of actual truth, meditators should not get hung up on gross concepts of them as polyhedra with faces, edges, and corners!

For the purpose of visualization, one should know that inside the palace appear two cakras, shaped like ten- and four-spoked throwing stars, respectively. In the first of these, the ten wrathful couples are positioned in the ten spokes. Inside that is the mandala of the four princes, with four spokes in the four directions.

In this explanation, I have briefly supplemented the words of the secret accomplishment text with some of the visualizations from the extensive practice manual. In that text, each stage of development is elaborated in fine detail. When the extensive sadhana is taken to its end point, one arrives at the secret accomplishment text we are practicing, which is like the condensed essence. While it is all right to visualize the elaborate mandala during the secret accomplishment, it is not necessary to do so. For our purposes, it is suitable simply to imagine the entire mandala suddenly arising in the mind, manifesting like rainbow appearances. The mandala's spontaneous presence should be understood in this way.

Visualizing the Deity

Then, in the center of the four-spoked cakra, there appears the principal deity with consort. When visualizing him, it is best if one has no thought at all of self versus other or inside versus outside. Similarly, it is unnecessary to enumerate distinctly each of the appearances of the mandala, thinking, "I am here; those deities are over there." In this regard, Lord Milarepa advised meditators not to distinguish between the one and the many. Otherwise, confusion will arise.

One should merely visualize oneself as the deity, having confidence that the entire mandala and retinue naturally and spontaneously appear like surrounding reflections. For example, when a ray of light strikes a faceted crystal, rainbow reflections spontaneously manifest due to the crystal's innate self-radiance. Similarly, the four princes, ten wrathfuls, the entire retinue, and the deities in one's own channel hubs naturally arise as the self-radiance of the principal deity. Thus, rather than fabricating visualizations based on concepts about the words read in the text, one should become confident that the mandala deities are actually present. A sādhaka who is confident need not discriminate between great or small, many or few, or a visualization that is clear or unclear. In this way, one should directly imagine whatever is described in the text without giving rise to many concepts.

The yidam deity continually abides in the expanse of space. One's mind is like a clear mirror that is always reflecting him or her. So, if it is difficult to visualize the yidam in the beginning, to be aware of this point alone is sufficient. Even if one does not know how to visualize anything at all, it is said that one can begin by imagining the color of the deity's form. Later, once the color has become stable, one can visualize the approximate form of the deity in a coarse way, gradually refining it over time. That form appears like a rainbow: although it is visible, it is entirely without substance. This is the pure illusory body. If one stabilizes this, there will be no error, even if there are imperfections in the visualization. Rather than focus on minute details, one should attend to the main point of empty appearance. Regarding visualization, even if there is only an unclear approximation of the deity in one's mind, it will be sufficient as long as the main point of insubstantiality is present.

Keeping the mind open, relaxed, and clear of many concepts, one should allow the visualization to unfold according to the words of the text:

> In its center on lotus, sun, moon,
> and four māras crossed is a blue HŪṂ.
> As light emanates and gathers back,
> the complete, unaltered body of
> the great sovereign, Glorious Vajra Youth,
> blue-black, with three faces and six arms,
> stands with four legs spread in champion's stance.

At the very center of the palace, inside the ten- and four-spoked cakras, is a seat of lotus flower, moon, sun, and the four māras. The lotus seat symbolizes freedom from defilement. The moon and sun represent method and wisdom, respectively. They are compassion and emptiness, the white and red constituents of the father and mother, through which the consciousness takes rebirth during the bardo of becoming. As mentioned before, the four māras are the māra of the aggregates, the māra of afflictions, the māra of the lord of death, and the māra of the son of the gods. Since they embody the afflictions of pride, aversion, jealousy, and desire, they are the causes of the sufferings of this worldly realm. However, they do not include ignorance, since Vajrakumāra himself is the purified essence of ignorance. When ignorance has been transformed into primordial awareness, then the four other afflictions are spontaneously brought down. Upon these four māras appears the HŪṂ syllable.

In the practice of Vajrakīla, the first point is meditation on the causal HŪṂ syllable that emerges from within the dharmatā, emptiness. This is the same as the visualization from the Yamāntaka practice manual, in which the three samādhis are set forth. These three are (1) the samādhi of suchness, (2) the causal samādhi, and (3) the samādhi of total appearance.

The first of these is the emptiness of all phenomena. This unfabricated mind totally free of all dualistic grasping—the samādhi of suchness—then takes the form of the blue-black HŪṀ syllable, the causal samādhi.

With regard to the causal samādhi, the extensive Vajrakīla practice manual says, "The wrathful vajra cuts off aggression."[13] Here, the wrathful vajra and the weapon that is the seed syllable are indistinguishable. All the excellent qualities of Vajrakīla's form are naturally complete therein. Thus, the term "complete" signifies the perfection of the deity's fully manifest form, which is inherent in the seed. His body, ornaments, and implements—symbols, meanings, and signs—are all primordially intrinsic to the seed itself. Because concentration on the deity's seed syllable is the cause of the third samādhi, it is referred to as the causal samādhi.

From the HŪṀ, light rays radiate outward, making offerings to all the buddhas and clearing away the wrongdoings and obscurations of all sentient ones. Then they return, gathering together all the buddhas' blessings. Through their power, "the complete, unaltered body of the great sovereign" emerges. This is the samādhi of total appearance, the physical manifestation of compassion.

Here, the word "unaltered" indicates the basic mind free of thought or emotion—the naked, ordinary mind that is the buddha nature. Not fabricated through dualistic grasping, rigpa is the basis of the development stages of every deity. This unfabricated mind itself arises as the body of Great Glorious Vajrakumāra. His blue-black complexion signifies the changeless dharmatā. His three faces symbolize the qualities of the buddhas' three kāyas. His six arms are the sign of the six transcendent perfections' completeness. His four legs represent the four immeasurables and also the four enlightened activities from within the emptiness of dharmatā. Since he is the essence of mindfulness, the four māras beneath his feet symbolize the suppression of afflictions by mindful awareness.

Once the complete body of the deity has emerged, one should

scan it in stages from head to toe and then back again, paying attention to the details of his ornaments, implements, and the like. Thus, sādhakas should visualize as follows:

> Middle blue, right white, and left face red,
> the five families beautify my head.
> The heart's vital force is the seed, HŪṂ.
> With nine glaring eyes, I look upon
> all the ten directions and my mouths
> gape with twisted tongues and canines bared.
> Nine- and five-pronged vajras in both right,
> massed flames and khaṭvāṅga in left hands,
> the last two hands roll a Meru stake.
> This completes the fearsome charnel gear.

Vajrakumāra's right white face represents the purification of aversion. The left red face symbolizes the purification of lust and the middle blue face the clearing away of ignorance. Once those three afflictions have been refined away, they manifest as the three kāyas: the nirmāṇakāya, the saṁbhogakāya, and the dharmakāya, respectively.

The deity is adorned with the five-pointed crown ornament, which signifies the five victorious ones' families. His nine eyes represent the nine successive vehicles. His bared fangs are the sign of cutting off from the root birth and death in samsaric existence. In his upper right hand, he holds a nine-pronged vajra, which is emblematic of the nine successive vehicles. In his middle right hand, he holds a five-pronged vajra, which symbolizes his guidance of the five family lines' sentient ones in ways appropriate to their dispositions. These five family lines refer to the beings of the six realms, with gods and demigods combined as one. In two of his left hands, he holds a heap of flames, the sign of burning all samsaric imprints, and a khaṭvāṅga, whose three prongs signify severing the three poisons at the root. His two lowest hands hold a kīla the size of Mount Meru, which symbolizes the subjugation of arrogant ones.

Although it is not mentioned in this text, Vajrakumāra also has two wings. The wing on the right is comprised of vajras and is paler in color. The one on the left is made up of precious jewels and is variegated. Symbolizing the skillful means of compassion, the vajra wing conquers the afflictions in the minds of all sentient ones. The jewel wing signifies the wisdom aspect that is emptiness. As the source of everything precious, it bestows all the buddhas' qualities. Together, the two wings represent the nondual union of method and wisdom. Similarly, they symbolize extraordinary unimpeded movement and activity that accomplish beings' benefit. In brief, the wings are a metaphor for the view that is dharmatā. When dharmatā, the state of Vajradhara, is realized, all the qualities of unified samsara and nirvana are spontaneously accomplished.

In general, all wrathful herukas have the eightfold charnel ground attire. This includes the three smeared substances of (1) great ash from human bones, symbolizing the dharmakāya; (2) fresh rakta, the saṁbhogakāya; and (3) great fat, the nirmāṇakāya. The three freshly flayed garments are (4) an elephant hide stretched behind the deity's back, (5) a shawl that is the skin of a human enemy of the teachings in whom the ten grounds are complete, and (6) a loincloth of tiger skin. In addition, there are the ornaments of (7) snakes and (8) fresh human heads and dried skulls.

Since the herukas of the Eight Sadhana Teachings are said to be endowed with the ten glorious accoutrements of wrathful ones, they display all of the above eight attires as well as (9) heaps of wisdom flames and (10) vajra wings.[14] Each of these accoutrements is endowed with symbolic meaning.

However many good qualities of body, ornaments, implements, and the like can be elaborated, they are all attributes of the deity's inner mindstream, which is primordial awareness. As such, they are complete and present from the beginning as the buddhas' five kāyas or five wisdoms. Expanding outward, all five are present within each one, making twenty-five, just as expressed in *The Aspiration of Samantabhadra*. To whatever degree one may elaborate the deity's good qualities, those attributes continue to increase infinitely. Whenever one cultivates pure recollection of the deity's body, speech, and mind according to the words of the extensive practice manual, one should again and again seal those pure perceptions with the view.

Gathering inward, the five kāyas are subsumed within the three kāyas, which are further contracted into the dharmakāya, the blue-black HŪṂ that is rigpa. After abiding in meditation on the seed syllable for some time, one should immediately recall the complete form of the deity again. In this way, it is suitable to alternate among a visualization of the deity's entire body, the seed syllable, and empty awareness.

As one recites the words of the sadhana from within the state of buddha nature, the sound conjoined with meaning arises in the mind. The words merely serve to remind the meditator of that which is already present. Thus, the stages of development spontaneously arise within the mind free of grasping. In this way, rather than generating the deity's form by means of many concepts, one should give rise to a secret, confident knowing.

The Deity's Names

The divine form that arises is a Vajra-family heruka known by different names. Samantabhadra, Vajrasattva, Vajrapāṇi, and Vajrakumāra all have the same meaning, which is inseparable and indistinct from one's buddha nature. This is the vast sphere of dharmas Kagyü practitioners call Vajradhara. The body, speech, mind, qualities, and activities of the three times' buddhas manifestly abide therein. Therefore, Vajrakumāra pervades the buddha nature of all wayfaring sentient ones. Although that buddha nature is perceived with greater or lesser clarity by individuals, it is singular in nature.

As for the name of the deity, the term *vajra* (*dorje*) refers to the ultimate adamantine nature that is emptiness. Even though the vajra is empty, it has profound symbolic meaning. Its five upper and lower prongs represent the fathers and mothers of the five families. Its eight upper and lower petals symbolize the eight male and female bodhisattvas. As emptiness, the vajra is the basis of all phenomena. It is similar to a crystal, from which refracted rays of white, yellow, red, green, and blue light spontaneously shine forth. Thus, every quality emerges from the mind, the empty tathāgatagarbha. This meaning is also taught in *The Aspiration of Samantabhadra*, which says, "Everything of all that appears and exists—samsara and nirvana—is an illusory display of knowing or ignorance with one basis, two paths, and two fruits."[15]

All the qualities of the grounds of nirvana have arisen from mind. Likewise, all the samsaric sufferings of the six realms' mother-beings have emerged from mind. The mind alone is emptiness. It is beyond having any part of the minutest particle. It is nothing whatsoever, yet it gives rise to all sorts of appearances.

The term *vajra* also appears in the Tibetan word for "diamond," *dorje phalam*, which cuts through and can destroy all other materials. This example illustrates a quality of the vajra mind. Under the influence of ignorance, grasping mind, and grasped-at objects, sentient wayfarers of the six classes experience existence—taking birth in unbounded samsara, living, dying, and being reborn again and again in countless bodies. Wandering throughout the six realms, they experience incalculable hardships. Because of some slight virtue in the past, they experience a bit of comfort in the three higher realms. Due to misdeeds, they endure countless sufferings in the lower realms. Yet, in spite of all this wandering, the adamantine mind is not subject to death.

When one cultivates the cause that is bodhicitta based on the condition that is the virtuous friend, the six classes' obscurations of karma, imprints, and knowable things are pierced through and scattered. In this way, the vajra mind traverses the pure grounds of the buddhas.

Conversely, when one befriends passion and aversion based on the condition of self-grasping, the qualities of the pure buddhafields are present in name only. Under such conditions, the adamantine mind assuredly goes to the three bad migrations. So, one should understand that the mind rises or falls within the wheel of existence, all the while remaining unbreakable and indestructible. For this reason, it is said to be adamantine, like the vajra. This kīla of awareness-rigpa is new in every moment, free of aging, and like space. Since the mind is uncompounded, it is free of conditions and not subject to destruction. Unborn and undying, changeless in the three times, it is unmingled and untainted. This is what the word *youth* means. The name Vajra Youth (Vajrakumāra) should be understood in this way.

More commonly, the deity is referred to as Adamantine Stake (Vajrakīla). Sometimes he is called by the name of one of his emanations, Adamantine Carnivore (Vajrarākṣasa). In this manifestation, he consumes the flesh that is sentient ones' ignorance. Regardless of which name is used, he is, in essence, Adamantine Courageous Attitude (Vajrasattva), the sovereign of all the buddha families. In particular, when destructive activities are required, he manifests as Accomplisher of the Meaningful (Amoghasiddhi). The master of all the buddhas' enlightened activities, he is the deity who dispels obstacles on the grounds and paths for present and future lifetimes.

Among the victorious ones of the five families, Amoghasiddhi is the lord of the family of enlightened activities. However, the New Treasure traditions have put Unshakable One (Akṣobhya) in that place. Since one buddha family encompasses all the others, in different contexts these buddhas exchange places depending on the activity being accomplished and the lineage tradition.

In the context of sutra practices, deities such as Avalokita are visualized in single form. In secret mantra contexts, those same deities are often visualized with consort. Why is this? Although the mind is nondual, in beings' samsaric experience, all phenomena are dualistically divided. Thus, the father and mother deities appear as two. By cultivating practice on the basis of this apparent duality, first, one experiences great bliss. Then, when one looks at the nature of that bliss—the innate, actual condition of the mind separated from all thought and all grasping—it becomes emptiness. When the empty nature becomes clear, the nonduality of mind is seen. Finally, the nondual fact that is the union of emptiness and flame-like clarity is realized. This is a special attribute of secret mantra practice.

Thus, after the body of Vajrakumāra has been generated, his mother-consort—the nature of emptiness—is visualized with the following verse:

The Great Consort Khorlo Gyedebma
is pale blue, with one face and two arms.
Utpala in hand, she clasps the neck
of the father and with her left hand
proffers to his mouth a blood-filled conch.

The Lady of the Sealed Cakra (Dīptacakrā) is known in Tibetan as Khorlo Gyedebma. This name signifies that the cakra that is her body, mind, channels, and constituents has been sealed with the experience of bliss. In essence, she is Liberatrix with Binding Commitment (Samayatārā). Light blue in color, she is unwavering from the nature that is the dharmakāya. In her left hand, she holds a white conch that is cut in half and contains wisdom-amṛita, symbolizing conquest of the four māras. As an oblation vessel, the conch has the same significance as a kapāla.

The Body Mandala

Next, one focuses one's attention inward on the main deities of the body mandala:

In our foreheads, a blue Hūṁkār pair,
and red Hayagrīva in our throats,
a blue Yama couple in our hearts,
o'er the navels, chartreuse Dütsi Khyilpa couple,
in the navels, a dark green Miyo pair,
in the privates, a blue Tobchen pair,
a white Namgyal pair in the right shoulders,
and blue Yug-ngön couple in the left,

a pink Dögyal couple in right thighs,
and dark gold Khamsum pair are in the left.

For the purposes of introduction, practitioners are taught that the fathers and mothers of the five families are present throughout the body mandala. However, these coarse forms of the deities are merely expedient symbols. In actuality, the deities are the nature of the five elements that make up the body: flesh and bones are the earth element, blood is water, warmth is fire, breath is wind, and mind is space. For example, the human body is naturally pervaded by warmth, the fire element. That warmth is none other than Vajravārāhī. By their very nature, the five elements are the subtle nirmāṇakāya emanations of deities.

In this regard, Lord Buddha taught that the human body is pervaded by 1.2 million microorganisms. Because of this, if one person becomes a buddha, 1.2 million microorganisms will also become buddhas. Conversely, if an individual should wander to the three bad states of hell denizens, pretas, and animals, the same number of microorganisms will travel there together with him or her. Thus, one need not have any doubt about whether one's actions can benefit or harm others.

More than two thousand years after Lord Buddha, scientists now know that countless bacteria and different organisms inhabit the human body. When magnified, these can actually be seen with the eye. Beneficial microorganisms have their origins in affection, love, and compassion. Harmful ones are manifestations of afflictions like anger, pride, and jealousy. The various helpful and harmful effects of these individual life forms can be directly witnessed, affirming the view that love is the cause of physical and mental well-being and afflictions are the cause of suffering. This is true even from the common, worldly perspective of the impure state.

In the context of secret mantra, innumerable deities are actually present in the body mandala of every deity. When viewed from an ordinary, unripe perspective, they are microorganisms. When viewed through the lens of bodhicitta and ripened pure perception, they are gods. When viewed through the lens of a grossly afflicted mind, they are demons. These features are brought into stark contrast in the bardo, or intermediate state between births, when one no longer has a physical form. Having only a mental body, one will perceive the hundred families of the holy peaceful and wrathful ones according to one's karmic imprints. Those who have cultivated bodhicitta will recognize them as divine. Those who have cultivated affliction will experience them as terrifying demons doing all sorts of harm—some coming to slaughter, others coming to strangle one, some eating one's flesh, and still others drinking one's blood.

In this way, although the deities are continuously present, their attributes change depending on the state of one's mind. Thus, life force, merit, health, great intelligence, and so forth will naturally come about in this life when the body mandala has been sealed with bodhicitta. Such are the benefits of secret mantra pure perception.

The divine couples of the body mandala should then be visualized in stages according to the words of the text. They appear superficially within the body; that is, they dwell more toward the surface than in the body's inner core. Although these deities are visualized within the self-generation, it is not necessary to imagine them in fine detail within the form of the visualized consort. It is sufficient simply to be aware that the body of the consort is also pervaded by deities. The main point is not to focus on all the different forms of the body mandala's deities; rather, it is that bliss arises in the body and mind on the basis of bodhicitta. The ten wrathful couples are merely symbols of this.

Reflections of the body mandala's ten wrathful ones appear throughout the visualization. On the innermost level, it is as though there were a crystal in Vajrakumāra's heart where they abide and from which they are also projected outward. They are innately present in the places of one's body mandala and the ten spokes of the inner mandala.

Beings in the Surrounding Mandala

Now that the bodies of the principal heruka Vajrakumāra and consort have been established, the sadhana lists some of the deities who appear in the surrounding mandala with these words:

> In four quarters are the four families
> and ten wrathful couples in ten spokes,
> each together with a *zasö* pair.
> With three faces, six arms, and wide-spread
> four legs, vajra wings, and charnel gear,
> these twenty-four wrathfuls hold diverse
> weapons with their own respective signs.

The "four quarters" refer to the previously mentioned four-spoked cakra that is immediately outside the heruka's body. In the cardinal directions of its four spokes dwell the princes of the four families: Vajrakīla, Ratnakīla, Padmakīla, and Karmakīla. In this constellation, the Buddha and Vajra families are merged together. These four princes represent the four enlightened activities. Thus, they are associated with the four activities' material kīlas, which are placed inside the material mandala: the pacifying silver of the Vajra family, the enriching gold of the Ratna family, the magnetizing copper of the Padma family, and the greenish-black iron of the Karma family.

Surrounding the four-spoked wheel is the ten-spoked wheel of sky iron, the seat of the ten wrathful couples. These ten are the natural expressions of the bodhisattvas' ten strengths and ten perfections. The ten strengths are listed as (1) reflection, (2) superior aspiration, (3) application, (4) discriminative awareness, (5) prayer or aspiration, (6) vehicle, (7) conduct, (8) transformation, (9) enlightenment, and (10) turning the doctrinal wheel.[16]

As for the transcendent perfections, although the systems of individual liberation and the Bodhisattva Vehicle speak of them as being six, in the context of secret mantra, they are listed as ten, which correspond to the ten *bhūmis*. They consist of the first six perfections with the addition of (7) means, (8) aspirations, (9) power, and (10) primordial awareness. In brief, these ten strengths and ten transcendent perfections are the conduct of all the enlightened ones.

Each of these great male and female wrathful ones emanates a smaller animal-headed servant of the same sex. With human-like bodies, the females have falcon heads and the males have the fanged heads of tigers and other beasts of prey. The females, known as "slayers" (*sö*), are like a falconer's trained hawks, in that they can be sent forth to carry out the deity's work. The males, called "devourers" (*za*), like the other deities in the mandala, consume enemies' and obstructors' flesh and blood. These servant couples, together called "zasö," stand like tiny retinues to the left and right of each of the wrathful couples and engage the activities of Vajrakīla.

All of these couples—the princes of the four families, the ten great wrathful ones, and the ten zasö—equal twenty-four. Holding implements and weapons appropriate to their activities, they comprise the concise retinue, which is the essence of the elaborate retinue described in the extensive Vajrakīla sadhana.

Since these deities naturally abide regardless of whether or not one is meditating on them, there is no need to visualize them in detail. It is sufficient to give rise to confidence that the wrathful ones are spontaneously present in the surrounding mandala as described.

The visualization then continues, listing additional inhabitants of the mandala:

> The four gates have four beast-faced guard maids.
> In the mandala's concentric spheres,
> emanations, princes, aides in wait,
> sovereigns, dog maids, earth maids, and the hosts
> of great men—Se, Chag, and Dung—appear.
> Thus, the chief and retinue have been
> visualized in their entirety.

Beyond the ten-spoked wheel are the four walls of the immeasurable palace. The outer guardians of the palace's four gates are unseen. However, they have female bodies, and each one has the head of one of the four kinds of birds, including an owl, a falcon, and the like.

Beyond the walls is an outer corridor surrounding the palace. It is filled with guardians and protectors. The sovereign maidens, dog-faced maidens, earth-owning maidens, and four great *kiṁkāra* beings comprise the twelve Kīla guardians. Of the great personages, Se is reddish, the color of copper. Chag is black, or iron-colored. Dung is the white color of a conch. Many such masters of earthly domains have physical forms that bear the characteristics of their territories. Each of these different types of beings leads a crowd of his or her own kind. Since these protectors are all enumerated in the extensive practice manual, if it can be read just once, then thereafter one can maintain a general idea of the different sorts of mandala deities. When reciting this verse, one should imagine that the entire protection circle suddenly and completely appears in a flash of light.

In this way, the various cakras with different numbers of spokes comprise the concentric spheres of the mandala of Vajrakīla. Within these spheres abide innumerable hosts of divine beings who are like the ministers, envoys, and troops who carry out the manifold activities of a great king. They are all subsumed within Vajrakumāra alone. One quality of the heruka's body is his extensive emanation of limitless light rays and hosts of divine servants. Thus, one should think of the principal deity as being like the sun and all the deities in the retinue as being like the sun's rays.

Throughout the meditation, one should visualize the principal, the consort, and the body mandala. As for the other deities in the surrounding mandala, it is sufficient just to be aware that they are present. Through this means, one gains mastery over the billion-fold universe, which is complete within the single mandala of the commitment being, or *samayasattva*.

To briefly review the development-stage visualization of the extensive immeasurable palace from outside to in, there is the mandala of the blue tetrahedron, inside of which is the expanse with charnel grounds and wisdom flames. Inside of that is the eight-spoked protective sphere of the ten wrathful ones, inside of which is the immeasurable palace surrounded by hosts of guardians. Therein is the ten-spoked sphere of the inner ten wrathfuls, inside of which is the four-spoked cubical mandala of the four princes, which surrounds the principal and consort.

Here, as I have described some features of the visualization that are not included in our text, it is important to note that—according to the needs of individuals of greater, middling, and lesser faculties—there exist extensive and abbreviated sadhanas. More extensive empowerments and practice manuals are set forth for those who wish to accomplish the four activities, uphold the teachings, and cause the Dharma to flourish and spread. In this regard, in *Gongchig: The Single Intent, the Sacred Dharma*, Jigten Sumgön said, "[Even] people of the highest acumen need extensive rituals."[17] In the supplemental verses to that same text, Drigung Dharmasūrya said, "Regardless of whether the approach is provisional or definitive, extensive liturgies are necessary. Once the mind has been subdued by the extensive, a concise liturgy is also acceptable."[18] These statements mean that practitioners should first understand and become familiar with the elaborate sadhana of a deity. Then, on the basis of that familiarity, they may practice abbreviated sadhanas.

For the purposes of training, one should have a rough understanding that the mandala is laid out in this way. However, since the saṁbhogakāyas of five certainties naturally and spontaneously appear like this, one need not fabricate them through visualization. Instead of actively visualizing every detail of the mandala, it is easy just to imagine its door being open. For example, when a Vajrakīla secret accomplishment is happening in the temple, if someone simply opens the door of the temple, that person walks into a vividly clear environment. Similarly, if the door of the saṁbhogakāya mandala is always open—if there is neither inside nor outside—then the container and contents are primordially established as the mandala of the deity. One should think of the mandala in this way.

The whole point of all this is that this planet Earth is one mandala; one's own body is a microcosm of that mandala. Every sentient one, down to the tiniest insect, is the principal at the center of a mandala. The outer and inner meanings are just that. The secret meaning is that all these appearances have been created by the self-radiance of mind alone. When this has been understood, then the secret accomplishment is perfectly fulfilled.

The Heart Visualization

Now that the visualization of the principal and mandala have been established, one again turns one's focus inward, to the visualization at the heart center.

Just as Americans obsess about water purity and have developed water purification systems, so too should practitioners purify the mind through the stages of development. Although there are some who doubt the qualities of deity yoga, it is through purifying the mind that great discerning intelligence arises. One who has such aware intelligence will fundamentally understand the qualities of bodhicitta—what its benefits are and whether or not it is truly able to clear away karma and obscurations.

If one really wishes to purify the mind, the following visualization should be the main focus of the actual development-stage meditation:

> In the principal's heart on a sun,
> a thumb-joint-sized *sattva* rolls a stake.
> On a sun within his heart is a
> grain-sized golden vajra, at whose core
> is a HŪṂ by mantra circumvolved.

The outer body of the deity is a nirmāṇakāya that naturally arises. It appears like a rainbow and is brilliant like the sun. At the heart of that deity is a tiny radiant sun disk, upon which abides the wisdom being, or *jñānasattva*, referred to as "sattva" in the text.

Since he dwells in the heart, one might wonder where this sattva is positioned in relation to the blue Yamāntaka couple of the body mandala. He abides at the center of one's heart cakra in the innermost axis of the body. Since the body mandala is somewhat like an armor, the Yama couple appears in front of the sattva at the heart center.

The wisdom being is the height of one's own thumb joint—that is, the joint at which the thumb nail is located. Dark blue in color, he has the naked and totally unadorned body of a plump eight-year-old child with one face, two arms, and a risen vajra. His hair stands on end. With three eyes and lips pursed, he wrathfully bares his teeth, biting his lower lip. His body expresses the nine moods of dance. Between his hands, which are placed palm to palm, he rolls a tiny kīla at the level of his heart. As he is the natural expression of the mind, his body is crystalline luminosity-emptiness—visible, yet insubstantial.

His appearance as an eight-year-old child—seven years for Westerners who do not count the time the infant spends in utero—reflects the stage of life at which one's physical faculties are undiminished and at their full potency. His nakedness and blue complexion symbolize the noncomposite dharmakāya, the ultimate essence. As such, he is the fully ripened *ātman*—dualistic consciousness brought to complete maturity as nondual primordial awareness.

It is taught that sustaining this sort of development-stage visualization is like threading the eye of a fine needle. This is an example of the extreme mental clarity it requires. One should cultivate this very clear, subtle visualization at the heart of the principal deity. When first visualizing the wisdom being, one needs only to imagine him approximately and larger in size. Then, once he can be visualized clearly, one can gradually imagine his body smaller and smaller. Since it is not possible to visualize such intricacies immediately, this is how one should proceed—slowly and gradually. Otherwise, people like us cannot do it. According to the instructions of the buddhas, one should train in this way.

The Wisdom Being

Within the wisdom being's heart is another sun disk, which is the size of a lentil split in half. Upon that stands a golden vajra, which is the size of a barley grain. Its gold color signifies bodhicitta. Mind you, this is not one of those skinny American barley grains! Rather, one should imagine the vajra being like one of our plump Tibetan barley grains!

The hollow spherical core at the center of the vajra is the size of a mustard seed. Within it is a tiny sun disk, on which a dark green HŪṂ syllable stands upright like a person. The syllable is as minute as if it had been written with a single strand of hair. It is three-dimensional, hollow, and translucent, as are all seed syllables.

These examples of scale are mere approximations; one should visualize the sun disk, vajra, spherical core, and seed syllable as being exceedingly fine. Such minute forms can be created by the mind when one's awareness is held extremely taut.

The Seed Syllable and Quintessence Mantra

The very subtle seed syllable, HŪṂ, is referred to in Tibetan as "the heart seed"—that is, the syllable dwelling in the heart of the sattva, who abides in the heart of the principal deity. It is visualized at one's heart center because the heart is the most essential of vital organs. A manifestation of mind, the HŪṂ is like a body of light without any substance. It is the nature of luminosity-emptiness—as though it had been formed from a hollow, transparent tube of light. As such, the seed syllable is the nature of fire, the essence of warmth. It is conjoined with wind energies, just like a flame that cannot burn unless supported by oxygen. It symbolizes the discerning intelligence of all the three times' buddhas. One's mind should abide upon it single-pointedly.

The moment the seed syllable—or life force syllable—shines forth, there is no self. In that instant, ignorance and the thoughts arisen from heedlessness do not arise at all. If one can focus on the seed syllable for even five minutes, it is of inconceivably great benefit. Conversely, when there is the notion of an "I," then there can be

The Concentration Being

no syllable, as the two are mutually exclusive. If one fails to focus on the life force syllable, afflictions accumulate like a continuous snowfall, gradually increasing. However, the moment one recalls the syllable, it is like the sun breaking through clouds, causing such karmic accumulation to begin melting away. The ongoing cultivation of awareness via the seed syllable is one of the greatest practices one can engage.

As one develops the stages of visualization, they become progressively finer. They must be habituated again and again in order to become clear and stable. To whatever degree one can visualize the sattva, vajra, and seed syllable as being extremely fine, one will experience a corresponding clarity and stability of mind. The essential meaning of this extremely minute detail is that samādhi, the wisdom of factual truth, is extremely subtle and difficult to see. Such infinitesimal objects of meditation are like the microfilm in a prayer wheel. Unless it is viewed with a microscope, one will not be able to see the letters that comprise the mantras. Similarly, as one cultivates clearer and clearer awareness by holding rigpa taut, it is like the microscope that enables one to see such fine details.

Although this world is inconceivably vast, it can fit entirely within a single eyeball. Although the mandala of the deity is comparably vast, it can fit entirely within the mind. Understanding this, one should train by giving rise to the complete mandala visualization again and again. Through repeated training—sometimes developing the visualization in progressive stages, other times causing it to arise completely in an instant—clear rigpa will arise.

After having stabilized this visualization, one should imagine that the HŪṂ̐ is surrounded by the nine-syllable quintessence mantra of Vajrakīla: VAJRAKĪLI KĪLAYA HŪṂ̐ PHAṬ. Since the main point is the sound—rather than the forms—of the syllables, it is acceptable to visualize the mantra in the alphabet or characters of one's choosing. Facing outward around the periphery of the sun disk, the syllables of the mantra are positioned in a counterclockwise fashion so that they could be read by an outside observer as the mantra revolves clockwise. This visualization of the sun disk, vajra, spherical core, HŪM̐ syllable, and quintessence mantra within the heart of the wisdom being comprise the concentration being, or *samādhi-sattva*. This visualization of the samādhisattva is the method whereby the sādhaka's body, speech, and mind become singularly concentrated.

One should develop these visualizations gradually, only progressing to the next step after the previous one has been stabilized. If one finds it difficult to visualize the sattva, sun, vajra, seed syllable, and mantra, one can begin by focusing on the HŪM̐ alone or even on the tiny circular dot at the top of the HŪM̐, particularly in the form of a flame. Once that has become stable, one should focus on making it as minute as possible. Just making that single visualization as fine and clear as one can is something that should be habituated over a period of weeks and months.

As the visualization becomes clearer, one can refine its size, shape, and color. As a support, an image of the HŪM̐ syllable inside a flame can be used as the basis for one's visualization. Through focusing on this again and again, one can gradually habituate the development-stage yogas.

Unless one maintains rigpa with taut, single-pointed focus, it will not be possible to generate this well. To the degree that one can visualize these fine details clearly, one will experience a correspondingly strong concentration. If one does so, the profound power of the development stages will arise. When this sort of minute visualization becomes stable, the sādhaka can manifest displays like Milarepa's miraculous appearance inside the yak horn. At that juncture, Milarepa's body did not become any smaller, nor did the yak horn become any larger. Such are the qualities of mastering the development-stage meditations, as great siddhas like Rigdzin Chökyi Dragpa and others have done. Although such minute visualizations seem extremely difficult, it is not a question of ability or inability to form mental pictures in this way. Since every development-stage visualization is subject to creation by the mind, one's present inability to imagine them clearly is solely due to the fault of inexperience. Those who have habituated such imagery will find it not so problematic, as the human mind has created tiny computer chips that can store many enormous volumes of the buddhas' words.

One should try to visualize as explained, testing one's ability to do it. In order to accomplish the visualization well, it is necessary to make concerted effort over a long period of time. Even if one can visualize nothing at present, one should abide in an undistracted mind, having confidence that the wisdom being is present. Even if the visualization is only hopeful or aspirational in nature, it will not be without results. In this regard, Guru Rinpoche taught that it is best if one reaches the result of the development stages. However, even if one does not, as long as one is intensely motivated to identify with the deity, one will gain inconceivable merits.

In this way, one should meditate to whatever degree one can. Even if one cannot visualize with great clarity, one should remain without wavering from the confidence "At the very basis, I am Vajrakumāra." The deity's life force is the union of compassion and emptiness. If the mind never parts from compassion, the deity will always be present. By one's remaining in undistracted recollection, there will be no error. To whatever degree one can meditate, there will be results.

One should visualize in this way, sometimes taking breaks from the visualization and cultivating mahāmudrā. Then, one can return to the fine visualization. It is not necessary to hold it continuously. Rather, the moment an aspect of it becomes clear, one should immediately place the mind in mahāmudrā. Sealing the development-stage meditation with the view causes the wisdom deities to pervade the visualization. If one seals a moment of clarity in this way, the virtue will not be exhausted until buddhahood has been attained.

What does it mean to seal with the view? This is accomplished when the sādhaka sees the nonduality of self and other. That is, however vast the outer mandala of the deity may be, all the appearances of the container and contents are mere reflections of one's mind. The individual who resolves the fact that appearances are mind recognizes the nonduality of the deity and his or her own mind. By alternating between the minute visualization and emptiness in this way, one will eventually become able to give rise to the complete and clear visualization suddenly and in all its fine detail.

Later, when returning one's focus to the deity visualization, one may imagine one's body as the principal deity, Vajrakīla, the consort, or both co-emergent and inseparable, according to individual preference and abilities. If one is visualizing oneself as the main deity, the HŪṂ syllable and so forth are all imagined according to the words of the text. Since the consort (the emptiness aspect) and the father (the clarity aspect) are nondual, there is no need to visualize another HŪṂ syllable in the heart of the consort. Otherwise, for those who visualize themselves in the form of the mother-consort, there is no need to imagine a second seed syllable in the heart of the heruka.

Some beginners do not understand what meditation is. For their sake, I can clarify it with the following example: Imagine someone is unaware that he or she has a hidden illness. That person visits a doctor who diagnoses an illness. Even if the diagnosis is wrong and that sickness is not actually present in the body, the patient starts to worry—ruminating on the illness, thinking about its location in the body, its causes, symptoms, and prognosis. In this way, through the power of mind, that person can give rise to a physical sickness that wasn't present before. That process is meditation. Similarly, if one starts repeatedly thinking, "I've got this HŪṂ syllable in my navel or in my heart," it will be there.

The Bhagavan Buddha taught, "Thoroughly subdue your mind."[19] Thus, in the Buddhist tradition, taming the mind is of greater importance than taming the body. The principal among all the methods of taming the mind is the cultivation of discerning intelligence. The diverse development-stage visualizations are also means of subduing the mind. When they are conjoined with discerning intelligence, they are particularly effective. This is one of the characteristics of secret mantra—having many methods that are yet free of hardship.

Calm Abiding and Special Insight

In the context of Vajra Vehicle practice, the entire visualization should be built on a foundation of bodhicitta. That is to say, through cultivating the four immeasurables, one gives rise to a vast mind within which the deity can emerge. Because of this, the stages of development are rooted in cultivation of the four immeasurables.

From a mantric perspective, the practice of calm abiding with support refers to all the different trainings of the development-stage yogas. For example, when one is practicing in an accomplishment retreat, one visualizes the clear appearance of the deity. In this way, the mind is engaged in the practice of calm abiding using the form of the deity as the object of meditation.

Without some kind of object, or support, it is difficult for the mind of a beginner to abide in place. The mind becomes confused by distraction toward outer phenomena. For this reason, the buddhas have taught the skillful means of visualizing the deity's seed syllable and the stages of developing the deity's form. When giving rise to the image of the deity in the mind, one should imagine him or her to be insubstantial—visible yet like a rainbow. In this way, to focus single-pointedly on the deity's clear appearance is the practice of calm abiding with support in the context of the Secret Mantric Vajra Vehicle.

The companion to calm abiding is special insight. It is nothing other than the cultivation of discerning intelligence, whereby the mind becomes exceedingly clear and free of thoughts or emotions. From within this state, one recognizes the nonduality of self and other. This causes one to understand all the dualistic views one has previously held to have been delusions.

In the context of deity yoga, at the very basis, Vajrakīla is the dharmakāya—the empty essence of mind itself. From within the dharmakāya, the deity manifests like rainbows in the sky. This manifestation is the saṁbhogakāya. Being without any substantial form, it is free of any object at which to grasp.

Just as one's entire surroundings can be reflected in a crystal ball, so too when one gives rise to the idea of the deity, that deity is reflected within the thinking mind. If there are a hundred crystal balls and one deity image, the deity appears in each of them. Similarly, when many people gather for an accomplishment retreat, inviting the mandala of the deity to be present, that deity mandala will be reflected in the mind of each one of those gathered. Furthermore, when one focuses on the seed syllable, the entire deity is complete therein. In this way, the deity is empty in essence yet clear in appearance.

To speak about all this is one thing; to give rise to an inner experience of it is another. If one looks in texts, there are many descriptions of the deity and his aspects—the empty essence, the clear nature, and so forth. Likewise, many ways in which one can go astray in the cultivation of these practices are elaborated. However, the best thing is for one to make effort to visualize the seed syllable and deity and thus—based on one's own experience—recognize what calm abiding is. Then, after having stabilized calm abiding, one should gain some direct experience of special insight.

The Threefold Sattva

The commitment being, the wisdom being, and the concentration being together comprise the threefold sattva, or heroic being. These three are not separate. Rather, they are of a singular nature.

The commitment being is the self-generation of the practitioner as the deity Vajrakīla. How does he manifest? The commitment, or samaya, is one's stated intent to benefit sentient ones. It comes from bodhicitta. Without bodhicitta, there can be no spoken commitment. Without the word that is the samaya, one cannot emerge as the deity. So, the mind set on attaining enlightenment (*bodhicitta*) gives rise to the word (*samaya*), which gives rise to the body of the deity, the commitment being.

As for the wisdom deities, in general, they pervade the entire sphere of dharmas. Even though their essence is emptiness, they appear like rainbows. Some people wonder whether pure fields and wisdom deities actually exist, but one need not have the slightest doubt. There are innumerable pure fields with divine inhabitants. Since they abide uninterruptedly, whenever one supplicates or imagines them, they immediately and spontaneously manifest. Otherwise, when they are not appearing, they naturally subside into the expanse of five-colored lights. In actuality, they are the saṁbhogakāyas endowed with the five certainties: (1) certain place, the Akaniṣṭha Dharmasphere; (2) certain time, the eternal wheel of continuity; (3) certain teacher, Vajradhara; (4) certain Dharma, the Great Vehicle; and (5) certain retinue, bodhisattvas of the ten bhūmis. These five certainties are ceaselessly present in the pure saṁbhogakāya buddha-fields—the inseparable union of the dharmakāya and saṁbhogakāya from which all deities arise. All the pure illusory bodies that have been sealed with bodhicitta abide in such pure fields.

These spontaneously present wisdom deities should be distinguished from the wisdom being of the threefold sattva. As mentioned previously, he is the thumb-joint-sized sattva who dwells upon the sun disk in the heart of the commitment being.

Finally, the concentration being is himself the visualization in the heart center of the wisdom being. So, there is the sun, upon which is the grain-sized golden vajra, at the center of which is the HŪṂ syllable that is surrounded by the mantra. While the sun, vajra, and HŪṂ are stationary, the mantra revolves. This entire visualization comprises the concentration being.

As for this threefold sattva, the commitment being is one's body, the yidam deity. The wisdom being is the mind. The concentration being is rigpa, the syllable HŪṂ. These last two together represent the natural qualities of the yidam's mind.

The three sattvas can also be understood in the context of the three features of ultimate fruition—essence, nature, and compassionate activity. The empty essence is the concentration being, the dharmakāya guru manifested as mind. The clear, luminous nature is the wisdom being, the saṁbhogakāya yidam. All-pervasive compassion is the commitment being, the physically manifest nirmāṇakāya deity. The activities of these three sattvas are carried out by innumerable spontaneously arisen ḍākiṇīs and guardians.

When one reads the sadhana, after the visualization of the commitment being, the wisdom being, and the concentration being have been established, one invokes the outer, spontaneously present wisdom deities and merges them into oneself with the syllables JAḤ HŪṂ VAṂ HOḤ. Then, all the subsequent offerings, praises, and the like are made to oneself as the deity Vajrakīla, who embodies all wisdom deities. In this way, the three sattvas—the commitment, wisdom, and concentration beings—are one.

Clarity, Purity, and Stability

When visualizing the clear appearance of the deity, you practitioners—my parents—will experience these three features: clarity, purity, and stability. Although these three are explained in the Vajrakīla tantra, they are not exclusive to Vajrakīla practice. Rather, they are essential attributes of any deity yoga.

Clarity manifests when the appearance of the deity's form arises distinctly in the mind. Such clarity applies to every detail of the deity's body—his complexion, hand implements, ornaments, attire, and so forth, from the crown of the head to his māra-suppressing feet. Once it has become stabilized, one meditates on the immeasurable palace, focusing on the outer surroundings up to the body of the deity and back. Reviewing this again and again many times, one trains the mind to become the artist who draws the deity and palace.

Usually, beginners are unable to generate the deity's complete body. At least, that's how it was for me. Even so, merely for the face of the deity to appear in one's mind is very efficacious. So, first, one should cause the deity's face to appear in the mind again and again. From one's doing so, clarity will gradually arise. When that clarity is combined with compassion and benevolence, the mind becomes cleansed.

As one trains in this way, the yidam will definitely appear in the mind. Then, sometimes, he will suddenly vanish like a rainbow.

Because he appears and disappears, some will give rise to doubt, thinking this illusory appearance must not be the real deity. But, in actuality, since the deities are the nondual union of clarity and emptiness, they truly manifest in just this way—appearing for a brief moment like rainbows and then suddenly vanishing. Such fleeting appearances in the mind are manifestations of the buddha nature itself, which is pure from the basis. One should develop trust that those junctures of appearance when the mind is free of thought, emotion, and imprints are actual manifestations of the yidam. The feature of the deity's clarity should be understood in this way.

The second feature of the deity's appearance involves the recollection of utter purity. According to the needs of beings to be tamed, the same deity can take different peaceful or wrathful forms, appearing with different numbers of faces and limbs and with appropriate accoutrements.

Peaceful deities are said to have thirteen different aspects of peaceful attire, which are the signs of having accomplished the vajra holder's thirteen bhūmis. When practicing peaceful ones, it is very effective to visualize them abiding within rainbow spheres, or bubbles. Since the afflictions' very nature is primordial awareness, afflictions are gradually pacified through love and compassion. The rainbow spheres symbolize this pacification in stages.

While peaceful deities gradually transform each affliction into its corresponding wisdom, wrathful ones use the fire of a single wisdom to consume all five afflictions suddenly and without discrimination. It is for this reason that wrathful deities appear within flame heaps and mountains of fire. When consciousness is ripened into primordial awareness, thoughts and afflictions are suddenly liberated into wisdom. They are instantly burnt away like a heap of dried grass. Whatever thoughts arise are rendered impotent through holding mindfulness. This clear, mindful awareness is rigpa, the view of mahāmudrā. It is self-illuminating self-awareness. Since fire and wisdom both accomplish instantaneous transformation, they have the same nature. By contemplating the inner meaning, one can understand the great power of the fire of wisdom. One can gain insight into why the wrathful ones appear within heaps of wisdom flames.

Those who are unfamiliar with wrathful deities—principal among whom is Vajrakumāra—may think that their wrath is one of aversion. This is not at all the case. All deities abide in a state that never wavers from the peaceful dharmakāya. Their hearts are great compassion, the four immeasurables, free of any fault or deception. According to individuals' karma, they can display wrathful aspects. In this regard, the scriptures say, "Though unwavering from the state of the peaceful dharmakāya, you arise as fearsome forms in the saṁbhogakāya state."[20]

Thus, the only difference between peaceful and wrathful deities is individuals' karma and afflictions. For example, in a truly just society, when a law-abiding person sees a policeman, he has nothing to fear, perceiving that policeman as a benevolent protector. On the other hand, when criminals see a policeman, they feel genuine fear and dread. Although it is the same policeman, their experiences of that person are completely different. In this way, one can understand the differences in individuals' perceptions, which are conditioned by circumstantial inner afflictions and self-grasping. Those who have strong self-grasping perceive nothing but faults in others. It is taught in the tantras that due to their afflictions and perverted views, they especially give rise to terror upon seeing wrathful ones.

When practicing deity yoga, one should repeatedly imagine the deity abiding within a rainbow sphere or a heap of flames, as appropriate, causing him or her to appear in various sizes. Deities can be as tiny as mustard grains or as vast as the expanse of the sky. Training in this way will result in autonomy of the mind. Later, after great autonomy has been attained, one will be able to imagine such wisdom kāyas filling all of space and will be able to transform them at will.

When one trains the mind's potential—mastering the liveliness of the mind—in these ways, diverse appearances will manifest. One need not give rise to hopeful expectation or doubtful apprehension about such pure appearances. Rather, one should understand them according to these lines from the lineage supplication:

> [Symbols,] meanings, signs—the union of
> wisdoms with the kāyas—radiate and
> gather dreadful, blazing wrathful ones.

For each aspect of the deity's clear appearance, one should contemplate the relationship between the outer sign and the inner meaning. For example, one can consider the heruka's garland of fifty-one human heads. It symbolizes the fifty-one mental arisings. When such thoughts go unrecognized, one accumulates afflictions and negative karma. This is similar to one's valuables—one's accumulation of merit—being plundered by thieves. Conversely, when afflictions and unvirtuous thoughts are recognized through awareness, it is as though the thieves and plunderers have been decapitated.

In the context of the deity's body with flame heaps, attire, ornaments, implements, and the like, each of these symbols, meanings, and signs is neither random nor arbitrary. Every outer appearance expresses a specific attribute of the deity's inner mind. The six bone ornaments signify the six transcendent perfections. The weapons the deities hold symbolize the slaughter of afflictions. The victorious ones of the five families and their consorts are complete in the five-pointed crown ornament. All such manifold appearances are self-knowing primordial awareness. They are the natural radiance of the mind itself.

For example, during empowerments or during the introduction to dzogchen *thögal*, a crystal is placed in a ray of light. The moment the sunlight touches the crystal, the room becomes filled with rainbow reflections. All the qualities of the rainbow are already inherent in the crystal; so it is with the mind's fundamental disposition. The form, ornaments, and attire of the deity—the union of the wisdoms and the kāyas—have many different meanings. However, all these should be understood as inner qualities outwardly shining forth.

To hold in mind these different meanings is the recollection of purity. In order to understand the meanings of pure symbols, one should study texts that praise the deity's signs. It is good to peruse and contemplate such instructions about clarity and purity, which are somewhat easy to understand.

Having given rise to clarity and purity through visualizing the deity's vivid appearance, one should cultivate the stability of divine pride, which is the principal point of this triad of clarity, purity, and stability. It is one of the most important signs of deity accomplishment. This pride is the confidence that oneself is the actually manifest deity. However, such confidence is not rooted in grasping at a self, since the mere concept "I am the deity" will not overcome faults.

If one considers an individual, his or her inner life force is more important than the outer body of that person. The nature that is the life force of every deity has already been discussed. This life force is the nondual union of emptiness and compassion, which is inseparable from the heart of the guru. It manifests through knowing the actual condition of the mind. Since the mind is the buddha nature, the deity, the guru's mind, and one's own mind have been inseparable from the very beginning. Because one's buddha nature is the same as that of the buddhas, the moment one gives rise to the altruistic motivation, one has become the deity. This is the best sort of divine pride. Regardless of whether or not the visualization is clear, when the mind is not separated from love and compassion, that is the actual deity.

One must investigate one's own mind to determine whether or not one has actually become the deity. As the singular basis was taught in Lord Buddha's pronouncements, I suppose everyone already knows about buddha nature, which is inherent in the minds of all beings and all buddhas.

The difference between ordinary beings and buddhas is that in their wish to benefit others, the enlightened ones' minds are suffused with vast love and compassion. As the minds of us ordinary beings are preoccupied with self-grasping and with the wish to find comfort for the self, we give rise to all the phenomena of samsara and nirvana, thus separating ourselves from the buddhas. In spite of this, the basis of mind itself is singular, like pure water.

Unless one has understood this singular continuum shared by buddhas and sentient ones, one has no basis for engaging secret mantra practices. However, for one who has understood it and has a true wish to accomplish the bodhicitta-yidam, the moment one gives rise to bodhicitta, even if it is only for an instant, one's mind actually becomes the deity's mind. When this has been understood, one can have assurance that the actual deity is the mind wishing to benefit others. Thus, that which distinguishes deities from demons is benevolence versus self-grasping.

Once a bit of self-grasping has been liberated, one gives rise to the intent to benefit others. As a result, the deity's life force—the union of emptiness and compassion—is made manifest. Every individual already has emptiness at the basis. So, when one abides within immeasurable loving-kindness and compassion, not falling under the power of afflictions, one can have confidence that one has truly seized the deity's life force. This is the actual yidam, the natural expression of compassion. Through generating a mind of great love for the yidam, one will reach a state of never forgetting him or her. Then, regardless of whether or not one can clearly visualize the deity, one will recognize the inseparability of the deity and one's own mind, thus gaining stability. By abiding in the view that is the nondual union of emptiness and compassion, one can give rise to trust in oneself as the deity. This is the meaning of confident divine pride, through which autonomy is actually accomplished.

Some people think that merely to remember the deity or to have the deity appear in a dream is insignificant. They think the real accomplishment is to meet the deity face to face and to converse with him as though he were an actual person. This is not at all the case! The actual deity, the saṁbhogakāya, is insubstantial, like a rainbow. In a single moment, he appears. In the next moment, he is gone. Thus, whenever the deity appears in the mind, that appearance is the actual yidam. At that juncture, the nature of the deity has been glimpsed. The sign of having seen the deity is the ongoing cultivation of divine pride.

When one knows benevolence to be the actual deity, one can participate in accomplishment retreats. Through the blessings of the gathered sangha, a certain positive feeling can arise in one's mind during such retreats. When, having had that sort of experience, sādhakas come together in small groups to practice the liturgy, it will be very effective. This will be the best way to practice in the future.

However, even if one cannot participate in such group practices, it is important to bring to mind the deity and the seed syllable during daily activities. The moment one gives rise to benevolence, one should understand, "Now I have the mind of the deity; now I have become the deity." This recollection at the instant of arising is important. Conversely, when afflictions arise, one should think, "Now I have become the demon." Through heedfulness and mindful awareness, one will recognize the distinction.

Yeshe Tsogyal once asked Guru Rinpoche, "From where have the deities come?"

He replied, "That which is called the deity is bodhicitta."[21] That is to say, the deity arises through the force of bodhicitta. The deity is present for anyone who cultivates bodhicitta. Thus, to have the certainty of bodhicitta is the best sort of divine pride. Regardless of whether or not one can clearly visualize the deity's form, one must give rise to certainty about this point. Even if one does not have the great opportunity to do extensive formal practice, one should clearly recall the deity in an instant, trust in him or her, and recite the deity's mantra throughout the course of daily activities. By again and again giving rise to confidence in bodhicitta as the singularity of one's own mind and the deity's mind, one will eventually emerge in the form of the deity.

The Mandalas of Wisdom Deities and of the Self-Generation

At this juncture, one has established the self-generation, emerging as the commitment being abiding in the mandala. There are many different sorts of mandalas. Planet Earth is one. A single person's body and mind is another. The only difference between the two is that one is great and the other small. One's own body is a microcosm of the world. Even though we ordinary beings are ignorant of it, the saṁbhogakāya forms with the five certainties are always present, abiding like fully blossomed flowers. Each individual innately possesses in his or her embodied form the seed of such a flower, endowed with all the qualities of the complete mandala. Outwardly, there is the body of flesh and blood. Inwardly, there is the eightfold group of consciousnesses. If these are simplified, outwardly, there are the five elements and, inwardly, the five afflictions. Secretly, there are the five wisdoms. The mandala is established in the completeness of these.

The secret accomplishment retreat focuses on the self-generation alone. Although the sādhakas may construct a mandala, the practice does not require one. When there is no material mandala, one simply imagines the mandala of saṁbhogakāya wisdom deities that naturally abides without ceasing in the sphere of space. That mandala then merges with the mandala of the self-generation.

The different ways sādhakas conceive of the mandala and the deities therein are reflections of their maturity. For beginners who are bound by self-grasping, the principal is the saṁbhogakāya mandala of wisdom deities. To whatever degree dualistic grasping at objects and their characteristics is present, one should visualize this vast, pure mandala abiding in space. One's focus should be on the principal deity therein; it is not necessary to consider every detail of the retinue. Until the grasping at self and other as separate has been exhausted, the primary focus should be on the heruka in the mandala of wisdom deities. Beginners should cultivate the idea "This is the actual divine mandala," since that perception opens the door to the deities. Although the ceaselessly abiding mandala of space is utterly beyond imagination, it is good even if one has a mere conceptual understanding of the saṁbhogakāyas of five certainties.

This mandala serves as the principal only circumstantially. Those who are more mature should focus on the self-generation of the commitment being. For the sake of expediency, first it is taught that the self-generation is like a mirror reflection of the continually abiding saṁbhogakāya mandala of wisdom deities. Eventually, however, these dualistic notions must be torn down. For one who understands the view, such a distinction is unnecessary. Once one has some experience of the completion stage, one knows the inseparability of self and other. When there is no dualistic grasping, these two mandalas become like two mirrors infinitely reflecting each other. In one's waking experience, one arises as the self-generation with all other beings appearing as the retinue. However, in one's meditation, the two mandalas have become indistinguishable. Thus, one no longer identifies one or the other as being the principal, nor does one perceive oneself as being located here or there.

In the end, since every mandala that can exist is pervaded by the five wisdoms, one must determine all the phenomena of samsara and nirvana to be like mirror reflections. Without making distinctions among them, one simply leaves them in equanimity, knowing them to be inseparable and singular in essence.

These different conceptions of the self-generation and the saṁbhogakāya mandala can be understood according to the Latter System's four classes of tantra. In action tantra, there is a clear distinction between self and other. Thus, the mandala of wisdom deities is principal. In conduct tantra, self and other have somewhat equalized. In yoga tantra, the self-generation is principal. In unsurpassed yoga tantra, the self-generation and the saṁbhogakāya mandala are nondual. These four also parallel the Earlier System's four branches of approach and accomplishment, which will be explained later.

Invoking and Merging with the Wisdom Deities

Every deity is subsumed within Vajrakumāra. As it says in the invocation,

> At each deity's crown is an OṀ,
> ĀḤ at the throat, and HŪṂ at the heart.
> As the ten directions' conquerors

grant empowerment-blessing, we're adorned
with Amoghasiddhi as its sign.

Since all deities are of a singular essence, each deity embodies every other deity as well as the five families of the victorious ones—all the buddhas of the ten directions and three times. Likewise, all the wisdom deities are complete within the syllables OṀ ĀḤ HŪṀ. Whenever wrathful activity is required, it is performed by Amoghasiddhi. When peaceful activity is called for, it is performed by Vajrasattva. Even so, their basic essence is the same.

During the invocation, one focuses mainly on oneself in the form of Vajrakīla, whose three places are marked with the syllables OṀ ĀḤ HŪṀ. However, if one wishes to visualize in greater detail, one may imagine all the deities in the retinue to be marked in the same way.

When the invocation is made, the wisdom deities completely dissolve into the forms of the three syllables, which fall like raindrops upon the commitment being—oneself as the principal deity. Those syllables then merge with the OṀ, ĀḤ, and HŪṀ in one's own three places.

The essential meaning of this is that the yogin is not alone in his or her meditation. Even though one's referential visualization of the mandala lacks force, it is backed up by the swift blessings of the ten directions' victorious ones, who think of nothing but the welfare of sentient beings. Thus, when a practitioner with bodhicitta and the three types of faith visualizes the mandala of Vajrakumāra, the deity bestows the force of his mandala upon that person. The buddhas of the ten directions give their power and support to his or her meditation. In this regard, in a mind accomplishment sadhana of Vajrasattva, there is a supplication that states,

You who know the three planes' miseries,
you who act to calm infernal fires,
holy ones, please grant your able force
when I go forth to swiftly act for beings![22]

Since the enlightened ones grant the power that accomplishes aspirations, it is important to accumulate vast wishful prayers. In the Sukhāvatī literature of the Sky Dharma (Namchö) Treasure, the Buddha said, "I create conditions conducive to accomplishment."[23] Thus, when one enters the door of Dharma and can accomplish results without difficulty, rather than wondering whether the good results are due to one's past virtuous accumulation or to the buddhas' blessings, it is good to remember these words of Lord Buddha. The empowerment-blessing granted by the ten directions' conquerors should be understood as this creation of favorable conditions by the buddhas.

The invocation continues:

> OṀ HŪṀ SVĀṀ ĀṀ HĀṀ, MŪṀ LĀṀ MĀṀ PĀṀ TĀṀ.
> Through the light rays from each of our hearts,
> wisdom beings are invited here.

All the buddhas of the ten directions and three times are subsumed within the five families. The first five syllables are the seed syllables of the father-buddhas of the five families. The second five are the seeds of their mother-consorts. There are many different ways of reciting and placing these syllables according to different systems of practice. In this system, the more common syllable TRĀṀ is replaced by SVĀṀ, the syllable of the Ratna family.

One should imagine that through the force of faith and love, rays of light stream forth from the hearts of the sādhakas visualized as Vajrakīla, stirring the wisdom deities' compassion from its vital point. This interaction among faith, love, and compassion is the nature of the samaya that binds sentient ones with the buddhas and yidams.

The mudrās that accompany the recitation of the syllables symbolize the five father-buddhas uniting with their five consorts in space and dissolving into light. Their blessings manifest as light rays, nectar, and the forms of great and small Vajrakumāras. The large ones are as great as Mount Meru; the small ones are as tiny as mustard seeds. In this way, divine forms actually appear, filling space. They descend like rainfall or like snowflakes, merging into the pores of the sādhakas, the commitment beings. As the radiant nectar of their union fills one's body, it overflows, transforming into a five-pointed crown. Thus, the empowerment is like a coronation in which the commitment being is adorned with the crown of the five families.

Even though this crown is usually depicted in thangkas as being like a tiara that partially encircles the deity's head, it is actually a circular crown with two arches that intersect at the center. There is one point in the center and one in each of the four directions. These five points are also represented by the mudrās. In the central point at the apex of the head appear HĀṀ TĀṀ, the syllables of Amoghasiddhi-Samayatārā. The lord and lady of the family, they abide at one's crown as the sign of empowerment. This crown, marked with the syllables of the five families, is the sign of bodhicitta having transformed one's five afflictions into the five primordial-awareness wisdoms.

By their very nature, the five afflictions are the five father-buddhas and the five elements are the five mother-buddhas. Through bodhicitta, they instantly manifest as such. Thus, since one is already endowed with a mind of afflictions and a body comprised of the five elements, one already possesses the cause of the five families. For example, if one gives rise to aversion, the moment it meets with bodhicitta, it is nothing other than Vajrasattva. Since there are countless afflictions, there are countless buddhas who are the ultimate purified essence of these emotions.

After the empowerment-blessing, the wisdom deities are requested to come with the following words:

> HŪṀ. Showing born miraculous displays—
> blazing forms from the completely pure
> unborn sphere of dharmas—Vajra Youth
> with your courts, please come here from that sphere!
> Wisdom Wrath King and courts, when you've come

to grant siddhis and empowerment to
attain existence-vajrakīla,
further, to show noble marks and signs
and bestow Kīla's accomplishments,
Wisdom Wrath King with your courts, please come!
JAḤ HŪṂ VAṂ HOḤ. VAJRA SAMAYA JAḤ. SAMAYA TIṢṬHA HLEN.

Free from arising, the dharmasphere is the empty space from which manifold saṁbhogakāya deities spontaneously emerge. They are unborn in the beginning, free of abiding in the middle, and without cessation in the end. Since the wisdom deities are without birth, they are utterly pure and not subject to an end.

Through blessing and due to their past commitments and aspirations, in an instant they emerge from within this unborn sphere as the "born miraculous displays" of great compassion. These miraculous displays themselves are the appearances of something out of nothing at all.

This is related to the following lines from the text *Taking Up Accomplishments*:

Vajrakīla from the natural sphere,
you lack concept or exertion; yet
like a precious jewel that grants all wants
is your blessing, nature of past oaths.

If one holds in mind these words alone, again and again taking empowerment, one will come to understand the nondual meaning. In accord with the wishes of faithful ones, Vajrakumāra with his retinue manifestly appear. People of pure karma will actually be able to see their divine forms with implements, ornaments, and attire.

However, regardless of whether one actually sees the wisdom deities, they most definitely appear whenever they are invoked. Thus, one requests that the wrathful king and retinue come in order to bestow all empowerments and actual accomplishments, to reveal marks and signs, and, finally, to cause sentient ones to realize existence—the three planes—as the mandala of Vajrakīla. This last point means that samsaric existence itself is the basis of Vajrakīla accomplishment. Existence-vajrakīla is the attainment of buddhahood. It is the fruition of deity yoga—the nondual union of samsara and nirvana, in which the container and sentient contents are established as the mandala of the yidam with its divine inhabitants.

The most crucial, fundamental point is this: by requesting the deities to come, sādhakas cause them to enact the samaya. With the syllables JAḤ HŪṂ VAṂ HOḤ, practitioners remind the deities of their past promise to benefit sentient beings through the enlightened ones' four immeasurables. With the syllables VAJRA SAMAYA JAḤ, sādhakas point out, "This is your adamantine commitment." Since the practitioners have also been cultivating the four immeasurables for the sake of sentient ones from the beginning of the practice, they are basically saying, "Because of your commitment, of course it is your duty to come. Were you not to come, you would be violating your own rules." Having pointed out that our own commitment is the same, the sādhakas then offer them seats with the words SAMAYA TIṢṬHA HLEN.

This is the heart of the matter: the link between the wisdom deities and the commitment being is the bond of the four immeasurables. The shared samaya is such that they are absolutely compelled to come. When one lacks the four immeasurables, they will not come. Actually, it is not appropriate to say that they will not come. Rather, it is that when the sādhaka fails to cultivate the four immeasurables, there is no seat for the wisdom deities. There is no place where they can abide. It would be the same as if I invited disciples to a Dharma center that lacked facilities for lodging, bathing, and cooking!

Since one already made the invitation and received the empowerment in the previous section, one might wonder why the empowerment is followed by yet another invitation. Generally, it is taught that in the lower tantras, the wisdom deities must be invited and, in the higher tantras, because the view of emptiness is utilized, the sādhaka is indistinguishable from the wisdom deity. Since the essence of awareness itself is the deity, there is ultimately no need for invitation. Regardless of whether or not one sees the mind's essence, rigpa is continually present. Although all of this is true, it is essential that practitioners distinguish between actual experience and mere conceptual understanding. Once this distinction is made clear, there is no contradiction between practicing higher tantras and repeatedly invoking the wisdom deities.

At the very basis, the five families are already complete within the psychophysical aggregate of an individual. Empowerment is a means of being introduced to and recognizing this. Whether it is a self-empowerment or one bestowed by a guru, empowerment is about obtaining the deity's blessings. This activity does not depend on the quality of the guru, since blessings are bestowed by the deities themselves. With the blessing-empowerment, the outer wisdom appearances of the five families in space subside into oneself, transforming into the crown adornment. Since bodhicitta is of a singular nature, the wisdom deities are not separate from oneself. Eventually, the sādhaka will become exactly the same as them. At present, one has only the causal basis. Therefore, the hot water of the wisdom deities' compassion is needed to melt away the ice of dualistic grasping that is continually forming. Only once it has been completely destroyed will nonduality be realized.

With the empowerment, the singular essence of buddhas and sentient beings is glimpsed; one identifies that the buddhas of the five families have been present from the very beginning. In spite of this, self-grasping has not yet been destroyed. Although the sādhaka has identified the buddha in self and others, the tathāgatagarbha possessed by beings is still very slight. For this reason, on top of that basic recognition, the sādhaka must again and again request the actual blessings, wisdom, and compassion of the deities in order to receive the warmth that melts away self-grasping. If one finds it difficult and tiresome to visualize the deity, it is a sign of dualistic grasping, which causes one to perceive the deity as something other than oneself. Until duality and self-grasping have been completely torn down, it is necessary to repeatedly supplement with nondual primordial awareness.

Even though empowerment is received, the afflictions in one's mindstream do not cease to exist. Hatred is most definitely mirrorlike wisdom. But to whatever degree one gives rise to it, a corresponding degree of harm will be experienced. Only when one can liberate afflictions on arising is hatred rendered harmless. At that juncture, there is no distinction between hatred and primordial awareness. It is fully realized as mirrorlike wisdom. Thus, the outer five elements manifest as the consorts of the buddhas of the five families, and the inner five afflictions are nothing other than the five wisdoms.

Empowerment is but an introduction. Once it has been received from the guru, individuals must then take empowerment for themselves. Month by month, year by year, one must continue to train the mind. Otherwise, merely comprehending the notion that oneself and the deities are the same will not be of benefit. It is something that must be continually cultivated through direct experience. The empowerment and invitation should be understood in this way.

Paying Homage

At this juncture, having established the visualization through the stages of development and having unified the wisdom deities into the commitment being, one must pay homage to, make offerings to, and praise the divine hosts of the mandala so that they will engage activities and bestow common siddhis. In the petition that is recited in the afternoon, one supplicates these beings to "protect the buddhas' teachings, glorify the Triple Gem, preserve the dominion of sanghas and Dharma," and so forth. So, first, they are visualized within the mandala. Then, one makes offerings to and praises them. Finally, one supplicates these beings to carry out desired activities. By doing so, they bestow common accomplishments upon the sādhaka. The following words of homage are found in the text:

> HŪṀ. To save the three planes from noxiousness
> and destroy our prideful clinging, we

prostrate with one-pointed, great respect
to you, Vajrarākṣasa and hosts.
ATI PU HOḤ, PRATĪCCHA HOḤ.

From the perspective of action tantra (*kriyatantra*), to offer prostrations is the best of all physical virtues. A practitioner with a dualistic view pays homage to the wisdom deities as distinct from himself or herself. However, when the mind has become free of duality, the commitment being and wisdom deities are void of meeting or parting. Thus, there is no object to whom one offers prostrations. From within the mind of nondual awareness, the one who pays homage and the ones to whom homage is paid are inseparable.

Making Offerings

Next, as an antidote to attachment to forms, sounds, smells, tastes, and sensations, one makes offerings of the flowers, incense, lamps, perfumes, foods, music, and the like that can be found in this worldly realm. These offerings of the five desirables pervade space in the manner of offering clouds of Samantabhadra. Even though the wisdom deities themselves have no need for them, sādhakas make outer, inner, and secret offerings in accord with worldly conventions. When making these symbolic offerings, one should imagine them being extremely vast in scope. Any offering made to the deities is a cause for becoming free of attachment. For example, just as one offers a mandala to clear away self-grasping, so too if a flower is offered, it diminishes one's attachment and clinging to outer forms. This is how siddhis are attained.

The first verse of offering is as follows:

HŪṂ. Varied offerings, real and formed by mind—
connate union, outer, inner, and
secret here arrayed—we offer you,
self-born, emanated deities.
Now partake of them nondually

and without discrimination, please.
OṀ VAJRA ARGHAṀ, PĀDAṀ, PUṢPE, DHŪPE, ĀLOKE, GANDHE, NAIVEDYE, ŚABDA PRATĪCCHA SVĀHĀ.

One should set out whatever material offerings are available. Although they are exhaustible, the imagined offerings are without limit. These two are of a singular essence. Even if there are no actual offering substances, one should have confidence that the offerings are naturally accomplished through visualization and mudrā. When offering flowers, for example, one should visualize this entire worldly realm and the expanse of space being utterly filled with colorful blossoms, vividly imagining their fragrance permeating everywhere.

The visualization should be accompanied by the lotus-circling mudrā, which ultimately symbolizes the union of the father and mother deities, from which Samantabhadra's offering clouds emanate and increase. Together with the mudrā, one imagines innumerable light rays streaming forth. Heroes emanate from the light rays of the right hand's fingertips. Heroines emanate from those of the left hand's fingertips. Then, from each emanation emerge more light rays tipped with more heroes and heroines, who again emanate light rays. In this way, the offering gods and goddesses multiply, filling all of space. For however many buddhas of the ten directions and three times there may be, there emanates one such god or goddess bearing offerings of forms, sounds, smells, tastes, and tactile objects. Holding their respective offerings in hand, the heroic ones make infinite offerings to the inconceivably vast buddha-fields. Understanding the potency of the lotus-circling mudrā, one should similarly engage body, speech, and mind in making the seven daily offerings of (1) water for drink (*arghaṁ*), (2) water for ablution (*pādaṁ*), (3) flowers (*puṣpe*), (4) incense (*dhūpe*), (5) oil lamps (*āloke*), (6) scented water (*gandhe*), and (7) food (*naivedye*).

After the offerings are made, the heroes and heroines then subside into the buddhas' bodies, speech, mind, and so forth, becoming one with them and delighting their minds. It is not the offerings themselves that please the enlightened ones. Rather, that which delights their minds is the essence of the light rays and offerings. That essence is bodhicitta. For example, when the natural radiance of a person's love touches his or her beloved, the beloved one experiences great delight. When the two are together, enjoying each other's company and conversation, their experience is joyful. In a similar way, the force of the practitioner's bodhicitta transforms into light rays that reach the pure realms and make pleasing offerings to the buddhas.

How can such offerings please the buddhas? All the enlightened ones think only about how to bring benefit and happiness to sentient beings. Having nothing but this motivation, they have attained buddhahood by accumulating merit for three limitless kalpas. Therefore, the moment one person gives rise to bodhicitta—the very source of benefit and happiness—it brings joy to all the buddhas. That bodhicitta manifests as actual offerings.

While one visualizes the deity and recites mantras, inexhaustible, manifold thoughts and afflictions continue to arise. Those very thoughts become diverse offerings as one visualizes the offering clouds of Samantabhadra. This brings about a twofold benefit—circumstantial and ultimate. The circumstantial benefit along the way is that ordinary concepts are transformed into purity through the stages of development. The ultimate benefit is that one comes to know the factual meaning. At the root, this factual meaning is the able potency of bodhicitta, which brings delight to all the buddhas.

The words "connate union" mean that the minds of the buddhas and sentient ones are not separate but are fundamentally one. That singular mind pervades everywhere, like space. Even though appearances are manifold, they are of the same nature as the all-pervading mind. Appearances are nothing other than mind.

Outwardly, the dualistic expressions of self, others, and diverse perceived objects and their characteristics appear to ordinary beings. Inwardly, however, there is no duality. These manifold appearances are nothing other than the eightfold group of consciousnesses. Secretly, there is the ultimate factual perspective, in which the offering, the one who offers, and the ones to whom offering is made are indistinguishable. This secret truth is meditation itself and is only knowable through meditation. It is important to understand clearly this introduction to outer, inner, and secret offerings.

The "self-born, emanated deities" are the divine forms that have arisen from one's own mind. It is to these deities that one makes offerings. Thus, *The Thirty-Seven Practices of Bodhisattvas* says, "The ways things appear are one's own mind. From the beginning, that very mind has been free from elaborated extremes."[24] Thus, all appearances are mind. Since the mind that is mahāmudrā pervades space, there is no duality. From within nondual mind, various appearances arise. When there is no dualistic grasping at that which appears, the view is present. When there is dualistic grasping, one becomes bound. When this single point has been understood well, everything else will also be understood. Conversely, for one who has not yet seen the basis that is ultimate factual truth, it will be difficult to grasp the meaning. Trying to understand each separate point by means of different explanations will only cause concepts to proliferate.

When beings make offerings to the deities with a mind of faith and love, those pure offerings are received without any bias. This is the nature of the samaya that is shared among humans and deities. When offerings are made through nondual awareness, the divine act of offering and the divine enjoyment of offering are simultaneous and free of discrimination.

Next, one makes the three inner offerings with these words:

> HŪṂ. Great amṛita made from eight main and
> thousand branch ingredients, secret great
> rakta, the afflictions' space-expanse,
> and the torma, foremost substance of
> great elixir—these we offer you.
> MAHĀ PAÑCA AMṚITA, RAKTA, BALIṄTA KHĀHI.

These inner offerings are common to highest yoga tantra practices. Amṛita—the method aspect—is the accomplishment medicine or nectar pills that are compounded from many precious substances, chief among which are the physical constituents of red and white bodhicitta. Rakta is the wisdom aspect.

The torma vessel is the outer container that is this universe. The torma itself is the inner contents—all sentient ones, along with our self-grasping and afflictions, in particular. Among all the afflictions, delusion is foremost. It comes down to not knowing the actual condition of the mind—not understanding how the mind is. So, with the torma, one offers sentient ones' delusive self-grasping to the wisdom deity, the sky-like dharmakāya. This offering is made without any grasping at perceived objects or their characteristics as being real. The offerings continue with the following verse:

> HŪṂ. Dullness like a flesh mountain brought down;
> lust, a wave-tossed, blood-filled ocean; and
> hatred, a bone heap—these offerings are
> made to Vajrarākṣasa and courts. OṂ ĀḤ HŪṂ.

Since delusion, lust, and hatred are the bases of all the other afflictions, these three should be imagined as being extremely vast like the sky. The words of the sadhana give a sense of this vastness by referring to them as a mountain of flesh, an ocean of blood, and a heap of bones. One should imagine that one is offering as much flesh, blood, and bones as can be found in this entire worldly realm. In this way, mentally gathering together all the afflictive three poisons of oneself and all the three spheres' sentient ones, imagine the offerings as vast and profound.

Finally, all offerings come down to the basic point of nonduality. The one who makes offering, that which is offered, and those to whom offering is made are singular in nature. They all arise out of the natural sphere that is emptiness. From this perspective, they cannot be seen as separate or distinct. Ultimately, knowing oneself to be inseparable from Vajrakumāra, one sends forth emanations of offering goddesses who make offerings of divine enjoyments to oneself, the divine body of great enjoyment. So, the offering goddesses and the offerings themselves are inseparable from the deity. Similarly, when partaking of the five desirables in daily life, one should never be parted from the clear appearance of the deity. This can be accomplished through mindfulness. In this context, one need not visualize the outer appearance of the deity's form as depicted in thangka images. Rather, the actual meaning of becoming one with the deity is that clear appearance and mindfulness are nondual.

Offering Praise

After the offerings, one praises the bodies, speech, mind, attributes, and activities of all the mandala deities with the following lines:

> HŪṂ. Wrath King, Glorious Great Vajra Youth,
> pure dharmasphere, Khorlo Gyedebma,
> from your method-knowledge body come
> the ten emanated wrathfuls and
> female wrathfuls dawned from natural space,
> zasö with symbolic heads and fangs,
> emanations, falcon hosts dispatched
> to activities and four gate guards
> who defend the mandala's quarters,
> slaying henchmen, twelve Kīla guards with
> great men, Se, Chag, and Dung, and the like—
> oath-bound hosts declared as Kīla's guards—
> praise and homage to you with your courts!
> Now it's time for your compassionate pledge:
> bring about direct, destructive acts!

Since it highlights the meanings behind some of the mandala's divine appearances, this praise has the same basic meaning as the *Sign-Based Praise of Mañjuśrī Yamāntaka*. The ten male wrathful ones symbolize the ten strengths. Their ten female counterparts symbolize the ten transcendent perfections. The guard maids of the four gates symbolize the four immeasurables. Although one supplicates them to engage "direct, destructive acts," one should understand that they carry out all the activities of the buddhas of the ten directions and three times. Those who wish to contemplate the deity's attributes in greater detail should read the praise in the extensive Vajrakīla sadhana.

The Recitation of the Charm

Depending on how the sādhaka is approaching the practice, the recitation of the charm* may or may not include an additional visualization. In general, the secret accomplishment retreat and the daily practice focus only on the self-generation, which is a reflection of the abiding mandala of wisdom deities described previously. Therefore, when reading this section, one need only contemplate the meaning of the words before beginning the mantra recitation.

Opening the Chamber of Recitation

However, at this juncture, one may also practice the unsurpassed yoga tantra method known as "opening the chamber of recitation," which is described in the extensive sadhana. Through this special method, it is suitable to visualize the complete and instantaneous appearance of any other mandala one wishes, including that of the facing generation, the Foremost Prince, and the vase generation. These are all features of the great accomplishment retreat. Even though these mandalas are not necessary for the secret accomplishment, I will speak about them briefly in order to give some context.

Having already established the complete mandala of the self-generation, one can spontaneously accomplish the facing mandala by abiding in a state free of duality and imagining the syllables PHAṬ JA. These syllables need not be recited aloud. With these words,

*The term "charm" (*dzap*) is a loanword from the Sanskrit *japa* and refers to a mantra that is repeated in meditation.

brilliant rays of light suddenly shine forth from the heart of oneself as the principal deity. They radiate throughout the ten directions, filling space and causing the facing mandala to appear completely in an instant. Then, the light rays gather back into the heart of the principal. This radiating out and gathering back happens as described in the visualization that accompanies the approach mantra.

The Mandala of the Facing Generation

In general, the self- and facing generations are recited and established independently in other tantric systems. However, they are brought forth concurrently in the context of the Vajrakīla great accomplishment. Thus, according to unsurpassed yoga tantra, the "inseparable self and facing are simultaneously accomplished through the development [stages]."[25]

If a facing generation is visualized, it appears suddenly outside of oneself—as vast as the sky and like a mirror reflection of the mandala of the self-generation. When imagining the facing generation, it is not necessary to visualize a second wisdom being or concentration being in the heart of the principal deity of the facing mandala.

Although this visualization is not required for the secret accomplishment retreat, those who wish to practice it should imagine the facing mandala of Vajrakumāra with retinue, without conceiving of self and other as being separate. This accords with the example mentioned previously: if there are many crystal balls and a single large buddha, that buddha will be perfectly reflected in each of them.

Similarly, one should meditate on the entire container and contents as being divine in nature. When one invites the deities, one should imagine the scope of the immeasurable palace to be as vast as the outer container. The inner contents are all the deities of the mandala. Sādhakas should remain within this view free of distraction. When the mind is devoid of self-grasping, all beings manifest as the nature of the deity. In this way, if one knows how to meditate on the facing generation, it is suitable to do so. If one does not meditate on it, it is also fine since it is present at the very basis.

The Mandala of the Foremost Prince

The same method can be applied to the mandala of the Foremost Prince. The light rays from the heart of the principal reach the material kīla of signs, which is the substantial support for the Foremost Prince's mandala. In this way, the mandala suddenly appears in its entirety with the opening of the chamber of recitation.

The Mandala of the Vase Generation

Similarly, although there is no vase visualization in the secret accomplishment, one can be imagined as necessary, for example, when one performs ablution during an inscription ritual for the deceased. Although the inscription is not part of the Vajrakīla practice, it can be performed as a supplement to any deity yoga.

The vase generation is exactly the same as the facing generation, except that it is not as elaborate. Instead of visualizing all the deities in the extensive mandala, one visualizes only the principal father-mother couple inside the vase. Those who are to be purified with the nectar of the vase are the immature. Those who do the purification are the five wisdoms, which ripen sentient ones, bringing them to maturity.

As for the vase visualization, there is a story of an ancient Indian *paṇḍita* who taught that one must clearly visualize the deity's blessings merging into the nectar of the vase. Hearing this teaching, Āryadeva disputed it, saying that one must know the nectar itself to be divine in nature. This is a profound instruction. When one knows the five elements to be deities, there is no need to visualize anything else. Such knowing of things as they truly are is the best method of practice.

Finally, it is important to remember that no matter how many mandalas one may generate, they all arise simultaneously, like mirror reflections of the single, principal mandala. Each one (except for the simplified vase generation) features the immeasurable palace, the heruka, the mother-consort, the body mandala, retinues, and the like. As each of them is exactly the same, one need only visualize the mandala in stages one time.

This describes the special secret mantra method known as "opening the chamber of recitation." The moment one gives rise to confident belief in the deity, the saṁbhogakāyas of five certainties are present. This occurs in a single instant. So, rather than focusing on exactly when to open the chamber of recitation according to the words of the text, one should know that the opening takes place on the basis of the authentic inner experience of certainty. In the context of unsurpassed yoga tantra, it is appropriate to cause entire mandalas to arise in an instant. When one realizes oneself and the deity to be inseparable, then that is a suitable basis for giving rise to mandalas. Once they have appeared, one can sustain their visualization throughout the approach mantra.

Meaning of the Words of the Recitation of the Charm

The recitation of the charm begins with the following words:

> HŪṀ. Glorious Vajra Youth, princes, and courts
> fiercely dance in Khorlo Gyedeb—space.

Among outer, inner, and secret offerings, the charm is a secret offering. While one visualizes oneself as the principal, each deity in the mandala has a consort like Khorlo Gyedeb (Dīptacakrā) with whom he is in sexual union. In the best circumstance, as one reads these words and throughout the mantra recitations, one will give rise to an experience of great bliss. In this way, the deities themselves will spontaneously feel pleasure. Whatever experiences one generates will be felt by the deities. The visualized deities receive one's own inner experiences of delight.

For example, in order to make tormas, one needs dough. If a delicious dough is prepared using butter and molasses, then all the tormas made will be delicious. Similarly, every deity is created with the same material that is the mind. When the mind is suffused with bliss, whichever deity one creates—the self-generation or facing generation—will be equally blissful. The fierce dance of the mandala deities is one's cultivation of bliss.

In this way, the entire mandala, including the body mandala, is experiencing the pleasures of union. However, the main focus is the sensations that are arising within the channels of Dīptacakrā. Her name, Lady of the Sealed Cakra, means that the cakra comprised of her body, mind, channels, and constituents has been sealed with the experience of bliss. Similarly, within one's own body, the deities in one's channels and constituents reverberate with the self-resounding *nāda*. When the mind is suffused with pleasure, all the organisms in the body also experience pleasure. When the principal experiences bliss, the entire mandala does as well. The verse continues:

> Sound and emptiness, the melody
> of the mantric charm, like thunder roars.
> Thus, I'll practice till our samaya
> is accomplished in the vast expanse.

When one abides in samādhi ("emptiness") conjoined with the recitation of mantra ("sound"), the mantras' vibration, like the deities' dance, is continuous. From that union of concentration with the energy of speech, rainbow light rays spontaneously radiate in every direction. From those rays of light, emanations appear, pervading the six realms and engaging activities for the sake of beings. In this way, through the mantra recitation itself, all the pure fields spontaneously become manifest, countless offerings are continually made to the objects of refuge, and so forth.

The "samaya" referred to here is one's personal commitment never to abandon love and compassion for beings from now until buddhahood is attained. When one takes a samaya, one speaks actual words of commitment. Those words are connected to one's mind of loving-kindness. So, the primary meaning of samaya is that no matter what conditions arise, one will never abandon the love, compassion, and faith one has generated. Since sādhakas and deities are unified in their singular commitment, the mantra recitations become an expression of their bond.

Approach and Accomplishment

Visualization of the Approach Mantra

The final heart essence of all the stages of development is the visualization of the delicate mantra strand, through which accomplishments are attained. Most of you probably know a bit about the revolving of the mantra strand in general. In the development-stage yogas of Kīla, the visualization that accompanies the approach mantra is clearly described in the following words of the text:

> Light rays radiate throughout ten directions from the life force and mantra strand at my heart, rousing the divine Three Roots' samaya from its vital point. Every blessing of body, speech, and mind comes like rainfall as white OṀ, red ĀḤ, and blue HŪṂ, merging ceaselessly into my three places. Further, I imagine all the blessings and potency of every victor's compassion as Vajrakīla's divine hosts in unfathomable great and small forms that gently fall and merge with me. Like opened sesame pods are the body mandala's gods and channel hubs' divine couples. They and all in the mandala recite the mantra, resounding like a beehive broken open.

Here, the words "the life force and mantra strand at my heart" refer back to the visualization of the wisdom and concentration beings at the heart center, which is found in the practice manual:

> In the principal's heart on a sun,
> a thumb-joint-sized sattva rolls a stake.
> On a sun within his heart is a
> grain-sized golden vajra, at whose core
> is a HŪṂ by mantra circumvolved.

This concentration being is really the main focus of the meditation. To whatever degree beginners can visualize the mantra strand, they will experience a corresponding purification of obscurations. Cleansing the mind is the ultimate purpose of this heart visualization, which was previously described in detail. Because it accords with Lord Buddha's instruction "Thoroughly subdue your mind,"[26] it is of extreme importance. In order to tame the mind, the method here is to gather awareness single-pointedly into the seed syllable HŪṂ̊, which is the "life force" mentioned in the visualization. Through focusing awareness in this way, the mind and wind energies will abide together in the HŪṂ̊ syllable. When mind and winds become mingled, the mind cannot wander.

Surrounding the HŪṂ̊ is the nine-syllable quintessence mantra of Vajrakīla: VAJRAKĪLI KĪLAYA HŪṂ̊ PHAṬ. This is the "mantra strand" referred to in the visualization. Each of the dark green syllables radiates brilliant rays of light without obstruction. Thus, the text reads, "Light rays radiate throughout ten directions from the life force and mantra strand at my heart."

One should stabilize this visualization as the approach mantra is recited. Then, the mantra strand begins revolving slowly in a clockwise direction while the sun, vajra, and HŪṂ̊ remain stationary. The purpose of this is to keep the mind from wandering toward outer things. Thus, the revolving mantra strand is a method of holding or fixing the mind. If it is difficult to imagine the strand revolving, one should give more attention to stabilizing the radiant clarity of the syllables.

For those who prefer to maintain the focus of their meditation at the navel cakra—the source of all the channels—it is acceptable to shift the visualization from the heart center down to the navel. In this case, the wisdom being and concentration being, as described in the text, should be imagined together at the navel.

Because the visualization is somewhat intricate, one cannot expect it to be complete or stable from the beginning. Rather, it is meant to be cultivated throughout an entire lifetime. Gradually, over a period of months and years, one should first stabilize the flame-like seed syllable HŪṂ. Once that has become clear, minute, and stable, one can add to it the nine-syllable mantra surrounding the HŪṂ. In the next stage, the mantra begins revolving, first slowly and then progressively faster until it becomes too fast for the mind to keep track of. At this juncture, one slips into empty awareness. Having stabilized the visualization as described, one should imagine light rays radiating outward and the wisdom deities' blessings dissolving back into oneself, according to the words in the text. Knowing that the mantra strand continues revolving, one should settle the mind in the view.

All of this can be understood with the following example: once a house has been constructed, it can be inhabited by people. Similarly, when the immeasurable palace has been established, the wisdom deities abide therein. Their very life force is the ceaseless revolving of the mantra strand. It turns extremely quickly, creating a streak of light in which individual syllables can no longer be distinguished and a constant, self-resounding drone that pervades this worldly realm. At this phase, one may also imagine that the light generated by the revolving mantra is like a fire whose warmth spreads throughout the body, giving rise to light rays that emanate outward. One should understand the light rays of the mind to be the natural radiance arisen from bodhicitta. The regular, principal visualization during the approach is just this. Other aspects are secondary.

Even a beginner who is struggling with visualization techniques can still maintain a broad overview of the purpose of practice, which is to cultivate bodhicitta. Even if one can visualize nothing more than a vivid blue, one should still give rise to the divine pride of knowing oneself to be the deity. On top of this, one should consider with compassion the suffering of all sentient beings. In this way, a connection is established between the deity and sentient ones. When these three conditions—divine pride, compassion, and connection—come together, one becomes endowed with great power to benefit others. This capacity is naturally conjoined with the radiating-out of light rays that make offerings to the objects of refuge and simultaneously alleviate sentient ones' sufferings, establishing them in the state of the yidam deity. Further, one can accomplish the two objectives, those of self and others, through the light rays that radiate out from and return back into the revolving mantra strand.

Having become frustrated by slow progress, sometimes students say things like, "I have been practicing for five years now. Why can I not see the wisdom deities?" But one cannot expect to perceive the saṁbhogakāyas until self-grasping has been cleared away. Thus, one should understand that achieving the desired result depends more on a mind of altruism and immeasurable love than on visualization techniques.

The guru, yidam, and ḍākiṇī have taken on a samaya for the sake of sentient ones and, on that basis, have attained buddhahood. When, from the conventional perspective, one gives rise to vast love for sentient beings, it brings extreme delight to the field of accumulation, since their objective is also to benefit all beings. For example, it is said that in the past if someone offered a pot full of gold to the Bhagavan Buddha, he wouldn't even look at it. However, if a person gave rise to just a bit of compassion for sentient ones, the Buddha would slightly smile. Thus, by generating immeasurable compassion for every sentient being, one pleases the enlightened ones. As the force of bodhicitta is born in one's own mind, it stirs the wisdom deities' hearts, causing them to bestow their blessings of body, speech, and mind. This is how the light rays, which are the nature of the deities' own altruistic intent, "rouse the divine Three Roots' samaya from its vital point."

In return, their blessings of body, speech, and mind are gathered together in a rainfall of OṀ, ĀḤ, and HŪṀ syllables, which merge into one's three places. Thus, their blessing, the nature of bodhicitta, enriches the sādhaka's altruistic mind. In this way, the buddhas and deities support and give backing to those who have the mind set on benefiting others. Since bodhicitta benefits sentient ones and delights the deities, the two objectives of self and others are simultaneously accomplished merely through cultivating love. One should imagine that this rainfall of seed syllables descends upon all sentient ones according to the visualization in the text. This example of rainfall has a great connection with the actual meaning. At the basis, immature sentient ones are like flower buds. When they are nourished by the rainfall, they will blossom and the qualities of the fully matured flower will become evident.

As for the syllables OṀ ĀḤ HŪṀ "merging ceaselessly into" one's "three places," in fact, all sentient ones possess the seeds of the buddhas' body, speech, and mind. At the very basis, their bodies are nirmāṇakāyas; their speech, saṁbhogakāyas; and their minds, the dharmakāya. Since they are endowed with the seeds of the three kāyas, if they make a connection with all the buddhas through generating great love, the buddhas' blessings dissolve into them ceaselessly. That is, OṀ syllables dissolve uninterruptedly into the OṀ at their crowns, ĀḤ syllables dissolve uninterruptedly into the ĀḤ at their throats, and so forth. Like snowflakes falling on the surface of a lake, they merge indivisibly on contact. Through this visualization, resplendent blessings will enter and one's mind will abide in comfort and ease. The mind will be cleansed through abiding with single-pointed focus. This is an extremely important point, which hearkens back to the need to continuously receive empowerment as the antidote to dualistic self-grasping.

The text continues, "Further, I imagine all the blessings and potency of every victor's compassion as Vajrakīla's divine hosts in unfathomable great and small forms that gently fall and merge with me." The heart-blessing of all the buddhas of the ten directions and three times thus descends in the forms of Vajrakīlas as large as Mount Meru to bless the entire worldly container. In addition, forms as tiny as atomic particles dissolve into the bodies, speech, and minds of the sentient contents. In this way, the entire universe is completely packed with wisdom deities' bodies, vast and small. As they dissolve into one, their immeasurable love and compassion destroys one's self-grasping, causing the four immeasurables to increase. Because the single intent of all the buddhas is nothing other than the welfare of sentient ones, they will endow with their strength whoever gives rise to the mind set on benefiting others.

It is on this basis that the supreme siddhi is realized. When the ice of sentient ones' self-grasping melts and merges with the vast ocean, that is buddhahood. Thus, one should understand the deities' blessing to be love and compassion.

Furthermore, with regard to the benefits of the accomplishment retreat, when there have assembled at least four members of the sangha—those who have entered the path of Buddhist practice according to the systems of individual liberation, the Bodhisattva Vehicle, or Mantric Vehicle—that assembly is invested with great strength. It is suitable to refer to them as "an order of the sangha." It is extremely efficacious for an order of the sangha to make aspirations. This is the reason why long-life prayers for eliminating obstacles are recited at the time of group accomplishment retreats. To make offerings to an order of the sangha is similarly powerful. This is why meals are often sponsored at such gatherings.

In particular, as beings of high, middling, and lesser faculties participate in such assemblies, whatever potency is present for those of highest faculties will be equally shared by each participant. For this reason, however vast the assembly, there is said to be a corresponding degree of potency. Thus, Guru Rinpoche taught that a seven-day group accomplishment retreat is more effective than an individual remaining in solitary retreat for seven years. Since these words are actually true for those who really practice, they help one to appreciate the great qualities of accomplishment retreats. Obtaining the buddhas' blessings and potency should be understood in this way.

Finally, the visualization of the approach mantra concludes, "Like opened sesame pods are the body mandala's gods and channel hubs' divine couples. They and all in the mandala recite the mantra, resounding like a beehive broken open." Just as during a secret accomplishment a temple houses many people who continuously chant the mantra, so too one's own body is like a building full of countless, ever-present deities, the murmur of whose voices is constant. Many hundreds of thousands of deities abide within the channels of the subtle body and comprise the body mandala.

Dwelling in the channel wheels at the crown, throat, heart, and so forth, the "channel hubs' divine couples" can be roughly understood as the ten wrathful couples and the other deities named in the practice manual. However, if one considers them in finer and finer detail, manifestations of the five wisdoms appear in each cakra. As each of the five wisdoms is present in a single wisdom, each of those five can be further subdivided into five, making twenty-five. Expanding outward from those, the hundred families of the holy peaceful and wrathful ones manifest. In this way, innumerable emanations of the deity emerge, just as countless rays of light appear from one sun.

In addition to the principal divine couple and the deities of the outwardly manifest mandala, the many thousands of deities of the body mandala also simultaneously recite the mantra. In this way, one should imagine the mantra resounding.

The Three Mandalas

A prominent feature of the extensive sadhana is the three mandalas. These are the mandalas of (1) the self-generation, the commitment being; (2) the facing generation; and (3) the Foremost Prince who is the implement, the material kīla.

Rather than being limited to the mandala of the commitment being, the mantra resounds throughout every Vajrakīla mandala. Even though these cannot be visualized in detail, one should give rise to confidence in their presence.

Methods of Meditation during the Approach Mantra

Now I have described in detail the visualization that accompanies the approach mantra. During the recitation, one should alternate one's focus between this visualization and the view. That is to say, after stabilizing an aspect of the visualization for a while, one should seal it by abiding in empty awareness. Later, when one's attention wavers from the view, one should return to the visualization. This is the means of cultivating the union of calm abiding and special insight described earlier.

One who wishes for the deity and one's own mind to become inseparable should understand the samādhi of the deity to be like a flame and the recitation of mantra to be like oxygen. By unifying fire and air when visualizing the revolving mantra strand, the mind becomes very clear. The fire will be able to consume every bit of grasping at perceived objects and their defining characteristics. This is a vivid example of how when the inner mind of discerning intelligence becomes clear, it can burn away thoughts, emotions, and propensities. Guru Rinpoche condensed all the efficaciousness of mantra into the following single point from the Vajrakīla texts: "The recitation conjoined with wind energies stirs the flame-like samādhi, setting fire to the kindling of obscurations."[27]

In order to set alight the kindling of obscurations, it is necessary to actually practice. At present, one has obscurations of three kinds: physical, verbal, and mental. First, physical obscurations are burnt through visualizing the development stages of the deity.

A person who fails to set fire to physical obscurations will grasp at the notion of "this body, my body" at the time of death. In the intermediate state following death, even though one no longer has a body, one will experience illness, hunger, fear, and whatever other propensities have been established by karma. The present sign of this is that the strongest imprints of one's waking state—whatever they are—manifest at night in the dream state as happiness, suffering, fear, and the like. In this way, such imprints will also emerge in the bardo.

However, when thoughts are suspended, the mind is no longer bound by happiness, suffering, or afflictions. Compassion and discerning intelligence emerge through giving the mind rest. Those who practice in this way and who cultivate a habit of continually recalling the deity can reach a state of never forgetting him or her in the present lifetime. Through the power of this imprint, they will not forget the deity in the bardo.

Generally, if a vase containing precious nectar is broken, its contents spill everywhere and are wasted. However, for a practitioner of deity yoga, tomorrow, when the time of death comes and the fragile vase of the body is broken, its precious contents will automatically flow into the form of the yidam, without need for one to take another birth. One will attain autonomy through immediately recalling the deity and mantra without any other intervening thought. Having left behind the body, one will emerge in the rainbowlike form of the deity. For this reason, stable, pure recollection is among the greatest qualities of deity yoga. For one who has a pure perception of both self and others, there is not the slightest chance of traversing perverted paths. Whatever illness, fears, sufferings, physical propensities, and the like one has in the embodied state can all be cast off like old clothing at the time of death.

If, on the other hand, pure perception is not accomplished, the development stages alone will not be of that much benefit. For those who have not stabilized the deity's clear appearance, karmic winds will follow whatever afflictive imprint suddenly arises. Thus, this is the dividing line between autonomy and dependence. It is important to consider this well and to investigate whether or not it is of benefit. Westerners are expert investigators, right? Does meditation on the deity burn away habits of embodiment or not? One should really inquire into this.

The obscurations of speech are purified by the beautiful self-resounding of the mantra, the union of sound and emptiness. One should think about the different kinds of pleasant and unpleasant sounds one hears. For example, when ordinary people listen to others' speech, if it is favorable, they like it. If it is disagreeable, they get upset. Any time such thoughts of attachment and aversion arise, they defile the mind and give rise to karmic imprints. However, if one continually recalls the murmur of mantra—not grasping at any particular sound—there is neither attachment to praise nor aversion to criticism. In this way, one cleanses the mind and blocks habits from being established.

Just as the development-stage yogas purify grasping at forms and the body, mantra purifies grasping at pleasant and unpleasant sounds and speech. Finally, obscurations of the mind are cleared away by meditation on the kīla of primordial awareness-rigpa—the nondual union of compassion and emptiness.

Meaning of the Approach Mantra

Here it is important to note that when we speak of secret mantras, the point is not that sentient ones should not hear the mantras. They are, after all, liberations through hearing. Instead, the point is that since the mantra's meaning is too profound to be fathomed, it should be kept hidden from those who cannot comprehend it. The mantra for the approach of Vajrakīla is OṀ VAJRAKĪLI KĪLAYA, SARVA VIGHNĀN VAṂ̊ HŪṂ̊ PHAṬ!

In brief, its meaning can be understood as follows: With the words OṀ VAJRAKĪLI KĪLAYA, one calls out and pays homage to the divine couple by name. KĪLI is the consort, Khorlo Gyedebma. VAJRA and KĪLA are the "adamantine stake," the heruka Vajrakumāra. The vajra is diamond-like, unbreakable, and unconquerable by others. Thus, the inner meaning of his name is actual, empty rigpa—the discerning intelligence that is the mind's actual condition. SARVA VIGHNĀN signifies everything that is obstructive in nature. In actual fact, the root of all obstruction abides in the mind. It is the concepts and afflictions that come from grasping at perceived objects and their defining characteristics as being true. These thoughts and afflictions are overcome by the kīla of primordial awareness-rigpa. When such inner demons are overcome, all outer demons are naturally subdued. In fact, since all of samsara has been created by thoughts, Vajrakīla overcomes samsara itself. The syllable VAṂ̊ is the same as that found in the words "JAḤ HŪṂ̊ VAṂ̊ HOḤ," which refer to the four activities and the four immeasurables. Thus, VAṂ̊ is the imperative, meaning "Magnetize!" or "Bring under your power!" It is associated with immeasurable joy. HŪṂ̊ means "Smash!" or "Shatter!" PHAṬ means "Sever!" or "Cut off!" So, the gloss on the mantra is "Homage to the Adamantine Stake and consort! Control, smash, cut off every appearance of perceived objects and their defining characteristics with the actual vajra that is emptiness!"

Similarly, when thoughts or emotions arise, by verbally or mentally reciting "HŪṂ̊ PHAṬ," one leaves the thoughts alone and the mind becomes clear. It is unnecessary to manipulate them in any way. Thus, one should simply remain within the actual condition of the mind. For example, when the lens of a film projector is covered, its projections will not appear on a screen. Similarly, when inner obstructors have been dispelled, outer hindrances will naturally disappear.

Recitation

Understanding the words of the mantra in this way, one may engage the recitation. As for the numbers of recitations, it is said that once the visualization has been established, each syllable of the mantra is to be repeated one hundred thousand times. This means that a ten-syllable mantra will require the recitation of one million syllables in total. This is the measure of what should be accomplished.

It is important to understand that these numbers do not refer merely to verbal recitation. While accumulating mantras, one should be free of distraction in body, speech, and mind, never mixing the mantra's syllables with ordinary speech. Having isolated one's three doors in retreat, one should recite while remaining within the clarity, purity, and stability of the yidam. In this way, the sādhaka becomes habituated to the deity's enlightened body, speech, and mind. This applies not only to one's self-perception, since all outer appearances will also manifest as the deity and all sounds will be perceived as mantra. Finally, when all thoughts are apprehended by mindful awareness, the mind will remain without distraction from divine sights, sounds, and thoughts. It is in this context that the texts speak of the numbers of mantras that are to be accumulated. It is also taught that after one has become well habituated to the modes of development-stage meditation, one need not focus so much on the numbers of recitations.

Those who think the numbers of mantra accumulations are of principal importance often abandon melody in favor of quick recitation. However, when reciting focused on numbers alone, those who lack the assurance of the view will become distracted by manifold thoughts, making it impossible to abide in single-pointed awareness. Because of this, they will follow whatever wandering thoughts arise.

A single-pointed meditation will never become stable when one is focused solely on numbers, counting mantras while totally distracted, with googly eyes wandering here and there. Some people accumulate many recitations in this way, mingling mantra with idle chatter. Although there are benefits from any mantra recitation and one will gain inconceivable merit, such practice will not result in accomplishment of the actual four activities or the supreme and common siddhis. This is because the method of practice itself is flawed.

In contrast, by looking at the essence of one's own mind, the buddha nature, one becomes free of attachment and aversion toward outer appearances. Thus, appearances are recognized as the deity. Through the method of mantra recitation, one is protected from thoughts of dualistic grasping toward sounds. Thus, the natural sounds of the five elements—water, wind, and so forth—are perceived as mantra. Then, if mindful awareness is not lost, thoughts and afflictions are overcome. This is the method for seeing the meaning that is mahāmudrā, the essence of ultimate bodhicitta. As a support to this, the emanating out and gathering back of light rays are methods for cultivating conventional bodhicitta, loving-kindness, and compassion. So, the meaning of the two types of bodhicitta is subsumed within these methods through which one accomplishes the yidam—perceiving appearances as the deity, sounds as mantra, and thoughts as awareness.

When reciting mantra, it is said one's chanting and articulation of the syllables should be free of fault, with exceedingly clear and pure pronunciation. As it is said in the scriptures,

> It is neither too loud nor too soft,
> neither too fast nor too slow,
> and neither too forceful nor too weak.
> Its phonemes are uncorrupted.
> It is without distraction, speech,
> or interruption such as yawning.[28]

Among all these faults of mantra recitation, yawning is the greatest, as it is a sign of boredom, which is characteristic of ignorance.

Yawning, which disrupts the life-sustaining wind that abides at the heart, is especially prohibited in the vinaya. By maintaining mindful awareness, one can keep one's mouth closed, suppressing the urge to yawn. Since sneezing can cause the life-sustaining wind to flow outward, it is also considered a fault and should be similarly suppressed.

To recite the mantra aloud with clear and uncorrupted articulation has many benefits. The movement of the tongue increases blood circulation, gives rise to warmth, and supports clarity of the mind. It benefits the entire body and dispels various illnesses, especially stomach ailments. Otherwise, if one sits there motionless and silent with closed mouth, digestive problems and phlegm-based diseases increase. Thus, during accomplishment retreats, sādhakas should make effort to recite well instead of sitting in silence.

The melody for the Vajrakīla approach mantra that is recited in our tradition is the same as that used in the Kīla Activity sadhana of *Gathering of Sugatas of the Eight Sadhana Teachings*, which was brought forth by the treasure revealer Nyangral Nyima Özer. It came to be practiced within the Drigung Kagyü lineage through the influence of the treasure revealer Rinchen Phüntsog.

During accomplishment retreats in Tibet, the practitioners were divided into two groups. About 20 percent of the assembly were more senior lamas, who were responsible for reciting the practice manual and mantras, while the other 80 percent were younger monks who chanted only the approach mantra.[29] This division reflects the principal importance of the mantra recitation, as it must be sustained day and night without interruption.

In my view, nowadays it is best if new students recite the practice manual in order to gain familiarity with the text. Once they know well the recitation and meaning of the practice manual, they can focus more on recitation of mantra. In this way of practice, meditators of both higher and lesser faculties can emphasize mantra recitation.

In addition, during Vajrakīla retreats in Tibet, the approach mantra was sometimes recited in a round, or as a canon. Since the melodic line runs through two recitations of the mantra, half of the sādhakas would chant the first mantra with melody. Then, when they reached their second recitation, the other half of the group would begin the melodic line of the first recitation. In this way, the sounds of the two recitations would mingle like waves in a choppy sea.

Chanting with melody is an extremely important point. In *The Exposition on the Great Accomplishment of Karuṇā Guhyasamaja from a Thousand Perspectives*,[30] there is a brief description of the visualization that accompanies the approach mantra. Therein, Guru Rinpoche says, "[Sādhakas] should not drone but express themselves with sweet melodies."[31]

Thus, to chant with melody is necessary for the actual experiences of approach and accomplishment. Guru Rinpoche taught that just as the meanings of the mantra's syllables are significant, the melody itself is also endowed with blessing. Whichever liturgy or mantra one practices, the force of its blessing depends to a great extent upon whether or not there is a melody.

One apprehends the mantra through the intelligence arisen from hearing. The majority of practitioners stop there. They think it is sufficient merely to have heard the words, regardless of the way in which those words have been heard. They completely disregard the intelligence arisen from contemplation, which can discriminate between the qualities of chanting with melody and the faults of chanting without.

To give an ordinary example, when two friends love each other, one may say the words "I love you," but when that love is expressed in song, so much feeling comes through the pleasing sounds of the melody. The mind becomes enticed by them. From the perspective of the intelligence that comes from contemplation, the great difference between these two ways of expression is obvious.

When one actually experiences the feelings evoked by recitation with melody, the intelligence born from meditation arises. If the words are merely read, there is no feeling at all; however, the mind becomes completely absorbed by words and meaning conjoined with melody. There is a kind of desire that is based on sounds. In actuality, when the deity's blessing interacts with one's attachment to beautiful sounds, the ear faculty becomes captivated by the pleasing melody and the mind is ravished by grasping at sound. This opens the mind, causing the inner meaning of the Dharma to make an imprint. If there is no beauty in the aural expression, the meaning will not be retained. For example, this is the same reason why so many medicines are sugarcoated.

When the sound is unpleasant or the recitation discordant, others' minds are immediately put in a state of unease. This is the reason why the entire assembly should chant in accord with the melody modeled by the cantor, without improvisation or harmonizing. When the melody is correct and the pitch and tempo stable, all the sādhakas can abide in a unified, single-pointed mind. In this way, the mind becomes extremely clear, having separated out purity from impurity. Thus, ordinary thoughts cannot arise, the deity's blessing is received, and the mind is purified.

Furthermore, one recitation with beautiful melody and clear pronunciation is equal to many recitations without. As it is said in the scriptures, "Just as one pure recitation exceeds a thousand adulterated ones, so does a single recitation with samādhi exceed a hundred thousand without."[32]

Through the vibration of the sound waves, it is as though each syllable is repeated multiple times. By contemplating the attributes of melodic chant alone, one can understand the good qualities of bodhicitta. Those who actually gain experience in practice will understand the importance of blessing-melodies. To assume that the style of recitation does not matter signifies a lack of experience.

The majority of the session, then, should be dedicated to the recitation of the approach mantra. Thereafter, the accomplishment mantra can be recited for a brief period. It is important not to mix up the visualizations of the two mantras. Rather, when reciting each mantra, one should hold in mind the accompanying visualization. Each of the visualizations must be done according to what is written in the text.

Visualization of the Accomplishment Mantra

The second mantra, the longer one, is for the purposes of accomplishment and activity engagement. Its visualization is extremely precious because it offers a method whereby samsaric faults can be transformed into good qualities, allowing practitioners to bring whatever arises onto the path of enlightenment. On the conventional level, this is accomplished by cultivating the primordial awareness that is bliss-emptiness in reliance on a partner. In this regard, most practitioners will be familiar with the following common prayer:

> May precious, foremost bodhicitta
> arise in whom it's not yet risen.
> Once born, instead of lapsing, may it
> increase higher and ever higher.[33]

As mentioned previously, this prayer lays out the three vehicles' intent. The methods that cause precious bodhicitta to increase ever further are the practices of the Secret Mantric Vajra Vehicle. The cultivation of yogic practice in reliance on a partner is one of many such methods. It employs visualization and meditation on the mantra strand and is related to the yogas of the channels, wind energies, and bodhicitta.

In order to understand this practice, it is necessary to first understand its relationship to the two types of bodhicitta. The human body is endowed with the six constituents: (1) earth, (2) water, (3) fire, (4) wind, (5) channels, and (6) seed essences. These six are the substantial bases for giving rise to great pleasure. Because these constituents are only complete in womb-born human beings, Lord Milarepa taught that the human body is even more precious than the forms of gods.

At the basis, conventional bodhicitta is indistinguishable from the seed essences that are inherent in the precious human form. From a scientific perspective, these reproductive fluids are the end result and the most refined essence of the six constituents' generative processes.[34] If this is true according to worldly understanding, how much more important is it from the perspective of the Secret Mantric Vajra Vehicle, whose yogic practices are entirely dependent on the channels, wind energies, and seed essences?

For mantrins, it is a downfall to view the seed essence as impure. In truth, conventional bodhicitta is the material basis for all physical well-being and love for others. Compassion and lust have the same nature, which is loving-kindness. The seed essence is the substantial basis of these. It is like a wish-fulfilling jewel that allows the meditator to achieve whatever could be desired. When one's own mind is blissful, it brings forth others' affection. For these reasons, it should never be wasted or perceived as ordinary.

Conventional bodhicitta can be transformed into ultimate bodhicitta. When lovers have the basis that is conventional bodhicitta, they can maintain their connection of mutual love and affection by visualizing each other as divine consorts. Through this practice, the same relationship that creates suffering for ordinary beings becomes a method of liberation for sādhakas. This happens through uniting the love and compassion of conventional bodhicitta with the primordial awareness that is ultimate bodhicitta by means of mantra recitation itself.

In this context, it is extremely important to make a clear distinction between the faults of dualistic grasping and the qualities of not grasping. If one considers the dualistic appearances conditioned by self-grasping, under the influence of adventitious confusion, there appear to be two bodies—those of oneself and one's partner. The moment one conceives of self and other as two, the notion of the "I" has entered. Even though a couple may have mutual love and affection, by apprehending a self in the other, they give rise to clinging to sexual pleasure. From that clinging emerge afflictions like mutual jealousy and aversion. Since such afflictions ruin love and affection, ordinary relationships become causes of limitless samsaric sufferings.

If one considers the connection between worldly lovers from the perspective of the seed essence, theirs is a pleasure with outflows.

As such, on the level of external samsaric appearances, the bliss of ordinary beings is contaminated and exhaustible. Not understanding this, worldly lovers become mutually dependent, clinging to the pleasure they think depends on the other, thus perpetuating cyclic existence.

So, in the beginning, one perceives one's lover dualistically. In the middle, one experiences sexual pleasure. In the end, one grasps at duality. In this way, with both partners grasping at perceived objects and their defining characteristics as real, their connection becomes a cause of mutual pain. Such are the samsaric faults of ordinary sexual relationships.

Conversely, when the couple knows self and other to lack inherent existence, when the blissful, fundamental disposition of the mind is mutually understood, then there is no point in grasping at a self. Free of grasping, the inner mind manifests as the actuality of buddha nature. That nature is singular despite the illusory appearances of two forms. Within the mind that is emptiness, there is no duality. When dualistic grasping is torn down, all thoughts of attachment and aversion that arise from it are also torn down to the very ground. Then, although one perceives illusory outer phenomena, one still maintains the thought "I must benefit beings." That thought itself brings benefit. In this way, both lovers share the mind that is set exclusively on benefiting others. Within that mind, there is no source from which jealousy or aversion can arise.

As the mantra strand circles between the two—the father and mother—self and other are known to be nondual. One realizes the nondual fact that is the actual condition of the sky-like mind. Thus, one can truly become liberated from samsara. When there is no samsara, there is no karmic accumulation. When karma is not accumulated, samsara becomes utterly without meaning. One gains mastery over the pure fields in that very instant. This gives rise to a state of physical and mental ease that is free of suffering and yet endowed with compassion for sentient ones.

This union of the divine father-mother couple, which is common in secret mantra yogas of any heruka, is referred to in the following verse from the lineage supplication, which reflects the qualities of the kīla of bodhicitta:

> [Symbols,] meanings, signs—the union of
> wisdoms with the kāyas—radiate and
> gather dreadful, blazing wrathful ones.
> When the mother's sky is planted with
> bodhicitta's kīla, may clouds of
> emanations, foremost heirs, stream forth!

As the mantra strand circles between them, their experience of bliss-emptiness causes the mind to become exceedingly clear. That clarity is the innate liveliness of primordial awareness—the pure portion of the seed essence—from which arises the mantra, the emanating and gathering back of light rays, and so forth. In this way, through liberation on arising, whatever thoughts or emotions emerge are spontaneously transformed into nirmāṇakāyas. Utterly free of outflows, the deities enjoy inexhaustible pleasure that spontaneously and instantly brings forth innumerable emanations who act for beings' purpose. This is the pure generative process of the deities, which comes from their bond of mutual love and affection and their mastery of rigpa's self-liveliness.

In contrast, for beings bound by dualistic grasping, this same liveliness manifests as a compulsion to procreate. The exhaustible bliss of ordinary beings is characterized by outflows, which lead to conception, lengthy gestation, and the sufferings of birth, aging, illness, and death. Through this example, one can see how dualistic grasping perverts the generative process, narrowing one's affections to one or two offspring who are near and dear. In this way, beings perpetuate samsaric wandering. One should deeply contemplate these ways in which secret mantra practice brings about realization of the fact of nonduality, while samsaric existence reinforces dualism. This is an extremely important distinction.

As for the seed essence, if it is allowed to degenerate, physical health is compromised, and luster and force are exhausted. One becomes easily angered and couples argue with each other. Pleasure, happiness, and the capacity to love others are all diminished. The basis for bliss in one's own body and mind is lost. This, in turn, provokes others' jealousy and aversion. In this way, when the view is not maintained, unmitigated afflictions will proliferate under the sole influence of lust.

Just as there are various kinds of subtle channels and wind energies, there are also different sorts of seed essences, which include the life-sustaining seed essence and the pervading seed essence. Because of this, degeneration is not defined exclusively by ejaculation. For example, in an experience of intense passion, some can lose the life-sustaining seed essence and die. On the inner level, degeneration depends on one's response to physical pleasure. On the secret level, outflows occur in the subtle body through the movement of wind energies from the wavering of attention. Thus, rather than focusing exclusively on gross outer phenomena, meditators should cultivate awareness of ever subtler movements of mind-winds, which are not visible to the eye. The main point is that the pure portion will not decline when one maintains mindful awareness-rigpa. By sustaining the view, one can bring down afflictions through vigilant mindful awareness. In this way, the various kinds of seed essences are preserved. This is the key point of utilizing lust in yogic practice.

The methods of nourishing seed essences are taught in detail in the practices of subtle channels and wind energies. Although they involve ingesting various kinds of medicines and substances, the principal method is simply disclosure—that is, laying bare all faults and misdeeds.

Thus, in order to cause bodhicitta to increase, sādhakas practice herukas like Vajrakīla and also Cakrasaṁvara—who is particularly associated with the yoga of *candalī*. The extremely precious meaning of secret mantra is taught through such practices, which can accomplish many diverse activities for the purposes of self and others through the revolving mantra strand. In these instructions, there are differences depending on whether the mantra circles clockwise or counterclockwise in relation to the descent or ascent of the seed essences when cultivating the four joys. These four are (1) joy, (2) supreme joy, (3) parted from joy, and (4) co-emergent joy. With the last two, the sādhaka experiences freedom from dualistic grasping. Parted from joy is a state in which there is neither an experiencer of delight nor any object that delights. Co-emergent joy is the fundamental, natural disposition of the mind. It is discriminating awareness-wisdom.

Thus, the ultimate point of such practices is to realize the inseparability of self and others by experiencing the nonduality of the father-mother couple. The resulting realization of nondual primordial awareness undermines the entirety of samsara, which is rooted in dualistic views of self and other. When lustful pleasure is recognized and mixed with practice in this way, it becomes the cause of accomplishing the rainbow body and attaining the ground of the buddhas. Such results can occur in this very lifetime. This is the reason why the buddhas have taught the yogic methods of subtle channels and wind energies. It is not for the purpose of causing lust to increase! How one manages pleasure is the dividing line between going up or down within samsara and nirvana.

The mantra for Vajrakīla's accomplishment and activity engagement is OṀ VAJRAKĪLI KĪLAYA, JAḤ HŪṀ VAṀ HOḤ KAṬAṄKAṬE JAYE VIJAYE AJITE APARĀJITE MĀRA SENA PRAMARDANĪYE SARVA VIGHNĀN VAṀ HŪṀ PHAṬ!

According to the text, the visualization that accompanies it is as follows:

> From the mantra strand radiate light rays and a second strand, which flow from the father's to the mother's mouth. Through the mantric self-resounding of unfathomable heroes and ḍākiṇīs in the mother's four cakras, the mindstream is roused. The mantra strand enters the father's vajra through the mother's secret place. The gods in one's channel hubs proclaim the mantra's sound. Visualize the mantra strand merging ceaselessly into the heart center.

In general, the methods for visualizing the mantra strand with its emanating light rays are the same in various wrathful deity yogas, regardless of which deity is being practiced. However, in this sadhana, the way in which the mantra strand arises is unique.

The first mantra strand is the nine-syllable quintessence mantra revolving on a horizontal plane in the heart center. As it ceaselessly revolves, one imagines that light rays and another mantra strand, that of the long mantra, arise out of the nāda, the fine, wavy line atop the circle of the HŪṂ syllable—the deity's life force at the heart. This second strand is extremely subtle like a fine golden thread and is the nature of light. One by one, each syllable of the mantra emerges from out of the nāda. That nāda is like the tip of a wavering candle flame. Tantric texts sometimes speak of the "self-resounding nāda." This means that the sound vibration of the mantra spontaneously manifests from the flickering nāda.

From there, the strand rises through the father's central channel. Emerging from his mouth, it enters the mouth of the mother, descending via her central channel. Then, the strand reenters the father at the couple's point of union and rises through his central channel. One by one, the syllables ascend like the steps of an escalator, returning to the HŪṂ via the hook at its base and dissolving nondually therein. Since a single accomplishment mantra is not long enough to complete the entire circuit, the mantra strand is made up of a number of mantras. It is not as though the same strand continuously revolves. Rather, the strand begins with a new, freshly arisen string of syllables and completely dissolves into emptiness when returning to the seed syllable. In this way, the second mantra strand should be visualized circling in a large vertical loop.

Although both mantra strands are circling simultaneously during the accomplishment mantra, the first one is turning so quick that individual letters cannot be distinguished. At this stage, it is not necessary to focus on the shorter quintessence mantra since it would be difficult to visualize both. One should focus only on the mantra being recited at the moment. For example, in order to brew tea, one needs a stove, a pot, water, tea, a cup, and the like. Once the tea has been brewed and poured, though, one can simply enjoy it without further concern about each of its different components.

If one finds it too difficult to visualize in this way, one should at least give rise to confidence that there is a brilliant strand of mantra circling between the deities in union. This visualization of the father and mother consorts in union should be stabilized regardless of whether one is practicing alone or relying on the body of another.

In the practice of Cakrasaṁvara, the circling of the mantra strand between the divine couple is similar to this. However, since the direction is reversed in Cakrasaṁvara practice, if one always meditates in this way, it can become a cause for the degeneration of the seed essence. So, if one is not careful, there is a danger of practicing in ways that are driven by sensation. For this reason, it is advisable for yogis to reverse the direction of the mantra strand as needed during Cakrasaṁvara meditation.[35]

In the yogic practice of Vajrakīla, since the seed essence rises and dissolves into the HŪṂ syllable, there is not the same danger. In this regard, although technically there is no seed syllable or mantra garland in the heart of the consort, those practitioners who choose to visualize themselves in the form of the consort Dīptacakrā should imagine the circling of the mantra strand independently from their partner's visualization. That is, each partner should primarily visualize the rising of the strand within his or her own central channel. This avoids the risk of degeneration, which can manifest as ejaculation for men and women or as increased menstrual bleeding in women. In this regard, if one engages the visualization undistractedly from within the view, realizing perceived objects as illusory, there will be no error or contradiction in the visualization that lacks reference point. Otherwise, if one conceives of the visualization scientifically, grasping at how things dualistically appear, it will become a cause for many concepts to emerge.

As the mantra strand circles through the consort's body, the many deities who reside in her channels are aroused. These "unfathomable heroes and ḍākiṇīs in the mother's four cakras" are manifestations of the aggregates and elements in the aspects of the five

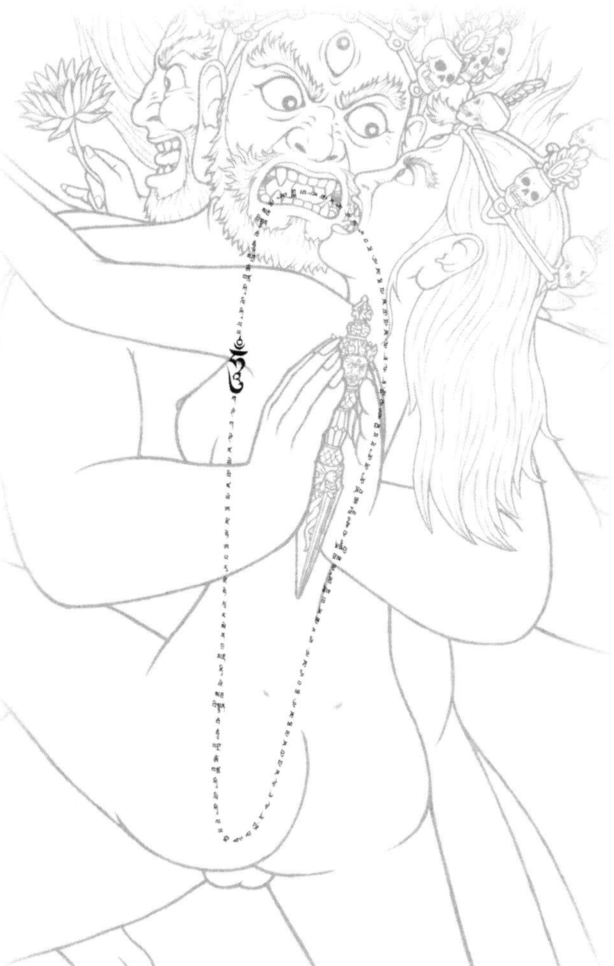

The Accomplishment Mantra Strand

victorious families' fathers and mothers. If one elaborates out from that, the channels and elements of the subtle body are incalculable, as is expressed in *The King of Aspirations for the Conduct of Samantabhadra*. In their impure state, they manifest as various thoughts and emotions. However, when they are conjoined with bodhicitta, the pure aggregates and elements are all divine in nature. Thus, from the basis that is bodhicitta, one knows one's own body to be full of tiny deities. This recognition alone gives rise to an experience of pleasure. The deities abide within spheres of rainbow bubbles in the channels and constituents of the subtle body. As the principal deity couple experience the pleasures of union, the deities dwelling in their crowns, throats, hearts, and navels are awakened. From each of these tiny wrathful couples emerge rays of rainbow-colored light, like reflections appearing from a crystal. These light rays fill the hollow bodies of the principal divine couple.

Through the experience of bliss—the self-resounding of the mantra—the deities' mindstream is roused. For example, when lovers experience sexual passion, they involuntarily cry out due to pleasure. For the deities of the body mandala, it is recognition of the great bliss of primordial awareness that rouses their mindstream. Their cries, which reverberate throughout the channels and cakras, are the "mantric self-resounding."

According to the text, this self-resounding occurs "in the mother's four cakras." These words from the recitation of the charm have the same meaning: "Glorious Vajra Youth, princes, and courts fiercely dance in Khorlo Gyedeb—space." The fierce dance gives rise to the passionate cries that arise from contact with her main channel.

To visualize oneself and one's partner as the nondual father-mother heruka in this way is the ultimate offering to the deities. This is the meaning of secret offerings—the empowerment of co-emergence (*sahaja*) according to the Latter System. By imagining the channels, the deities abiding therein, the wind energies, the revolving mantra strand and seed syllable, and the blazing and dripping of the seed essences, the sādhaka makes great offerings. The actual offering is simply to meditate on the yidam while directly experiencing the empty nature of great bliss. Since the mind of the deities and the mind of the yogi are inseparable, the deities themselves receive whatever pleasure one experiences. For example, just as people become sexually aroused when looking at pornography, so too the deities experience pleasure looking at sādhakas in union. This is especially so for saṁbhogakāya deities, who are characterized by great enjoyment of the passionate offerings of great bliss. This is what is meant by the words "The gods in one's channel hubs proclaim the mantra's sound." Such is the spontaneous resounding of the mantra's natural sound.

By practicing in this way, half of one's attention remains grounded in the skillful means of the deity's clear appearance while only half becomes lost in the experiences of pleasure. Through the yidam's compassion and the potency of deity yoga, both partners can gather the accumulations of merit and wisdom.

During such practice, whenever one recognizes that one has become bound by grasping, one should inquire, "Whose pleasure is this? Where has it come from?" In reality, it has both conventional and ultimate aspects. Although on the conventional level, the father and mother experience great bliss, the ultimate nature of their pleasure is the cessation of ordinary concepts—the pleasure of the actual condition of the mind itself, free of any thought or emotion. It transcends grasping mind and grasped-at objects. It is the bliss of the dharmakāya—the mind's fundamental disposition—not the bliss of another. It is merely due to conditions that it appears to depend on outer objects. The nature of bliss is singular; what is mistaken is one's way of perceiving it. When recognizing that one has become dependent in the experience of pleasure, one should think, "I've become confused. This bliss is the actual condition of my own mind. Self and other, father and mother, are inseparable. The actual condition is without duality."

By placing the experience of great pleasure in the view, one will know a bliss beyond change or transition. When one cultivates uncontaminated, inexhaustible great bliss free of grasping, all thoughts and emotions are suspended, causing the sky-like nature of mind to be laid bare. In this way, the consorts in union support each other in the recognition of the actual condition of the mind. In this regard, Lord Milarepa said in his *Hundred Thousand Songs*,

> In the state of bliss, there is emptiness.
> In the state of emptiness, there is clarity.
> In the state of clarity, there is rigpa.[36]

Thus, great pleasure is a skillful means for seeing the mind's nature. Through this method, nonduality is recognized. When one is utterly free of self-grasping in the moment, there is no distinction to be made between self and other. If in this way one can cultivate inexhaustible bliss recognizing nondual awareness, then there will be no basis for the proliferation of afflictive minds.

The fundamental disposition of one's own mind goes by many names—Samantabhadra, Vajradhara, inseparable method and wisdom, nondual father and mother. Regardless of which label is applied, when its meaning has been realized, one has understood the intent of secret mantra. As is said in *The Aspiration of Samantabhadra*, "If just that is known, such is buddha."[37] This is not hyperbole. If in this life one maintains the clear appearances of oneself and one's partner as divine, then those imprints will remain tomorrow when the bardo comes. As the memories of one's beloved arise in the mind, the form of the deity will appear together with such recollection. At that moment, through the potency of the deity's compassionate blessing, one will be able to attain buddhahood within the deity's saṁbhogakāya pure realm.

In contrast, those who lack the skillful means of such pith instructions become no different from common beings, giving rise to ordinary, impure perceptions, unmitigated desires, and clinging. Since clinging itself obscures the mind's nature, oneself and one's companion—mutually bound by dualistic grasping—will circumstantially wander in samsara.

Meaning of Approach and Accomplishment

Previously, I mentioned the importance of understanding the four branches of approach and accomplishment when practicing Earlier System treasures like this sadhana of Vajrakīla. Secret mantra teachings often speak of maturing empowerment and liberating instructions. As for the former, the difference between immaturity and maturity is like the difference between a flower bud and a flower that has fully blossomed. Although the seed of the flower, the buddha nature, is present in all sentient beings of the six realms, it only finds the proper conditions for maturation among humans. Thus, this precious human birth is like a flower bud. Through practice, one can cause the bud to open, revealing the qualities of buddhahood in a single lifetime. In the context of deity yoga, the maturation of the sādhaka occurs in four stages: approach, close approach, accomplishment, and great accomplishment.

Approach is a way to connect the enlightened bodies, speech, and mind of the wisdom deities who abide in the sphere of phenomena with the ordinary bodies, speech, and minds of us common beings. That connection is established through devotion. By practicing on the basis of devotion, the sādhaka comes to understand his or her three doors to have been the three secrets from the very beginning. In this way, the entire container and contents are realized as naturally pure at the basis.

There is an inverse relationship between an individual's self-grasping and his or her maturation. For example, when one feels sad or depressed, it is a result of self-obsession. However, the moment one meets a loving friend, forgetting the self, one immediately feels better. Due to the power of love, one becomes temporarily free of ego, experiencing the bliss of selflessness. If this is true from an ordinary worldly perspective, how much truer is it for sublime beings? The love that is shared between two close friends, no matter how strong, is still trifling compared to the deity's great love, which extends to all beings and is without measure. Through secret mantra approach and accomplishment, one cultivates a connection with the yidam who abides in the bliss of selflessness. Thus, the four branches reflect the progressive stages in the relationship between the practitioner and the deity who is being practiced. This relationship is based on love.

During approach, the deity is like an acquaintance. First, one must become familiar with the deity, looking at, visualizing, and recognizing his or her form. Gradually, through visualization, supplication, and the recitation of the approach mantra, one becomes better and better acquainted with the deity.

Some people focus only on the number of mantra recitations as the measure of accomplishment. However, instead of calculating the numbers of recitations, one should assess one's degree of familiarity with the development-stage visualizations and mantra. When accomplishment is measured by the degree of habituation, one need not be so concerned with the number of accumulations.

However familiar with the practice one becomes, one will experience a corresponding habituation to the stages of development. During the approach, the main point is to familiarize an extremely fine, subtle mantra strand while reciting the approach mantra. In this regard, Guru Rinpoche taught that the approach involves a visualization like the moon with a garland of stars. This is like imagining a crystal māla upon a moon disk. Just as each bead would be fully illuminated by moonlight, the syllables of the mantra strand are like distinct, tiny stars encircling the periphery of the moon disk. At this stage, the mantra strand does not move. One should accumulate as many hundreds of thousands of recitations as possible while clearly visualizing the radiant syllables of the mantra garland abiding stationary. This, then, is the first stage: that of approach.

Having familiarized oneself again and again in this way, one experiences the second stage, that of close approach. At this juncture, one gives rise to bodhicitta. With it comes some understanding that oneself and the deity are not so different but are like kith and kin, who share the singular basis that is mutual love and affection. This is accompanied by some experience of the transformation of afflictions and impure appearances. It is not as though the development stages involve taking on new perceptions. Rather, they simply transform one's own mistaken, impure notions into pure perceptions of things as they truly are. At this stage, the image of the deity's form arises more naturally and can remain in one's mind with greater ease.

As for the mantra recitation, according to Guru Rinpoche, the close approach involves a visualization like a sparkler's circle, that is, the image that would appear when drawing a quick circle with a lit sparkler in darkness. So, in close approach, the fine mantra strand one has visualized begins to revolve, at first slowly and then progressively faster. Eventually, like the turning blades of an airplane's propeller, the individual syllables can no longer be distinguished. From this there arises the constant drone of the mantra's self-resounding. Although the revolving wheel can no longer be perceived by the eye, the ceaseless hum of the mantra is all-pervading. At this stage, there is no need to focus on the details of the visualization. As one hears the resounding of all outer sounds as mantra, the mind abides in ease and stability.

The sparkler's circle is also used to describe the exchange of the mantra strand between the father and mother consorts. During the recitation, the mantra strand circles between them based on the love and affection they share. Some people think the distinguishing feature of secret mantra is the notion that every practitioner must have a lover. But this is not the point. To beings in samsara who perceive phenomena dualistically in terms of male and female, the father and mother consorts appear separate. The entire macrocosm of samsara arises on the basis of such dualistic perceptions. This samsaric duality plays out microcosmically in the relationship between two lovers.

However, from the ultimate perspective, one can realize the fact of nondual mind on the basis of the divine couple. Even though one perceives the bodies of self and other as two, when one arrives at the actual condition of the mind, there is no duality. The term *bliss-emptiness* means that the essence of the father, bliss, is the essence of the mother, emptiness. The empty sky of the mind is without duality. Although there is the illusory appearance of two bodies, one knows self and other to be inseparable. Thus, the point of the circling of the mantra strand between the couple is to destroy the confusion of dualistic grasping through the unions of bliss-emptiness, clarity-emptiness, and awareness-emptiness. Since the affliction of lust is the nature of bliss-emptiness, aversion, the nature of clarity-emptiness, and delusion, the nature of awareness-emptiness, this circling of the mantra strand undermines samsara itself.

The third stage, accomplishment, is marked by the pacification of self-grasping and certainty about bodhicitta. Through cultivating vast altruism, the mind abides in greater stability. To whatever degree the mind can abide, discriminating intelligence will increase and the mind will become clearer and clearer, causing one to recognize the inseparability of oneself and the deity. Thus, accomplishment involves a feeling of great intimacy. At the ground, one's own mind, the buddha nature, is emptiness. When conjoined with love and compassion, it is the very life force of the deity. Although outwardly oneself and the deity appear in two different aspects, from the ultimate perspective, self and deity are nondual. Thus, free of grasping at duality, one need not visualize the deity as being separate. Rather, self and deity are like two crystal balls perfectly reflecting each other. In this way, one should perceive oneself to be the actual yidam. Together with this perception, one's faith in the Three Jewels naturally increases, as does compassion for sentient ones who do not yet understand cause and effect.

Accomplishment is also characterized by great delight in the recitation of mantra. Guru Rinpoche taught that accomplishment involves emanating and gathering like a king's envoys. At this stage, rainbow-colored light rays emanate outward, giving rise to offering goddesses who make offerings to the pure buddha-fields. During accomplishment, one need not actively visualize the five lights in any deliberate way. Rather, one should know the light rays to be spontaneously present as the five wisdoms' natural radiance; they are not something that needs to be fabricated. For example, if one looks into the sun while squinting to protect the eyes, one will naturally see the light refracted as rainbow colors. If this is experienced even once, it can serve as a reference point that illustrates the five lights' natural radiance. Unlike ordinary light, these light rays appear through the force of one's faith in the buddhas above and one's love and compassion for sentient ones below.

Then, those rays of light return to oneself in the aspects of seed syllables, implements, and deity forms. These are the blessings of the deities' bodies, speech, and mind, which clear away sentient ones' obscurations. One should understand that regardless of which yidam is being practiced, when the wisdom deities are invoked, one is actually inviting the buddhas of the ten directions and three times. So, when making the invitation in the practice of Vajrakumāra, one is invoking all the ten directions' and three times' buddhas in the aspects of Vajrakumāra's divine hosts. Then, when the light rays are gathered back, it is their blessings that subside into the fast-revolving mantra strand. In this way, the four activities are accomplished through the radiating out and gathering back of light rays. Thus, the light rays are like the ministers, envoys, and troops of a powerful king.

What are the actual blessings of enlightened body, speech, and mind? They are all the buddhas' immeasurable bodhicitta and great compassion. At present, one's compassion is very limited in scope. However, when the force of the buddhas' compassion reaches one's mind, it gives rise to immeasurable compassion. The moment its rays of light reach sentient ones, they are suddenly and clearly transformed into the divine hosts of the mandala of Vajrakumāra. Each time one visualizes in this way, sentient ones are guided in stages to more fortunate karmic conditions. Thus, emanating and gathering in the context of accomplishment should be understood in this way.

When accomplishment has become stable over years of practice, the fourth and final stage, that of great accomplishment, manifests. It is marked by the realization of nondual meaning, in which oneself and the deity have become indistinguishably one. The entirety of appearance and existence are known to be the nature of the deity.

The outer container—every world in the universe—is comprised of the five elements, the five great mother-consorts. The inner contents—all sentient ones—are endowed with buddha nature, the basis of buddhahood. When, in a single instant, they have become freed from self-grasping, their afflictions are nothing other than the five wisdoms. Thus, all beings without exception are deities. In this way, the container and contents have truly become the immeasurable palace replete with divine inhabitants. One abides as the principal deity surrounded by the retinue—all sentient ones—within the inconceivably vast palace. Clear, ongoing experience of this is great accomplishment, through which the able potency of the deity becomes manifest. Thus, having achieved the royal seat that is one's own purpose, one becomes capable of accomplishing the purpose of others. Through the four activities, the deities liberate every sentient one into the status of buddhahood, in which all appearances are recognized as the deity and all sounds are perceived as mantra.

As for the mantra recitation in great accomplishment, Guru Rinpoche taught that this final stage is like a beehive broken open. For example, the circling propellers of an airplane's engines cannot be individually distinguished, yet they give rise to a drone that pervades the entire aircraft. Similarly, in great accomplishment, the container and contents reverberate with the self-arisen sound of mantra.

This is like an entire evergreen forest comprised of deities that resounds with the sound of mantra. How can a forest be divine? Although we ordinary beings perceive only trees, the molecules that compose them are actually divine emanations. This point is explicitly made in the practice of Mañjuśrī Yamāntaka, in which the deity's protective spheres are made up of the five elements. These minute particles lack any inherent existence. Every such manifestation of emptiness is the nature of the deity.

Thus, the Yamāntaka text reads, "White wrathfuls wielding water lassos fill the entire space within a swirling sphere of ocean waves."[38] We perceive merely ordinary water. Of course, it is extremely beneficial; it quenches thirst and cleanses. But, in actuality, water is the nature of emptiness. This is the meaning of the tiny wrathful ones; they are the molecular physical expressions of primordial awareness. They are truly emanations of the buddhas. From the perspective of secret mantra, the five elements are inconceivable. They are objects in whom one can cultivate great faith. In this way, in the context of great accomplishment, the rainbowlike outer container of this world is said to be the immeasurable palace. The inner contents, sentient ones, are said to be divine heroes and ḍākiṇīs. Such are the qualities of a single mandala.

If one condenses the meaning of unsurpassed yoga tantra into one point, the outer container of this world—the macrocosm—is complete within one's own body. All the inner contents, sentient beings, are complete within one's own mind. Thus, oneself alone is inexpressible, being beyond description or conception. This recognition of phenomena as being pure at the very basis is the purpose of practices employing the sudden method. This is the meaning of great accomplishment, the intent of the four branches of approach and accomplishment. It is good if one understands these methods of liberation.

These four stages are central to the secret mantra practices of the Earlier System. Their equivalents in the Latter System are the four classes of tantra. Thus, one should understand approach to be action tantra, close approach to be conduct tantra, accomplishment to be yoga tantra, and great accomplishment to be unsurpassed yoga tantra. Although the two systems use different terminology, their basic meanings are the same. As the meditator progresses through the four stages or four classes, there is a corresponding decrease of self-grasping and increase of bodhicitta, discriminating intelligence, and wisdom.

Textual Notes Following the Accomplishment Mantra

After the accomplishment mantra, the following meditation instruction is found in the text:

> When one needs to practice the facing generation, from the beginning, one should open the chamber of recitation and respectively radiate and gather back rays of light. One should engage a back-and-forth recitation, in which the mantra strand emerges from the mouths [of oneself as the father-mother couple, enters] those of the facing generation, [and returns] via the navels or nexus of union. Finally, imagining that the four activities will be accomplished through the rays of white, yellow, red, and green light that radiate therefrom, one engages activities.

As mentioned previously, since the sādhaka focuses only on the self-generation in the secret accomplishment retreat, there is no need for a facing generation. However, if one wishes to give rise to any additional mandala—including a facing mandala—one may do so by "opening the chamber of recitation." Described earlier, this is the special method of unsurpassed yoga tantra, in which a complete mandala is instantaneously projected from the heart of the self-generated deity. Through this means, the mandala suddenly appears in space before one. Thus, it is not necessary to generate the mandalas in stages nor to generate each one individually.

Here, the text says this should be done "from the beginning." This means that one should give rise to any additional mandala with the section of text known as "the recitation of the charm" at the beginning of the approach mantra. Although the text above only mentions the facing generation, one can generate as many mandalas as are needed via the method known as "opening the chamber of recitation."

This "back-and-forth recitation"* involves visualizing the wisdom deity of the facing generation at the center of the facing mandala. He is extremely large, pervading the expanse of space before one. In this context, the self- and facing generations are like crystal balls

*The "back-and-forth recitation" mentioned here is a loanword that comes to Tibetan from the Sanskrit *doli*, meaning "palanquin, stretcher, hammock, or swing." In this context, the swing is a metaphor for the exchange of mantra and light rays between the self- and facing visualizations. The term also has sexual connotations.

infinitely reflecting each other. When the bodhicitta of the facing deities reaches oneself visualized as the yidam, it destroys dualistic grasping and purifies faults. Since it is very difficult to visualize the mantra strand circling between the self- and facing generations and since this visualization is not a feature of the secret accomplishment retreat, it is not necessary to do. It is sufficient merely to think that the mandala of the wisdom deity is always present in the expanse of space. However, for practitioners who understand and wish to do the facing generation, it is fine to engage it.

The Four Nails That Pin the Life Force

The visualized stages of development and recitation of mantras are special methods of uncommon secret mantra practice that are related to the four nails that pin the life force. In this context, the term *nail* means "heart essence" and refers to essentialized methods of practice. These four nails are required to accomplish any sadhana of any deity, whether of the Earlier or Latter System. They are associated with the four branches of approach and accomplishment.

Although the minds of immature sentient ones are veiled by the adventitious stains of self-grasping, at the very basis, their minds and the deity's mind are one. Affliction and suffering characterize the minds of the immature; however, through the practice of these four nails, their minds become occupied with bodhicitta and thus mature into the five wisdoms.

The meaning of all four nails is subsumed within the first one, "the nail of changeless intent," which is the ultimate fruition of the other three. Milarepa referred to it as "the nail of the view," the single ground of both samsara and nirvana. It is the factual meaning that is mahāmudrā. To accomplish it, one should leave the mind in its actual condition, free of grasping at any thought or emotion. This purifies the obscuration of afflictions and the obscuration to knowable things, causing the nail of changeless intent to be realized. Experientially, it is the recognition that one's own mind free of all thoughts—yet endowed with compassion—is the buddha nature.

This ultimate bodhicitta that arises on the basis of conventional bodhicitta is the greatest power imaginable.

Sustaining awareness of the mind's essence, one settles the mind in a nonreferential state. If one is able to abide in undistracted, lucid recollection, even though thoughts and emotions may arise, they will do no harm. Within self-illuminating reflexive awareness, thoughts are liberated on arising.

For example, when one looks at the outer forms of the divine father and mother, since they have two bodies, they appear as two. However, that appearance is only on the relative, fictional level. In truth, since their minds are free of dualistic grasping, they are one. This realization of the ultimate nondual nature of oneself and all beings is the nail of intent. The inner guru, the life force of the deity, is just that. Like the single trunk of a vast tree with many branches, this fundamental buddha nature is the essential point required for practice.

In order for divine forms to appear in the mind, the mind must be free of defilements. For example, although there is only one moon in the sky, if there are a thousand bodies of water on the earth, the moon will be reflected in each of them. When the moon is eclipsed, the thousand reflected moons will also be unseen.

Similarly, the underlying reality of both samsara and nirvana will be known only through understanding the actual condition of the mind. It is taught that the entirety of appearance-existence—samsara and nirvana—should be perceived as the mandala of Vajrakīla. Even though the outer worldly container and the inner sentient contents are manifold, all these diverse appearances have manifested through the mind—through shared and individual karma. The creator of these appearances, the mind-essence that is buddha nature, is devoid of good or bad quality. Thus, the entirety of appearance-existence is known to be one's own mind. Since phenomena lack inherent existence, when grasping at a dualistic reality is torn down, whatever is desired can be imagined. For example, when one closes one's eyes, if there is no grasping at this building, there is no distinction between being indoors or out. Similarly, when practicing the development stages, first one must cultivate this sort of view free of grasping at duality. That is the basis on which the deity can emerge.

With such experience, the mind becomes free of grasping at phenomena as real and true. Even though appearances are unreal, the worldly container and its sentient contents are still perceived. From within this state, the second nail, "the nail of samādhi," or concentration on the body of the deity, emerges. It is the meditation of the development-stage visualizations, which point to the essential meaning of secret mantra—the fundamental purity of container and contents.

By abiding in a mind free of grasping at any object and closing one's eyes, one can roughly give rise to the notion that all beings are Vajrakīla. Likewise, the outer worldly container is made up of the five elements, which are like divine emanations. At the very basis, they are the nature of the five families' mother-consorts. Fundamentally nonexistent, they are emptiness. In this way, the mindstreams of sentient ones are ripened through first transforming ordinary appearances into purity. Then, the nature of that purity is realized as emptiness.

As for the inner contents, when they are perceived impurely, they appear as sentient beings. However, at the ground, the inner contents are primordially pure, since their basis is the buddha nature. It is only due to temporary circumstances that delusions arise in sentient ones. Such adventitious stains are due to thoughts of attachment and aversion that arise from grasping at a self. However, the moment one looks at afflictions' essence, primordial awareness, they disappear. At the very basis, the inner mind of all sentient beings is pure. The outer aggregates and five elements are the primordially pure nature of the five families of victorious ones. Seeing this, one gives rise to the certainty of knowing things as they truly are. This purity is the body of the development-stage deity. The nail of samādhi of the deity, which is connected with the branch of approach, should be understood in this way.

If the development-stage samādhi is like a flame, then the recitation of mantra is like oxygen. This is the third nail, "the nail of the essence mantra." It involves visualizing the seed syllable—together with the revolving mantra strand surrounding it—in the heart center of the thumb-joint-sized sattva. This is the actual point to be meditated upon.

When one has given rise to the clear appearance of the deity and remains undistracted from the mantra visualization, the mind will follow. The body is engaged by telling the beads of the māla. The speech is involved in the actual recitation of mantra. The mind is absorbed in samādhi. In this way, body, speech, and mind abide single-pointedly. By focusing on the mantra strand, the mind remains in its own nature without thoughts arising. One settles in the view that is mahāmudrā. Thus, one should recite the approach mantra within the state uninterrupted by thoughts or emotions. This nail of the essence mantra is connected with the branch of close approach.

Then, when thoughts begin to arise again, one can employ the fourth nail, "the nail of the activities of emanating and gathering." This is done by visualizing the light rays that radiate forth from the revolving mantra strand. Just as a faceted diamond gives off multicolored reflections when struck by sunlight, with the fourth nail, rays of rainbow-colored light emanate outward from one's heart center to all the pure fields. These light rays pervade as far as one's love is vast.

At the tip of each light ray is a god or goddess, each bearing an offering of forms, sounds, smells, tastes, or tactile objects—all the desirables of this world. From each of the gods emanate innumerable others from whom emanate still others. In this way, many generations of emanations infinitely make offerings of the eight auspicious symbols and so forth to all the buddhas. Such offerings are referred to as "offering clouds of Samantabhadra." Once one is habituated to this way of offering, the visualization will spontaneously arise whenever it is needed. In this way, one will become able to imagine vast offering clouds that pervade all the infinite pure fields of the ten directions. Wherever there is space, the mind pervades. Wherever there is mind, such clouds of offerings become manifest.

Then, all the buddhas' blessings and siddhis of body, speech, and mind fall like rain in the forms of diverse seed syllables and merge into oneself, enabling one to fulfill the purpose of all sentient beings. Thus, through the emanating out and gathering back of light rays, the two objectives are accomplished. These activities of emanating and gathering back are associated with the previously described branch of accomplishment.

One should meditate in this way, resting in the view focused on emptiness alone, without thoughts proliferating. Then, when thoughts again begin to arise, one can transform them by turning one's focus to either the development-stage visualization of the deity's body, or the mantra strand, or the emanating and gathering of light rays. In this way, the meditator should alternate among the nail of changeless intent and the other three nails according to arising conditions.

Finally, since the nail of changeless intent is the nondual wisdom of the deity's enlightened mind, it is associated with the branch of great accomplishment. If this single nail is seized, all the other three nails will naturally be mastered. All sights will spontaneously emerge as the deity, appearance-emptiness. All sounds will be heard as mantra, sound-emptiness. All thoughts will be known as awareness-emptiness. Through abiding within the nail of intent, there will be no error, regardless of whether or not one visualizes the development stages. Since it is supreme among meditations, there will be no error even for those who do not imagine the emanating and gathering back of light rays.

These four nails that bind the life force are described in the tantras. However, when they are actually taught, they are explained in the context of the four branches of approach and accomplishment, since their meaning is inseparable from it. Likewise, when one engages the practice of the four nails, it must be done according to the four branches.

Doubting the Qualities and Results of Secret Mantra Practice

Some beginners may question whether there is any power in meditation and visualization since their benefits cannot be seen with the eye. But for those who truly accomplish the practice, there is no doubt whatsoever that the fruition will be made manifest. For example, there are life stories of past knowledge holders of the Vajrakīla lineage who displayed signs of accomplishment such as thrusting their kīlas into stone or having locks of hair that were like tongues of flames.

Although doubters may wonder whether such signs are attainable in the present or if they only appeared in times past, I can personally attest to the efficaciousness of mantric practice. For example, I have met a lama who actually accomplished the fruit of recitation. Having accumulated many mantras for the purpose of alleviating illnesses, now he can cause any object—even his thumb—to become as hot as a branding iron by reciting mantra over it for a couple of minutes. When another person is touched by the object, it will burn and leave scars, even though it does not feel hot to the lama. I have experienced this firsthand when the lama treated me for an illness. The treatment was very healing for me. This is an example of the true blessings of mantra. Such abilities will actually manifest for those who accomplish secret mantra practice. Buddhist or not, there is no one who, having directly observed such powers, will fail to accept them. It is important to be free of doubt about the amazing potency of secret mantra practices. To believe in the possibility of gaining such accomplishment through real practice is the basis for achieving similar results. For this reason, the wise will give rise to belief in the power of the deity and mantra.

The Four Activities

Of the two Vajrakīla mantras, the longer one is for the purposes of accomplishment and engaging activities. Regarding the four activities, one should take extreme care about one point in particular. Whichever activity one engages, it is of primary importance to do it in a state of selflessness. This means one must have as one's objective the purpose of every sentient being. For this reason, those who wish to accomplish the four activities must do only one thing: cultivate compassion. It is through compassion that selflessness is realized. When one's compassion ceases to be about subject and object—when the one who is generating compassion and the one for whom compassion is being generated collapse into one—compassion becomes boundless, as in the four immeasurables of boundless love, compassion, joy, and equanimity. Within these, the four activities that benefit beings are naturally and spontaneously accomplished. Furthermore, just as all five afflictions are complete within one and all five families are complete within one, so too all enlightened activities are present in a single activity.

Thus, there is no need for a sublime being like Vajrakīla to expend any effort to engage the four activities. Rather, they are naturally realized through the power of mind, which is the nondual union of emptiness and compassion. For example, if a great tree is provided with water, its diseases will die and it will flourish, bearing fruit and flowers. Similarly, through the power of the mind that has been nourished by the waters of compassion, illness and affliction will spontaneously be pacified. Wealth, vitality, and abilities will be enriched, and sentient ones will be magnetized by the five perfectly complete sense objects.

Although Vajrakīla's compassion spontaneously accomplishes the four activities, he is perhaps most renowned for destructive activities. In this context, where words such as *harmdoers* and *hostile enemies* often appear in the mantras or the drawings in, benevolence is of particular importance. If one is never separated from love and compassion—even at the cost of life—one will maintain the life force of conduct. For the destructive activities of Yamāntaka and Vajrakīla, this is essential. Otherwise, unmitigated aggression can arise.

When one reads in the liturgy words such as "every harmdoer, oath transgressor, and opportunistic spirit—into this ruddy flesh and blood torma be drawn!" one should not be thinking of the outer physical forms of harmdoers and hostile enemies. Rather, that which is drawn into the torma are the inner afflictions of hatred and jealousy that come from perceiving self and other as two. Thus, the afflictions of oneself and others must be drawn in simultaneously.

Since enemies' hatred and one's own hatred are of a singular nature, Ngülchu Thogme Zangpo says the following in *The Thirty-Seven Practices of Bodhisattvas*:

> When the enemy of one's own aggression has not been tamed, subduing outer enemies will only make them multiply. Therefore, to conquer one's own continuum with the army of love and compassion is the bodhisattvas' practice.[39]

Similarly, in *The Way of the Bodhisattva*, the prince of the conquerors, Śāntideva, says,

> Harmful beings are everywhere like space itself.
> Impossible it is that all should be suppressed.
> But let this angry mind alone be overthrown,
> and it's as though all foes had been subdued.[40]

Due to ignorance, sentient ones grasp at the notion of killing embodied enemies. However, knowing hatred to be the greatest enemy of the mind, the enlightened ones slay hatred. Even if one were to kill another, one would not eliminate that person's mind. That individual would again take form and do harm to one. For this reason, the practitioner should slay his or her own afflictions and dualistic grasping.

In brief, hatred cannot be overcome by hatred. It can only be slain by love and compassion. Destructive activities should be understood in this way.

Offering the Charm

Toward the end of the session, after the recitation of both mantras has been completed, the Sanskrit vowels and consonants are chanted to compensate for all the errors in one's recitation of the practice text and mantras—excesses, omissions, interruptions, and mispronunciations. Next, through the hundred-syllable mantra of Vajrasattva,[41] one purifies all wrong or mistaken actions and confesses the heedlessness and afflictions that have arisen during the practice. As for the afflictions, they are purified through meditation itself. Third, one recites the essence of dependent relations,[42] a statement declaring Lord Buddha's exposition of karmic causality.

Then, in offering the charm, one makes offering and praise, discloses, and supplicates with the following lines:

HŪṂ. Glorious Great Kīla's divine hosts, come!
We make offerings—outer, inner, and
secret—and extol your attributes,
activities, bodies, speech, and mind!
Heedlessness, confusion, transgressions,
breaches, and impairments we disclose.
Lovingly and with compassion, please
think of us and grant accomplishments!

Although with these words one discloses and amends faults in the practice and offers all the virtue of one's practice, the actual offering of the charm is taking place continually during the mantra recitations and particularly during the *kaṭaṅkaṭe*, the accomplishment mantra.

The outer, inner, and secret offerings referred to here are exactly as described in the restoration ritual with these words:

. . . outer offerings, massed enjoyment clouds,
inner offerings, strewn desirables,
secret offerings, dance of the *rigma*.

The bliss of the sādhaka is simultaneously experienced by all the deities in the channels and cakras as well as by all those in the mandala. The actual offering of the charm—the secret offering—is just that.

Subsequent Rites

Offering and Praise

On each day of the secret accomplishment retreat, the subsequent rites should be practiced at the end of the third session of the day and again at the third session of the night.

If one wishes to understand the qualities of the deity to be practiced, they are clarified in this praise in the subsequent rites:

> HŪṀ. All the ten directions' and three times'
> buddhas' unified activities
> rise up as your body of great force!
> Praise and homage—Kīla deity,
> māra tamer with changeless and firm
> body void of aging or decline!

Every buddha of the ten directions and three times is complete within the divine wisdom deity. A single deity is pervaded by all the buddhas.

The dharmakāya and saṁbhogakāyas are the pure factor of enlightened manifestation. Nirmāṇakāyas appear among beings of the six classes and manifest both purely and impurely. The sentient beings to be subdued and the virtuous friends who subdue them are all the same in that they are all human beings appearing together in this worldly plane. All the sentient ones to be subdued are pure at the very basis. This is taught in *The Aspiration of Samantabhadra*.

Having realized primordial awareness-rigpa—the fact of the state beyond birth and death—one becomes an immortal knowledge holder. This is the mastery of reflexive rigpa—the actual Vajra Youth who is "void of aging or decline."

Disclosing Wrongs

One must know with certainty the connection between oneself—the practitioner—and the deity to be practiced. Because there are many different schools of thought with diverse views, some people give rise to doubts, wondering whether deities exist or not, whether the deity is just a ruse, and so forth. But there is no need for confusion. This question is definitively resolved by buddha nature. Since time without beginning, one's mind that is the buddha nature—the cause—has been the same as the mind of Vajrakumāra. This point is clarified in the disclosure:

> From the start we've been inseparable,
> yet whate'er declines, nonvirtues, breaks,
> breaches, and confusions I've amassed
> through confused ignoring while I've roamed
> in samsara, I disclose them and
> lay them down with full remorse and shame.

Instead of merely reciting these words, one should deeply reflect on their meaning. This is something that cannot be done by relying on Tibetan transliteration alone. In order to gain experience, one must conjoin one's recitation with an understanding of the meaning.

The text says, "From the start we've been inseparable." Thus, when the singular basis of one's own mind and the deity's mind has been understood, whatever samsaric confusion one experiences is a result of having temporarily forgotten the sameness of oneself and the deity. Although one's mind is veiled by adventitious stains, those stains are nothing more than self-grasping and afflictions. Apart from them, the basis is singular. The mind that is buddha nature itself, when not recognized, is consciousness. When the actual condition of the mind is realized, that same consciousness goes by the names "mahāmudrā" and "dzogchen." This is the fundamental actuality of the mind—the naked, ordinary awareness utterly free of thoughts. In brief, this clean mind is the view. Whoever has understood the clean mind knows it to be the sky-like union of clarity and emptiness completely free of the faults of permanence and nihilism.

It is within that very sphere that the wisdom deities continually abide. Thus, it is said, "All the conquerors are one within the sphere of primordial awareness."[43] What is that oneness? We posit space as an example, since it is without center or limits, birth or death, or decline from aging. When one looks inward at the actual condition of the mind and understands there to be no distinction between the clear, empty mind and space, one will know its primordial nature. This is the meaning of the words "From the start we've been inseparable."

Once the essence of consciousness has been seen, that itself is nondual with the mind of the deity. The singular continuum of sentient ones and the buddhas is like the one strand that binds together the beads of a māla. Even so, beings are yet unaware of this buddha nature. Perceiving everywhere the duality of self and other, not realizing the actual condition of the mind, they experience the confusion of ignorance. On the basis of that, the six poisonous afflictions emerge, causing suffering births among the six classes of wayfarers. Thus, beings conditionally wander within samsara like ice floes in the vast ocean. This is what is meant by the words "confused ignoring while I've roamed in samsara."

One should consider how one's experience became dualistic in the first place. Even though the mind is like space, one habitually grasps at that which is selfless as though it were a self. So, by grasping at an "I," one has fabricated a self out of that which inherently lacks self. However, this is a mere fiction. In actuality, the mind is utterly devoid of self.

With the disclosure, one is declaring, "Today, I have finally understood that all my confused actions have resulted from not recognizing that I have buddha nature." In this way, the disclosure expresses the very heart of one's connection with the deity.

In order to purify the confused habits of dualism, one must disclose and lay aside the karma one has accumulated and the obscurations arisen from suffering and afflictions—the seeds of rebirth in the six realms. Self-grasping is the dwelling place of all of these. Since bodhicitta is the supreme antidote to grasping at an "I," it is the king among all methods of disclosure. To scatter self-grasping severs the root of the six afflictions. For this reason, the heart of all Buddhist practice is bodhicitta. All the eighty-four thousand collections of Dharma are included within bodhicitta. Thus, even more than disclosing "declines, nonvirtues, breaks, breaches, and confusions," the sādhaka is confessing and laying aside self-grasping through his or her commitment to cultivate bodhicitta.

Immediately following the disclosure, one again recites the Sanskrit alphabet, the hundred syllables, and the essence of dependent relations.

The Departure or Request to Remain

After these amending recitations, one should mentally draw all the wisdom deities together into the sole principal wisdom deity. Then, one supplicates him with the following words:

> Though you've dwelt in cyclic existence
> here with this support, please duly grant
> life without disease, the wealth of power,
> in addition to all things supreme!
> OṀ SUPRA TIṢṬHA VAJRĀYA SVĀHĀ.

When a statue, thangka, or other representation of the deity has been used as a material support for practice, one supplicates the deity to continue to abide within that representation. Otherwise, if one has been practicing without the support of a deity image, one should simply imagine that the only remaining visualized wisdom deity now merges back into the unborn sphere.

Gathering In

The extremely profound completion stage of Vajrakīla is expressed in the following lines:

> All-pervading mercy's hosts divine
> merge into the nature—five lights' sphere.

Clear, complete enjoyment, rainbow light,
contents and container now subside
into dharmakāya's vast expanse.

The sky-like dharmakāya is the mind that is inexpressible, being beyond description or concept. Although space is empty, it is pervaded by vast love. The words "all-pervading mercy's hosts divine" refer to the fact that rainbowlike saṁbhogakāya wisdom deities spontaneously appear from within the dharmakāya and pervade everywhere through the power of love and compassion. Thus, the dharmakāya is the empty factor and the saṁbhogakāya the clarity factor.

This verse points to the actual accomplishment of the deity, who is endowed with knowing wisdom, loving compassion, the activities of enlightened action, and the able force that gives protection. His form is visible yet insubstantial, like a rainbow.

Knowledge manifests as the omniscient wisdom that comprehends the sufferings of all others. Loving compassion spontaneously arises for all who have not yet realized the nature of mind. The activities of enlightened action are the capacity of the deity to destroy the grasping of those who supplicate him. Able force comes from the altruistic mind, which overcomes self-grasping. The powerful altruism of the deity is established through the union of immeasurable compassion with rigpa. When this is understood, one gives rise to certainty. On that basis, faith and belief in cause and effect become unshakable.

The line "merge into the nature—five lights' sphere" should be understood in the following way: Ever present in the sky, the saṁbhogakāya deities are continually arising out of space and dissolving back into it. Whenever one recalls the deities, they are present. If one wants them now, they are here right now. In actuality, they continually pervade the entire space-like dharmakāya, manifesting as the cloud-like saṁbhogakāyas, from which appear rain-like nirmāṇakāyas. Thus, without effort or fabrication, the three kāyas naturally and spontaneously arise from and dissolve back into one another.

This was expressed by Protector Jigten Sumgön in one of his vajra songs: "Without center or bounds, you pervade all phenomena in the vast sky, the glorious dharmasphere."[44] Thus, there is no place the dharmakāya does not pervade, including one's own buddha nature.

At the time of gathering in, the development-stage visualizations, which have appeared like rainbows, simply return to their source. One should look inward at the mind's essence. By one's doing so, all those rainbow appearances of divine saṁbhogakāya hosts—the entire mandala of the deity—will naturally subside into the principal, who then melts into rainbow light and vanishes into the dharmakāya-sky. Looking nakedly at the mind free of thought, one will see that there is no distinction between mind and space.

Stated another way, the deity is like a saṁbhogakāya wave that has arisen out of the vast ocean of the dharmakāya. In the completion stage, the development-stage deity instantaneously returns, merging back into his place of origin. Within the expanse of the dharmakāya, all deities are one. In the saṁbhogakāya expanse, different deities rise like waves to perform various activities that benefit beings. This is the outer level of understanding.

Its inner corollary is that when the mind looks at itself, all appearances subside into the view. The moment thoughts and afflictions arise, they are recognized through mindfulness. With recognition, they perish. When one see's the mind's actual condition, remaining in the depths of the kīla of primordial awareness-rigpa, every thought is self-mastered. Even though there are many tens of thousands of mental arisings, they all have but one nature. The method for conquering just one of them is the method for conquering them all. Like a great fire that consumes everything, this is the principal among the four kīlas, the actual Vajrakumāra. In this way, development and completion are both the mind; the difference is in the shining forth or merging back.

As for the line "clear, complete enjoyment, rainbow light," the scriptures refer to the "bhagavan buddha—personification of the three kāyas."[45] All buddhas are the same in that they have become inseparable from space. Like the reflections from a diamond in a ray of sunlight, the saṁbhogakāyas spontaneously manifest as the buddhas of the five families. Their various colors arise as the five wisdoms' natural forms. The words "complete enjoyment" point to their actual pure-field realm—indestructible, rainbowlike clarity and emptiness.

Usually, one thinks that the phenomena of this human life are real, whereas the pure realms must be insubstantial. This is a great delusion! Tomorrow when one dies, other than the bondage of one's grasping at the outer container and inner contents as being real and true, there will be nothing at all remaining of this life's appearances. Like rainbows, all phenomena are composite and impermanent in nature. The moment body and mind have separated, the bardo consciousness will appear in its rainbowlike natural form.

The last Tibetan line of the gathering in is "*nö chü chö kü long du-o*," which means

> ...contents and container now subside
> into dharmakāya's vast expanse.

Although one generally dissolves the mandala in stages, in this practice it is also appropriate to gather the entirety of appearance-existence into the dharmasphere in a single instant, just as it is suitable to cause the complete mandala to appear out of emptiness in one moment.

This points to the ultimate lack of inherent existence of self, others, the container that is this world, and its sentient contents—all of which are nothing other than the yidam's mandala. When all these appearances subside into the dharmakāya, one recognizes things as they truly are. Directly experiencing the nonconceptual mind, one will perceive all phenomena as inseparable from space. In the Tibetan, there is a final "o" sound at the end of this line indicating that there is no distinction between that which subsides and that into which it subsides. The perceiving mind and that which is perceived are nondual. This is the union of appearance-emptiness at the very basis. Thus, it is said,

> This primordial awareness is exceedingly subtle and equal to space, the adamantine essence. It is tranquility, the furthest limit of immaculacy. Although yourself, you are also your father.[46]

Here, the words "exceedingly subtle" refer to a state in which mind, phenomena, and space cannot be distinguished. Since the mind is the perceiver of phenomena as well as the perceived phenomenon, the object and its source are one. Since both the seer and the seen are the mind, the child is also the father. Within the mind's sky-like expanse, there is neither a grasping mind nor grasped-at objects. This is the meaning of nonduality. With such realization of singularity, one attains the ground of the vajra master—the ground that is Vajradhara.

If beginners cannot conceive of this, another method is to deconstruct the visualization in stages, first imagining the entire mandala as a substantial entity, then imagining that its solidity gradually fades into radiant light. Thereafter, one can gather the visualization together in stages, from the outside in, until it merges into oneself as the divine couple in union. Then, the mother-consort dissolves into the father, who then subsides into the syllable HŪṂ̐ at the heart, which disappears from the bottom up. Finally, through the power of buddha nature, the mind of great love and compassion that is Vajrakumāra pervades everywhere. Free of any shape or color, it liberates self-grasping. So, at the time of the completion stage, everything becomes like ice melting into the vast ocean, just as, in the future, all appearing phenomena will become one—nondual and empty. It is entirely suitable to visualize the dissolution in this manner.

After the verse of gathering in has been recited, a bell is rung. With the first strike, all thoughts are thoroughly severed and the mind naturally becomes space-like clarity and emptiness. One recognizes this to be the actual condition of the mind, which is the same as the dharmakāya. At this juncture, one should think of nothing whatsoever. In this regard, it is said in the introduction to mahāmudrā, "Not pondering things in the mind, look at resolved truth."[47] Having suspended all mental arisings, one should regard the sky-like mind of clarity and emptiness. That itself is the fundamental view. Although there are many aspects to the stages of development and completion, the final completion stage is to place the mind within that view. By again and again releasing all dualistic grasping into nondual wisdom, one will habituate the basic unity of samsara and nirvana, happiness and suffering, self and other. Meditators must gain this sort of experience.

Then, with the final bell strike, one reemerges in the form of the HŪṂ syllable or the deity. This is the meaning of the terms "gathering and reemergence" (*dudang*). This momentary placement of the mind in the view and sudden emergence of the deity is the instantaneous union of development and completion. In this way, the union of appearance-emptiness and the union of development-completion must be practiced together in a single instant.

Dedication

At the conclusion, one gives rise to a mind of dedication, reciting,

> Having changed and made complete the two
> gatherings massed throughout the three times through
> my and others' bodies, speech, and minds,
> they're transferred for great reality.
> May the fruit—nondual essence—be gained!

Here, the text speaks of the "two gatherings," or two accumulations, of merit and wisdom. As for the accumulation of merit, now and in the past oneself and others have had mixed positive, negative, and neutral motivations for accumulating even a single virtue. In addition, it goes without saying that countless past and present virtues have not even been dedicated.

So, first one must "change," or transform, past and present virtues by bringing one's former motivations into accord with the path that leads to the buddhas' status. Also, since it is unknown whether one will have mixed pure and impure motivations in the future, it is appropriate to dedicate now all those virtues that have not yet been accumulated.

Second, one must "make complete" all the three times' virtues by sealing them with emptiness. This is nothing other than the accumulation of wisdom. In this regard, *The Sutra of the Three Heaps* says, "Just as the past bhagavan buddhas fully dedicated, just as those bhagavan buddhas not yet come will fully dedicate, and just as those bhagavan buddhas now present fully dedicate, so too shall I fully dedicate."[48]

Among the three strengths, the transformation of the merit accumulation is related to the strength of one's intention and the strength of the tathāgatas. The second point, making virtues complete, signifies the strength of the sphere of dharmas, which is inherently pure and inconceivable. This is the wisdom accumulation referred to in the dedication prayers of the Drigung Kagyü as "this existent root of virtue."[49]

Having dedicated or transferred all the accumulations of merit and wisdom in this way, one makes the aspiration "May the fruit—nondual essence—be gained!" The final fruition of the two accumulations is buddhahood, the primordial awareness free of dualistic grasping.

By dedicating merit with genuine loving-kindness and compassion for sentient beings, one merges one's aspiration with the intent of the buddhas of the three times. The entire realization of all the buddhas is dedicated for the welfare of others. Because one is not alone in the generation of bodhicitta and dedication, one should have no doubt that one's practice will benefit all beings. The dedication based on this shared intent is like a drop of water cast into the ocean. No matter how small it may be, it merges with and becomes a part of the vast whole.

The Prayer of Auspiciousness

The Bhagavan Buddha said, "Sentient ones are the very nature of buddhas."[50] That point has already been resolved. Sentient beings exist, yet they are not merely ordinary. All of samsara, nirvana, and the buddhas' three kāyas are included within every sentient one. Thus, the view of secret mantra is that phenomena are pure from the very basis. This same meaning can be found in the prayer of auspiciousness that appears at the conclusion of the liturgy. It begins,

> OṂ. May auspicious, spontaneous vastness
> of primally pure dharmakāya...

The dzogchen teachings, especially, speak of primordial purity. That which has been pure since time without beginning is the buddha nature, the mind itself. It is the mind of all sentient ones of the three planes of existence. That mind is the empty dharmakāya.

Where is the dharmakāya? To find it, one must look inward at one's own mind. Thoughts and emotions emerge in the mind like the countless dust particles that are seen in a ray of sunlight. Yet those things that appear and the sphere in which they appear are like various reflections mirrored in a looking glass. The mind is just that. When no thought or emotion at all arises, one abides in the clear, empty essence of mind, which is like a transparent crystal.

It is said that the dharmakāya is like space. This is the buddha nature, the single basis underlying both samsara and nirvana.

With regard to the saṁbhogakāya, the text continues,

> ...ĀḤ. be present in luminosity's
> self-born state, the sambhogakāya!

This body of complete enjoyment is endowed with the quality of luminosity. So, although the buddha nature is empty in essence, its nature is clarity. Due to the samsaric, dualistic grasping that sees self and other as separate, one does not perceive it at present. However, by giving rise to love and measureless compassion, one can experience selflessness, which causes the mind to become extremely clear. Within that clear luminosity, one perceives the incalculable saṁbhogakāya forms and pure fields, which have come into existence through compassion. This is the unity of emptiness and compassion.

Those who do not recognize it may wonder, "Where is this luminosity?" For those who have not seen it, it manifests as consciousness—the clear, aware quality of mind that engages worldly activities, thinking thoughts like "I need to do that. I want to eat or drink this. That is an actual fact." It is what distinguishes self from other. It is also the clear thinking involved in analysis and scientific inquiry. Until luminosity is realized, it manifests in this way as ordinary consciousness.

When both seeing and not seeing become equalized, it is as stated in the text:

> HŪṂ. May auspicious tamers of beings, the
> manifold nirmāṇakāya forms...

Diverse nirmāṇakāyas have both pure and impure aspects commingled. This is understood by all those virtuous friends who perceive the mind's nature. Through the view, they give introduction to those who have not yet seen the view. First, they introduce karma, cause and effect, love, and compassion. Thereafter, the disciple can see the fact of emptiness on his or her own. That which is called "emptiness" should be understood as the nonduality of self and other. Such is luminosity. As soon as dualistic grasping arises and phenomena are perceived as two, luminosity is absent.

The six classes of beings, all sentient ones, are included within the "manifold nirmāṇakāya forms" referred to in the text. These inhabitants of the six realms are the ones to be subdued. Those who do the subduing are the six *munis*.[51] Through their skill, they guide beings in the stages of the paths of individual liberation, bodhisattvas, and secret mantra.

The term "manifold" means that nirmāṇakāyas appear in infinitely diverse ways. Born nirmāṇakāyas are gurus, virtuous friends, physicians, and the like. In order to reveal the path, they take on the forms of each of the six realms' beings, appearing as animals in the animal realm and so forth. For example, in this human realm, born nirmāṇakāyas introduce deity sadhanas and mantras, bestow empowerment, and grant practice instructions and transmissions.

Created nirmāṇakāyas appear as statues, paintings, and other deity images. When looking at statues and thangkas, some people merely regard their material attributes, thinking, "This is metal. That is cloth." Such a view is completely mistaken. For those who know how to practice, created nirmāṇakāyas are no different from actually manifest deities.

In this regard, Protector Jigten Sumgön said, "Even false, fictional [appearances] serve a purpose."[52] So, although some may think an image is just a drawing—a false representation of the actual deity—there are accomplished masters, such as Jowo Atiśa, to whom thangkas and statues directly and repeatedly spoke. It is only due to doubts and perverted views that one remains oblivious to the qualities of created nirmāṇakāyas. Even if the deity himself or herself were standing right next to such a person, he or she would go unrecognized. For example, although His Holiness the Dalai Lama is an actual emanation of Avalokita, there are people who perceive him as ordinary.

Those who wish to practice sadhana must first rely on created nirmāṇakāyas to become acquainted with the form of the deity. They look at an image and, on that basis, the deity's form arises in the mind. For the image merely to appear in the mind is extremely powerful. As the self-radiance of dharmatā, such peaceful and wrathful deities arise in the bardo for all beings. Those who have become habituated to them in life will recognize them as refuges—as the self-manifesting forms of bodhicitta—during the bardo. Those who have not will perceive them as terrifying and threatening. So, when viewing images of the deity, even though the clarity, purity, and stability of the development stages may not yet have become fully manifest, one can still give rise to some devotion. Because they create the conditions for one to recognize the deity in the bardo, such created representations are extremely precious.

Even if one has at home a buddha statue as tiny as a thumb joint, one should consider it to be the actual body of the buddha and should repeatedly think, "This buddha is the owner of my home and everything in it." By applying the antidote of mentally offering one's body, possessions, and enjoyments, one will become free of self-grasping. Such is the power of created nirmāṇakāyas that appear in the mind.

Furthermore, since the five elements themselves are among the diverse nirmāṇakāya manifestations, all those sentient ones to be subdued are merely circumstantially confused. For example, when one sees an animal, one usually perceives it as a mere animal. However, someone who understands the Dharma will know that that being was born in such an animal form due to karma. If one considers a poisonous snake, under the circumstantial influence of karma and propensities, that being has taken a body that is the natural expression of aversion. Despite this, the buddha nature of that snake can never go to waste. It is not subject to birth or death. Once negative karma has been exhausted, that being will eventually attain buddhahood. Knowing this, one can understand the perspective of secret mantra.

In this way, every peril and suffering experienced by beings is just such a circumstantial arising. The text mentions "auspicious tamers of beings, the manifold nirmāṇakāya forms." This means that one who aspires to tame wayfaring beings must be able to eliminate their suffering. The method for accomplishing this is to subdue one's own self-grasping. The principal subduers of self-grasping are love and compassion. Thus, the text reads,

> . . . HRĪḤ. be present as skill in loving means
> in the state of [beings'] compassion!

It is important to understand the meaning of these final two lines. Although I myself have none of the qualities that come from having studied, since I believe in cause and effect, I have great trust in the pure deities and in bodhicitta. My belief in the pure buddha-fields is unwavering. Since I have considered well the attributes of bodhicitta, the existence of buddha-fields is entirely plausible to me.

It is taught that on the basis of aversion and hostility, the hell realms come into being. So it is that the animal and human realms visible to us have also been shaped by stupidity and desire, respectively. Because of this, I trust that all the forms of the six realms' beings are the natural expressions of their afflictions. Just as the samsaric appearances of the six realms have become manifest through affliction, so too have the buddhas' pure fields come about through the power of their bodhicitta. In this regard, Protector Jigten Sumgön taught, "Cause and effect are embodiments of momentary thoughts."[53]

One who believes this must give rise to belief in love and compassion. The entire spiritual heap of the eighty-four thousand Dharmas—the complete words of the Buddha—is subsumed within the root that is bodhicitta. The Buddhist view for self and others is bodhicitta, or *jangchub sem* in Tibetan. *Jang* means to "clear out" or "purge." *Chub* means to "have complete and perfect mastery" of something. These two terms together are translated as "enlightenment." When conjoined with *sem*, they refer to the "mind of enlightenment."

That which must be purged is the self-cherishing mind. When this has been accomplished, benevolence—the wish to benefit others—will arise. Then, even though one must do physical activities for one's own sake, the mind will have gained perfect mastery of benevolence, becoming stable—firmly planted like the footstep of an elephant. To have loving-kindness and compassion, with the patience to maintain them—this is what I request of you Dharma friends.

Henceforth and until buddhahood is attained, the deity who is the form of love and compassion abides with the sādhaka. The yidam deity is the supreme companion. As the deity is the natural expression of love and compassion, one should understand these two to be the actual deity. For this reason, no matter what, one must have one deity and one mantra to rely on.

Although skillful means can be defined in many ways, in brief, it is compassion—the counterpart to emptiness. In other contexts, it manifests as bliss. Thus, the significance of the "skill in loving means" mentioned in the prayer of auspiciousness is that anyone who has great love will be endowed with corresponding great skill in benefiting sentient ones. Just as a mother's love makes her skillful at nurturing her child, so too the buddhas' love and compassion make them unrivaled in benefiting sentient ones.

Summary of Deity Yoga

In brief, from one's entry into the Buddhist path and henceforth, whichever practice one does, whichever tenet system one follows, whichever Dharma one cultivates, as long as it is engaged with love and compassion, it will become authentic Dharma. Understanding this, one can discern with confidence whether one's practice is the true Dharma. If so, it will benefit both self and others. It will accomplish one's own purpose, which is attainment of the higher existences along the way and, ultimately, attainment of the buddhas' status. Through these, one will spontaneously bring benefit to others.

There is no great difference among deities and tenet systems. Even though there are many different deity forms, the single life force of them all is love and compassion. For one who has these in one's mindstream and understands them to be the deity's life force, it is sufficient merely to recall the deity and to recite his or her mantra. You Dharma companions, please practice in this way.

Regarding the confidence of divine pride, there are some quotes from the Mañjuśrī Yamāntaka literature that are relevant for Vajrakīla practitioners. The Yamāntaka liturgy says, "Appearance-existence, samsara and nirvana have arisen from me"[54] and also, "As I am all the buddhas' timeless awareness, I abide in their mind."[55] The entire meaning of divine pride is complete in these two lines alone. The buddhas' primordial awareness is free of duality, like the expanse of space. Thus, it is said, "All the conquerors are one within the sphere of primordial awareness."[56] By realizing the view, one will settle this point for oneself.

The following lines can be found in the Yamāntaka praise known as *Great Bliss, Supreme Means*:

> May those like myself who dwell in samsara's darkness,
> glimpsing but fragmented light rays of the Ārya's love,
> reach awakening by offering this praise with devotion,
> naturally fulfilling our own and others' aim![57]

This glimpse of the radiance of the exalted one's love is also referred to in the *Taking Up Accomplishments* text of Vajrakīla:

> From the glorious knot within your heart
> dawns primordial wisdom's secret sun
> on the bodies, speech, and minds of us
> yogins, great sādhakas, SIDDHI HOḤ!

The dawning of the secret sun of primordial awareness is the heart essence of all the methods of accomplishing Vajrakīla. Unlike the earthly dawn, it is utterly without reference point. It occurs only once. Thereafter, it is known—stable and unchanging. This is nothing other than what Protector Jigten Sumgön meant in his *Song on Realizing Fivefold Mahāmudrā*, in which he sang, "Unless your own body, king of divine forms, has seized the immutable seat—the basis—the retinue of mother-ḍākiṇīs will not gather 'round."[58]

In the practice of secret mantra, the deity only becomes manifest on the basis of that stable, immutable seat. That seat is Vajradhara, the changeless ground on which thoughts and afflictions have been destroyed. In this regard, Jigme Lingpa spoke the following words to the wisdom ḍākiṇī:

> As long as aware knowing does not lose its autonomy, nothing more than this is needed. Though one may encounter a hundred revered experts, a thousand siddhas, ten thousand *lotsawas* and

> paṇḍitas, a hundred thousand pith instructions, and a billion treatises, one need not doubt. SAMAYA DHA THIM.[59]

Although others will not see it, the immutable basis is just that. The royal seat is just there. One must determine for oneself whether or not one has seized it.

CHAPTER 5

White Torma Offering Instructions

I included the white torma offering text as a supplement to the practice manual. Since it is extremely important to understand the meaning rather than just to mimic Tibetan sounds, it has been translated for recitation in English. The white torma offering is particularly necessary when sādhakas must consecrate a new place for Buddhist practice. Meditators should understand that the local deities, earth goddesses, and landholding spirits of mountains, waters, and the five elements have been there long before one arrived and will be there long after one has departed.

Secret mantra sadhanas must absolutely be practiced in places where the Dharma has never been heard before. When such new places are being consecrated, nonhumans may cause hindrances for practitioners. These are beings whose experience with humans may be limited to contact with people who were too self-absorbed even to be aware of their existence. Thus, from a worldly perspective, the white torma offering is a sign of civility—an acknowledgment of the landholders and their circumstances—and an offering made with kindness. Through practicing the generosity of the white torma and smoke offerings, sādhakas allay the doubts of nonhumans and fulfill their wishes through bodhicitta, thus dispelling obstacles to the practice.

Even those humans who are aware and who know to make offerings often approach landholders with a materialistic or transactional attitude. For example, when people are undertaking a construction project, they commonly think they should offer the white torma as a means of communicating, "I need to erect a building here, so don't give me any trouble!" But that is not the purpose at all! What one is accomplishing with the white torma and golden libation offerings is far more profound than that.

The ritual begins with cleansing and refining the offerings through mantra, mudrā, and meditation. One imagines a vast jeweled vessel containing the torma, which transforms into nectar and is then consecrated with the three syllables. Next, one summons the earth goddesses and other landholders, offering them seats. Then, one makes the initial offering of the torma and the outer offerings.

The recipients of these offerings, the holders of many different kinds of places, are diverse in their names, forms, characteristics, and activities. Some of them are extremely long-lived. Others hold great wealth and power. Still others are timid, withdrawing and hiding as soon as humans appear. A few of these beings are listed in the text:

> HŪṂ. Gods, *nāgas*, kinglies, furies, harmdoers,
> planetary spirits, smell eaters,
> aquarians, demons, men-or-whats,
> carnivores, *mātarīs*, bulbous ones,
> *mu* demons, receptacle girls, and
> urban flesh eaters with female ghosts,
> local gods and lords of regions and
> places, treasures, wealth, and all the rest,
> bands of spirits, elementals, gods,
> all lay folk who keep commands and oaths—

Among these, bulbous ones are a type of preta with short, rounded bodies. They experience gain and loss in games of chance. Receptacle girls are like beggars who hold out a container to receive offerings. Perhaps they are prostitutes. Although it is not necessary to know about each of these different types of beings, a bit of understanding can help in relating to them with compassion.

These beings experience great suffering and hardship. Through the ritual, one assures them that one is practicing in order to accomplish their purpose. Thus, from a spiritual perspective, the main point of the white torma is to approach the landholders with a mind of love and compassion, wishing to clear away their circumstantial sufferings and the hardships of all beings. Since one is not motivated by one's own aims, the practice is really for the sake of the country, the land, and its inhabitants. Thus, the text says,

> ...as you take this golden libation
> and torma comprised of all things clean,
> harmful, wicked thoughts are pacified.
> Thus, always be my wholesome allies.
> In this country's lands and regions, I
> practice unsurpassed supreme *bodhi*
> and make effort for sentient ones' sake.
> Thus, make my conditions favorable!

Although the material offering appears in the form of a torma, one should understand that it actually emerges as whatever diverse offerings will please the local deities. The same is true of the golden libation, which has traditionally been a small vessel of beer or tea, sometimes garnished with shavings of pure gold. Regardless of the outer appearances of these offerings, their nature is bodhicitta. It isn't that one bribes the landholders not to do harm by offering them gifts. Rather, one wins them over through the force of bodhicitta that accomplishes the purpose of all sentient ones, themselves included. For this reason, one must have completely pure intentions from the bottom of one's heart to benefit the land and its inhabitants.

Since the earth lords can clearly perceive people's motivations, they understand when beings give rise to conventional bodhicitta. They recognize the intentions that accord with their own aims. Similarly, when practitioners are insincere, merely mouthing the words of the text without pure intent, this too is obvious to them.

The white torma offering text concludes with the following aspirations:

Steadfast earth goddesses and the like,
earth lords' kings with ministers and courts—
as you take this golden libation
and torma comprised of all things clean,
these, my wished-for hopes, will be fulfilled.
Neither bothered, nor begrudging, nor
jealous, please provide me this ground of
precious treasures! Actualize all hopes
and accomplish aspirations, please!
Bring forth my activities' results!

When, with loving-kindness, sādhakas assure the earth goddesses and holders of the land that our purpose is to free them from suffering, they feel delighted. The natural consequence of that delight is that they become allies, helping and supporting practitioners' work. As one chants the words and offers the white torma with pure motivation, they receive bodhicitta into their mindstreams through the buddhas' blessings. If practitioners hold on to the view of "making effort for sentient ones' sake," the meaning and purpose of the peaceful torma offering will be achieved.

CHAPTER 6

Kīla Consecration Instructions

Composed by Jamgön Kongtrül Lodrö Thaye and drawn from the extensive sadhana, the text *Consecration of the Material Kīla Mandala: The Development Stages of the Foremost Prince* is endowed with great blessing. It describes the means of sanctifying the implement, which is known in Sanskrit as *kīla* (*phurba*). In general, the term refers to a sharpened stake or peg that can be driven into the ground to secure a tent or to tether an animal. By extension, it also refers to self-arisen or man-made ritual daggers.

The Implement, the Material Kīla

Having cultivated the clear appearance of the deity through the development stages, the sādhaka then utilizes the kīla of the four activities, through which he or she can benefit all beings. On the surface, this kīla of the four activities is the kīla of the Foremost Prince, which is created with material substances like metal or wood. This consecrated implement, often referred to as the "compounded, material kīla," is required as an accomplishment-support for the practice of Vajrakīla.

Different sorts of created kīlas—the materials and ways of fashioning them, the types of beings who should create them, the various colors, sizes, shapes, and markings necessary for different activities, and so forth—are extensively detailed in the Vajrakīla literature. These diverse attributes of the material kīla symbolize the inner qualities of the deity's mind and the outer activities through which he benefits sentient ones.

In addition, the texts explain in depth the appropriate means of consecrating the different kinds of implements—the requisite substances, meditations, visualizations, and retaining mantras for the approach and accomplishment of each type. Each kīla of the four activities is said to require certain causes and to have eleven characteristics. Although it is not possible for me to elaborate on all of these details here, it is good if practitioners have a general appreciation of the scope of this practice. Thus, I would like to give a brief introduction to the kīlas of the four activities.

The Pacifying Kīla

First is the pacifying kīla, which should be fashioned from the basic material of silver, white sandalwood, or other white wood. It is eight fingerbreadths in height. Below the handle, it is shaped like a peg, round at the top and tapering to a point. It must be consecrated over a long period of time through recitation of peaceful mantras and visualization of white light rays emanating from and gathering back into the assembly of peaceful deities within it. When a master plants this sort of kīla in a place where the inhabitants are experiencing great hardships, it pacifies all discordant factors, the eight or sixteen great perils, and the sufferings of sentient ones.

The Enriching Kīla

The enriching kīla should be made from gold or yellow woods like barberry and should be six fingerbreadths in height. Below the handle, it is shaped similar to an obelisk—square at the top, with a four-edged blade tapering to a point. Its consecration involves visualizing enriching deities, such as those of the Ratna family, within it and imagining the shining forth and gathering back of light rays for extended periods. This visualization must be accompanied by the appropriate mantras. Through these means, the kīla becomes

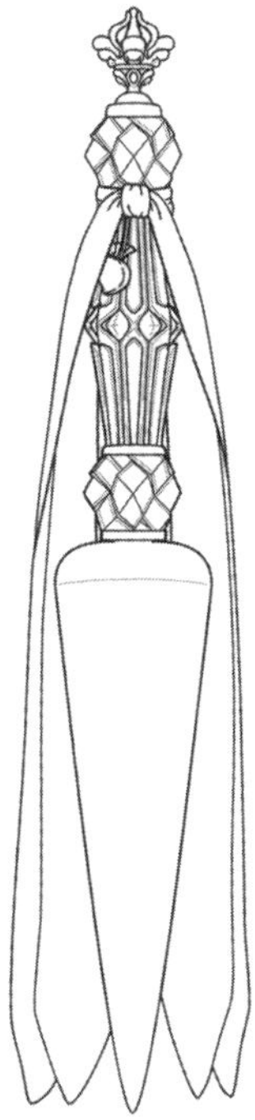

Pacifying, white

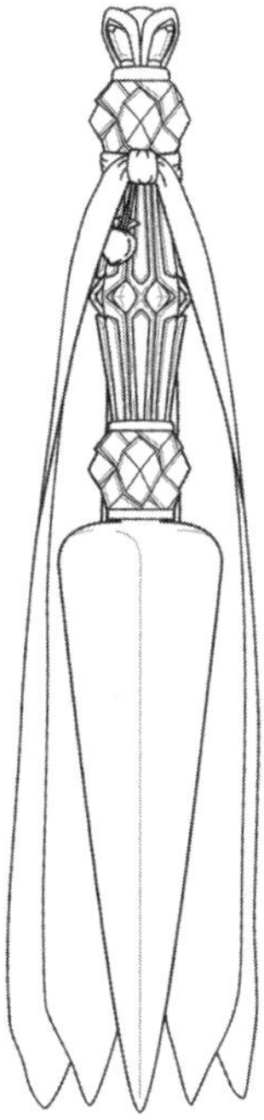

Magnetizing, red

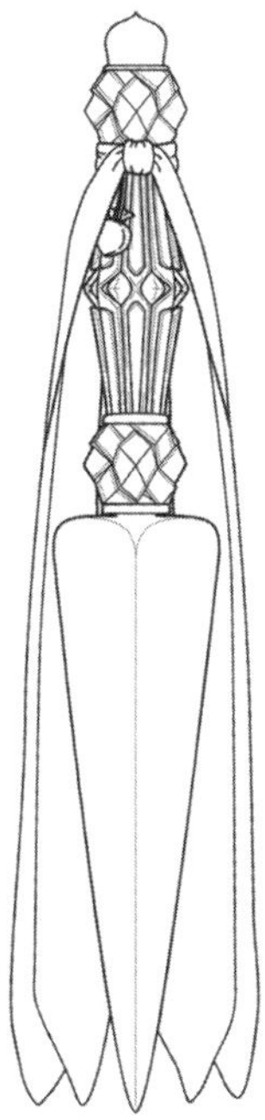

Enriching, yellow

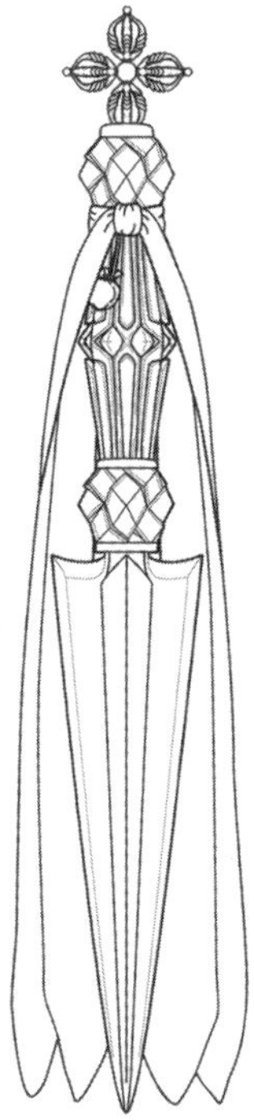

Destructive, black

Kīlas of the Four Activities

endowed with the ability to enrich life, merit, wealth, power, experience, realization, wisdom, qualities, and the like.

The Magnetizing Kīla

As for magnetizing kīlas, they should be crafted from copper, red sandalwood, acacia wood, or other red-colored materials. Ten fingerbreadths in height, they have a half-moon-shaped blade that tapers to a point. One should visualize divine assemblies of magnetizing families therein. Through the emanating and gathering back of red light rays, the kīla becomes empowered to magnetize the minds of those who have heavy misdeeds and obscurations—prideful, arrogant, deluded ones, and the like—binding them to that which is virtuous.

When mindful awareness has become stable through engaging magnetizing practices, it will be able to exert control over afflictions. As it is said, "When self-appearances have been brought under control, others' appearances will be overpowered."[1] Control of self-appearances means subduing one's inner afflictions. Overpowering others' appearances means that because of the force of one's love, others will naturally have faith in one. Magnetizing activities should be understood in this way.

The Destructive Kīla

Finally, the destructive kīla is made of iron, black hardwood, poisonous wood, or the wood of a thorny tree. According to some sources, it should be eight fingerbreadths in height. Others say it should be twelve. Below the handle, its blade is triangular, with three edges that taper to a sharp point. It should be consecrated through visualization, recitation, and the samādhi of approach and accomplishment appropriate to destructive activities.

It is said that the destructive kīla is suitable for use on those enemies in whom the ten grounds are complete—those who destroy the buddhas' teachings, plunder the comfort and ease of sentient ones, demean the status of the Three Jewels, fail to reciprocate the kindness of parents, and so forth. Since such beings claim the Dharma is without benefit and pay no heed to karmic causality, they cannot be subdued by peaceful means. Therefore, only destructive methods can benefit beings with such great delusion. Although their embodied forms are liberated by the kīla, their consciousnesses are ultimately the buddha nature and cannot be killed. Thus, through being liberated, obstructors are blessed to attain the ground of the buddhas or else to take rebirth as bodhisattvas.

Although it is taught that material kīlas are made from different substances that accord with the four activities, it is not necessary for practitioners to think, "I need one of each!" One can accomplish all activities through the use of a single kīla alone. The four material kīlas fashioned from the four different substances are merely outer symbols of the four activities. Of course, people create each of these different kinds of kīlas, but one must understand that they are not required for the actual practice. Since the entire mandala is complete within a single kīla, it is best for sādhakas to use one kīla as a support for recollection, samaya, and respect.

Although this introduction to the compounded, material kīlas of the four activities is only a small fraction of what is taught in the tantras, I offer it in the spirit of an auspicious connection. In spite of its brevity, *Consecration of the Material Kīla Mandala* is endowed with the complete qualities of more extensive consecration texts.

Aspects of the Implement According to the Tantras

With regard to foremost princes, it is said that there are four distinct categories, which emerge as the four extremes: Some are princes, but not foremost. Some are foremost, but not princes. Some are neither foremost nor princes. Some are both foremost and princes.

Further, it is said that there are three ways of accomplishing the wisdom deities, ḍākiṇīs, kiṁkāras, and the like. Accomplishing the wisdom deities involves accomplishing (1) the hundred and eight Kīlas, (2) the two Kīla family lines, and (3) the sole hero Kīla, that is, the principal heruka alone, without consort or retinue. The ḍākiṇīs and kiṁkāras are the mandala inhabitants who carry out diverse activities. All of these divine beings are accomplished by outer, inner, and secret means. The outer accomplishment refers to the ritual methods of practicing the great accomplishment retreat. The inner accomplishment is one's own practice in personal retreat. wThe secret accomplishment occurs through the view, which is the main point of the secret accomplishment text we are practicing.

As for the development stages of the compounded, material kīla, it is said that there are eight mandalas. First, the mandala of the development stages is the body. Second, the mandala of the seed syllable is speech. Third, the mandala of the knot is the mind. Fourth are the four mandalas, in which the ḍākiṇīs of four types are gathered. Fifth is the slaughtering mandala. The last three mandalas are those of destructive methods—the tail end of the four activities, which eliminate enemies' force and splendor through various methods. Among these, the sixth is the mandala of suppression, whereby enemies and obstructors are thoroughly oppressed. Seventh is burning in fire. Finally, the eighth is the casting or hurling of malign repelling tormas, which will be described in the teachings on liberation in the gaṇacakra. All of these different mandalas are subsumed within the compounded material kīla.

Consecrating the Implement

The implement, the kīla who is the Foremost Prince, is endowed with all the attributes of the principal deity. Complete within him is the entire mandala of beings who engage the activities to liberate sentient ones from samsara. As such, the material kīla of signs is the substantial basis on which the four activities can be accomplished and the eight common siddhis achieved. One should honor the material kīla in the same ways one would respect the actual deity. To regard him as merely an object made of wood or metal is a sign of the mind's ignorance that needs to be purified. The main point of the kīla consecration is to establish the mandala of the Foremost

Prince in purity, so that the implement is not perceived as an ordinary object.

A kīla that has been properly consecrated in our tradition will bear red and blue cloths with a small pouch of mustard seeds knotted around the upper neck of the implement. The cloths symbolize emptiness and compassion and ideally should be cut into points so that the ends of the cloths fall to the tip of the kīla. The mustard seeds are nirmāṇakāyas that bear the blessings of Vajrapāṇi and symbolize the subjugation of obstructive forces and hindrances. The cloths and the charmed substances are like garments and ornaments for the Foremost Prince and are a means of honoring him.

After the cloths and substances have been affixed to new kīlas and the initial consecration completed, the implements can then be placed inside the material mandala to be consecrated over the course of the retreat and returned to their owners at the end. However, since the text *Consecration of the Material Kīla Mandala* has now been well translated, the ritual can be performed by practitioners daily during the secret accomplishment. In this case, new implements should be adorned, blessed, and returned to their owners at the outset of the retreat. Through practicing the ritual each day and meditating on the meaning of the text, one can learn how to consecrate the implement for oneself without depending on a master to do so.

Those who do not have a material kīla may simply visualize the stages of consecration or may use a māla as a support. Although there are many different types of blessing-supports, one of the most precious among them is the māla. All the deities of the mandala are truly complete within it. The guru bead is like the principal deity, while the smaller beads on the strand represent the deities in his or her retinue. If one imagines each mantra recitation as an offering to the mandala deities, those divine beings will become one's companions, since they delight in the mantra.

In addition, a coiled māla placed on one's altar or practice table is a suitable support for making offerings and meditating on the mandala of the deity. When one wears a māla, it should not be worn outside of one's clothing but should always be kept next to the skin so that it is not separated from the warmth of one's body. Since it symbolizes the presence of the entire mandala on the body, the māla is a most excellent protection. Because of these great qualities, the māla may be used as a support instead of a kīla when requesting blessing-empowerment.

Meaning of the Words of the Text

As for the actual practice, regardless of whether a māla, a kīla, or another support is used, it is initially consecrated in three stages, each of which requires its own mantra, substance, and meditation. As one recites the first mantra, one imagines that the tip of the implement is tempered by the smoke of black frankincense. Thus, it becomes like an extremely sharp weapon carried into battle.

Next, with the MAGUTALA mantra, one pelts the kīla with charmed mustard seeds, imagining that the body is covered in an armor whose very particles are tiny wrathful ones. Because each round seed is naturally marked with a single line, it looks like a head with a mouth whose lips are wrathfully pursed. Thus, each mustard seed is like a tiny wrathful one capable of driving out obstructive forces.

Finally, one imagines that by reciting the RAKTA mantra and smearing the implement with blood, the weapon is empowered to accomplish with a mere touch whatever activity is required. Then, after returning the kīla to its stand, one should visualize according to the words of the text, which do not require explanation.

At this juncture, the actual consecration of the implement happens concurrently with the development stages of the Foremost Prince. The father-mother buddha couples of the five families are present in the fingers of the right and left hands of oneself as Vajrakīla. Through their union, their red and white bodhicitta mingle, giving rise to rays of multicolored light. As the implement is picked up and held between the hollows of one's palms, it is pervaded by these light rays.

If it is difficult to visualize in this way, one can use the material mandala as a visualization support. In this case, one should imagine that the blessings of the entire divine assembly—inseparable from the three mandalas—appear in the form of light rays that emanate from the principal deity dwelling together with his retinue. So, as one performs the consecration, all the deities inside the material mandala radiate rays of light that enter the implement in one's hands.

In either case, the light rays instantaneously melt the physical substance of the material kīla. At this juncture, it is no longer ordinary metal or wood. Rather, it manifests as the divine seed syllable HŪṂ, the embryo of the buddhas. From the appearance of the HŪṂ, there is the secret manifestation of the Foremost Prince as the deity. This is the first of the three perceptions, which is described with the following words:

> From the HŪṂ's transformation appears a blue-black wrathful with one face, two arms, and three eyes, holding a kīla in his right hand and ankus in the left. His lower body is a sky-iron kīla with sharp, tempered triangular tip. Like metal drawn out of a smith's embers, he emits sparks of fire.

Here, the text indicates that the upper portion of the kīla appears as the torso of a blue-black wrathful one with one face and two arms. However, it is not necessary or even practical to visualize him in this way. Rather, one should understand the HŪṂ to transform into the implement itself, with three faces like the principal deity, but no torso. This is the outer manifestation of the Foremost Prince as the implement, the second perception.

The kīla, whose upper half represents wisdom and whose lower blades symbolize skillful means, is utterly pervaded by divine beings. It is said that the mandala of the deity is complete within the material kīla, who is the Foremost Prince. Below his three-faced head is the handle, which consists of the upper knot, the contracted eight flanks, and the lower knot. Inside the upper knot, in the center and the four directions, dwell the couples of the five families of victorious ones, who are the nature of the five wisdoms. The contracted eight flanks symbolize the eight emancipations. These are the eight stages of becoming freed from samsara, beginning with emancipation from grosser to progressively subtler states.[2] In the four directions of the lower knot are the four female gatekeepers, who symbolize the four immeasurables.

According to another explanation, the mandala described in the development stages is present within the material kīla. Thus, the implement's handle is like the conjoined, eight-spoked domes of the outer mandala, wherein the ten wrathful couples abide. This is described as follows:

> In his upper knot is Hūṁkāra; in the contracted eight flanks, the eight wrathfuls; and in the lower knot, Mahābala. These ten wrathful couples each have falcon types. In the lower knot's four facets are four gatekeeping maids. Beneath the water dragon are four kiṁkāra men. The twelve Kīla guard maids manifest in the three blades.

In this configuration, the wrathful father and mother Hūṁkāra appear with their animal-headed emanations above in the kīla's upper knot. Eight of the ten wrathful ones with their consorts and emanations abide in the eight cardinal and intermediate directions of the contracted eight flanks. Below, the wrathful Mahābala couple with emanations inhabit the center of the lower knot. Thus, the ten wrathful couples of the inner mandala and the falcon types—their emanated zasö servants with animal heads—fill the implement's handle. In the four superficial sides of the lower knot are the four female gatekeepers.

Below the handle is the head of the makara, who symbolizes holding all sentient ones with compassion. Its mouth opens onto the three-sided blade ornamented with three pairs of entwined snakes. The three blades are symbolic of establishing all beings of the three planes—above, below, and upon the earth—in the status

The Kīla as Implement and Immeasurable Palace

of the three kāyas. The six snakes represent the six transcendent perfections, which subdue the hatred of those to be tamed. Within the blade dwell the twelve Kīla protectresses. Since each of these parts of the implement houses countless deities, to meditate on the material kīla alone is of inconceivable benefit. This is the inner manifestation of the Foremost Prince as the immeasurable palace, the third perception.

Just as the sphere of the outer mandala is mirrored within the handle of the implement, the yogi who is practicing the inner fire of *candalī* can also imagine the mandala sphere mirrored within his or her navel. This can be understood in the following way: When the abdominal muscles are contracted, the entire body is held firm and upright. If the spine is the inner support of the body, the contracted musculature of the abdomen is the outer support. This parallels the contracted eight flanks of the kīla's handle. This contracted core is the basis of the bellows breathing. Instead of expanding the belly toward the front like a rounded pot as is often taught, one should bind it, so that the breath is forced downward into a constricted point. Then, binding the lower doors, one draws the wind energies upward. Simultaneously pressing down on the upper winds, one draws the upper and lower together, like the two domed halves of a spherical amulet. Having bound the winds on all quarters, there is no alternative but for them to feed the flame at the navel. In this way, the eight-ribbed sphere of the outer mandala is mirrored within the sealed amulet of candalī. The eight wrathful ones in the eight sides, with above and below making ten, are all present in this tiny mandala.

Since the entire mandala is complete within the ritual dagger, it is the same as the main torma. Even a kīla as tiny as that held by the thumb-joint-sized sattva in the deity's heart is the dwelling place of all the deities. Such material kīlas can be worn on the body as representations of the deity himself. When wearing them, one should give rise to the divine pride of being Vajrakīla. The material kīla may also be placed on one's altar as a protection for the home.

Each aspect of the implement can be explained in terms of outer sign, inner meaning, and secret symbol mentioned earlier. For example, the outer sign that is the three blades of the kīla symbolizes wisdom-rigpa, which is free of all faults and endowed with all qualities. The inner meaning is the transformation of the three poisons into the buddhas' three kāyas. The mind endowed with the empty essence is the dharmakāya. The clear nature is the saṁbhogakāya. The compassion that pervades everywhere like space is the nirmāṇakāya. Finally, the secret symbol is the convergence of the three blades into a single point. The tip of the kīla symbolizes all the myriad qualities subsumed within the singular mind.

The visualization of the implement concludes with the following words:

> In every pore of myself and the Foremost Prince are tiny blue-black wrathfuls the size of barley grains. With gaping mouths, bared fangs, one face, and two arms, they wield diverse weapons. As Kīlaya's sound is resoundingly proclaimed, they fill us without interstice.

Thus, not only are the forms of Vajrakumāra and the Foremost Prince armored with adamantine tiny wrathfuls, they are also densely packed with them.

Now that the implement has been fully consecrated, arising as the Foremost Prince, the sādhakas supplicate the wisdom deities and take the empowerments of body, speech, and mind using the kīla as a support. Since the written meaning is explicit, one should meditate according to the words of the text.

Following that is a textual note, which contains a few key points:

> Then, having the three perceptions of the Foremost Prince himself as the immeasurable palace, the deity, and the implement, one should place him in the seat of É, imagining that his blade has been planted between the light and dark portions of enemies' and obstructors' hearts.

Throughout the secret accomplishment retreat, one should maintain the three perceptions of the kīla as the immeasurable palace, the deity, and the implement. These three perceptions explained earlier are distinctive features of Vajrakīla practice.

Here, the text mentions placing the kīla back into its triangular stand—"the seat of É." However, when performing the actual ritual, one continues holding the implement at this juncture. Later, when one does return the kīla to his seat, one should imagine that his three-edged blade slides between the heart muscle, "the dark portion," and its surrounding fat, "the light portion," of obstructors' hearts. The red muscle symbolizes samsara, and the white fat nirvana. As the kīla is planted between the two, it severs dualistic grasping at samsara and nirvana. In this way, it performs the activity of the kīla of primordial awareness-rigpa.

Some years ago, I designed a kīla stand in the shape of the mandala of a blazing blue-black triangle, which signifies the source of dharmas. Its three inner planes are marked with the syllables OṀ ĀḤ HŪṀ. On its six outer panels are the syllables of the six classes of wayfarers, whose sufferings have all been caused by the six afflictions. When performing the kīla consecration, one should imagine that all sentient beings, along with their afflictions and ill-being, are gathered into their respective syllables, A NRI SU TRI PRE DUḤ, which then dissolve into the OṀ ĀḤ HŪṀ. The visualization in the text continues with the following words:

> The light arisen from the seeds of the three mandalas' three vajras pervades the three realms, bestowing the empowerment of every sentient one's life force as primordial awareness. The six realms' beings, the afflictions' dwelling places, have been cleansed, turning into the six seeds: A NRI SU TRI PRE DUḤ. Those six also melt into light, transforming into OṀ ĀḤ HŪṀ.
>
> Having gathered back, the light merges into the three places of myself and the Foremost Prince, bringing the three realms and three planes under our control. OṀ ĀḤ HŪṀ.

Visualizing the OṀ seed syllable of vajra body, the ĀḤ of vajra speech, and the HŪṀ of vajra mind in the three places of every divine

The Foremost Prince in Kīla Stand

being in the three mandalas, one imagines that rays of light emanate from them, pervading everywhere. When the light rays make contact with sentient beings, their ordinary life force—consciousness—is transformed into awareness. Thus, those beings change into the seed syllables of their respective realms: A for gods, NRI for humans, SU for demigods, TRI for animals, PRE for pretas, and DUḤ for hell denizens. These six then transform into OṀ ĀḤ HŪṂ, whose light returns and subsides into the three places of the heruka and the Foremost Prince. Thus, all beings of the desire, form, and formless realms below, upon, and above the earth are magnetized.

The transformations above have the same meaning as the protection mantra visualization in the Yamāntaka practice manual, which reads,

> From the HŪṂ letters at the hearts of the entire divine assembly, multicolored light rays and hosts of working envoys—first, second, and third emanations and male and female wrathfuls—unfathomably issue forth. The life force and life span essences of everyone to be protected, others and myself, are in the form of NRI syllables, which have been stolen away by all the eight classes' gods and demons.
>
> ...Turning into forms of HŪṂ, the NRI syllables—those stolen life force essences—penetrate the hearts of everyone to be protected, others and myself.[3]

In actuality, that which causes the life force and life span essences to be stolen away in the first place are the six afflictions. Appearing in the aspect of NRI syllables, the precious life essences are carried off and hidden by negative emotions like aversion and jealousy themselves. The life essences are recovered only after the NRI syllables have been transformed into the seed syllable HŪṂ. Thus, they merge back into the hearts of those who are to be protected, restoring their well-being.

Although the Vajrakīla and Yamāntaka examples above use different words as means of expression, their inner meaning is the same. So it is with all the buddhas' teachings. As it says in *The King of Samādhis Sutra*,

> Whichever sutras I've explained
> in thousands of worldly realms—
> though their words differ, their meaning is one.
> If even a single word has been fully contemplated,
> every one of them will become contemplation.[4]

At this juncture, the kīla is returned to his seat with the words SAPAŚVARI SAMAYA JAḤ HŪṂ VAṂ HOḤ. Finally, the kīla consecration concludes with the empowerment of the five wisdoms, which the sādhakas request through the following supplication:

> HŪṂ. Means, your conduct for beings' purpose, is
> love and compassion that rightly tame.
> Now grant siddhis and empowerment to
> make buddha activities complete!

Since the meaning is self-explanatory, one should simply meditate according to the words of the text. Then, as one recites the syllables OṂ HŪṂ TRĀṂ HRĪḤ ĀḤ, MŪṂ LĀṂ MĀṂ PĀṂ TĀṂ, the empowerment-blessing of the fathers and mothers of the five families is bestowed. Although the syllables differ slightly from those in the practice manual, the accompanying meaning, mudrās, and visualization are exactly the same as those described in the empowerment section of the practice manual.

CHAPTER 7

Bringing Down Blessings Instructions

Although profound, the supplemental ritual of bringing down blessings is simple to understand. Since we have not yet recognized ourselves as inseparable from the deity, we lack confidence that the deities are one with us. One of the compassionate methods of secret mantra is the construction of a physical mandala, wherein the deity and his or her retinue can come and reside for a time. For this reason, the great accomplishment retreat requires an elaborately constructed mandala with vast outer offerings. For beginners, this mandala is a support for meditation. Without such a support, it would be difficult to know or to relate to the saṁbhogakāya deities.

By hosting the deities, practitioners develop a connection with them. Even though we cannot see them, they are actually present within the mandala. At this stage, we are like blind children, unable to see the face of our own mother. However, through the skillful means of this imagined support of all-encompassing purity, our doubts will gradually be dispelled, and we will come to know with confidence the sameness of ourselves and the deities.

The mandala is the deity's palace. It is like a grand hotel for the yidam and retinue. When one invites into the material mandala the divine wisdom deities who naturally abide in the expanse of space, it is good to imagine that they actually appear. In this way, the deities consecrate the mandala, making it a holy site worthy of circumambulation and offerings. Thus, the material, constructed mandala becomes a support for developing pure perception and gathering the merit accumulation. It brings about results commensurate with the cause. What this means is that by erecting the mandala and making offerings to it, one is creating the causes to be reborn in the pure realm that is the actual, ultimate mandala.

The Material Mandala

The way of constructing the mandala is described in detail in the scriptures. The various practice manuals disagree about the number of deities in the assembly of Vajrakīla. Some say there are seventy-two; others say there are seventy-eight. Still others give different enumerations. For the most part, these discrepancies are due to the way the number of Kīla guards is tallied. For our purposes, the material mandala includes seventy-two material kīlas having certain attributes that represent each of the mandala deities. Once these have been properly consecrated, they are placed inside the assembled mandala, arranged in their correct constellation. This represents the mandala of the commitment being. Then, through mudrā, recitation, and visualization, one invites the mandala of wisdom deities, which is continuously present in the expanse of space. It then merges with the mandala of the commitment being, becoming inseparable in essence and like a mirrored reflection in aspect. On the basis of this fully consecrated mandala, the sādhakas practice to accomplish the four activities as well as the common and supreme siddhis.

Such reflected mandalas can be simple or elaborate. It is said that the mandala for the approach is an eight-spoked iron wheel of destructive activities. The mandala for Vajrakīla accomplishment is named the "Twenty-One Crosses of É" (*É tram nyer chig*).* As for the word "crosses," X marks or cross-hatched markings are associated with kill lists in tantric black magic rites. In this case, the term

*In some of the earliest Indian scripts that predate Devanāgarī, the letter É had the shape of a downward-pointing triangle. Even the modern form of the letter (ए) still bears a resemblance.

"crosses" signifies the twenty-one spokes of the Vajrakīla accomplishment mandala. These spokes are shaped like long isosceles triangles. In each one stands a single kīla. More elaborate mandalas can have seventy-two spokes with the same number of kīlas.

When the kīlas are properly laid out for the great accomplishment retreat, the mandala becomes a slaying wheel that accomplishes destructive liberating activities. Even though these details are not particularly relevant to the ways we practice at present, I mention them to give a glimpse of the vastness of the practice. When one understands the meditation methods of great sādhakas of highest faculties, it can become an inspiration for one's own practice.

Obviously, a complete mandala requires many different implements, causes, and conditions, which are difficult to assemble. Even when a mandala is not quite complete, every torma, vase, deity image, and so forth becomes a seat for divine beings—a place where the deities can abide. In addition, each article of the mandala is endowed with meaning. The longevity arrows in each of the four corners, for example, represent the gathering of long life and merit.

Along each of the four sides of the mandala, there is a torma. In the eastern direction is a peaceful white torma, symbolizing the pacification of illness, evil spirits, and the like. In the south is an enriching yellow torma, which symbolizes the increase of wealth, life span, merit, and so forth. In the west, there is a magnetizing red torma, which brings all sentient beings of the three realms under one's control. In the north, there is a destructive dark green torma, which repels obstacles, hindrances, and those who would harm the Dharma or its practice. In this way, the mandala itself performs the four activities.

As for the main torma, one should understand it to be a representation of the immeasurable palace—from the four elements under the four-sided base up through the mansion with cakras of the ten wrathful couples and the four princes. These cakras surround the lotus seat with moon and sun, where the principal deity and consort abide.

Visualization and Meditation

Since this material mandala is the deities' dwelling place, according to my thinking, it is best to practice imagining that the door of the mandala is always open. Otherwise, one reinforces dualistic habit as one does the practice day by day with the notion that the door of the mandala is closed. Since the gathering-in mentions "all-pervading mercy's hosts divine," there is no such thing as a door that separates inside from outside. As space is beyond coming and going, how can the door be closed? In actuality, the only thing that can close the door is one's own heedlessness and dualistic grasping. In this regard, the extremely precious dedication says, "May the fruit—nondual essence—be gained!" If one aspires to accomplish the essence that is buddhahood, transcending samsaric duality, then every aspect of one's practice should reflect that aspiration.

In some traditions, the sādhakas rise when performing the ritual of bringing down blessings. Since practitioners must cultivate respect and devotion in any case, perhaps it is better to remain seated. Then, whether standing or seated, at the start they beckon the divine wisdom deities with various desirables that please their minds. Incense compounded from substances of their liking, chant, music, mudrā, and dance—all these are the outer expressions of practitioners' inner devotion, love, and longing for the deity. Just as a mother comes when her child cries out, the saṁbhogakāya deities' enduring compassion and affection are roused by the sādhakas' mind of yearning. Thus, they are drawn from the expanse of space to the mandala site. This interaction between the sādhakas' devotion and the deities' compassion is the samaya. The moment a practitioner calls upon the wisdom deities, they are present due to their loving commitment. This is reflected in the words of the text:

> Having densely massed like clouds in the sky through the power of their heart-samayas of old, all gurus, knowledge holders, deities, skyfarers, and oath-bound ones, send down great blessings on yogins and the mandala site and think of us with great affection.

The Vajrakīla Torma

Once the wisdom deities have gathered, the practitioners may invoke Guru Rinpoche—who is their very source—with the *Seven-Line Supplication*. In order to even out the number of lines, an extra line is added at the beginning of the prayer. Then, the supplication is chanted to accompany a dance with four or eight dancers. Although the dance is traditionally a feature of the great accomplishment retreat, since it is endowed with blessing, I introduced it to the secret accomplishment for sādhakas' benefit.

In this regard, in a great accomplishment four senior lamas are assigned the roles of regents, which are similar to the role of the vajra master. Each regent holds a vase containing the accomplishment substance of one of the four activities and each has an awareness-consort who holds a skull cup. Further, each one is responsible for certain duties during the retreat. Although such roles are not their day-to-day activities, they are necessary for the purposes of the great accomplishment.

It is these four who perform the dance. Depending on the size of the mandala, their consorts may accompany them. With their steps, they circumambulate while waving silk streamers and ringing bells to draw the saṁbhogakāya deities' blessings into the mandala. According to this tradition, the dance can be done each evening of the great accomplishment.

Since there is no need for people to play the roles of regents in the secret accomplishment retreat, sādhakas may serve as dancers according to their interests and abilities.

To whatever degree one can perceive the mandala and its inhabitants purely, one will become correspondingly receptive to their great blessings. It is not as though blessings just randomly fall down on sādhakas. Rather, they are actively invoked and brought down through the force of faith, love, and the bond of samaya, which are enhanced by recitation of the words of the text. The first verse begins as follows:

HŪṂ. Vajra Youth's mandalas, barring none,
and you, deity who's accomplished

existence-vajrakīla in the
mandala whose limits equal space,
through compassion great, you act without
obscuration or isolation.

With these words, the sādhakas are invoking the saṁbhogakāya wisdom deities who abide in the limitless expanse of the all-pervasive dharmakāya. The accomplishment of "existence-vajrakīla" is the realization that the entirety of samsara—the container and contents—is nothing other than the deity abiding at the center of the immeasurable mandala. When bodhicitta has melted the ice of dualistic grasping, the whole of samsara is realized to be the deity Vajrakīla, the buddha nature. In this way, the three seats of the aggregates, elements, and sense fields mentioned in the lineage supplication are naturally pure for all sentient ones. It is only through circumstantial self-grasping that they have become tainted. Anyone who seals these three with bodhicitta will become a buddha. Thus, the primary cause of accomplishing the pure appearing form of the deity is the cultivation of bodhicitta. Since the yidam has realized the nonduality of samsara and nirvana, he has accomplished existence-vajrakīla. This is the all-pervasive deity to be realized by the sādhaka.

The words "mandala whose limits equal space" give a sense of the unfathomable scope of the spontaneously present mandala of the facing generation. Wherever there is space, the dharmakāya pervades. Wherever there is the dharmakāya, the five buddhas' attributes pervade. The dharmakāya of the buddhas has the very nature of the five wisdoms. Therein dwell the principal and retinues whose bodies are unimaginably vast, filling the sky. Why are the wisdom deities imagined on such a grand scale? One will recall that in the offering section, the practice manual refers to "dullness like a flesh mountain brought down; lust, a wave-tossed, blood-filled ocean; and hatred, a bone heap." The afflictions of all sentient ones of the three realms are exceedingly vast. Since the wrathful wisdom deities revel in consuming the flesh, blood, and bones of beings' afflictions, they must be ever-present and similarly vast in scope. The actual meaning of their enjoyment of the offerings is that all afflictions are destroyed by wisdom.

"Without obscuration" means that due to his vast compassion, the deity is free of the fault of laziness in his activities benefiting beings. Since that compassion is also completely free of dualistic grasping at notions about what will benefit beings, the deity is impartial and without discrimination in his actions. His compassion is directed toward all sentient ones without exception. This immeasurable equanimity free of bias is the meaning of being "without isolation."

The sādhakas continue to supplicate with the following lines:

> You with timely vajra samaya,
> on this unsurpassed, great mandala
> of accomplishment, send down great waves
> of compassionate activities and
> blessings on this secret mandala!
> Please send down the great resplendence of
> body, speech, and mind and grant us the
> five wisdoms' supreme empowerment!
> OṀ SARVA TATHĀGATA BHAGAVAN, SAMAYA HOḤ. SAMAYAS TVAṀ.

Here, it is worth noting that there is an alternate reading of one line of this section. I have chosen the words "You with timely vajra samaya,"[1] since that is how I remember the old terma text. An alternate reading, which appears in Tenzin Chökyi Gyaltsen's rearrangement of the Ratna Lingpa Vajrakīla termas for practice in the Drigung lineage, is "You with timely compassionate samaya."[2]

Then, having invoked the samaya of all the tathāgatas with mantra and music, the sādhakas recite,

> HŪṂ. Now, the time to grant empowerment's come,
> sending great resplendence down from the
> secret sphere itself—Vajrakīla.

Here, the yidam is referred to as "the secret sphere itself." From within the space that is emptiness, there arises secret primordial awareness. Emptiness-wisdom is just that. It is Vajradhara. This is the same meaning as the dawning of the secret sun of primordial awareness mentioned in *Taking Up Accomplishments*. It is resolving the point of the mind's actual condition through practice. It is the certainty and complete freedom from doubt about the view that come from direct experience. Finally, the text concludes:

> Vajra Lord, bhagavan, with past pledge,
> the vajra empowerment samaya
> you bestow is unsurpassable.
> Deity whose sole declared oath is
> ne'er to stray from being a refuge, please
> bless us with the great resplendent waves
> of the conquerors—all excluding none!
> GURU DEVA ḌĀKIṆĪ KĪLI KĪLAYA, SAMAYA HŪṂ. SAMAYA JAḤ.

In order to understand these words, first one must know that all the stages of approach and accomplishment are for the purpose of reinforcing the connection between the deities and sentient ones. That connection is rooted in the three strengths—the basis underlying all deity yoga practices.

Sādhakas who have trust in the deity's qualities are endowed with the first of these, the strength of one's intention, which depends on faith. Since the deities have from the beginning given rise to the mind set on supreme enlightenment for the sake of sentient ones, their samaya and commitment are to maintain the second of the three strengths—the strength of the tathāgatas' great love and compassion. Whenever practitioners invite the wisdom deities, we are asking them to come by invoking the strength of their compassionate commitment.

Finally, since all deities and all human beings share the singular basis of mind, the fundamental connection that is buddha nature is inherent. This is the strength of the sphere of dharmas.

At the very basis, samsara, nirvana, and all the beings therein are devoid of inherent existence. When one has purified some karmic imprints through meditating on the deity, one realizes that the self has been fabricated merely through grasping at that which is selfless. When one's own lack of inherent existence has been understood, it becomes as simple to change into the deity's form as to change clothes. Thus, the strength of the dharmasphere—the great mind connection between deities and humans—is the very nature of emptiness.

As the sādhakas invoke the deity's "vajra empowerment samaya," reminding him that his "sole declared oath is ne'er to stray from being a refuge," we call upon the strength of the dharmasphere, the singular basis of buddhas and sentient ones. We call forth the innate connection between the mind of the wisdom deities and the minds of all beings.

That which we request is to be blessed "with the great resplendent waves of the conquerors—all excluding none!" When one actually engages the practice of meditation, sometimes there will naturally arise moments of definite certainty, in which one knows without doubt, "This is it." Such certainty about the view comes from within; it is not based on anything anyone else has said. This is the nature of direct, personal experience. On the basis of the three strengths—one's faith, the tathāgatas' compassion, and the sphere of dharmas—such certainty can definitely be accomplished.

Finally, circumambulating the mandala while waving silken streamers of five colors, the ritual master—sometimes accompanied by the vajra master and dancers—draws down the blessings and potency of the five families.

CHAPTER 8

Petition Instructions

The purpose of the petition is to invite, make offering to, and mobilize all oath-bound guardians and protectors of Vajrakīla. Some practitioners have the notion that petitioning Dharma guardians is something separate from deity yoga. But this is really not the case! The deity's body, speech, mind, attributes, and activities are unified. Thus, the protectors who carry out the deity's enlightened activities cannot be distinguished from the principal himself. For example, if a master wants to bestow empowerment, since he or she cannot do it alone, the master must rely on attendants. Similarly, guardians and protectors should be seen as helpers in the accomplishment of activities.

If one wishes to understand the guardians, one should consider the words of the following Vajra Guru refuge prayer from an extensive mind accomplishment sadhana of Guru Rinpoche:

> In the essence, the guru, dharmakāya, buddha;
> the nature, saṁbhogakāya, the pacifying, true Dharma;
> and compassionate activity, nirmāṇakāyas, ḍākiṇīs, the sangha,
> I go for refuge until attaining enlightenment.[1]

These words of the Drigung treasure revealer Nüden Dorje acknowledge the singular essence of the Three Jewels, Three Roots, and three kāyas. Although the protectors are not mentioned directly, one should understand them to be included within the nirmāṇakāyas, the ḍākiṇīs.

Some practitioners focus on the histories of each individual protector, thinking that they are distinct from one another. But such dualistic concepts just lead to confusion. It is said that as wisdom expands, one takes up the costumes of samsara. So, one should understand that regardless of how they may appear, the guardians are inseparable from the divine wisdom deities.

Even if the yogin who understands this were to visualize a demon, it would transform into a wisdom deity. Conversely, even though a wisdom deity may be visualized by one who does not understand this, it will not result in accomplishment of the common and supreme siddhis. Although the mode of practice is important, on the outer level, there is no great distinction between wisdom deities and worldly appearances. This was taught by Jamgön Kongtrül.

When requesting the guardians' help to accomplish activities, it is appropriate to offer them a torma. It is also fine to prepare offerings of cookies, fruit, tea, liquor, and the like as substitutes for a torma.

Because I wished to make the petition text complete for the secret accomplishment retreat, I supplemented it with a drawing in, which reads,

> NAMO! By the truth of the Three Jewels, Three Roots, and yidam Vajra Youth's divine assembly of seventy-eight, every harmdoer, oath transgressor, and opportunistic spirit—into this ruddy flesh and blood torma be drawn! JAḤ HŪṂ VAṂ HOḤ.

With these words, all obstructive forces are drawn into the torma that is to be offered. Although harmdoers and oath transgressors may be familiar, "opportunistic spirits" are those who are constantly on the lookout for chances to create obstacles for human beings. They are like sharpshooters who have taken aim and are waiting for the right moment to fire.

The torma is imagined as an inconceivably vast mountain of flesh, ocean of blood, and heap of bones. That which is drawn into the torma is ultimately the ignorance, desire, and aversion of oneself and all sentient beings. The syllables JAḤ HŪṂ VAṂ HOḤ represent the four immeasurables. Thus, it is the sādhaka's mind of loving-kindness, joy, compassion, and equanimity that involuntarily draws in these afflictions in the aspects of harmful spirits.

The torma is then consecrated with the syllables OṂ ĀḤ HŪṂ, transforming it into a mass of whatever desirable things will delight the protectors' minds.

Next, reciting these words, one summons the different types of oath-bound guardians, together with their assemblies:

> JOḤ. You who've pledged as Kīla guards before
> the great master, Padma Thötreng Tsal—
> dog maids, sovereigns, four earth-owning *se*,
> mighty four kiṁkāras, blazing ones,
> mothers, sisters, and such—numberless,
> glorious messengers with your hosts, please
> come to this place through samaya's power!

Apart from the kiṁkāras, these messenger-guardians—referred to as "mothers, sisters"—are female. As they assemble, one welcomes the messengers by offering them seats, the seven outer offerings, and the inner offerings of amṛita, rakta, and torma.

Finally, one petitions them to accomplish activities. These are stated explicitly in the text:

> Accepting these superior offerings, you twelve oath-bound Kīla guards and hosts, protect the buddhas' teachings! Glorify the Triple Gem! Preserve the dominion of sanghas and Dharma! Dispel this world's decline! Increase sentient ones' ease and benefit! Be yogins' allies! Accomplish mantra holders' activities! Vanquish hostile enemies! Conquer harmful obstructors! Especially for those with samaya gathered here, pacify outer, inner, and secret adversities, increase and enrich favorable conditions and every good thing desired, and engage activities to swiftly accomplish supreme and common siddhis, barring none!

Then, with the final verse, one praises the different classes of guardians with their retinues and incites them to activities:

HŪṂ. Glorious Great Blood Drinker Kīlaya's
guards, obedient servants, oath-bound ones,
dog maids, sovereigns, earth maids, kiṁkāras,
mothers, sisters, female envoys with
awesome charnel-ground gear—mistresses
of unhindered, forceful actions' skill—
praise to you with hosts innumerable!
Now accomplish deeds entrusted you!

CHAPTER 9

Feast Offering, Restoration, and Repelling Instructions

For the purpose of the secret accomplishment retreat, restoration and repelling texts have been inserted into the gaṇacakra. Although the meaning of the texts is mostly self-explanatory, there are a few points that merit clarification.

Meaning and Purpose of the Gaṇacakra

The Sanskrit word *gaṇa* (*tsog*) means "accumulation" or "gathering." Thus, the gaṇacakra is a cause of accumulating merit. This happens primarily through the altruistic mind.

In this regard, there is one important point about which all practitioners should be heedful. It is taught that whenever sādhakas give rise to afflictions like aversion and jealousy during accomplishment retreats, it ruins the virtuous accumulation of the entire assembly. Guru Rinpoche taught that this is similar to how one drop of rotten milk can spoil a whole container. Thus, the tantras explain,

> Just as a single drop of rotten milk will spoil an entire vessel of fresh milk, if even one person with impaired samaya is seated in a row of the feast assembly, though a hundred or even a thousand others who hold the samaya may be present, not as much as the slightest fruit of accomplishment will come forth due to the samaya taint of that one.[1]

That is to say, because of interdependence, even the slightest taint of one can ruin the accomplishment of the whole. If one disciple gives rise to an instant of affliction, the samaya is broken in an instant. Thus, when one practitioner has a moment of aversion or jealousy, everyone loses out. Such afflictions and disharmony among practitioners make everyone else feel ill at ease. Not only that, but these afflictions have an adverse effect on the entire surrounding region.

Understanding the importance of samaya, sādhakas must be strict with their discipline from the start. When we speak about how the merit of an entire retreat can be wasted by an instant of affliction, it offers an insight into how careful practitioners must be to guard the mind against negativity. This point, which accords with the individual liberation precepts, must be understood correctly. Seeking to avoid harming others, meditators will again and again make effort to block afflictions. When such afflictions do arise, a sādhaka will think, "I have gotten angry and broken the samaya! As a result, the whole retreat will be ruined!" By recalling this as soon as affliction has arisen, one will immediately feel remorse and think, "What can I do now? How can I make it right?" Otherwise, if this point were not emphasized, practitioners would find themselves unable to suppress their negative emotions in retreats.

On the other hand, once one has received this instruction, if one believes that a single affliction has ruined everything and that there is no way to correct the problem, this is also a mistake that will lead to discouragement. To avoid this error, one must understand that the method of laying aside faults and misdeeds was taught by Lord Buddha as a way to purify negativities whenever one's discipline falls short. In fact, the only good thing about misdeeds is that they can be confessed. In particular, vajra siblings must lay aside their afflictions daily through means of the gaṇacakra. Each afternoon of the secret accomplishment, the confession of the fourteen mantric downfalls is recited during the gaṇapūja. Such confession is a method of repairing samayas. Through it, sādhakas can immediately restore harmony within the mandala. Thus, it is taught that like a chain of pure gold, the samaya of bodhicitta is easily broken, yet easily restored. This is a distinctive feature of the bodhisattva's vow.

From a mantric perspective, whenever aversion arises, if it is recognized in the moment of arising, it becomes mirrorlike wisdom. Similarly, every affliction can be transformed into wisdom. When this occurs, the samaya cannot be broken and the affliction itself becomes beneficial. Finally, since secret mantra practice is rooted in the mind of all-encompassing purity, meditators are taught to perceive phenomena as being dreamlike. When all phenomena are perceived as illusory, one will be able to maintain the samaya regardless of what happens.

In brief, samayas can degenerate both on the conventional fictional level and on the ultimate factual level. For those who hold aversion and other afflictions within, there really can be no secret mantra samaya, since every samaya comes down to loving-kindness and nonduality. The samaya of the bodhisattva is to maintain love and affection. That commitment is damaged whenever loving-kindness and affection are lost to the enemy of anger. The secret mantra samaya is to be free of dualistic grasping. That commitment is damaged each time one gives rise to the notion of a self. So, on the fictional level, one's commitment is to protect the mind from aversion. On the factual level, it is to guard against dualistic grasping. The gaṇacakra restores both of these commitments as sādhakas cultivate love and affection conjoined with nondual awareness.

Making Offerings

By making offerings to the deities by means of the gaṇapūja, one practices generosity. In the context of secret mantra, the entire mandala is complete within one's own body-mind continuum. For one who knows this, the outer Vajrakumāra is this worldly realm of Jambudvīpa. The inner Vajrakumāra is fully complete within one's own body. The other, the secret, Vajrakumāra manifests when bodhicitta ripens into the pure-field realm. Through partaking of enjoyments while maintaining this view, one makes great offerings. In this regard, a common prayer for offering food states,

> In one's body, the mandala of gurus and yidams,
> the channels and constituents, the retinue of heroes and heroines, have circled.
> Through the virtue of having turned the wheel of gathering with this food and drink,
> may all wayfaring beings attain the state of herukas![2]

By remaining aware of this, continually recalling the deity while enjoying sense pleasures, the mind is free of grasping at the "I" who is enjoying. Being free of self-grasping, one will not experience the complete karmic ripening of such enjoyment. Another common offering prayer reads as follows:

> The teacher unsurpassed, the precious Buddha;
> protector unsurpassed, precious true Dharma;
> and the guides unsurpassed, the precious Sangha—
> to Three Jewels, source of refuge, I make offering.[3]

When a meal is accompanied by these prayers, it becomes a small gaṇapūja. Such offering prayers cut through the habitual thought "This food is mine. It is for me to eat." In this way, the offering to the Three Jewels and Three Roots scatters the thought of "I," diminishing self-grasping. This is how the gaṇacakra has the power to purify karmic imprints.

Of principal importance is the HŪṂ syllable. When visualized, it causes the mind to abide in a state free of thoughts. Thus, the extensive Vajrakīla practice manual says, "The HŪṂ is clearly visualized by the vajra eye. May unsurpassed enlightenment be attained as we consume the offerings!"[4]

This vajra eye is the nondual view; it is actual truth. Through meditation on the HŪṂ syllable whose nature is clarity-emptiness, the mind becomes free of dualistic grasping; thus, the five desirables are spontaneously transformed into a gaṇacakra. In the best case, this manifests as the purity of the deity's clear appearances. Regardless of which of the five desirables one enjoys, one remains inseparable from the view. In this way, one brings onto the path whatever secret mantra activities are engaged.

Likewise, when practitioners become selfless through recalling the yidam deity or the HŪṀ syllable, the ones who offered the food accomplish the merit accumulation, while practitioner-recipients diminish desire and self-grasping. Through this means, the wisdom deities can partake of the enjoyments. From the ultimate factual perspective, the offering, the ones who offer, and those to whom offerings are made are indistinguishable. The basic meaning of the gaṇacakra can be understood in this way.

Ritual Practice of the Gaṇacakra

At the beginning of the ritual, the gathered offerings are cleansed by fire, wind, and water with the syllables RĀṀ YĀṀ KHĀṀ, respectively. Then, the divine guests are invited with the following verse:

> HŪṀ. To take up empowerments and siddhis
> to accomplish existence-kīla,
> you great wisdom-wrathfuls, please come here!
> Having come, you beings of wisdom wrath,
> please reveal your marks and signs and grant
> the accomplishments of Kīlaya!

Thus, sādhakas' aspiration in offering the gaṇapūja is that the deities will reveal themselves, bestowing accomplishments on the assembly and causing existence to be realized as the mandala of the deity. The gaṇapūja accomplishes this by restoring the bond of samaya among human practitioners and the divine beings in the mandala. This is expressed in the following lines:

> OṀ ĀḤ HŪṀ. Outer vessel, inner contents, and
> secret offerings—enjoyments displayed—
> have been consecrated for the feast.

As they're offered to you, Glorious, Great
Father, mother, your courts, Kīla guards
with ten wrathful couples, take them, please,
to restore our bond in the expanse!
GAṆACAKRA MAHĀJÑĀNA PUJĀ HŌḤ.

The Restoration

This theme of restoring the samaya is further clarified by the supplemental text *The Māra-Subduing Secret Mantra Sanctuary*, the restoration ritual composed by Jamgön Kongtrül. It is inserted at this point in the gaṇacakra. With this ritual, sādhakas make outer, inner, and secret offerings, which include restoring substances. They are described with these words:

...outer offerings, massed enjoyment clouds;
inner offerings, strewn desirables;
secret offerings, dance of the rigma.

Since one cannot know all the different sorts of material substances desired by the diverse types of beings in the Vajrakīla mandala, one should imagine that the gaṇacakra offerings spontaneously transform into whatever will delight the minds of the assembled guests. As mentioned before, the main point of the secret offerings is the physical pleasure of the sādhaka who has trained in the yogas of the channels, winds, and seed essences. Since such bliss is simultaneously experienced by all the deities inside one's body and in the mandala, it is the actual offering. Thus, through making pleasing offerings of bodhicitta, the connections among human practitioners and the divine beings in the mandala are fully restored.

The causes from which the Vajrakīla deities have arisen and the conditions on which they depend are clarified in the following verses, which describe some of the mandala beings' activities:

Actual ten perfections, ten virtues,
you wrath kings tame demons on ten sides.

With your emanated servant hosts—
twenty falcon types—our bond's restored!

You rise from mind, speech, and body as
mudrās penetrating noxious ones.
Through the families' boundless projection
and gathering—princes—our bond's restored!

The explicit four immeasurables,
four beast-faced ones who perform four acts—
four gates' blazing guards—our bond's restored!

Friends who guard the word of Kīla and
nurture yogins with samaya, you're
hindrances' and foes' great antidote!
You four canine maids—our bond's restored!

The first of these verses refers to the ten wrathful couples, who are embodiments of all the buddhas' ten strengths. They appear through sentient ones' accomplishment of the ten virtues—fruitions that depend on their practice of the six or ten transcendent perfections. Causes and conditions such as these are the origins of all the pure deities. Similarly, the subsequent verses point to the divine manifestations arisen from the nail of the activities of emanating and gathering and from the cultivation of the four immeasurables. One should contemplate well the meaning of these words.

Having made offerings, sādhakas then request the deities to reciprocate by restoring the bond through bestowing siddhis and empowerments:

To restore our grave commitment from
root and branch samayas' breakages,
faults' downfalls, confusion, and the like,
grant the eight great siddhis, four actions,
and great jewels of body, speech, and mind—
siddhis and empowerments, barring none!

The restoration concludes with the following supplication:

Wisdom-wrathfuls, grant resplendence to
yogins with our courts who practice you!
Marks and signs of the accomplishment
of existence as vajra soon show!
Consummating penetrating mind,
tame four māras and slay the three foes!
In the unborn sphere, enlightened, make
the two aims spontaneously achieved!

The term "existence" (*sipa*) signifies all the possibilities in cyclic existence—everything that could come to be within samsara. When the "vajra" nature of the three planes is laid bare, whatever could appear manifests as the yidam's mandala. Thus, one supplicates the deities of wisdom-wrath to bestow accomplishment of this union of samsara and nirvana.

Although the four māras have already been clarified, the "three foes" should be understood as (1) impeding outer embodied and formless demons, harmdoers, and enemies; (2) unimpeded inner enemies that are the six afflictions; and (3) the secret enemy that is dualistic grasping. In other words, dualistic grasping is the essence, afflictions are the nature, and obstructing harmdoers are the capability aspect.

Since all of these afflictions and sufferings are subsumed within dualistic grasping, they are nothing other than the māra of the lord of death, which is ultimately slain when one gives rise to nondual wisdom. Once enemies' bodies have been destroyed, the HŪṂ syllable arises in place of self-grasping consciousness—the ordinary life force. In this way, the kīla of unfurled and pervasive wisdom liberates the māra of the lord of death by seizing the ordinary life force of sentient ones. This is the meaning of the words "Tame four māras and slay the three foes!" The final fruition of this will be enlightenment, the accomplishment of one's own purpose. From within that state, the four activities that spontaneously accomplish others' purpose will also be complete.

The restoration is then followed by a verse of disclosure and the hundred syllables, which are part of the original gaṇacakra text.

Drawing In

Then, before the liberation, the sādhakas call upon the authority of the Three Jewels' and Three Roots' truth to draw enemies and obstructors into the torma effigy. Specifically, that which is being drawn in are the three poisons—the afflictions in the mindstreams of all sentient ones of the three realms—delusion, the nature of flesh; lust, in the aspect of blood; and aversion, in the aspect of bones.

As symbols of the authority of the Three Jewels' and Three Roots' truth, the ritual master dons a fringed brocade and a hat. There are a couple of different hats that may be worn for this ritual. The Kagyüpas adopted the Mohawk-like style of the Gelug tradition's yellow hat (*tsezha*), changing the color to red. Since this hat has a connection with vinaya holders of the past, it is not appropriate to be worn by the laity. Instead, lay mantrins may wear the poison hat of Zhangtrom (*zhang trom dug zhu*) for the drawing in and for lower activities. It was designed by the treasure revealer Gya Zhangtrom, a holder of the Yamāntaka lineage. Resembling the enchanted projectile torma, it consists of a large red triangle, which is shaped like a poisonous flower. It symbolizes the activities of the three kāyas. On its left and right sides, it has smaller black triangles that rise to about one-third of the height of the red peak. They represent the blades of an iron throwing star.

As black frankincense is burned, the assembly recite,

> NAMO! By the truth of the Three Jewels, Three Roots, and yidam Vajra Youth's divine assembly of seventy-eight, every harmdoer, oath transgressor, and opportunistic spirit—into this liṅga of the final gaṇacakra be drawn!

To accomplish the drawing in, one must understand that when others do harm, it is a result of their afflictions; at the very ground, they have the buddha nature. Thus, the sādhakas are supplicating the deity to separate beings' afflictions from the buddha nature. In this way, all the afflictions, sufferings, and three poisons of all sentient beings—oneself and others—are gathered together as one and drawn into the torma effigy. Just as the kīla consecration makes use of the syllables A NRI SU TRI PRE DUḤ, so too one can imagine that all the afflictions of the six realms' beings, in the aspects of these six syllables, are being gathered up and drawn into the feast liberation.

Imagining the afflictions to be like oil and all the deities' forms to be like heaps of flames, one should think that the deities have consumed the sufferings and three poisons of all the three spheres' sentient ones, just as a great fire consumes oil that has been poured into it. One should cultivate this visualization not only in the context of Vajrakīla practice, but in every secret mantra gaṇacakra liberation.

Liberation

The liberation and proffering, which come next, are part of the original gaṇacakra text. Because the practice of liberation is easily misunderstood, it is important to clarify its outer, inner, and secret meanings. As it says in *The Thirty-Seven Practices of Bodhisattvas*, "What worldly god, himself also bound in samsara's prison, is able to give protection?"[5] Thus, one who wishes to accomplish liberating activities must first free oneself from the fetters of samsara. This is accomplished through the kīla of bodhicitta, which involves control over the channels and winds. Mastery of bodhicitta is necessary for the fourth kīla, the material kīla of signs, which is associated with liberation. In order to liberate beings, one must have the ability to lead their consciousnesses to the pure realms. Otherwise, liberating activity is indistinguishable from killing. Ultimately, it is only through the sādhaka's view that sentient ones can be guided to the pure buddha-fields.

When one sees the mind that is buddha nature, one gives rise to the view of inseparable samsara and nirvana. Then, one understands the single underlying basis that is described in *The Aspira-*

tion of Samantabhadra. By developing certainty in that view, one recognizes all sentient beings to be endowed with buddha nature. It is only through conditional delusion that self and other appear as two. In actuality, self and other cannot exist as two. This understanding frees one from the fetters of dualistic ego-grasping.

First, this point should be understood. Then, it must be experienced. Finally, it must be stabilized through meditation. The person who does this comes to liberate afflictions in their own place—to liberate the five poisons into the five wisdoms. In this way, everyone, self and others, is freed from samsara. As it says in a famous praise, "Freed, you then show freedom's path."[6] Thus, having become free oneself, one shows others the methods and practices to liberate themselves.

So, on the secret level, one first liberates oneself from dualistic concepts and self-grasping. Then, on the inner level, one becomes able to free all others from the bonds of afflictions. Finally, on the outer level, one can engage the direct, destructive actions that liberate—through immeasurable great loving-kindness and compassion—outer enemies, harmful elementals, and those in whom the ten grounds are complete. In this way, the entirety of appearance-existence becomes evident as the mandala of Vajrakīla. This is the sort of potency that can be developed through practice of the deity's approach and accomplishment.

If one contemplates the different sorts of beings in this worldly realm, there are some who have great pride. Others have great ignorance. Still others have great hatred. Considering only the phenomena of this life in this world, they think, "Whatever happens when I die doesn't matter." Completely self-absorbed, they have no knowledge of anything beyond the present lifetime. When they hear that all phenomena are emptiness, they understand it nihilistically, thinking, "When I die, my consciousness will dissolve into nothing." Having no concept of karmic imprints, they are angrily opposed to spiritual practitioners and to religious systems, labeling religious people as feeble-minded losers, misfits, and weirdos. Their view is that all religions are useless.

What is a practitioner's view? Someone who is practicing Kīla could give rise to mistaken views about such people, thinking, "Since he has such perverted attitudes about the Dharma, he is really a suitable object of liberation!" However, there is no reason whatsoever to become angry at these types. In fact, there is no need to have anything but compassion. Due to gross ignorance, such beings cannot control their extreme arrogance.

For example, one can consider spiders. I met a tarantula on the road the other day. Among all insects, they are the most arrogant, killing and eating whatever other bugs they can. They stay in their places, thinking, "There is really no one more terrifying than me!" Their arrogance is such that they can hardly bear to meet a human being walking on their path. Because they seem threatening, others avoid them.

To protect the spider, I tried to move him away from the road with a spoon. In reaction, the poor guy started biting the spoon, trying to take on such an enormous human! Being totally confused by great arrogance, he had no idea that all it would take is a single stamp of the foot to wipe him out. Bless his heart; he was just like that! That prideful bug was like that. I really felt sorry for him!

So it is with prideful, arrogant ones. I mean, in this world, one would not find anyone with greater reason to be prideful than Lord Buddha, right? But what did he teach? The Bhagavan Buddha taught that there is a direct correspondence between the greatness of one's attributes and being peaceful, restrained, and harmonious with all. Those endowed with good qualities are meek, showing humility to all. For this reason, it is said that the sign of spirituality is to be peaceful and restrained.

Conversely, arrogance is a mark of being devoid of attributes. Thus, Sakya Paṇḍita said, "Inferior qualities equal great pride."[7] Such are the faults that come from ignorance. When encountering such beings, one must cultivate affection.

The buddhas have taught all sorts of different activities that are appropriate for different types of beings. The mindstreams of most will be freed through peaceful methods. Other demonic types who do harm to countless sentient ones are not subdued through peaceful means. The beings to be liberated, known as "those in whom the ten grounds are complete," are those with gross afflictions like great hatred, those who are difficult to tame, and those who do grave harm to others. The mode of activity that is suitable for such beings is destructive in nature. It is a reflection of the coarseness of their own mental outlook.

There is not the slightest difference between the buddhas who have taught the Dharma of cause and effect and the yidam Vajrakīla who subdues māras. The minds of all sentient ones and the minds of all māras are also the same in regard to their buddha nature. However, one who has befriended his or her own afflictions is like a person with an incurable disease. Having become habituated to creating unvirtuous causes lifetime after lifetime, he or she becomes trapped, unable to escape those imprints. Destructive activities are for the purpose of liberating such beings from entanglement in their afflictions.

For example, someone who intends to harm a hundred others must be stopped, both for the sake of the hundred potential victims and because of the karmic weight of such negative deeds, which would cast the perpetrator into the lower realms. Those who bomb public places and harm the inhabitants of a country, inflicting injury on the general populace, are examples of such types. Though one may explain to them the Dharma of cause and effect, they do not listen. Having contempt for the teachings, lacking respect for humanity, such beings cut off their own life force through great ignorance. Under the influence of afflictions, they accumulate grave misdeeds. The only way to change the karmic trajectory of those who have extremely heavy afflictions is for them to change bodies and to take another birth. Even though the unripe aggregates, elements, and sense fields are pure at the basis, inferior bodies must be ripened. Thus, the compassionate ones have established actual practices to liberate those beings who are suitable fields for liberation.

The lower activities cause such beings' brutal code of conduct to be applied to themselves. Causing obstructors' ill will to fall back on their own heads, the lower activities speed up the ripening of misdeeds. If such ripening is not expedited, in the future, harmdoers will endure extreme suffering. Thus, the duration is shortened, and the weight of their karmic burden is lightened. It is not as though one is making them suffer; they have already created the causes of suffering for themselves. By considering this, one can give rise to a mind of immeasurable compassion for those ten grounds of liberation. When one truly has compassion, then beings will be tamed by whatever means are appropriate to them.

Some may ask, if afflictions abide in the mind and not in the body, how can killing obstructors separate them from their afflictions? The body has been created on the basis of karmic habits. As long as one is embodied, one will not become free of the circumstances of happiness and suffering conditioned by these latent imprints. Such habits have been accumulated through karma, which has been accumulated through positive and negative emotions. Thus, the compassionate buddhas have taught the skillful means of development and completion, through which practitioners can purify latencies and the obscurations of body, speech, and mind. However, since those with great delusion do not have the good fortune of faith in the Dharma, they are bereft of such methods. Because of this, they have no other recourse but to change bodies.

Among the destructive actions of the divine hosts who carry out enlightened activities, the liberation is principal. Within the Vajrakīla texts, there are various methods of liberation, such as suppression, burning, and casting of malign repelling tormas. There are also mantras for the lower activities of siccing, killing, and sorcery. These are employed during the great accomplishment retreat that is done at my monastery. In such rituals, it is essential that the vajra master and the various lamas maintain their focus. This focus requires not even the slightest wavering from loving-kindness and compassion. It is nothing but the mind of the four immeasurables.

Therefore, it is not at all appropriate to engage liberation with a mind of aggression. These methods do not involve killing with attachment- and aversion-based views about those one likes and dislikes. That would be an exceptionally grave misdeed and a fault more severe than shooting someone dead.

Since the buddhas' teachings are entirely unadulterated by self-interest, during the practices of drawing in and liberation, one should not hold on to any such notions as "This should be liberated. That should be liberated. This one is no good. That one is no good." Rather, since the deities are endowed with the eye of wisdom, one can leave everything to the three times' buddhas to adjudicate, asking them to bear witness. One should think, "May you draw in and deal with all the beings in this worldly realm who are suitable for liberation—all those in whom the ten grounds are complete."

Then, after the enlightened ones have drawn in beings according to their karma, one should recite the mantras and perform the liberation from within a state free of reference point. Otherwise, if one tries to engage destructive actions based on one's own judgment, it is said that there is great danger of going astray and taking the form of a destructive, demonic force (*rūdra*) in the future. This is an extremely grave point.

From the perspective of one's grasping at things as real, it is easy to think, "This person is doing harm to others. He is really engaged in bad actions." But whether or not someone is truly a bad actor can only be known by the Three Jewels. With their omniscient wisdom, they can adjudicate that. Thus, one should supplicate, "May you Three Jewels judge it. May you divine assemblies adjudicate. May you Dharma protectors and guards see to it." In this way, one can leave everything to them to determine appropriately. One should consider this point well.

Just as there are special substances known as liberations through taste, seeing, contact, and the like, malign tormas are said to be liberations through being struck. When malign tormas are cast, they make contact with enemies and obstructors, delivering them from samsaric sufferings. First, throughout the retreat, sādhakas should regard the torma as the immeasurable palace of the deities. Over a week of continuous practice, they should make offerings to the torma, using it as a meditation support. At the end of the retreat, after the deities have departed into space, one imagines the torma as a mass of poison, weapons, and armed troops. Then, having previously calculated the year, month, day, period, time, life-spirit weekday, direction, and so forth of the object at whom the weapon is aimed, the torma should be cast. When such astrological calculations have been made and the practice has been properly accomplished, the weapon will effectively reach its intended target, no matter the physical distance.

Even though the method of liberation appears to be the same as killing, the sentient ones to be liberated are led to the pure buddha-fields. In this way, the *phowa* transference for the deceased and the liberation of those in whom the ten grounds are complete are fundamentally the same. The only difference is that one is a peaceful method and the other is a destructive one. But, in fact, the destination to which they are guided is the same. Such obstructors have buddha nature. When that nature is forcibly separated from afflictions, they are established on the ground of the buddhas. Thus, one should understand that this activity is not beating and killing. Even though the sadhanas for the liberating activities of suppression, burning, and casting use extremely terrifying language that can make one's hairs stand on end, finally, they all come down to the enlightened activity of the buddhas. Liberation takes place through the force of great love alone. Thus, it is said in the Vajrakīla tantras, "The commitment to liberate through compassion is neither slaughter nor suppression."[8]

Through these means, the māra of the aggregates is conquered by bodhicitta. The liberation rite is not so much a killing as it is the destruction of obstructors' afflictions. Through the use of mantra, charmed substances, and the like, the sādhaka causes obstructors to become free of suffering and fear. The transformation of thoughts and afflictions into primordial awareness-wisdom is the inner liberation. Stabbing the torma effigy with the material kīla, one forcibly separates the mindstreams of those to be liberated from their karma and afflictions. In this way, consciousness is transformed through the interdependent arising that is the outer liberation. Finally, emerging as divine children of Vajrakīla and consort, they are established on the ground of the buddhas, the buddha nature having become fully ripened in them.

One who understands the liberating activity of Vajrakīla will know that it occurs only through compassion. Hatred cannot liberate. Only a practitioner who has become free of his or her own inner afflictions will be capable of conquering the outer afflictions of others through loving-kindness. For example, when one returns another's hostility and anger with love, that person's anger will spontaneously be exhausted. Liberating activity should be understood in this way.

Giving rise to a mind of great compassion for those who must be tamed, one should recite the following words of the liberation:

> Having suitably released them through
> manifest behavior and reduced
> their bodies and speech to particles,
> cause them to experience suffering!

Although obstructors must experience suffering during the liberation, that suffering is exceedingly brief and serves to exhaust their negative karma. Once that karma has been experienced, it is expended. For example, one endures some pain as a result of a surgery, but it is minor compared to the greater illness that is cured. Similarly, when demonic beings are liberated through illusory destructive activities, they experience an instant of suffering due to their grasping and then, in the very next instant, are delivered into the awareness of the buddhas—the pure realm of Sukhāvatī. In that brief moment of relatively small suffering, their vast accumulation of negative karma is completely exhausted.

Hearing this, some may wonder why accomplished practitioners of Vajrakīla don't just liberate all sentient beings, establishing everyone in the state of buddhahood. However, if one wants to grind grain that is mixed with stones, one must first remove the stones from the grain. It is unsuitable to grind the stones and the grain together. Similarly, one must apply antidotes appropriate to the conditions. The vast majority of sentient ones will definitely be freed through peaceful, enriching, and magnetizing activities. For example, those who are greatly afflicted but do not do great harm to others or to the buddhas' teachings can be tamed by means of magnetization. One should use the least invasive means necessary, reserving destructive methods only for those unfortunate ones who cannot be tamed any other way.

For example, the heap of dharmas—the tantras and sadhanas taught by the three times' buddhas—are literally inexhaustible and without limit. This is because the different sorts of individuals of high, middling, and lesser faculties are inexhaustible and limitless. The methods of establishing sentient ones in the status of the buddhas are equally diverse. Whichever methods are used, they should suit the faculties, dispositions, and karmic fortunes of each kind of individual. This idea is reflected in a common prayer to request Dharma teachings:

> Please turn the Dharma wheel of *yānas*—
> the great, the smaller, and the common—
> according to specific ways of
> sentient ones' reasoning and intentions.[9]

All the progressive stages of different vehicles are like different sizes of clothing. One should consider that one would not dress an adult man in an infant's onesie! Similarly, if one clothed an infant in a grown man's suit, it would die of suffocation! In this way, it is good to reflect on the vastness of the buddhas' knowledge. Otherwise, one may be mystified and feel doubtful about the enlightened ones' actions. Unless one has great intelligence, the buddhas' enlightened activities are incomprehensible. This is the explanation of liberating activity.

After the liberation is the proffering, which occurs with the following verse:

HŪṂ. Open wide, Great Glorious One and courts!
These five skandhas of delivered foes
and obstructors we serve to your mouths—
glorious couple, you ten wrathful ones,
and your emanated retinues.
Please partake of harmdoers, hostile foes,
and their hosts, with not an atom left!
VAJRA YAKṢA KRODHA KHA KHA KHĀHI KHĀHI.

Here, one should imagine that all the divine servants in the mandala of Vajrakīla consume the flesh, blood, and bones of the enemies and obstructors who have been liberated. Since these are the nature of the five afflictive poisons, that which is consumed is ultimately the afflictions of sentient ones.

Repelling

Next, the assembly recites another supplemental text, that of repelling. The demons, māras, furies, kinglies, and so forth who are mentioned in the repelling text should not be thought of as external entities. Rather, they are manifestations of one's own inner afflictions. As such, these harmful forces can arise anywhere. It is not so much that these beings should be repelled by sādhakas; rather, it is their negative actions that must be turned back.

These various spirits and demons are not entirely bad. One should understand that they are extremely diverse. For example, in a vast country, there are many different nationalities and various sorts of groups. So it is with the different kinds of beings in the repelling practice. Through their self-grasping, they do harm to sentient ones. As a result, they create the causes of their own suffering. Through the interaction of their negative karma with one's own conditions, they appear as beings to whom one owes karmic debts. So, that which is really being turned back are self-grasping and afflictions. When one's own self-grasping and afflictions are repelled, all negative conditions are repelled. Thus, there is no outer demon to be subdued. Those who have discerning intelligence understand that the cause of the so-called demon is the karma they themselves have accumulated through afflictions. That negative karma is turned back by the power of compassion. All repelling activity should be understood in this way.

Gaṇacakra Offerings

Once the repelling is complete, it is time to enjoy the offerings. When one offers food to the wisdom deities, they do not actually consume it. However, since oneself and the deity become indistinguishable when one's actions are virtuous, offering food to the assembly of sādhakas is no different from making offerings to the actual divine mandala. Through this means, the wisdom deities can partake of enjoyments. Because offering in this way will become a cause for one to experience perfect enjoyments for many lifetimes, it is one way that merit is accumulated in the context of the gaṇapūja.

Particularly when partaking of the enjoyments, one should perceive all men as the father deity and as heroes. Likewise, one should think of all women as the mother deity and ḍākiṇīs. Seeing self and others as divine in this way, one's perceptions should be conjoined with the vivid appearances of the deity. Everyone has been transformed into the yidam abiding at the center of the mandala, and all the offerings have become divine enjoyments. Thus, there is no difference between the mandala deities partaking of the offerings and the gathered sādhakas doing so.

In the context of gaṇacakra offerings, we speak of the five fleshes and five nectars. The fleshes—(1) human, (2) cow, (3) dog, (4) elephant, and (5) horse—are the nature of the buddhas of the five families. The nectars, naturally present in one's own body, are (1) excrement, (2) urine, (3) red bodhicitta, (4) white bodhicitta, and (5) brains. They are the nature of the five buddhas' consorts. From the perspective of the Vajra Vehicle, these are all considered to be precious medicines. Since this notion would be shocking for ordinary people who do not understand secret mantra, this view is kept hidden and should not be disclosed. Because ordinary beings give rise to afflictions by perceiving such substances as impure, the point for meditators is to realize their fundamental purity.

Thus, when presented with the five fleshes and five nectars, one must purify the dualistic concepts "this is clean; that is unclean." Such notions only do harm. The idea that something is unclean is merely subtle aversion. The idea that something is tasty is subtle desire. These dualistic concepts of attachment and aversion follow one after the next like a continuous snowfall. Of course, dualistic grasping arises in the mind. Even if something is filthy, people will eat it as long as it tastes good! But when it's filthy and tastes nasty, then what? The yoga is to partake impartially, without regard for clean and unclean. This is a special feature of the gaṇapūja. Everything must be received in the state of great equanimity. For this reason, the following words are recited when offering to the vajra master: "Look! To have doubt in this beautiful true Dharma would not be right! Partake, regarding Brahmins, dogs, outcastes, and pigs as singular in nature!"[10] Then, the master responds, "AH LA LA HOḤ! Priceless is the *sugatas'* Dharma! Free of taint by desire, I fully reject grasped at and grasping! To thusness I bow with respect!"[11]

The principal point of this yoga is that the imprints of grasping at desirables not be reinforced in the mind. Even though one enjoys desirable objects, one should practice in ways that do not cause imprints to be laid down. In the context of the two accumulations, the accumulation of wisdom means not allowing imprints to be established. Thus, it is said, "One should neither take up clinging to passion nor abstain from the downfall of desirables."[12] This means that one must partake of the enjoyments. Even so, one must be free of clinging to the gaṇacakra. Experiences of pleasure must be liberated on arising. In this context, everything dawns as the pure appearance of the deity. When partaking of the five desirables, it all comes down to the essential point of not losing oneself in the enjoyment. One should only lose oneself halfway. The final benefit of the gaṇacakra is just that.

As the ritual master gathers the residual of the gaṇacakra, it is important that the sādhakas take great care with it, perceiving the divine ḍākiṇīs to whom one makes the offering as being like loving mothers, sisters, and companions. Because sādhakas share a singular samaya with them, one should offer the remainder with a mind of great affection. For example, if someone is very dear to you, you will take a bite of food before feeding that person the rest. This is also the reason the vajra master must offer saliva with the remainder: it is a sign of extremely great love for the heroes and ḍākiṇīs. Because of this, it is unacceptable to offer carelessly the discarded peels from fruits or throw the foods one dislikes into the offering vessel.

After the residual has been gathered, it is consecrated with the words OṀ VAJRA AMṚITA UCCHIṢṬĀYA HŪṂ PHAṬ, and then music is played. At the start of the music, the sādhakas should whistle softly—not harshly—to gather nonhuman guests to come and partake of the offering. The recipients require this self-arisen sound, which is like a gentle wind. Because demons and other nonhumans respond to such sounds, they are often regarded as scary by Tibetans. But there is no need to hold superstitious views about empty echoes.

Then, the residual is offered with the following verse:

HŪṂ. First, we offer gods' hosts the choice part.
Next, the feast restores the siblings' bond.
Finally, through this torma of remains,
may deserving ones be satisfied!
OṀ UCCHIṢṬĀ BHAKṢA KHĀHI.

Taking in hand the vessel containing the residual, the ritual master dances out of the assembly while music is played. It is taught that the residual should be set outdoors in a clean place. Since animals and insects will eventually eat the coarse food that has been set out, these offerings become the practice of generosity.

The gaṇacakra concludes with verses to invoke the samaya and rouse the deities, oath-bound guardians, and earth-keeping maidens each to fulfill their respective promises. Finally, after another drawing in, the following lines are recited:

> HŪṂ. Imprints born through ignorance and the
> mass of four conditions, six causes,
> and afflictions are suppressed beneath
> Meru—self-born knowing-emptiness—
> seamlessly upon completion's ground!
> OṂ ĀḤ HŪṂ LAṂ STAMBHAYA NAN.

Even though no dance is performed at this stage, this verse is called "the horse dance." It refers to Hayagrīva, whose wrathful movements suppress harmdoing spirits as though they were being trampled by the striking hooves of a horse. In actuality, these harmdoers are the bases of dualistic consciousness, the afflictions, and karmic imprints. Collectively, they give rise to all the samsaric phenomena of the six realms. As the empty torma vessel is forcefully turned upside down, one imagines that all such obstructive forces have been suppressed by the Mount Meru that is the view.

The Gaṇacakra in Daily Activities

Once one has understood the meaning of the gaṇacakra, one can call it to mind at all times during daily activities. Whatever delight or pleasure among the five desirables one experiences, one should never part from the vivid appearance of the deity. It is said that food or any other pleasurable phenomenon becomes a gaṇacakra offering when it is enjoyed while recalling the deity. So it is with the sexual pleasures that are experienced with the mantra recitation: by vividly imagining the deity, one makes the supreme secret offering. This essential point is called the instruction on perceiving pleasures as the gaṇacakra. Even if one has no time for formal practice, one must not forget the deity when partaking of desirables.

CHAPTER 10

Taking Up Accomplishments Instructions

As the taking up accomplishments text is drawn from the extensive sadhana, its ritual is a feature of the great accomplishment retreat. The consecrated kīlas should be used as supports for this ritual, which is ideally done at the break of day. If personal material kīlas have been kept inside the material mandala for the duration of the retreat, they should be removed and returned to the sādhakas before the ritual of taking up accomplishments. In the absence of a kīla, a māla may be used as a support.

The note at the beginning of the text mentions the vajra master and regents. Even though there is no need for regents in the secret accomplishment retreat, I wanted disciples to gain experience of the empowerment known as "taking up accomplishments." The purpose of this ritual is for sādhakas to gather up all the siddhis that have been generated during the course of the retreat.

When taking up the accomplishments, it is good to reflect on the connection between the wisdom deities and practitioners. In general, the term *mudrā kīla* refers to the meditation on the deity's form in the development stages. It is divided into two aspects: the natural, self-arisen kīla and the kīla of samādhi. As for the first, the natural, self-arisen kīla consists of the actual wisdom deities who emanate from the enlightened mind of the three times' buddhas and abide in the Akaniṣṭha Dharmasphere. Thus, the qualities of the mind of all the buddhas dwell within the dharmakāya. The forms of the principal, retinues, palace, mandala, and pure field that supports them all emerge within the dharmasphere. These wisdom deities are the objects of sādhakas' meditation—the supports of accomplishment. Through the force of all the buddhas' compassion interacting with the force of practitioners' faith and insight, the wisdom deities' blessings actually come forth like rainfall from clouds.

The second aspect, the kīla of samādhi, becomes manifest when the common outer container and inner contents—all worldly realms and the beings therein—are known to be the very nature of purity according to the view of secret mantra. The kīla of samādhi seals all appearances with purity. Through the stages of development, impure perceptions are transformed into pure ones. In this way, the entirety of appearance-existence dawns as the mandala of the deity. It is on this basis that one can attain the siddhis of accomplishing the four activities.

With this understanding, the sādhakas should begin by offering incense and reciting the charm of accomplishments a few times: OṀ VAJRAKĪLI KĪLAYA, SARVA VIGHNĀN VAṀ HŪṀ PHAṬ! KĀYA SIDDHI OṀ, VĀK SIDDHI ĀḤ, CITTA SIDDHI HŪṀ, SARVA SIDDHI HRĪḤ. Then, with mudrā, music, melody, and a mind of devotion and longing, they should chant the verses, which call forth the yidam's commitment, and request desired accomplishments. Since the meaning of the text accords with the words for the most part, not much explanation is needed. However, the following lines are noteworthy:

> HŪṀ. Knowledge holders of Vajra Youth, make
> existence as vajra manifest!
> You existence-vajrakīla gods,
> bring primordial wrathful wisdom forth!

Here, the sādhakas supplicate the assemblies of Vajrakumāra to "make existence as vajra manifest" and to "bring primordial wrathful wisdom forth." Although existence as vajra has already been explained, what makes primordial awareness wrathful? Consciousness is dualistic—always dividing phenomena into self and other. Dualistic grasping is ignorance; it is the lack of clarity. When one looks at the mind with the mind, that which appeared as two collapses into one and duality is suddenly rendered nonexistent. Since primordial awareness impartially slaughters dualistic mind, along with every thought and emotion arisen from it—gross or subtle, virtuous or unvirtuous—it is referred to as wrathful. The moment one recognizes the actual condition of the mind, this happens instantaneously.

The wrath of primordial awareness will be understood through ongoing practice. For example, when an affliction arises, the practitioner of individual liberation blocks it. The practitioner of the Bodhisattva Vehicle transforms it. For the secret mantra meditator, the very instant it arises, the affliction is recognized as affliction. In this way, it ceases to be. Thus, the recognition itself is like killing. In this way, the nature of wisdom is wrathful.

For example, when anger arises, if the angry person glimpses the singular basis of his or her mind and the other person's mind, then the object of anger disappears. There is no one who becomes angry, nor is there anyone at whom to get angry. One's emotion becomes empty, as though one were trying to feel angry at a sketch on paper. At that instant, there is no dualistic grasping at all. Such awareness arises in a single moment. If one plants the kīla of primordial awareness-rigpa into mental arisings, they die and no longer elicit any feeling. When the mind becomes mirrorlike, one is left without any trace of aversion. The sensations of rage and anger are entirely absent. When the affliction suddenly disappears, its energy can transform into laughter. By training in this way, it becomes easy to let go of afflictions, because one begins to experience their illusory nature.

Incineration by fire and slaughter by wisdom-wrath have the same significance. Wisdom becomes like fire, which can instantly burn away afflictions. For example, the moment a flame and a piece of paper meet, they become one. The paper becomes the flame and is no more. All wrathful deities are analogous to that fire. So, without need of relying on the methods of individual liberation and the Bodhisattva Vehicle, one can immediately slaughter afflictions. In this way, wrathful wisdom should be understood as the kīla of primordial awareness-rigpa.

The next lines of the taking up accomplishments text are endowed with great meaning:

> These days, as the dawn's first light appears,
> Vajrarākṣasa's daybreak, too, dawns.

Although the first light of dawn is a fleeting phenomenon, it is referred to with the words "these days." In order to understand the significance of this, one should know that this dawn has outer, inner, and secret aspects. On the outer level, it is the fresh propagation of the Buddhadharma in so-called foreign lands. This has occurred through the ripening of the collective merit and aspirations of beings. Without a doubt, the pervasion of the buddhas' teachings throughout the world has been the most meaningful consequence of the Tibetan diaspora. Thus, the appearance of the first light of dawn is the emergence in foreign lands of the teachings that encompass the meaning of the three successive paths. This emergence is gradually destroying even the notion of primitive border areas where the sounds of Dharma teachings are unheard. Next, the inner dawn occurs when the beings who inhabit these lands actually enter the door of Dharma by receiving the vow of refuge.

Together with this dawn, the teachings of the Secret Mantric Vajra Vehicle—the uncommon daybreak of Vajrarākṣasa, Adamantine Carnivore—have emerged. This is the secret dawn that occurs through the practice of extraordinary mantric methods of accomplishment, whose ritual systems of practice are complete and grant especially great blessing. Whoever practices these methods will give rise to discriminating intelligence and authentic feeling in the mind. Through this daybreak, the flesh, blood, and bones of sentient ones' ignorance, desire, and aversion are consumed, laying them bare as the nature of primordial awareness. This uncommon daybreak, then, is nothing less than attainment of the buddhas' status. Finally, the text concludes with these words:

> From the glorious knot within your heart
> dawns primordial wisdom's secret sun
> on the bodies, speech, and minds of us
> yogins, great sādhakas, SIDDHI HOḤ!

Through supplicating one-pointedly and meditating, one gives rise to great feeling when gathering the accomplishments. That feeling is characterized by utter freedom from doubt about the view. In other cases, it manifests as great devotion or as great compassion. At such junctures, one arrives at the ground of the buddhas. This is the dawning of "primordial wisdom's secret sun."

That sun is actual luminosity. It is the omniscient, primordial awareness of all the buddhas. Why is it secret? It is something hidden—something not to be seen with the eye. Indeed, it is utterly beyond the senses of sight, hearing, recollection, or contact. Only through realization of the view will one be able to perceive it. If one has doubt about realizing the view, the doubt itself prevents one from seeing. It is through direct insight alone that this point can be settled. The wisdom that transcends rational mind is entirely outside the scope of rationality. Thus, when it comes to seeing this secret sun, inquiry and investigation, which are activities of the rational mind, cannot help. They merely perpetuate doubt. Manifest understanding will come only through one's own direct experience.

According to the phenomena of this material world, the sun rises in the east and sets in the west. However, the sun mentioned in this verse has nothing to do with the way things appear on the four continents. Such outer appearances bear the hallmark of confusion. This sun, which is without waxing or waning, increase or decrease, remains invisible unless one has cleared away dualistic grasping through realizing the view. Since this sun neither rises nor sets, the word "dawn" in the text signifies the potential to become a buddha in one lifetime. This perpetual dawn is the import of the term *youth* in Vajrakumāra's name. The Yamāntaka texts refer to this extremely profound point with the words "Glimpsing but fragmented light rays of the Ārya's love."[1] The meaning of these words is precisely the same as the dawning of the secret sun. The point is the realization of nondual awareness.

Although it is known by different names—the kīla of unfurled and pervasive primordial awareness, the kīla of primordial awareness-rigpa, and the symbolic kīla of blessing—its meaning is singular. This ultimate view is the fundamental oneness of buddhas and sentient ones. For anyone who comprehends it, the sun of wisdom dawns. Beyond being an object of sight, hearing, memory, or physical contact, this secret sun is to be directly perceived. Subject to neither birth nor death, it is Vajrakumāra, Vajra Youth, whose adamantine appearance can be seen only by the reflexive mind.

Like Samantabhadra and Vajradhara, he is the ground of all the buddhas. Since his qualities are too numerous, they are inexpressible. They can be fathomed only by looking inward at one's own mind. Each one of us has a Vajradhara who can be perceived by the mind without reference point. Through seeing him, one will know Vajradhara's qualities and Vajrakumāra's distinctive features. Since all phenomena have arisen from the mind, Milarepa taught, "Do not try to resolve phenomena; resolve the mind."[2] By rooting out the mind and realizing the view, one can understand all phenomena as they truly are. This is the Kagyü system.

How is the root of mind to be recognized? Free of both subject and object, one should look at the mind—the buddha nature—just as it is. Seeing the very essence of the inner mind, which is exemplified by the outer sky, one will recognize its nature. That nature is neither existent nor nonexistent. Since it is empty—beyond having any part of the minutest particle—it is said to lack existence. It has not even an atom of substance, yet since both buddhas and sentient ones appear from it, it is also not nonexistent. So how should one identify it? The mind is endowed with a clear nature. The one that perceives the empty essence is the clarity aspect of the mind. So, that which is seen is the emptiness aspect; the seer is the clarity aspect. These two are called "the inseparable union of clarity and emptiness."

When this essence has been perceived, one comprehends what is said in *The Aspiration of Samantabhadra*—that the entirety of samsara and nirvana have been established from it. What are the qualities of Vajrakumāra? All those who have departed to the pure grounds of the buddhas dwell within the attributes of innumerable kāyas and pure buddha-fields. The qualities of the buddhas' three kāyas have arisen from Vajrakumāra. As far as space extends and until samsara has been emptied out, this adamantine one will not abandon his enlightened activities.

The dawning of the secret sun of primordial awareness from within his heart is the essence of all the methods for accomplishing Vajrakīla. It occurs but once. Thereafter, it is known to be stable and unchanging. After having dawned, this secret sun continues to shine throughout this life, the next, and the bardo.

Finally, while holding the consecrated support—the kīla or the māla—between one's hands, one should repeatedly touch it to the four places while reciting the Sanskrit syllables OṀ VAJRAKĪLI KĪLAYA, SARVA VIGHNĀN VAṀ HŪṀ PHAṬ! KĀYA SIDDHI OṀ, VĀK SIDDHI ĀḤ, CITTA SIDDHI HŪṀ, SARVA SIDDHI HRĪḤ. Since the main point of this latter recitation is to bestow the empowerment of actual accomplishments, it is extremely important to maintain the visualization at this juncture. One should imagine blessings in the form of brilliant light rays radiating from the three mandalas of the deity—the self-generation, the facing generation, and the Foremost Prince, whom one holds in hand. These light rays are the essence of the deities' blessings of loving-kindness and compassion. Having filled the entire container and contents, the rays of light then subside into the four places of each of the gathered sādhakas, granting the empowerments of body, speech, mind, and qualities conjoined with activities. One should visualize in this way while supplicating one-pointedly to receive empowerment.

Those who have participated even once in the secret accomplishment have gained experience of the deity's blessings. As devotion arises for the deity, the mind's obscurations are cleared away. Thus, one naturally feels joy. Having gained this experience, one becomes like the seed of a flower that has sprouted. Although there are many different signs of accomplishment, such as never forgetting the yidam and the increase of joy and wisdom, the foremost sign of having received the deity's blessings is the increase of love and compassion. This is the result that should come from practice. The greater one's love and compassion for beings, the greater one's receipt of the deity's blessing. Taking up accomplishments is the means whereby sādhakas actively realize the yidam. This does not mean that one's gross physical body will morph into the deity's form. Rather, it means that the deity will be constantly present in the mind, and his or her love will take root in one's heart. When supplicating to receive empowerment, one is actually praying with yearning to take up the love of the yidam. The practice of taking up the accomplishments should be understood in this way.

In Tibet, the ritual is done somewhat differently and is more extensive. As the entire assembly recites the charm of accomplishments, the vajra master bestows empowerment on the sādhakas by touching his kīla to the four places of each of them. Thereafter, the ritual master distributes the accomplishment substances.

Following the taking up accomplishments are the gaṇacakra and the concluding rituals of the secret accomplishment retreat.

CHAPTER 11

Practical Applications of the Instructions

Carrying Retreat Experience into Daily Life

For a practitioner who wishes to give rise to the clear appearance of the deity, group accomplishment retreats are particularly important. If one is able to participate in even one such retreat, it creates imprints in the mind that can serve as future points of reference. Reciting the mantra and hearing its syllables and melody, reading the sadhana, and giving rise to the deity's clear appearance—all these trainings establish the mind in a state of great purity, which helps to clear away dualistic propensities. Through the force of engaging the practice with others, one can gain an experience of nonduality, which can be carried into daily life.

The mind of the deity is the dharmakāya—the empty nature. The appearance of the deity is the nondual union of clarity and emptiness—the saṁbhogakāya. The way the deity manifests among beings out of great love and compassion is the nirmāṇakāya. Through practicing together with the vajra master and other sādhakas who have stable meditation experience, one can receive the blessings of the deity's three kāyas and can give rise to the supreme and common siddhis. Even if one were to practice deity yoga consistently alone in one's home—chanting and playing the bell and *ḍamaru*—it would be difficult for an individual to give rise to the same sort of beneficial experiences that can arise in a group setting.

When meditators come together to do a practice like this, they temporarily set aside ordinary worldly activities in order to engage in visualization and mantra recitation. Through the power of this practice, combined with the blessing of the deity's love, ordinary thoughts and emotions are suspended. When, in this way, attachment and aversion temporarily cease, one's suffering also ceases. The fact that one can have this sort of experience of bliss and ease during the retreat is a sign of receiving the deity's blessing. This is like a small child feeling comfortable and at ease in the presence of his or her mother. It is because of the mother's love that the child feels such ease. Similarly, when engaging the practice, meditators directly experience the deity's love.

Once one has been exposed to this sort of group retreat and its benefits, that experience carries forward into one's daily activities. The moment one merely recalls the mantra and its melody, it can bring back a vivid experience of being together with the vajra master and one's vajra siblings in the mandala of the deity. When this is understood, one realizes the preciousness of group accomplishment retreats, since they create the causes for sādhakas to accomplish together the deities' kāyas and pure fields.

It is important that practitioners not become fixated on the outer condition of group retreats, though. Many people assume these good experiences are a result of being in the physical presence of the guru. This is not at all the case. This error arises due to gross fixation on outer phenomena as being real and true. One must understand that it is through the mind of the guru that one experiences blessings. This mind is not subject to birth or death. When one knows the mind of the guru to be the deity, the physical location of the master becomes irrelevant. Even in the future, when the guru transitions from this life and he or she is no longer physically present, one can have confidence that the blessing of the guru's mind endures. Now that the secret accomplishment retreat has been established, whether I am here or not, you students must cherish it, carry it on, and see that its continuity not be broken.

In addition, to carry the retreat experience into daily activities, one must call to mind the form of the deity and the sound of the mantra again and again. Through the power of having done a retreat like this even once, the sādhaka can reestablish his or her body as the deity, speech as mantra, and mind as samādhi through mere recollection. Especially when feeling sad or encountering troubles, one should play an audio recording of the mantra. When various afflictions and sufferings arise, if one calls vividly to mind the retreat experience, remembering the mantra or listening to a recording of it, this recollection will cut through all ordinary conceptual thoughts. In this way, one will immediately receive the blessing of the deity, the vajra master, and all the sādhakas who shared the retreat experience. If this is done many times each day, there is no need for the retreat experience ever to fade. When this recollection is conjoined with a mind of compassion for all those who have not had such fortunate experiences, one can bring manifest benefit to beings suffering in samsara.

Outside of retreat, there are many ways to maintain the continuity of practice without reading the entire sadhana. Indeed, in his *Hundred Thousand Songs*, Lord Milarepa summarized the essence of daily conduct in his instruction to cause the delusion of the dream state to arise as luminosity, to perceive food and drink as the gaṇacakra, and to perceive physical movement and stillness as circumambulation.[1] As supports to this, throughout daily activities, one can recite the mantra and recall the development-stage visualizations. At home, one can play the recording of the mantra while sleeping at night.

For those who wish to do a daily practice of Vajrakīla, there is a very brief and accessible sadhana that was composed by Khenpo Jigme Phüntsog.[2] Another option is to recite only the verse of praise from the subsequent rites of the present text, which reads,

> HŪṂ. All the ten directions' and three times'
> buddhas' unified activities
> rise up as your body of great force!
> Praise and homage—Kīla deity,
> māra tamer with changeless and firm
> body void of aging or decline!

Thereafter, one can immediately begin the recitation of mantra. Otherwise, once in a while, as time allows, one can recite the sadhana, always bringing to mind the continually abiding mandala. Within the naturally present saṁbhogakāya pure field that pervades space is the immeasurable palace of wisdom deities, whose door always remains open. As a practice support, one can set out a single kīla, since the entire mandala is complete therein. Thus, it can stand in for a material mandala.

For personal practice, one can rely on the practice manual without supplemental texts.* It is not necessary to make tormas or to recite other texts, such as the bringing down blessings text or the white torma offering text, which are read only in the context of the accomplishment retreat. Since recitation of the lineage supplication is optional, one may read it or not depending on time and interest. If groups of students can occasionally gather and do the practice together, this is also of great benefit.

Visualizing the Deity

Even when one is going about one's daily activities and not engaged in formal practice, one should bring to mind throughout the day the shape of the HŪṂ syllable or the form of the yidam. It is a good idea to keep an image of the deity on one's person and to look at it from time to time. By practicing this way in conjunction with the wish to benefit all sentient ones, the mind can become very clear such that when one closes one's eyes, the image of the deity will spontaneously appear. At first it is a mere approximation, but as one continues to cultivate the visualization, it will become more and more stable in the mind. In this way, the mind comes to abide on the visualized deity, using it as a support for meditation.

The point is that one should become able to recall the visualization instantaneously and on demand. One should aim for the visualization to appear clearly as soon as one thinks of the deity.

*This means that for daily practice, the practice manual can be recited without the sections marked by the vertical khaṭvāṅga icon.

For this reason, one should call the deity to mind as often as one can.

To carry the clear appearance of the yidam to its end point is difficult. However, along the way, one should continually make effort not to separate from the deity's pure appearance, remembering that one's own aggregates, elements, and sense fields are divine. If one does so, pure perception will gradually progress and increase.

What lies between the perception of oneself as divine and the perception of oneself as ordinary? The dividing line is vigilant mindful awareness. When it is present, afflictions are transformed into wisdom. When it is absent, there arise unmitigated afflictions—negative emotions to which no antidote is applied. For example, if someone who doesn't know how to observe the mind becomes angry, karma is accumulated at the very moment of the affliction's arising. A yogin, on the other hand, has an observer—an aspect of the mind that can sense the arising. This distinction is taught in dzogchen instructions. When the observer is present, the affliction itself is rendered impotent. In that moment, mindful awareness captures its own seat.

So it is with all the other afflictions. They continue to arise for the duration of one's life. To whatever degree one does not separate from mindful awareness—the clear appearance of the deity—when experiencing negative emotions, one will achieve a corresponding fruition. Through cultivating the observer again and again throughout daily activities, it will become possible for one to attain the saṁbhogakāya in the bardo. Even though the manifold aspects of the deity's clear appearance may seem complex, the practice becomes easy when one understands this key point. Through mindful awareness, one will come to know the aggregates and elements of all other sentient ones of the three realms to be innately pure gods and goddesses. Then, through recognition, one's own thoughts based in passion and aversion will naturally diminish. Such practice has great potency.

Mantra Recitation

During the secret accomplishment, we practice using a recording of the mantra with melody. When a large group chants a mantra together, some will tend to chant fast and others slow, some will hold the melody well and others will be tone-deaf, and some will chant very loud while others will be almost silent. One benefit of the recording is that it helps keep the group on track despite these differences. It protects the group from going too far astray in their recitation.

In addition, when humans and nonhuman elementals, insects, animals, and the like hear the sounds of the mantra with melody, it causes their thoughts to be suspended and the imprints of bodhicitta to be established in their minds. Likewise, it diminishes afflictions rooted in passion, aversion, and delusion. When those who have participated in past retreats have had the sounds of their voices captured in a recording of the mantra, then every time the recording is played, it continues to benefit all those who hear it even after they have died.

Because of this, wherever in the six realms one may travel, one will continue to reap the merit of aiding all those beings who hear the mantra. Even when it is not possible to be physically present for a retreat, those whose voices are on the recording will continue to receive the same advantages as if they were actually participating. If the recording is played in people's homes, there are similar benefits. In this way, use of the recording becomes a practice of compassion.

Furthermore, if there are a hundred people reciting in the assembly while listening to a hundred voices on the recording, each individual receives the benefit of having done two hundred recitations.

Following the retreat, the sounds of the mantra can spontaneously arise in the mind, dispelling thoughts and afflictions. The imprints established through the entire group's recitation can transform ordinary outer sounds into mantra in accord with the experiences of great accomplishment. These are some of the excellent qualities of mantra.

For those who have experience in meditation, it is all right to do without the recording. Even so, practitioners should be aware of the special benefits of utilizing recorded mantras. In addition, sādhakas must not think that mantra recitation is to be sustained only when one is participating in accomplishment retreats or meditation sessions. Rather, for all secret mantra yogas of any deity, it is necessary to cultivate meditation and recitation of mantra continuously and at all times. This is one of the primary means whereby the development stages transform ordinary consciousness into awareness-wisdom.

Since the mantras in the text, with their corresponding visualizations, are specific to the sadhana, it is not necessary to recite or visualize them outside of sessions. Among the many different kinds of mantras, the quintessence mantra (*nyenying*) is the one that should be recited during daily activities. This mantra is: VAJRAKĪLI KĪLAYA HŪṂ̐ PHAṬ. When reciting it, there is no need to include the syllable OṀ. The quintessence is like calling out the name of a divine friend. Each time one calls a friend's name, his or her face arises in the mind, reinforcing the connection between friends. In this way, the deity becomes a stable reliance who helps one to accomplish whatever work must be done.

Generally, when speaking with others, one loses the recitation. However, for sustaining awareness during conversation, the following two methods have been helpful for me.

Vajra Recitation

The first is the vajra recitation of the syllables OṀ ĀḤ HŪṂ̐, in which every mantra is subsumed. This can be practiced throughout all one's daily activities. Obviously, during conversation, one need not verbalize the syllables. Rather, one should conjoin mental recitation with the natural breath. With the in-breath, one's focus is on the syllable OṀ. When the breath descends, reaching the belly, one mentally recites the syllable ĀḤ. At that juncture, the pure essence of the breath is absorbed into the ĀḤ syllable, which is the nature of fire that abides at the navel. Then, with the out-breath, one focuses on the HŪṂ̐, exhaling only the remaining impure portion of the breath.

With this method, there is no need to visualize any letters at all. Rather, one should simply conjoin the in- and outflow of breath with the natural resounding of OṀ ĀḤ HŪṂ̐. When one practices in this way, the act of breathing itself becomes the mantra recitation. Since one must breathe in order to speak, every word that one utters is conjoined with mantra.

Practitioners should also train in recalling the vajra recitation when falling asleep. Eventually, one will become able to remember it in dreams, which is a great accomplishment. Once the vajra recitation has become stabilized to the point where it is remembered in the dream state, one should focus on the recitation of HŪṂ̐ alone.

Finally, having become well habituated to the HŪṂ̐ recitation, one will understand one's own pulse to naturally reverberate with the sound HŪṂ̐. When mind and wind energies are conjoined, the pulse throughout one's entire body spontaneously resounds throughout the channels. When one abides in meditation alone, it is unnecessary to do anything in the way of outer recitation. As a sign of having conjoined mind and winds, the mind will not wander outward. The accomplishment of mantra should be understood in this way.

The Seed Syllable

The second method is to focus on the HŪṂ̐ flame abiding at the navel. The flame pulses with one's natural heartbeat. Together with each pulsation is a spontaneous resounding of the syllable HŪṂ̐. This is a simple method one can practice in order to sustain the flow of mantra even while interacting with others.

Antidoting Afflictions and Self-Grasping

No matter how extensive or concise the methods of visualization and mantra recitation may be, they all come down to the cultivation of vigilant mindful awareness. Thus, there is no need for practitioners to become overwhelmed by the diversity of secret mantra methods. Disciples who really want to practice should do nothing but cultivate an undistracted mind. By doing so, they will definitely accomplish greater or lesser siddhis according to their capabilities.

When afflictions arise, it is best to look at the empty nature of the mind. Those who know how to meditate should apply this method to every affliction. By doing so for a couple minutes, one will cause the affliction to dissipate. Then it will return. Meditate again and it dissipates again. One must meditate over and over and over with diligence.

Otherwise, those who prefer to use mantra to antidote afflictions such as aversion must cultivate the awareness that recognizes the aversion in the first place. Generating such awareness is more than half the battle. As soon as the affliction has been recognized, one can recall the mantra in the next moment. With the mantra itself, one calls out to the deity Vajrakīla. As a result, his power will immediately arise in one's mindstream. In this way, any affliction can be antidoted.

Another method, appropriate for beginners who are not skilled in meditation, is to reflect on the six afflictions as being the seeds of the six realms, where the six types of suffering are experienced. Through contemplating the six sufferings, practitioners can use the six transcendent perfections to tame the six afflictions. Yet another approach is to cultivate stable love and compassion, in whose presence afflictions cannot arise.

When people who are suffering ask for my advice, I instruct them to supplicate Ārya Tārā. Sometimes they reply, "I have already recited so many Tārā mantras and there was no benefit at all!" How does this happen? Those who only approach the deity when they are completely miserable become very narrow-minded, grasping at suffering and hardship as though they were real. Although they verbally recite the mantra, their minds still dwell upon suffering. In this way, each recited mantra becomes a meditation on misery. If one contemplates suffering again and again, it binds the mind, rendering one stupid and discouraged. This causes one to despair, making things worse and worse. How is suffering on top of suffering supposed to be of benefit?

Practitioners who aspire to achieve results must first cast aside suffering. For example, if I want to benefit a disciple, I need to single-pointedly supplicate the yidam such that the disciple himself or herself is forgotten. One can only benefit another by abiding in an unobjectified mind. In this regard, some say it is necessary to supplicate Amitābha for the dead but supplicate Amitāyus for the living. In truth, there is no distinction among deities; they are one. Since the deity is the natural expression of bodhicitta, there will be benefit to beings in this and future lives regardless of which deity one practices. So, rather than praying to Jambhala for wealth and Amitāyus for longevity, one should focus on whichever deity is one's own principal yidam—visualizing, supplicating, and reciting his or her mantra without discriminating between the living or the dead and without thinking of helping this being or that one. Since the able force and bodhicitta developed by the yidam are the nature of the four immeasurables, they pervade all beings without exception.

For example, when disciples pray and practice White Tārā for the longevity of a guru, they often think they are aiding that guru alone. This is not at all the case. Deity yoga first brings benefit to the practitioner. Then, peripherally, the guru's life force is enriched through those roots of virtue. In particular, the connections of bodhicitta shared among disciples benefit guru and disciples together.

Whenever one gives rise to the notion of wanting to help a particular individual, such as a parent or a companion, since that very concept is conjoined with self-grasping, it will result in part benefit and part harm. It is for this reason that practitioners should aspire to benefit all beings in all circumstances.

An unobjectified mind is similarly important when supplicating to accomplish a particular purpose. In order to truly achieve something, casting away all thought of one's desired goal, one must think of the yidam with single-pointed focus. Then, when one's mind is touched by the force of the deity's great love and compassion, it clears away negative karma, habits, self-grasping, and afflictions. One's aims can be achieved because all the causes of suffering are dispelled by giving rise to love for the yidam. Here, I am speaking from experience. If one knows how to supplicate, it will bring great benefit.

We speak of grasping mind and grasped-at objects. More important than the fleeting experience of suffering—the object at which the mind is grasping—is to scatter the grasping mind itself. The point of visualizing the deity and reciting his or her mantra is to forget one's hardships. It is to scatter the notion "I am suffering." This is how karma is purified and discriminating intelligence arises. This is the method of antidoting suffering, which allows the mind to rest. That which we call the deity's blessing is the arising of discriminating intelligence, compassion, and love in one's mind. It is in this way that the deity conquers practitioners' self-grasping.

If this is habituated, sufferings will be perceived as dreamlike and illusory. Even when hardships are experienced, they will not be perceived as pain. This sort of fruition is definitely achievable.

When positive experiences and signs of accomplishment arise, practitioners should recognize them as indications that self-grasping is being purified. The moment attachment to or expectation of positive experiences arises, the grasping itself will cause such good experiences to vanish. So, although one can be grateful for a sign that one's practice is not mistaken, one should think it is nothing particularly special. Due to the blessings of the Three Jewels and Three Roots, it is fitting that self-grasping should diminish.

The Guru

The practitioner's view of the master can also become a support in integrating practice with daily life. One should see the guru as being full of good qualities. The greater one's realization, the more qualities one will perceive in the guru. When an individual lacks wisdom, he or she sees nothing but faults in others.

Regardless of how the guru may act or what words he or she may say, disciples need only concern themselves with the Dharma the guru teaches. It is this Dharma that one carries after guru and disciple part. Since karmic causality is incontrovertible, the guru is ultimately responsible for his or her own actions.

For example, Master Yangga was a great Yamāntaka yogin. Of his own guru, he said, "In all of this world there is no guru better than Ösal Dorje; in all of Tibet there is no man worse than Ösal Dorje."

Thus, a skillful disciple will understand how to distinguish worldly qualities from spiritual ones. Very few teachers combine both. Most of the time, someone with worldly qualities will lack spiritual ones and vice versa. A guru must have the spiritual qualities of compassion, wisdom, experience, and, most importantly, love for his or her disciples. If the guru lacks love, no matter how great his or her attributes, they will not arise in disciples' mindstreams. Thus, of primary importance is the guru's love; other qualities are secondary.

In the past, during the fortunate age, disciples were instructed to examine gurus for years before making a commitment and vice versa. However, in this present time, if gurus started examining disciples, they wouldn't find a single suitable follower. If disciples started investigating teachers, they wouldn't find a single suitable guru. Therefore, the less disciples investigate and evaluate the conduct of gurus, the greater their chances of staying focused on that which is meaningful—receiving the sublime Buddhadharma bestowed by the guru in spite of his or her personal shortcomings. For their part, gurus themselves should also avoid looking into disciples' conduct.

Maintaining the Samaya

Just as guru and disciple must maintain their bond of samaya, so too must sādhakas preserve the samaya among one another. This is done by maintaining love and compassion—the deity's blessing. If these are lost through jealousy and aversion, although one may practice deity yoga, one will end up accomplishing a demon. In particular, demons can manifest as competitiveness among disciples, which leads practitioners astray. When such jealousy and competitiveness are present, if somebody treats one friend well, another friend is lost because he or she feels betrayed. When befriending one sangha member, one loses another who cannot bear that one has other friends.

When these sorts of problems arise, they transform into demons who produce many sufferings. In this way, practitioners themselves create their own demons with the jealousy and aversion in their minds. Conversely, that which is called the deity is bodhicitta. Whoever has bodhicitta emerges as the actual deity right now. Thus, although the basis that is buddha nature is without good or bad qualities, it is veiled by adventitious stains. From the very beginning, gods and demons have lacked inherent existence. It is only under the influence of momentary conditions that the god or the demon appears in an instant. Such adventitious stains are like pure water suddenly becoming tainted by impurity. As a result, one circumstantially experiences the sufferings of the three lower realms.

The buddha nature shines forth in its innate purity when such defilements have been refined away. As the basis for attaining the status of the buddhas, it is never lost or spoiled. It is important that practitioners understand this. As long as one has self-grasping, aversion and jealousy will arise of their own accord. Thus, one must take care to guard the samaya among vajra siblings.

Pure Perception

By understanding the singular basis of the mind of the buddhas and sentient beings, one can recognize confusion as confusion whenever it arises. Through recognition, delusion will be destroyed in its own place. In this regard, the All-Knowing Longchen Rabjam said in his *Treasury of Experiential Pith Instructions*, "When thoughts are liberated in their own place, then there is no need to abandon samsara."[3] This is a very profound point of mantric practice. There is no instruction on secret mantra that is not included in this statement.

Generally, when people engage in ordinary talk, if the words are pleasing, one laughs; when the words are unkind, one cries. So, based on sounds, different feelings and emotions arise. Through the recitation of mantra and visualization of the deity's form, imprints of body, speech, and mind are refined away. The effect of this is that one becomes free of good and bad feelings.

Whenever there arises grasping at things as real, practitioners should leave it in the natural state. By abiding in the space-like union of clarity and emptiness, the mind thinks nothing at all—neither that things exist nor that they do not exist. The final point of secret mantra is to become free of grasping. This causes appearances to spontaneously arise as the deity. Even though the outer container and diverse objects may appear, and even though one is capable of distinguishing between good and bad, one remains free of grasping at those distinctions as being real and true. So even the notion of superior and inferior quality is an illusion, like a program on a television screen.

On that basis, sounds manifest purely, causing whatever is heard to be indistinguishable from self-resounding mantra. Since all the different kinds of talk based on attachment and aversion are meaningless, one need not become attached to praise or get angry about insults and unkind words. Thus, being free of attachment to sounds is the realization of sounds as mantra.

Freedom from grasping at forms and sounds comes from the ground of mind itself. When the mind is free of grasping at things as being real, the manifestations of forms as the deity and of sounds as mantra naturally arise. Thus, we speak of the three vajras: (1) vajra body, empty appearance; (2) vajra speech, empty sound; and (3) vajra mind, empty rigpa. Practitioners of secret mantra must sustain the samaya of these three. Merely through abiding in the view, all three are naturally accomplished.

Those who have entered the door of secret mantra must train in the pure perception of self and others. This does not mean that one should superimpose a concept of purity on that which is tainted. Rather, it means that one must do away with the deluded views of ordinary beings, whose impure minds have not yet recognized the primordial purity of phenomena. From the secret mantra perspective, pure perception is simply the recognition of things as they truly are. The moment one comprehends this, one realizes, "Oh! My failure to understand basic purity was my own error. My impure perceptions were reflections of my own confusion!"

By calling to mind the purity of phenomena, one instantaneously experiences the potency of secret mantra's meaning. Thus, pure perception is of principal importance for all you Dharma companions. Even a single moment of pure perception brings about inconceivable merit. Pure perception itself is the fruition of secret mantra practice. Whoever conceives of the container and contents as being pure in nature will experience emancipation. For such individuals, the ground of the buddhas is close at hand. This is my heartfelt advice.

Benefiting Beings

Those who have given rise to the altruistic intent will still face doubts such as "Even though I wish I could benefit beings, how can someone with my limited abilities actually accomplish others' purpose? I am not really capable of liberating beings from suffering." Such doubts should be recognized as manifestations of self-grasping.

In the development-stage trainings one imagines oneself as a heruka of inconceivable power and might. His capacity to benefit beings through enlightened body, speech, and mind—symbols, meanings, and signs—is without limit. From his terrifying form, there stream forth myriad emanations great and small who spontaneously accomplish the four activities. Thus, through the skillful means of development and completion, one receives the wisdom deities' actual blessings. In this way, ego-based defeatism and doubt are overcome, causing one to act swiftly and without hesitation in benefiting others.

Someone who has fixed ideas about how the benefit to beings should appear sets oneself up for discouragement, thinking that one's practice has had no positive effect. It is important to understand that when the state of buddhahood has been attained, the mind pervades all phenomena without any obstruction at all. The five elements are completely pervaded by the buddhas of the five families and their consorts. Since every substantial thing is comprised of the five elements, there exists no material phenomenon that is not an emanation of the buddhas. So, for example, whenever someone is benefited by food and drink, that person is actually experiencing the buddhas' blessings. When buddhahood is attained, the sādhaka realizes this.

Even right now, before the fruition has become manifest, one can spontaneously accomplish beings' benefit and ease merely through the power of the mind itself. Each time one gives rise to compassion, one accomplishes actual benefit for beings, even though the results are not perceived. So, at present, when realization has not yet been attained, it makes no sense to search for a result. Such searching will only increase dualistic views. Cause and result will not be understood until buddhahood has been attained. Only at that juncture will one perceive all the virtue one has accumulated before as well as the spontaneously accomplished benefit resulting from one's actions.

Concluding Points

In his "Four Dharmas," Lord Gampopa—the Precious One from Dagpo—taught, "The mind turns to Dharma. Dharma becomes the path. The path dispels confusion. Confusion dawns as primordial awareness."[4] It is easy for one's mind to turn to Dharma; however, after that, one's Dharma must become the path. This happens through the force of the altruistic intent, the path of the four immeasurables.

In general, there are countless diverse branches of Dharma practice and it is not possible to cut through to the essence of them all by means of words and concepts. However, by relying on the four immeasurables, one will traverse an unmistaken path, regardless of which spiritual tradition, tenet system, or master one follows. It is only through engaging the actual practice that one will be able to gain direct experience and thereby settle the point of the teachings' and yogas' inner meaning. Since the essence can only be understood through looking inward at the mind, there is no benefit to talking a lot about it.

Furthermore, within the Vajrakīla practice manual one finds vast and detailed visualizations. If one thinks about each individual aspect separately, it can cause concepts to proliferate. Since it is not possible for beginners to engage every detail of this vast visualization, it is important to focus on the most essential point. That point is to visualize the seed syllable HŪṂ.

Through the actual practice of focusing the mind on the seed syllable, the qualities of the development stages will naturally arise by degrees. For example, when a seed is planted in the ground and is nurtured with moisture, sunlight, and the like, it will naturally sprout, give rise to a bud, and bear fruits and flowers. The practice of meditation is similar. When one focuses on the seed and cultivates it through awareness, all the myriad aspects of the visualization described in the text will spontaneously arise.

There exist extensive commentaries on this practice and there is much about it that I do not know. If one wishes to focus on all the fine details, I would suggest reading the texts that are available in translation and asking questions of knowledgeable gurus. As for me, the one thing I know is this: if one wants to experience the actual essence of the practice, it must be cultivated through meditation. The door of entry into that meditation is to visualize the letter HŪṂ, which is inseparable from loving-kindness and compassion. That causal HŪṂ syllable, the nature of bodhicitta, is the very basis on which the complete deity clearly appears.

In this regard, in Tibet we say that once one has been satisfied by eating bread, there is no need to be concerned with the details about what sort of seed the farmer planted, how it grew, how the grain was harvested and ground into flour, and so forth. Similarly, if one gets a new car, one must give it basic maintenance in order for it to run properly. Yet, if one obsesses about every single detail of how the car was put together, where its parts came from, and what they look like, one will end up disassembling the car piece by piece until it becomes a useless heap that cannot carry one from one place to the next. Thus, rather than focusing on every small outer detail, sādhakas must gain confidence about the inner meaning.

This sadhana, or method of accomplishment, comes to us through a lineage of blessing and practice. Thus, there will be very little benefit from mere conceptual understanding that arises through study without practice. Conversely, even if one does not have much understanding of the details, if one merely practices the main point of the sadhana, the other aspects will gradually be revealed through practice.

Every single facet of the inner meaning of Vajrakīla practice is subsumed within the four kīlas. Those four kīlas can be further condensed into the following three points: the life force that is conduct, the abyss of meditation, and the fortress of the view. Those three can be further condensed into the fortress of the view alone. That view, which is the nature of mind, is the essential basis on which all other Vajrakīla practices have evolved.

Dedication

In conclusion, I can make no greater dedication than the one found in the practice manual itself:

> Having changed and made complete the two
> gatherings massed throughout the three times through
> my and others' bodies, speech, and minds,
> they're transferred for great reality.
> May the fruit—nondual essence—be gained!

Past, present, and future samsara and nirvana—no matter how deep and vast they may be—come down to dualistic grasping at self and other. As long as self and other exist, there will be the apparent duality of samsara and nirvana.

The entirety of sentient ones' merit is manifested through actions of body, speech, and mind. These include even the smallest actions, such as placing one's palms together in faith, speaking even one word that accords with the teachings on karmic causality, and giving rise to even the slightest virtuous thought. Such physical, verbal, and mental actions arisen through loving-kindness, compassion, and affection are the causes that bring happiness and ease to the sentient. One should dedicate all such virtues of body, speech, and mind—those that have been gathered in the past, those being gathered right now, and all those yet to be gathered.

In truth, the altruistic mind is the accumulation of merit. Whenever the merit accumulation is gathered, the wisdom accumulation also occurs. How? To whatever degree one exhausts self-grasping through the altruistic mind, primordial awareness will become correspondingly clear. Thus, the merit accumulation leads to the fruition that is the wisdom accumulation. Eventually, when one becomes entirely devoid of self-grasping, one will be freed of grasping at duality. The wisdom accumulation should be understood as becoming nondual.

For example, when someone with clinging and attachment to self and others trains by thinking of nothing but benefiting others again and again, the self gradually becomes exhausted. Eventually, through the power of immeasurable loving-kindness, the purpose of all sentient ones will remain constantly in one's mind—without one even being aware of the shift. Over and over, the well-being of this entire world will suddenly shine forth in one's mindstream. At those junctures, one is free of a self. When the actual condition of the mind is seen, that is the accumulation of primordial awareness-wisdom. In this way, the mind becomes like space. One becomes able to comprehend the all-encompassing nature of space, in which there is no duality. This is the accumulation of wisdom.

In brief, what is the connection between the two accumulations? The root of all sentient ones' suffering is the self. Each time one gives rise to compassion for others, it benefits oneself. To whatever degree one has compassion for another, one's self-grasping becomes correspondingly diminished. This is called the accumulation of merit. When one repeatedly exhausts the self, causing it to become less and less, discerning intelligence becomes greater and greater, just as when a block of ice melts, the volume of free-flowing water increases, merging into the vast ocean. Finally, the entire ocean will become free of any ice floes. Such is the wisdom accumulation. In this way, the two accumulations are conjoined. The purposes of oneself and others are accomplished together.

Beings have all sorts of pure and impure motivations for accumulating merit. The omniscient buddhas, through their compassionate blessings, are capable of transforming all motivations tainted by impurity into unmixed, unadulterated intentions. Once all such roots of virtue have been made complete, they are transferred for great reality. This ultimate, nonreferential, nonconceptual threefold purity is completely free of any individual who dedicates or any act of dedication.

The final fruition will be the ability to fathom the mind that is the indivisibility of self and other. That nonduality is the status of all the buddhas. By these virtues, may the fruit—nondual essence—be gained!

PART THREE

Liturgical Source Texts

This is the intent of Guru Padmasambhava as transmitted to Yeshe Tsogyal. It is based on an arrangement of the practice manual by Jamgön Kongtrül Lodrö Thaye (1813–1899), who combined the root terma of Ratna Lingpa (1403–1478) with Karma Chagme Rinpoche's (1613–1678) abbreviated edition of the extensive sadhana by Sanggye Lingpa (1340–1396). The current edition is an arrangement for the secret accomplishment retreat by the 8th Garchen Trülku, Könchog Gyaltsen, using supplemental texts by Jamgön Kongtrül.

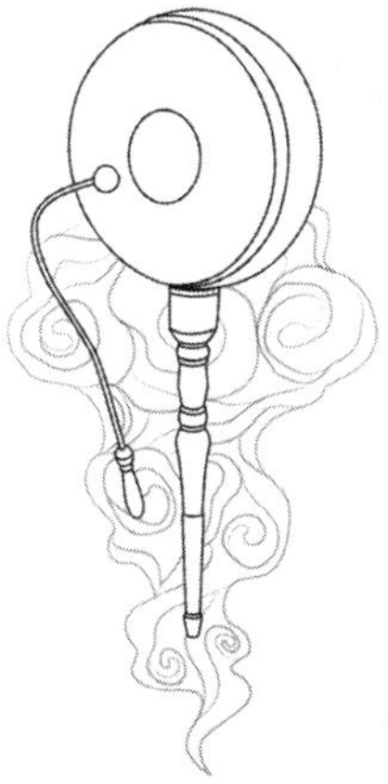

CHAPTER 12

Lineage Supplication

Melodious, Māra-Destroying Vajra Song: The Lineage Supplication That Encompasses the Buddha-Word and Treasure Transmissions of Vajrakīla

To the buddha-word lineage I pray:
primal Küntuzangpo-Dorje Chang,
five families' blood-drinking herukas,
great Lekyi Wangmo, Prabhahasti,
Vajra Thötreng Tsal, Vimamitra,
Queen of Great Bliss, māras' subduer,
Śīlamañju, worship's great object,
lord and subjects, you the twenty-five,
in particular, Nanam and Chim,
Shübu, Rongzom, and the clan of Khön—
may I gain the fortress of the view!

To the treasure lineage I pray:
Chökyi Wangchug, plumed Rigdzin Gödem,
Sanggye Lingpa, Drime Dorje, and
Rinchen Palzang, self-freed Padma Ling,
Düdül Nüden, Dzamling Dorje Tsal,
Ratön, Choggyur Lingpa, and the rest—
may I cross meditation's abyss!

To the Dharma keepers, transmitters, I pray:
Ma, Nyag, and the eight named Glorious,
Nub, So, Zur, Odren, Lang, Venerable
Ācārya Nuru, Langlab Jangdor,
four supreme and honored disciples,
Darchar, Rinzang, Rogchal, Terdag Ling,
Venerable Chagme, and all the rest—
may I seize the conduct, the life force!

To Kīla's divine mandala hosts I pray:
Vajrasattva, who's comprised of peaceful and
wrathful families' illusory displays,
Dharmevajra, Master of the Secrets, and
Dorje Namjom who cuts out confusion's root.
Dharmasphere-born body of compassionate wrath,
actor of a hundred moods, the blazing, great
māra tamer, god who's perfected as one
the activities that suitably tame beings,
Glorious, Great Vajrakumāra most supreme,
space and wisdom's union, Khorlo Gyedebma,
ten strengths and perfections, ten wrathful pairs' mode,
falcon hosts, gate guards, almighties, and oath-bounds—
may I conquer māras completely!

Self-arisen rigpa's mastery—the
blue-black weapon—shines forth in place of
life force as primordial wisdom-wrath.
When the dharmasphere is planted with
all-pervasive wisdom's kīla, may
all dualistic concepts be cut off!

Skandhas, dhātus, [āyatanas]—the
three seats—pack the vajra channel wheels.
Unelaborated consciousness
is fulfilled as the vajra, great bliss.

When the six wayfarers are struck by
measureless compassion's kīla, may
they possess compassion's great lifeline!

[Symbols,] meanings, signs—the union of
wisdoms with the kāyas—radiate and
gather dreadful, blazing wrathful ones.
When the mother's sky is planted with
bodhicitta's kīla, may clouds of
emanations, foremost heirs, stream forth!

Sentient contents of existence grasp
at three poisons and appearances;
yet as vajra wrathfuls they're complete.
When harmdoers are pinned by material
kīlas of signs that won't let them go,
may the pangs endured be finalized!

The aggregates' māra, conquered, is
freed into the ripened deity.
The afflictions' māra, conquered, is
marked with the seal of bliss-emptiness.
The lord of death's māra, conquered, finds
the empowerment of immortal life.
May the gods' son's māra, conquered, yield
spontaneous attainment of the grounds!

Swiftly may I manifest the eight
qualities and four activities!
Specially, having burnt the noxious hearts
of hinderers, foes, and obstructors with
fierce mantras—direct acts' fiery point—
may I gain Glorious Heruka's state!

Out of necessity, this was composed at the Śubha Sanctuary of Nine

Dragons by Yönten Gyamtso [a.k.a. Jamgön Kongtrül], who made a path of his preference for the yogas of this particular supreme deity. May virtue and goodness increase!

CHAPTER 13

Practice Manual

Essence of Display: A Regular Secret Accomplishment Liturgy of the Unsurpassed, Most Secret Vajrakīla

Having bowed to that method whereby
nondwelling wisdom dharmakāya—
existence as vajra—is achieved,
I shall clarify our forebears' views
regarding its regular practice.

When one engages the great treasure revealer Ratna Lingpa's Unsurpassed, Innermost Secret Sadhana of Kīla, *the sadhana and practice manual from the terma texts left pristine must be combined according to the meaning of their own textual systems and the earlier and latter commentarial notes on the practice.*

When one cannot carry out the regular practice, the self-empowerment for the actual empowerment and the like in their elaborate and extensive forms, it seems convenient to do this abridged activity liturgy for regular Kīla practice composed by Sanggye Lingpa, the development-stage verses of which were put into abbreviated form by Chagme Rinpoche. Accordingly, at the outset are refuge and bodhicitta:

NAMO! Sentient ones, wayfaring beings and I,
with respectful three doors, take refuge

in the guru, yidam, and Three Jewels
with the victors' oceanic hosts.
Recite three times.

Alas! For me to release all wayfarers
by upending samsara into
the mandala of Karmakīla,
I'll rouse mind—the four immeasurables.
Recite three times.

Setting the boundaries:
HŪṂ. In the measureless, spontaneously
present nature, even labels like
"hindrance" and "misguider" don't exist.
That's been clearly known primordially;
thus, the boundaried mandala has been
naturally, spontaneously produced.

The disclosure:
OṂ. Features of disclosure and disclosed
come undone in their own place within
the authentic, spontaneous expanse
of primordial purity unfurled.
Yet, should there be the delusions of
ignorant, dualistic grasping, they've
been disclosed before you naturally
emanated hosts of deities. SAMAYA A ĀḤ.

Consecrating the offerings:
Primally self-born, pure amṛita,
great redness, six causes freed into
the expanse, and mahābaliṅta,
appearance-existence structured in
basic ground—these three great essences
cannot be exhausted! OṂ ĀḤ HŪṂ.
OṂ VAJRA PUṢPE, DHŪPE, ĀLOKE, GANDHE, NAIVEDYE, ŚABDA ĀḤ HŪṂ.

Generating the commitment being:
HŪṂ̊. The immeasurable and manifold
palace is the object that appears.
A fiery blue three-point mandala,
wherein the eight charnel grounds surround
an expanse that flares with wisdom flames,
is where there appears the measureless
palace through wisdom projections formed.
In its center on lotus, sun, moon,
and four māras crossed is a blue HŪṂ̊.
As light emanates and gathers back,
the complete, unaltered body of
the great sovereign, Glorious Vajra Youth,
blue-black, with three faces and six arms,
stands with four legs spread in champion's stance.
Middle blue, right white, and left face red,
the five families beautify my head.
The heart's vital force is the seed, HŪṂ̊.
With nine glaring eyes, I look upon
all the ten directions and my mouths
gape with twisted tongues and canines bared.
Nine- and five-pronged vajras in both right,
massed flames and khaṭvāṅga in left hands,
the last two hands roll a Meru stake.
This completes the fearsome charnel gear.

The Great Consort, Khorlo Gyedebma,
is pale blue, with one face and two arms.
Utpala in hand, she clasps the neck
of the father and with her left hand
proffers to his mouth a blood-filled conch.

In our foreheads, a blue Hūṃ̊kār pair,
and red Hayagrīva in our throats,
a blue Yama couple in our hearts,
o'er the navels, chartreuse Dütsi Khyilpa couple,

in the navels, a dark green Miyo pair,
in the privates, a blue Tobchen pair,
a white Namgyal pair in the right shoulders,
and blue Yug-ngön couple in the left,
a pink Dögyal couple in right thighs,
and dark gold Khamsum pair are in the left.

In four quarters are the four families
and ten wrathful couples in ten spokes,
each together with a zasö pair.
With three faces, six arms, and widespread
four legs, vajra wings, and charnel gear,
these twenty-four wrathfuls hold diverse
weapons with their own respective signs.

The four gates have four beast-faced guard maids.
In the mandala's concentric spheres,
emanations, princes, aides in wait,
sovereigns, dog maids, earth maids, and the hosts
of great men—Se, Chag, and Dung—appear.
Thus, the chief and retinue have been
visualized in their entirety.

In the principal's heart on a sun,
a thumb-joint-sized sattva rolls a stake.
On a sun within his heart is a
grain-sized golden vajra, at whose core
is a HŪṂ by mantra circumvolved.

At each deity's crown is an OṂ,
ĀḤ at the throat, and HŪṂ at the heart.
As the ten directions' conquerors
grant empowerment-blessing, we're adorned
with Amoghasiddhi as its sign.
OṂ HŪṂ SVĀṂ ĀṂ HĀṂ, MŪṂ LĀṂ MĀṂ PĀṂ TĀṂ.

Through the light rays from each of our hearts,
wisdom beings are invited here.

Inviting the wisdom beings:
HŪṂ̊. Showing born miraculous displays—
blazing forms from the completely pure
unborn sphere of dharmas—Vajra Youth
with your courts, please come here from that sphere!
Wisdom Wrath King and courts, when you've come
to grant siddhis and empowerment to
attain existence-vajrakīla,
further, to show noble marks and signs
and bestow Kīla's accomplishments,
Wisdom Wrath King with your courts, please come!
JAḤ HŪṂ̊ VAṂ̊ HOḤ. VAJRA SAMAYA JAḤ. SAMAYA TIṢṬHA HLEN.

Paying homage:
HŪṂ̊. To save the three planes from noxiousness
and destroy our prideful clinging, we
prostrate with one-pointed, great respect
to you, Vajrarākṣasa and hosts.
ATI PU HOḤ, PRATĪCCHA HOḤ.

Making outer, inner, and secret offerings:
HŪṂ̊. Varied offerings, real and formed by mind—
connate union, outer, inner, and
secret here arrayed—we offer you,
self-born, emanated deities.
Now partake of them nondually
and without discrimination, please.
OṂ VAJRA ARGHAṂ, PĀDAṂ, PUṢPE, DHŪPE, ĀLOKE, GANDHE,
NAIVEDYE, ŚABDA PRATĪCCHA SVĀHĀ.

HŪṂ̊. Great amṛita made from eight main and
thousand branch ingredients, secret great

rakta, the afflictions' space-expanse,
and the torma, foremost substance of
great elixir—these we offer you.
MAHĀ PAÑCA AMṚITA, RAKTA, BALIṄTA KHĀHI.

HŪṀ. Dullness like a flesh mountain brought down;
lust, a wave-tossed, blood-filled ocean; and
hatred, a bone heap—these offerings are
made to Vajrarākṣasa and courts. OṀ ĀḤ HŪṀ.

Next is the praise:
HŪṀ. Wrath King, Glorious Great Vajra Youth,
pure dharmasphere, Khorlo Gyedebma,
from your method-knowledge body come
the ten emanated wrathfuls and
female wrathfuls dawned from natural space,
zasö with symbolic heads and fangs,
emanations, falcon hosts dispatched
to activities and four gate guards
who defend the mandala's quarters,
slaying henchmen, twelve Kīla guards with
great men, Se, Chag, and Dung, and the like—
oath-bound hosts declared as Kīla's guards—
praise and homage to you with your courts!
Now it's time for your compassionate pledge:
bring about direct, destructive acts!

The recitation of the charm:
HŪṀ. Glorious Vajra Youth, princes, and courts
fiercely dance in Khorlo Gyedeb—space.
Sound and emptiness, the melody
of the mantric charm, like thunder roars.
Thus, I'll practice till our samaya
is accomplished in the vast expanse!

Light rays radiate throughout ten directions from the life force and mantra strand at my heart, rousing the divine Three Roots' samaya from its vital point. Every blessing of body, speech, and mind comes like rainfall as white OṀ, red ĀḤ, and blue HŪṂ, merging ceaselessly into my three places. Further, I imagine all the blessings and potency of every victor's compassion as Vajrakīla's divine hosts in unfathomable great and small forms that gently fall and merge with me. Like opened sesame pods are the body mandala's gods and channel hubs' divine couples. They and all in the mandala recite the mantra, resounding like a beehive broken open.

OṀ VAJRAKĪLI KĪLAYA, SARVA VIGHNĀN VAṂ HŪṂ PHAṬ!
This recitation is the approach.

From the mantra strand radiate light rays and a second strand, which flow from the father's to the mother's mouth. Through the mantric self-resounding of unfathomable heroes and ḍākiṇīs in the mother's four cakras, the mindstream is roused. The mantra strand enters the father's vajra through the mother's secret place. The gods in one's channel hubs proclaim the mantra's sound. Visualize the mantra strand merging ceaselessly into the heart center.

OṀ VAJRAKĪLI KĪLAYA, JAḤ HŪṂ VAṂ HOḤ KAṬAṄKAṬE JAYE VIJAYE AJITE APARĀJITE MĀRA SENA PRAMARDANĪYE SARVA VIGHNĀN VAṂ HŪṂ PHAṬ!

By reciting thus, one has combined into one the mantras for accomplishment and engaging activities.

When one needs to practice the facing generation, from the beginning, one should open the chamber of recitation and respectively radiate and gather back rays of light. One should engage a back-and-forth recitation, in which the mantra strand emerges from the mouths [of oneself as the father-mother couple, enters] those of the facing generation, [and returns] via the navels or nexus of union. Finally, imagining that the four activities will be accomplished through the rays of white, yellow, red, and green light that radiate therefrom, one engages activities.

At the end of the session one should read the lines that follow every thousand recitations as usual.

The vowels and consonants: [OṀ] A Ā I Ī U Ū Ṛ Ṝ Ḷ Ḹ E AI O AU AṀ AḤ / KA KHA GA GHA NGA / CA CHA JA JHA ÑA / ṬA ṬHA ḌA ḌHA ṆA / TA THA DA DHA NA / PA PHA BA BHA MA / YA RA LA VA / ŚA ṢA SA HA KṢAḤ [SVĀHĀ]. *Recite three times.*

The hundred syllables: OṀ VAJRA SATTVA SAMAYAMANUPĀLAYA / VAJRA SATTVA TVENOPATIṢṬHA / DRIḌHO ME BHAVA / SUTOṢYO ME BHAVA SUPOṢYO ME BHAVA / ANURAKTO ME BHAVA / SARVA SIDDHIMME PRAYACCHA / SARVA KARMASU CA ME CITTAṀ ŚREYAḤ KURU HŪṀ / HA HA HA HA HOḤ BHAGAVAN SARVA TATHĀGATA VAJRA MĀ ME MUÑCA / VAJRĪ BHAVA / MAHĀ SAMAYA SATTVA AḤ. *Recite three times.*

Essence of dependent relations: [OṀ] YE DHARMĀ HETU PRABHAVĀ HETUṀ TEṢĀṀ TATHĀGATO HYAVADAT, / TEṢĀṀ CA YO NIRODHA EVAṀ VĀDĪ MAHĀŚRAMAṆAḤ [SVĀHĀ] *Recite three times.*

Offering the charm:
HŪṀ. Glorious Great Kīla's divine hosts, come!
We make offerings—outer, inner, and
secret—and extol your attributes,
activities, bodies, speech, and mind!
Heedlessness, confusion, transgressions,
breaches, and impairments we disclose.
Lovingly and with compassion, please
think of us and grant accomplishments!

The abridged subsequent rites of offering and praise:
OṀ ŚRĪ VAJRAKUMĀRA SAPĀRIVĀRA ARGHAṀ, PĀDAṀ, PUṢPE, DHŪPE, ĀLOKE, GANDHE, NAIVEDYE, ŚABDA PRATĪCCHA SVĀHĀ.

HŪṂ. All the ten directions' and three times'
buddhas' unified activities
rise up as your body of great force!
Praise and homage—Kīla deity,
māra tamer with changeless and firm
body void of aging or decline!

Disclosing wrongs:
From the start we've been inseparable,
yet whate'er declines, nonvirtues, breaks,
breaches, and confusions I've amassed
through confused ignoring while I've roamed
in samsara, I disclose them and
lay them down with full remorse and shame.

One should make amends for excesses and omissions and stabilize the blessings by uttering the hundred syllables, the vowels and consonants, and the essence of dependent relations three times each.

If the facing generation has been done without a support, the manner in which the wisdom being departs and the commitment being is gathered in should be in accordance with the sadhana framework. However, as nowadays one will not be without a support, one should recite the extensive request to remain steadfast according to the sadhana framework. If abbreviated, the request is:

Though you've dwelt in cyclic existence
here with this support, please duly grant
life without disease, the wealth of power,
in addition to all things supreme!
OṀ SUPRA TIṢṬHA VAJRĀYA SVĀHĀ.

The stages of gathering in:
All-pervading mercy's hosts divine
merge into the nature—five lights' sphere.

Clear, complete enjoyment, rainbow light,
contents and container now subside
into dharmakāya's vast expanse.

The dedication:
Having changed and made complete the two
gatherings massed throughout the three times through
my and others' bodies, speech, and minds,
they're transferred for great reality.
May the fruit—nondual essence—be gained!

The prayer of auspiciousness:
OṀ. May auspicious, spontaneous vastness
of primally pure dharmakāya
ĀḤ. Be present in luminosity's
self-born state, the saṁbhogakāya!
HŪṀ. May auspicious tamers of beings, the
manifold nirmāṇakāya forms,
HRĪḤ. Be present as skill in loving means
in the state of [beings'] compassion!

Having uttered this, scatter flower petals.

It seems certain that up through the recitation of the charm, this text was composed by Chagme Rinpoche. Since that time, unlearned city-dwelling-type mantrins have rearranged the practice, tacking on labels like "incorporating restoration and repelling." As it seems such texts are suffused with errors, I have combined the actual root treasure text—the heart quintessence—and the definitive speech of Chagme Rinpoche into an immaculate regular practice of secret accomplishment of the Ratna Lingpa system. This was written by Pema Garwang Tsal in Palpung at the upper hermitage of Devīkoṭi.

Like turquoise well set in the fine gold
of the māra-subduing queen's speech,

this secret accomplishment method
has become a beautiful necklace
for youthful ones, holders of knowledge.
Through this, may the excellent teachings'
youth-like resplendence blossom anew!

May virtue and goodness increase!

CHAPTER 14

White Torma Offering

As for the white torma's activity mantras, one should cleanse with: OṀ VAJRA AMṚITA KUṆḌALI HANA HANA HŪṀ PHAṬ *and refine with* OṀ SVABHĀVA ŚUDDHA SARVA DHARMA SVABHĀVA ŚUDDHŌ HAṀ.

From the empty state appears a BHRŪṀ, from which comes a jeweled vessel. Therein is an OṀ, from which appears a torma that has transformed into nectar. *Recite* OṀ ĀḤ HŪṀ *three times.*

OṀ PṚITHIVĪ DEVĪ LOKA PĀLA SAPĀRIVĀRA VAJRA SAMĀJAḤ.

Recite OṀ PṚITHIVĪ DEVĪ LOKA PĀLA SAPĀRIVĀRA IDAṀ BALIṄTA KHA KHA KHĀHI KHĀHI *three times.*

OṀ PṚITHIVĪ DEVĪ LOKA PĀLA SAPĀRIVĀRA ARGHAṀ, PĀDAṀ, PUṢPE, DHŪPE, ĀLOKE, GANDHE, NAIVEDYE, ŚABDA PRATĪCCHA SVĀHĀ.

HŪṀ. Gods, nāgas, kinglies, furies, harmdoers,
planetary spirits, smell eaters,
aquarians, demons, men-or-whats,
carnivores, mātarīs, bulbous ones,
mu demons, receptacle girls, and
urban flesh eaters with female ghosts,
local gods and lords of regions and
places, treasures, wealth, and all the rest,
bands of spirits, elementals, gods,
all lay folk who keep commands and oaths—

as you take this golden libation
and torma comprised of all things clean,
harmful, wicked thoughts are pacified.
Thus, always be my wholesome allies.
In this country's lands and regions, I
practice unsurpassed supreme bodhi
and make effort for sentient ones' sake.
Thus, make my conditions favorable!

Steadfast earth goddesses and the like,
earth lords' kings with ministers and courts—
as you take this golden libation
and torma comprised of all things clean,
these, my wished-for hopes, will be fulfilled.
Neither bothered, nor begrudging, nor
jealous, please provide me this ground of
precious treasures! Actualize all hopes
and accomplish aspirations, please!
Bring forth my activities' results!

Thus the torma is offered outside.

CHAPTER 15

Kīla Consecration

Consecration of the Material Kīla Mandala: The Development Stages of the Foremost Prince

One should fumigate with guggula and recite: OṂ VAJRAKĪLI KĪLAYA, SURU SURU PRASURU ADHI TIṢṬHA MUG MUG HALA HALA. Foes, obstructors, and elementals: putrefied CITTA MĀRAYA HŪṂ PHAṬ!

One should pelt obstructive forces with mustard seeds and recite: OṂ VAJRAKĪLI KĪLAYA, MAGUTALA MAGUTALA PRATALA PRATALA ŚATA RĀCA HŪṂ. Foes, obstructors, and elementals: MĀRAYA HŪṂ PHAṬ!

One should smear the kīla with rakta and recite: OṂ VAJRAKĪLI KĪLAYA, RAKTA JVALA MAṆḌALA MAṆḌALA RAKṢA RAKṢA. Foes and obstructors: VAŚAṂ KURU MĀRAYA HŪṂ PHAṬ!

Having thought Noxious ones, their hearts disturbed, have grown fond of the three spheres' wayfarers, *one should place the kīla in its stand.*

I manifest as the Great Glorious Lord. In my right hand is a moon mandala with a white A; in the left is a sun mandala with a red MŪṂ. On the right hand's five fingers are moon circles the size of split lentils. On those five are OṂ HŪṂ SVĀṂ ĀṂ HĀṂ. On the left five fingers are sun circles of the same size. On those five are MŪṂ LĀṂ MĀṂ PĀṂ TĀṂ. Melting into light, the seed letters change into the five implements. From those, the five families suddenly manifest as ten fathers and mothers.

With OṀ MAHĀŚŪNYATĀ JÑĀNA SVABHĀVA ATMAKŌ HAṀ, *the kīla is refined into emptiness. The fathers rouse with the words* SAMAYA HOḤ! *The mothers rouse with* SAMAYAS TVAṀ! *One should take hold of the kīla between the hollows of the palms.* VAJRA AÑJALI.

Having melted and leveled out through bodhicitta's light rays from the couples who've entered equilibrium, the kīla becomes a blue HŪṂ letter. OṀ VAJRAKĪLI KĪLAYA, HŪṂ JAḤ!

From the HŪṂ's transformation appears a blue-black wrathful with one face, two arms, and three eyes, holding a kīla in his right hand and ankus in the left. His lower body is a sky-iron kīla with sharp, tempered triangular tip. Like metal drawn out of a smith's embers, he emits sparks of fire.

In his upper knot is Hūṁkāra; in the contracted eight flanks, the eight wrathfuls; and in the lower knot, Mahābala. These ten wrathful couples each have falcon types. In the lower knot's four facets are four gatekeeping maids. Beneath the water dragon are four kiṁkāra men. The twelve Kīla guard maids appear in the three blades.

In every pore of myself and the Foremost Prince are tiny blue-black wrathfuls the size of barley grains. With gaping mouths, bared fangs, one face, and two arms, they wield diverse weapons. As Kīlaya's sound is resoundingly proclaimed, they fill us without interstice.

Since this system—a profound key point of Kīla practice—amounted to something unusual, it was generally not expounded in most Kīla practice manuals but was buried elsewhere. Because of this and in order to bring it forth in this dark age, a few khenpos said this kīla consecration should be written. As, under the circumstances, it appears that some have not even heard of it, I extracted this from the extensive teachings. Thus, you who have the pretense of being Kīla yogins, do not dismiss this basic point.

Then, for the activities of the common consecration-empowerment, one should think: The foreheads, throats, and hearts of the three mandalas' divine hosts are respectively marked with white OṀ, red ĀḤ, and blue HŪṀ.

HŪṀ. Nature of all buddhas are your forms,
blazing, terrifying wrathful ones
from the vajra dharmasphere's state born.
Cause me to arise as body's jewel!

Having recited thus, one should think: From our foreheads' OṀ letters radiate white light rays, making pleasing offerings to the bodies of the ten directions' victors. Their bodies' every compassionate blessing is gathered back in the aspect of OṀ letters. As they merge into our foreheads, physical luster supremely blazes forth. I've become the great lord who is every sugata's form vajra. OṀ BUDDHAKĪLI KĪLAYA, KĀYA VAJRĀ NĀN. JVALA JVALA. PRAJVALA PRAJVALA. SPHUṬA SPHUṬA. SARVA NASA PANAYE HŪṀ PHAṬ. *As one has recited thus, blessing has been bestowed on the body.*

HŪṀ. Nature of all buddhas is your speech,
blazing, terrifying wrathful ones
from the vajra dharmasphere's state born.
Cause me to arise as speech's jewel!

Having recited thus, one should think: From our throats' ĀḤ letters radiate red light rays, making pleasing offerings to the speech of the ten directions' victors. Their speech's every blessing is gathered back in the aspect of ĀḤ letters. As they merge into the ĀḤ at our throats, verbal potency supremely blazes forth. I've become the great lord who is every sugata's speech vajra. OṀ PADMAKĪLI KĪLAYA, VĀK VAJRĀ NĀN. SARVA DUṢṬAN HRĪḤ ŚO DHANAYE HŪṀ PHAṬ. *As one has recited thus, blessing has been bestowed on the speech.*

HŪṀ. Nature of all buddhas is your mind,
blazing, terrifying wrathful ones

from the vajra dharmasphere's state born.
Cause me to arise as the mind's jewel!

Having recited thus, one should think: From our hearts' HŪṂ letters radiate blue light rays, making pleasing offerings to the mind of the ten directions' victors. Their mind's every blessing is gathered back in the aspect of HŪṂ. As they merge into our hearts, mental strength and force supremely blaze forth. I've become the great lord who is every sugata's mind vajra. OṀ VAJRAKĪLI KĪLAYA, CITTA VAJRĀ NĀN. PETALI MANDHALA MAGUTALA PRATALA HŪṂ PHAṬ. *As one has recited thus, blessing has been bestowed on the mind.*

Then, having the three perceptions of the Foremost Prince himself as the immeasurable palace, the deity, and the implement, one should place him in the seat of É, imagining that his blade has been planted between the light and dark portions of enemies' and obstructors' hearts.

Once again, one should think: The light arisen from the seeds of the three mandalas' three vajras pervades the three realms, bestowing the empowerment of every sentient one's life force as primordial awareness. The six realms' beings, the afflictions' dwelling places, have been cleansed, turning into the six seeds: A NRI SU TRI PRE DUḤ. Those six also melt into light, transforming into OṀ ĀḤ HŪṂ.

Having gathered back, the light merges into the three places of myself and the Foremost Prince, bringing the three realms and three planes under our control.

Recite OṀ ĀḤ HŪṂ *three times. One should stabilize this by reciting* SAPAŚVARI SAMAYA JAḤ HŪṂ VAṂ HOḤ. *Then, to bestow the five wisdoms' empowerment, one should recite the following with the vajra uṣṇīṣa mudrā:*

HŪṂ. Means, your conduct for beings' purpose, is
love and compassion that rightly tame.
Now grant siddhis and empowerment to
make buddha activities complete!

With SPHARAṆA PHAṬ, light rays from the HŪṀ at my heart radiate in ten directions and strike the ten directions' victors, the five kāyas' great lords, together with their courts. As their mindstreams have been roused and they've been entreated to grant empowerment, the essence of every sugata's body, speech, mind, attributes, and acts descends like a rainfall that is the nature of heroes as five seeds.

With SAṀHARAṆA HŪṀ, they've gathered at the five places on my head and merged therein, transforming into OṀ HŪṀ TRĀṀ HRĪḤ ĀḤ, MŪṀ LĀṀ MĀṀ PĀṀ TĀṀ. From those appear the chief Karma Heruka and court, who become the forms of the five families' father-mother pairs. My body is filled as amṛita streams descend from their points of union. Dwelling in the small skull chambers, the blood-drinking couples become crown ornaments, making fully complete the five wisdoms' empowerment.

Through the light rays from each of our hearts,
wisdom beings are invited here.

Thus visualizing, one should recite: OṀ VAJRAKĪLI KĪLAYA, SARVA SAMAYA JA JAḤ. ĀVEŚAYA A ĀḤ, *inserting it into the invitation.*

CHAPTER 16

Bringing Down Blessings

Bringing down blessings upon the mandala is as follows. Having arranged their adornments and attire, the practitioners should sound forth diverse musical instruments, burn great fat and frankincense, blow thighbone trumpets, beckon waving black flags, locks of hair, and human skins and, giving rise to superior faith, imagine: Having densely massed like clouds in the sky through the power of their heart-samayas of old, all gurus, knowledge holders, deities, skyfarers, and oath-bound ones send down great blessings on yogins and the mandala site and think of us with great affection.

The Seven-Line Supplication:
[HŪṂ HRĪḤ.] In the past, the kalpa's origin,
on Uddiyāna land's northwest frontier
on a stamened lotus flower's pistil,
you found marvelous, supreme siddhi.
Famed as Lotus-Born, you're circled by
retinues of many skyfarers.
I shall practice emulating you.
Come to bless me with resplendence, please!

Circumambulating the mandala burning compounded incense and accompanied by music, recite:
HŪṂ. Vajra Youth's mandalas, barring none,
and you, deity who's accomplished
existence-vajrakīla in the

mandala whose limits equal space,
through compassion great, you act without
obscuration or isolation.
You with timely vajra samaya,
on this unsurpassed, great mandala
of accomplishment, send down great waves
of compassionate activities and
blessings on this secret mandala!
Please send down the great resplendence of
body, speech, and mind and grant us the
five wisdoms' supreme empowerment!
OṀ SARVA TATHĀGATA BHAGAVAN, SAMAYA HOḤ. SAMAYAS TVAṀ.

HŪṀ. Now, the time to grant empowerment's come,
sending great resplendence down from the
secret sphere itself—Vajrakīla.
Vajra Lord, bhagavan, with past pledge,
the vajra empowerment samaya
you bestow is unsurpassable.
Deity whose sole declared oath is
ne'er to stray from being a refuge, please
bless us with the great resplendent waves
of the conquerors—all excluding none!
GURU DEVA ḌĀKIṆĪ KĪLI KĪLAYA, SAMAYA HŪṀ. SAMAYA JAḤ.

CHAPTER 17

Petition

At the start of the petition is the drawing in: NAMO! By the truth of the Three Jewels, Three Roots, and yidam Vajra Youth's divine assembly of seventy-eight, every harmdoer, oath transgressor, and opportunistic spirit—into this ruddy flesh and blood torma be drawn! JAḤ HŪṂ VAṂ HOḤ.

That which is in essence enemies' and obstructors' flesh and blood has become in aspect an inconceivable wealth of desirables. *Recite* OṂ ĀḤ HŪṂ *three times.*

One should think: Through the light rays arisen from the HŪṂ letter in the heart of myself clearly manifest as the Great Glorious One, Kīla guards and oath-bound ones with their hosts are each invited from their own places.

JOḤ. You who've pledged as Kīla guards before
the great master, Padma Thötreng Tsal—
dog maids, sovereigns, four earth-owning se,
mighty four kiṁkāras, blazing ones,
mothers, sisters, and such—numberless
glorious messengers with your hosts, please
come to this place through samaya's power!

OṂ VAJRAKĪLI KĪLAYA, MOHA GHĀTAYA MAMA ŚĪGHRAM KARMA KĀRAYE SAPĀRIVĀRA VAJRA SAMĀJAḤ.

OṀ VAJRA PUṢPE, DHŪPE, ĀLOKE, GANDHE, NAIVEDYE, ŚABDA PRATĪCCHA SVĀHĀ.

MAHĀ PAÑCA AMṚITA KHĀHI, MAHĀRAKTA KHĀHI.

Recite OṀ VAJRAKĪLI KĪLAYA, MOHA GHĀTAYA MAMA ŚĪGHRAM KARMA KĀRAYE SAPĀRIVĀRA IDAṀ BALIṄTA KHA KHA KHĀHI KHĀHI *three times.*

Accepting these superior offerings, you twelve oath-bound Kīla guards and hosts, protect the buddhas' teachings! Glorify the Triple Gem! Preserve the dominion of sanghas and Dharma! Dispel this world's decline! Increase sentient ones' ease and benefit! Be yogins' allies! Accomplish mantra holders' activities! Vanquish hostile enemies! Conquer harmful obstructors! Especially for those with samaya gathered here, pacify outer, inner, and secret adversities; increase and enrich favorable conditions and every good thing desired; and engage activities to swiftly accomplish supreme and common siddhis, barring none!

HŪṀ. Glorious Great Blood Drinker Kīlaya's
guards, obedient servants, oath-bound ones,
dog maids, sovereigns, earth maids, kiṁkāras,
mothers, sisters, female envoys with
awesome charnel-ground gear—mistresses
of unhindered, forceful actions' skill—
praise to you with hosts innumerable!
Now accomplish deeds entrusted you!

CHAPTER 18

Feast Offering, Restoration, and Repelling

Feast Offering

If a feast offering is to be made, sprinkle the materials for the gaṇa-cakra with nectar and recite: OṀ SARVA DRA BYAṀ VIŚVA DHAYA HŪṀ PHAṬ. The feast substances are at the heart of a precious thousand-branched offering tree, the gaṇacakra vessel. From a blazing blue-black HŪṀ dwelling on a sun, moon, and lotus come RĀṀ YĀṀ KHĀṀ; thus, every impure thing has been burnt, scattered, and washed.

HŪṀ MŪṀ, OṀ LĀṀ, SVĀṀ MĀṀ, ĀṀ PĀṀ, HĀṀ TĀṀ. Music of all desirables—nature of the five families' couples' great samaya—becomes manifest. *Recite* OṀ ĀḤ HŪṀ *three times.*

HŪṀ. To take up empowerments and siddhis
to accomplish existence-kīla,
you great wisdom-wrathfuls, please come here!
Having come, you beings of wisdom wrath,
please reveal your marks and signs and grant
the accomplishments of Kīlaya! *Thus invite.*

OṀ ĀḤ HŪṀ. Outer vessel, inner contents, and
secret offerings—enjoyments displayed—
have been consecrated for the feast.
As they're offered to you, Glorious, Great

Father, mother, your courts, Kīla guards
with ten wrathful couples, take them, please
to restore our bond in the expanse!
GAṆACAKRA MAHĀJÑĀNA PUJĀ HOḤ.

Thus the select portion of the feast gathering is offered.

Restoration

The Māra-Subduing Secret Mantra Sanctuary: The Restoration Ritual of Great Glorious Vajrakīla

HŪṂ. This gathering hall of Glorious Ones' play,
charnel ground of cruel rūdras' release,
is resplendent with adornments decked—
outer offerings, massed enjoyment clouds,
inner offerings, strewn desirables,
secret offerings, dance of the rigma.

Dazzling are reflected images
of common appearance-existence,
specially wondrous pledge substances—the
great and small supreme endowed with signs,
zali female yak, crystal-rock sheep,
lustrous eagle, blackish goat, *jagad*,
great redness, and baliṅta. When these
feast things through samādhi are refined,
stable realization will blaze forth.

Through unmatched restoring substances,
which have spread to equal the sky's reach
and been blessed by the mind of sameness,
Lekyi Wangmo, Mistress of Secrets,
Prabhahasti, Vajra Thötreng Tsal,
Queen of Great Bliss, Choggyur Lingpa, you
knowledge holders who've achieved Kīla—

three kāya-, nine lineage-endowed ones—
our grave bond's restored in the expanse!

Vajrasattva, lord o'er all families,
Glorious One emerged in blazing form,
māras' foe and tamer, slayer of
transgressors, Blood Drinker Vajra Youth,
Space Queen Khorlo Gyedebma—nondual
father and mother—our bond's restored!

Actual ten perfections, ten virtues,
you wrath kings tame demons on ten sides.
With your emanated servant hosts—
twenty falcon types—our bond's restored!

You rise from mind, speech, and body as
mudrās penetrating noxious ones.
Through the families' boundless projection
and gathering, princes—our bond's restored!

The explicit four immeasurables,
four beast-faced ones who perform four acts—
four gates' blazing guards—our bond's restored!

Friends who guard the word of Kīla and
nurture yogins with samaya, you're
hindrances' and foes' great antidote!
You four canine maids—our bond's restored!
You four sovereign maids—our bond's restored!
Four earth-owning maids—our bond's restored!
Four kiṁkāra men—our bond's restored!
Twenty-eight mighties—our bond's restored!
Twenty-one lay folks—our bond's restored!
Steadfast plague-keepers—our bond's restored!
Chief and courts with emanated hosts—
our grave bond's restored in the expanse!

To restore our grave commitment from
root and branch samayas' breakages,
faults' downfalls, confusion, and the like,
grant the eight great siddhis, four actions,
and great jewels of body, speech, and mind—
siddhis and empowerments, barring none!

Foreign onslaughts, conflicts, and the like,
human and nonhuman demons' tribes
who abuse the teachings and all beings,
spirits of loss ruining Tibet,
practice-hindering oath-transgressors' hordes
are crushed by a kīla-substance hail,
burnt in your mouths' blazing homa hearths!
Making even the term *atom* naught,
put an end to them through savage play!

Wisdom-wrathfuls, grant resplendence to
yogins with our courts who practice you!
Marks and signs of the accomplishment
of existence as vajra soon show!
Consummating penetrating mind,
tame four māras and slay the three foes!
In the unborn sphere, enlightened, make
the two aims spontaneously achieved!

When doing the accomplishment-repelling ritual of the New Treasures' Vajrakīla in association with temporal longevity ceremonies at the glorious, inconceivable Māra-Subduing Secret Mantra Sanctuary, Pema Garwang Lodrö Thaye wrote down whatever arose of its own accord in order that suitable vessels for this Dharma might get relief. May it benefit others! May virtue and goodness increase!

Feast Offering

HŪM̐. Samaya for kalpas is restored!
The bond with the father, appearance,
the bond with the mother, emptiness—
we've restored through great, nondual play!

HŪM̐. In self-born rigpa's dynamic state,
unconfused and free of thought, I've dwelt
from the start; thus, violations and
breaches have come free in their own place.
If I've grasped at mind-appearances,
I disclose it in the vast expanse. *Thus restore and disclose.*

The hundred syllables: OṀ VAJRA SATTVA SAMAYAMANUPĀLAYA / VAJRA SATTVA TVENOPATIṢṬHA / DRIḌHO ME BHAVA / SUTOṢYO ME BHAVA SUPOṢYO ME BHAVA / ANURAKTO ME BHAVA / SARVA SIDDHIMME PRAYACCHA / SARVA KARMASU CA ME CITTAṀ ŚREYAḤ KURU HŪM̐ / HA HA HA HA HOḤ BHAGAVAN SARVA TATHĀGATA VAJRA MĀ ME MUÑCA / VAJRĪ BHAVA / MAHĀ SAMAYA SATTVA AḤ.

Imagining the final gaṇacakra, recite: NAMO! By the truth of the Three Jewels, Three Roots, and yidam Vajra Youth's divine assembly of seventy-eight, every harmdoer, oath transgressor, and opportunistic spirit—into this liṅga of the final gaṇacakra be drawn!

OṀ VAJRAKĪLI KĪLAYA! Foes, obstructors, and harmdoers: JAḤ HŪM̐ VAM̐ HOḤ. ŚĪGHRAṀ ĀNAYA HŪM̐ PHAṬ! *Thus draw them in.*

HŪM̐. The time for great samaya has come!
The time for emanations has come!
The time for great servant maids has come!
The time for you dog-faced maids has come!
The time for great sovereign maids has come!
The time for earth-owning maids has come!

The time for your samaya has come!
The time to show forceful skill has come!

Through your blessing, great wrathfuls, at once
draw here noxious foes, obstructors, and
hordes of māras and disrupters who,
plundering siddhis, harm those who've aroused
the mind of supreme enlightenment—
we, the knowledge holders who are the
three times' victors' lineage successors!
Having suitably released them through
manifest behavior and reduced
their bodies and speech to particles,
cause them to experience suffering!

Having thus urged them, one should recite: OṀ VAJRAKĪLI KĪLAYA! Foes, obstructors, and oath transgressors: MĀRAYA HŪṂ PHAṬ, *while stabbing with weapons such as kīlas.*

Proffering to the deities' mouths:
HŪṂ. Open wide, Great Glorious One and courts!
These five skandhas of delivered foes
and obstructors we serve to your mouths—
glorious couple, you ten wrathful ones,
and your emanated retinues.
Please partake of harmdoers, hostile foes,
and their hosts, with not an atom left!
VAJRA YAKṢA KRODHA KHA KHA KHĀHI KHĀHI.

Repelling

At the conclusion of the proffering, while the two vajra helpers stand to the northeast of the mandala facing outward, everyone in the assembly should recite the following, clapping the hands at the ends of the lines:

HŪṂ. All you with dynamic potency
in this billionfold cosmos, heed us!
As we've thus petitioned and restored,
now engage the acts of turning back!

For us yogins with our circles, please
turn back those above who change to fiends!
Turn back those below who rise as *si!*
Turn back counter-charms of intimates!
Turn sicced evil spirits back on foes!
Turn back cross-hatched targets, dagger rites,
sickening magic weapons, bloody blades,
quarrelsome spirits of paternal lines,
yāmas' yantras, and mātarīs' plagues,
māras' X marks, demons of adults,
furies' teasing, earth lords' noxiousness,
kinglies' maddening spirits, the malign
and eclipsing planetary gods,
evil mantras of the *tīrthikas*,
bulbous ones' scrimping and pilfering,
rites that cause contagion and disease,
evil-fated years and months—all these
cause to be turned back on enemies!

Bad dreams, divinations, evil signs,
eighty-one bad omens, primordial
baggage of three hundred sixty kinds,
ninety-and-one adventitious things,
eighteen manners of untimely death,
arrows shot by the right's hundred males,
the left's hundred females' poisoned meals,
mockery from black-clothed lay folk, and
cursing lips of all inferior slaves—
cause [each one of these] to be turned back!

JOḤ! Repel! Deliver enemies!
JOḤ! Turn back obstructors and reduce
[each and every one of them] to dust!
Thus should one engage the repelling.

OṀ VAJRAKĪLI KĪLAYA, MA RAGMO YAKMO KĀLARŪPA. NYING TSA LA YAṀ YAṀ. SOK TSA LA YAṀ YAṀ. NYING LA TRIL TRIL. SOK LA CHUṀ CHUṀ. CITTA SOK LA TUNG TUNG. NYING TRAK SHE. JAḤ THUM RI LI LI. NYING TSEK TSEK! UR UR! SHIK SHIK! GÜL GÜL! NYAK NYAK! SÖ SÖ! DHADDHI MAMA KARMA ŚĪGHRAM KĀRAYE. MĀRASENA PRAMARDANĪYE HŪṀ PHAṬ!

OṀ VAJRAKĪLI KĪLAYA, HŪṀ HŪṀ HŪṀ! DÜ PRA MĀRAYA BE NAN! KHA LA JAMALI BE NAN! RĀJA DU LING SHAK BE NAN! SHIK SHIK DUM DUM BE NAN! TSAL PA TSAL PA BE NAN! KHROṀ KHROṀ JO BE NAN! MUK MUK BE NAN! TIR TIR BE NAN! TSAL DU TSAL DU BE NAN!

Feast Offering

Here, supplemental texts such as the disclosure of the fourteen mantric downfalls may be recited together with:
Having turned the gaṇacakra wheel
in Heruka's mandala, may I
and all wayfarers, excluding none,
be accomplished in one mandala!

Having enjoyed the gaṇacakra, consecrate the remainder with OṀ VAJRA AMṚITA UCCHIṢṬĀYA HŪṀ PHAṬ.

HŪṀ. First, we offer gods' hosts the choice part.
Next, the feast restores the siblings' bond.
Finally, through this torma of remains,
may deserving ones be satisfied!
OṀ UCCHIṢṬĀ BHAKṢA KHĀHI.
Thus it is taken outside.

Inciting the heart samaya:
HŪM̐. Rise up! Rise up! From the sphere arise!
Be roused! Be roused! From the point be roused!
Vajra Youth with courts, engage acts of
peace, enrichment, magnetism, force!

The covenant:
HŪM̐ JOḤ. You command guards and you oath-bound ones—
whether of this world or transmundane—
thinking on your former promises,
take this torma and engage actions!

Entreating the steadfast ones, protectresses:
JOḤ. Steadfast guard maids who dwell in this world
of appearance-existence, come here!
As you take up this adorned torma,
now accomplish deeds entrusted you!

 Drawing in: NAMO! By the truth of the Three Jewels, Three Roots,
and yidam Vajra Youth's divine assembly of seventy-eight, every
harmdoer, oath transgressor, and opportunistic spirit—under the
torma vessel like blazing Meru be drawn! JĀḤ HŪM̐ VAM̐ HŌḤ.

The horse dance:
HŪM̐. Imprints born through ignorance and the
mass of four conditions, six causes,
and afflictions are suppressed beneath
Meru—self-born knowing-emptiness—
seamlessly upon completion's ground!
OM̐ ĀḤ HŪM̐ LAM̐ STAMBHAYA NAN.

CHAPTER 19

Taking Up Accomplishments

The master and regents circumambulate the mandala and stand to its east while the charm and melody that draw together actual accomplishments are recited: OṀ VAJRAKĪLI KĪLAYA, SARVA VIGHNĀN VAṀ HŪṀ PHAṬ! KĀYA SIDDHI OṀ, VĀK SIDDHI ĀḤ, CITTA SIDDHI HŪṀ, SARVA SIDDHI HRĪḤ.

Then, invoking the heart samaya and making supplication for one's desired aims, with palms placed together, recite:

HŪṀ. Most superior wisdom, Deity
Vajrakīla from the natural sphere,
you lack concept or exertion; yet
like a precious jewel that grants all wants
is your blessing, nature of past oaths.
You, empowerment god of timely grace,
dwelling in your sole oath ne'er to stray
from protecting, please grant here and now
to the fortunate accomplishments,
common and supreme, excluding none,
from the inexhaustible jeweled wheel!

Grant attainment of immortal life!
Grant attainment of successors' rule!
Grant attainment of unending wealth!
Grant the treasures inexhaustible,
miracles, clairvoyant knowledge, and

four activities' accomplishment!
Grant attainment of mahāmudrā!

Having thus implored with longing melody, the sādhakas should burn incense and great flesh and sound forth musical instruments to reach the deity's vital point. Then, as the approach and accomplishment have been completed, the assembly—with lotus-circling mudrās, palms placed together, and minds of intense yearning—should invoke the siddhis via the break of day:

HŪṀ. Knowledge holders of Vajra Youth, make
existence as vajra manifest!
You existence-vajrakīla gods,
bring primordial wrathful wisdom forth!
These days, as the dawn's first light appears,
Vajrarākṣasa's daybreak, too, dawns.
Favored deity, consider this:
grant attainments, common and supreme,
and those of enlightened body, speech,
mind, attributes, and activities!
From the glorious knot within your heart
dawns primordial wisdom's secret sun
on the bodies, speech, and minds of us
yogins, great sādhakas, SIDDHI HOḤ!

OṂ VAJRAKĪLI KĪLAYA, SARVA VIGHNĀN VAṂ HŪṂ PHAṬ! KĀYA SIDDHI OṂ, VĀK SIDDHI ĀḤ, CITTA SIDDHI HŪṂ, SARVA SIDDHI HRĪḤ.
In this way, one should take up accomplishments.

Notes

Note to Practitioners

1. *dus ngan me ltar 'bar ba'i dus/ gsang sngags nus pa me ltar 'bar.*

Chapter 1. Contextualizing These Teachings

1. Jigten Sumgön, "The Song on Realizing Fivefold Mahāmudrā," verse 2.
2. *sangs rgyas thams cad thugs brtse ba chen pos dgongs par gyur.*
3. Gyalse Thogme Zangpo, *The Thirty-Seven Practices*, 41, verse 16.
4. *bdag med rtogs kyang sangs mi rgya.*
5. Jigten Sumgön, *Abridged Prayers of Refuge, Bodhicitta and Dedication of the Glorious Drigung Kagyü*, 7.
6. *bla ni sems can kun gyi bla/ ma ni sems can kun gyi ma.*
7. *yi dam dkyil 'khor bye ba sgom pa las/ bla ma lan gcig sgom pa lhag pa dang...*
8. *shes rig rang tshugs ma shor na/ 'di las lhag pa gzhan ma dgos.*
9. Garchen Triptrül, *An Unelaborate Liturgical Arrangement.*
10. *Rin chen gter mdzod chen mo.*

Chapter 2. Teachings Common to All Mantric Paths

1. *theg chen dpe tshad rgya mtsho bzhin/ theg pa chung ngu ba rjes chu.*
2. *sems can rnams ni sangs rgyas nyid/ 'on kyang glo bur dri mas bsgribs/ de nyid bsal na sangs rgyas nyid.*
3. Thogme Zangpo, *The Thirty-Seven Practices,* 39, verse 11.
4. Ibid.
5. *sems can rnams ni sangs rgyas nyid.*
6. *sems can rnams ni sangs rgyas nyid/ 'on kyang glo bur dri mas bsgribs.*
7. Rigdzin Gödem, *The Aspiration of Samantabhadra*, 18–19.
8. *snang srid lha skur go bar bgyis/ gsang sngags bskyed rim phun sum tshogs.*
9. Tibetans generally believe that the buildup of bilirubin in jaundice taints visual perceptions so that they appear yellow.

10. *khams gsum sems can bsad las sdig che ba/ byang chub sems dpa' rnams la skur ba btab.*
11. The teachings of the Earlier System were the first to appear in Tibet, having been translated under the patronage of the Tibetan Dharma kings Songtsen Gampo, Trisong Detsen, and Tri Ralpachen. Those of the Latter System were propagated after having been translated into Tibetan by the great translator Rinchen Zangpo in the mid-tenth century and others thereafter. Thus, one should understand that the terms *earlier* and *latter* refer to the periods in which their associated scriptures were translated and introduced to Tibet.
12. *Bka' brgyad bde gshegs 'dus pa'i rgyud.*
13. *dang po lha'i rnam pa bsgom/ rnam pa sems su shar tsa na/ tha mal rtog pa 'jig par 'gyur/ bar du lha'i nga rgyal bsgom/ nga rgyal brtan por gyur tsa na/ rang dbang rang gis thob pa yin/ mthar ni lha yi byin brlabs bsgom/ byin brlabs nus pas gzhan snang bsgyur.*
14. *sangs rgyas thams cad 'dus pa ni/ mgon po spyan ras gzigs sku yin/ sgom dang yid la dran pas kyang/ mtshams med sdig pa 'dag par byed.*
15. *sdug bsngal rgya mtsho'i snod gyur pa'i/ lus 'di...*
16. *lha zhes bya ba byang chub sems.*
17. *kun tu khyab pa byams pa dag gi stobs.*
18. Rigdzin Chökyi Dragpa, "A Collection of Scriptures," 8.
19. Thogme Zangpo, *The Thirty-Seven Practices,* 36–37, verse 3.
20. Ibid.
21. *Rdo rje phur pa'i sgrub chen gyi stong thun.*
22. *Bka' brgyad kyi rnam bshad.*
23. Thogme Zangpo, *The Thirty-Seven Practices,* 37, verse 4.
24. *lha la cig car 'jug pa zab mo'i gnad.*
25. *tha mal rtog pa 'gyur ba la/ bskyed rim ming du btags pa yin.*
26. *thang gcig bsam gtan thun bzhugs na/ khams gsum gang ba'i sems can la/ srog byin bas ni 'di don che.*
27. *mthar ni lha yi byin brlabs bsgom/ byin brlabs nus pas gzhan snang bsgyur.*
28. Rinpoche is referring to Karma Gyurme Rinpoche, the 8th Lharig Sigtrül Tülku, who has connections with the Nyingma and Karma Kagyü lineages.
29. *gzugs stong pa'o/ stong pa nyid kyang gzugs so.*
30. *ma 'ongs dus kyi mtha' ma la/ nga nyid yi ge'i ris su 'byon.*
31. *rgyal ba mnyes mchod rgyun mi 'chad/ sems can sgrib sbyong rgyun mi 'chad/ bdag la dngos grub rgyun mi 'chad.*

Chapter 3. Lineage Supplication Instructions

1. Although it is taught that the nature of the five afflictions is the five wisdoms, the term *unmitigated afflictions* refers to negative emotions as they are, without the mitigating influence of primordial awareness-wisdom.

2. *gdon du rnam rtog che'o gsung.*
3. *dngos grub thob khar bar chad sna tshogs 'byung.*
4. *bar chad bgegs rnams rdo rje phur pas bsgral/ phyag rgya chen po'i dngos grub gnas der thob.*
5. *gzhan gnod gzhi bcas spang na so thar sdom pa tshang/ gzhan phan gzhi bcas bsgrub na byang sdom tshang/ snod bcud dag snang 'byong na sngags sdom tshang.* These words come from Lama Garchen Rinpoche's refuge vow cards, which read, "When harm to others and its cause are abandoned, the individual liberation vows are complete. When help to others and its cause are accomplished, the bodhisattvas' vows are complete. When one is adept at the pure perception of the vessel and contents, the mantric vows are complete."
6. Tilopa, *The Ganges*, 22.
7. *lta ba nam mkha' bas kyang mtho/ las rgyu 'bras bag phye bas kyang zhib.*
8. Thogme Zangpo, *The Thirty-Seven Practices,* 42, verse 18.
9. *shes rig rang tshugs ma shor na/ 'di las lhag pa gzhan ma dgos.*
10. *lta ba lung rigs dang 'bral ba/ sgom pa nyams myong dang 'bral ba/ spyod pa dus tshod dang 'bral ba/ bla ma snying rje dang 'bral ba/ slob ma mos gus dang 'bral ba.* Although I have not been able to locate a source for this quote, Lama Garchen Rinpoche has said that it is from one of the songs of Milarepa, suggesting that perhaps it comes from a source other than those assembled by Tsangnyön Heruka. Rinpoche also insisted that the verb "to be free from" (*'bral ba*), rather than its occasional homonym "to be related" (*'brel ba*), is the correct term in this quote.
11. Thogme Zangpo, *The Thirty-Seven Practices,* 48, verse 36.
12. *ye nas yod pa ye zhes bya/ thams cad shes pas shes ces bya.*
13. Rigdzin Gödem, *The Aspiration of Samantabhadra,* 15.
14. *ma rtogs dus na ma rig pa . . . rtogs na rang rig ye shes te.*
15. *gcig shes kun grol.*
16. *ye shes me stag chung ring la/ dran pa'i me gso yang yang dgos.*
17. *nyon mongs ye shes khyad med na/ rtogs tshad klong du gyur pa yin.*
18. *hūṁ/ rdo rje khros pas zhe sdang gcod/ mtshon chen sngon po 'bar ba yi/ nam mkha'i dkyil nas thig pa shar/ srog gi go ru shar ba dang/ snying gi dkyil du bsgom par bya.*
19. *de ltar rtogs pa'i mkhas pa yis/ rnam shes ma mthong ye shes mthong.*
20. *chos kyi rtsa ba ma gcod sems kyi rtsa ba chod.*
21. Although the *skandhas* and *dhātus* were named in the original Tibetan text, the term *āyatanas* was omitted in order to preserve the meter of the line. However, it is implicitly understood.
22. Rigdzin Gödem, *The Aspiration of Samantabhadra,* 16.
23. *nam mkha'i mthar thug gyur pa ji tsam par/ sems can ma lus mtha' yang*

de bzhin te/ ji tsam las dang nyon mongs mthar gyur pa/ bdag gi smon lam mtha' yang de tsam mo.

24. Chökyi Drakpa, "Protection and Repelling Practices of Mañjuśrī Yamāntaka," 8.
25. *stong nyid rtogs na snying rje skye/ snying rje skyes na bdag gzhan med/ bdag gzhan med na gzhan don 'grub.*
26. Jigten Sumgön, *Prayers of Refuge, Bodhicitta and Dedication*, 7.
27. The words *dön tak*, "meanings, signs," in the Tibetan text are two parts of a three-part phrase. Although implied, the third term, *da*, "symbol," is omitted in order to preserve the meter of the line.
28. Tilopa, *The Ganges*, 20.

Chapter 4. Practice Manual Instructions

1. *rang gi snying ga'i hūṁ las 'od zer 'phros pas bla ma rig 'dzin dpal chen rdo rje gzhon nu'i dkyil 'khor gyi lha tshogs mkha' khyab kyi 'khor lor sad par gyur.*
2. *dang po nges gnyis 'dra 'dra yin pa la/ khyod ni brtson 'grus che bas mngon sangs rgyas/ nga ni le lo che bas 'khor bar khyams/ nga le lo can gyi 'brug pa kun legs kyis brtson 'grus can gyi shākya thub pa khyod la phyag 'tshal lo.*
3. *yid gnyis the tshom med par gsol ba 'debs.*
4. Jigten Sumgön, *Prayers of Refuge, Bodhicitta and Dedication*, 3.
5. *phyogs bcu dus gsum sangs rgyas thams cad kyi/ phrin las gcig bsdus drag po'i skur bzhengs pa.*
6. *gzhan gyi mi zab pa rnams 'dir zab ste.*
7. *rang gi sems ni yongs su 'dul.*
8. Once, there was a faithful old Tibetan woman who had a habit of making daily prayers and offerings. Since her son traveled regularly to India on business, she asked him to bring her an object of veneration from the Holy Land. After forgetting her request many times, the son finally remembered it just as he was returning home empty handed yet again. Feeling desperate, he looked around for something that could serve as a relic and spotted the skull of a dog on the ground. He pulled out one of its teeth, wrapped it in nice cloth, and when he reached home, presented it to his mother as a tooth of Lord Buddha himself. The woman continually made prostrations and offerings to it with a mind of faith. So great was her faith that the buddhas' blessings entered the ordinary tooth, causing secondary relics to spontaneously come forth from it. Through the force of her belief, the material substance of the dog's tooth became indistinguishable from an actual relic of the Buddha. This was confirmed by the appearance of auspicious signs

like rainbow lights and the like at the time of her passing. For the full story see Paltrül Rinpoche, *Kun bzang bla ma'i zhal lung*, 356–58.

9. *'di la bsal ba gang yang med/ gzhag par bya ba ci yang med/ yang dag nyid la yang dag lta/ yang dag mthong na rnam par grol.*
10. *snang ba snod kyi 'jig rten gtor gzhong du/ srid pa bcud kyi sems can gtor mar sbyang.*
11. *bskyed pa'i rim pa gdod nas yongs su grub.*
12. Here, it might be helpful to list the Sanskrit names of these ten wrathful ones with their Tibetan equivalents and their locations in the outer mandala.

    Hūṁkāra, Hūṁkāra (zenith)
    Hayagrīva, Tamdrin (west)
    Yamāntaka, Shinje She (south)
    Amṛitakuṇḍali, Dütsi Khyilpa (north)
    Acala, Miyowa (southwest)
    Mahābala, Tobchen (nadir)
    Vijaya, Namgyal (east)
    Nīldaṇḍa, Yug-ngön (southeast)
    Ṭakkirāja, Dögyal (northwest)
    Trailokyavijaya, Khamsum Namgyal (northeast)

13. *rdo rje khros pas zhe sdang gcod.*
14. Beer, *The Encyclopedia of Tibetan Symbols and Motifs*, 316.
15. Rigdzin Gödem, *The Aspiration of Samantabhadra*, 14.
16. Dudjom Rinpoche, *The Nyingma School of Tibetan Buddhism*, vol. 2, 167.
17. Jigten Sumgön, *Gongchig*, 17.
18. *drang nges med par cho ga rgyas par dgos/ de yis 'dul na bsdus pa yang ni bzhed.*
19. *rang gi sems ni yongs su 'dul.*
20. *chos sku zhi ba'i ngang las ma g.yos kyang/ longs sku ngang 'jigs tshul du skur byung pa.*
21. *lha zhes bya ba byang chub sems.*
22. *srid gsum sdug bsngal ci 'dra khyed kyis mkhyen/ dmyal tshogs me dpung zhi bar bgyid la sogs/ sems can don du myur du bdag mchi na/ dam pa khyod kyis nus mthu bstsal du gsol.* See *The Excellent Path of Complete Liberation.*
23. *'grub pa'i mthun 'gyur nged kyis byed pa yin.* See *An Arrangement of the Empowerment for Accomplishing the Pure Field of Great Bliss According to the Sky Dharma Treasure.*
24. Thogme Zangpo, *The Thirty-Seven Practices*, 43, verse 22.
25. *bdag mdun dbyer med dus gcig bskyed pas sgrub.*
26. *rang gi sems ni yongs su 'dul.*

27. *ting 'dzin me dang 'dra ba la/ bzlas brjod rlung dang 'dra bas bskyod/ sgrib pa'i bud shing bsreg par bya.*
28. *sgra chen ma yin chung ba min/ mgyogs par ma yin bul ba min/ drag par ma yin zhan par min/ yig 'bru yan lag nyams pa min/ yengs pas ma yin smra bzhin min/ glal sogs bar du chod pas min.*
29. Here, Rinpoche is referring to the great accomplishment retreat. Obviously, this practice of having one group responsible for chanting the practice manual with mantras and another for chanting only the mantras is not done in retreats in the West. Since Rinpoche mentioned it frequently in our discussions about Vajrakīla practice, I include this point to give some idea of how the retreat was conducted in a monastic setting in Tibet.
30. *Thugs rje gsang 'dus kyi stong thun.*
31. *'ur klog mi bya snyan po'i dbyangs kyis brjod.*
32. *dag dang ma dag stong 'gyur la/ ting 'dzin yod med 'bum du 'gyur.*
33. Jigten Sumgön, *Prayers of Refuge, Bodhicitta and Dedication,* 21.
34. According to the Ayurvedic and Tibetan medical systems, there are seven dhātus, or tissues (*lüzung dün*), in the body. After nutrients have been digested, the dhātus are generated sequentially from (1) *rasa* or plasma (*dangma*), to (2) rakta or blood (*trag*), to (3) *mamsa* or muscle and connective tissue (*sha*), to (4) *medha* or fat (*tsil*), to (5) *asthi* or bone (*rü*), to (6) *majja* or marrow (*kang*), and, finally, to (7) *śukra* or reproductive tissues (*khuwa*). A refinement takes place at each stage, yielding both a pure portion (*dangma*) and a waste product (*nyigma*). This process is said to take about a month to complete. See "lus zungs bdun" in Zhang Yisun's *Bod rgya tshig mdzod chen mo.*
35. This advice applies to those who are visualizing themselves in the form of the heruka.
36. *bde ba'i ngang nas stong pa/ stong pa'i ngang nas gsal ba/ gsal ba'i ngang nas rig pa.*
37. Rigdzin Gödem, *The Aspiration of Samantabhadra,* 15.
38. Chökyi Dragpa, "Protection and Repelling Practices of Mañjuśrī Yamāntaka," 12.
39. Thogme Zangpo, *The Thirty-Seven Practices,* 42–43, verse 20.
40. Shantideva, *The Way of the Bodhisattva,* 55.
41. "OṂ/ O Vajrasattva honour the agreement! Manifest as Vajrasattva!/ Be steadfast for me! Be very pleased for me!/ Be fully nourishing for me!/ Be passionate for me!/ Grant me all success and attainment/ and in all actions make my mind more lucid!/ HŪṂ/ HA HA HA HA HOḤ/ O Blessed One, diamond of all those in that state, do not abandon me! Become real O great agreement-being./ ĀḤ." Dharmacārī Jayarava, "The Hundred Syllable Vajrasattva Mantra."

42. "Of those experiences that arise from a cause/ The Tathāgata has said, 'this is their cause,/ And this is their cessation':/ Thus the Great Śramaṇa teaches." Dharmacārī Jayarava, "Ye Dharmā Hetuprabhava - Causation."
43. *rgyal ba thams cad ye shes klong du gcig.*
44. *dpal chos dbyings kyi nam mkha' yangs pa la/ chos mtha' dbus med pa kun la khyab.*
45. *sku gsum bdag nyid sangs rgyas bcom ldan 'das...*
46. *ye shes 'di ni ches phra zhing/ rdo rje snying po mkha' dang mtshungs/ rdul bral mtha' ste zhi ba nyid/ khyod kyi pha ni khyod yin no.*
47. Tilopa, *The Ganges,* 24.
48. *ji ltar 'das pa'i sangs rgyas bcom ldan 'das rnams kyis yongs su bsngos pa dang/ ji ltar ma byon pa'i sangs rgyas bcom ldan 'das rnams yongs su bsngo bar 'gyur ba dang/ ji ltar da ltar bzhugs pa'i sangs rgyas bcom ldan 'das rnams da ltar yongs su bsngo ba mdzad pa de ltar bdag gis kyang yongs su bsngo bar bgyi'o.*
49. Jigten Sumgön, *Prayers of Refuge, Bodhicitta and Dedication,* 25.
50. *sems can rnams ni sangs rgyas nyid.*
51. The six munis are (1) Indra Kauśika (Wangpo Gyajin) of the god realms, (2) Vemacitra (Thag Zangri) of the demigod realms, (3) Śākyamuni (Śākya Thubpa) of the human realm, (4) Śravasiṃha (Sengge Rabten) of the animal realm, (5) Jvalamukhadeva (Khabar Dewa) of the preta realms, and (6) Dharmarāja (Chökyi Gyalpo) of the hell realms. See "thub pa drug" in Tony Duff's *The Illuminator Tibetan-English Encyclopaedic Dictionary.*
52. *log pa'i kun rdzob kyis kyang don byed nus.*
53. Jigten Sumgön, *Gongchig,* 17.
54. Chökyi Dragpa, "Protection and Repelling Practices of Mañjuśrī Yamāntaka," 14.
55. Ibid., 15.
56. *rgyal ba thams cad ye shes klong du gcig.*
57. Chökyi Dragpa, "Protection and Repelling Practices of Mañjuśrī Yamāntaka," 19.
58. Jigten Sumgön, "Song on Realizing Fivefold Mahāmudrā," verse 2.
59. *shes rig rang tshugs ma shor na/ 'di las lhag pa gzhan ma dgos/ mkhas btsun brgya dang grub thob stong/ lo paṇ khri dang man ngag 'bum/ bstan bcos bye ba sa ya dang/ mjal yang the tshom bca' ma dgos/ sa ma ya/ dha thim.*

Chapter 6. Kīla Consecration Instructions

1. *rang snang dbang bsdus gzhan snang zil gyis gnon.*
2. The eight emancipations (*aṣṭavimokṣa*) are (1) emancipation from viewing that which has form as form, (2) emancipation from viewing the formless as form, (3) emancipation from the attractive, (4) emancipation from the

āyatana of infinite space, (5) emancipation from the āyatana of infinite consciousness, (6) emancipation from the āyatana of absolute nothingness, (7) emancipation from the āyatana of neither presence nor absence of perception, and (8) emancipation from cessation. Numbers 4 through 7 are the emancipations related to each of the four formless states and their absorptions. See "rnam par thar pa brgyad" in Zhang Yisun's *Bod rgya tshig mdzod chen mo.*

3. Chökyi Dragpa, "Protection and Repelling Practices of Mañjuśrī Yamāntaka," 15.
4. *'jig rten khams ni stong dag tu/ ngas ni mdo sde gang bshad pa/ tshig 'bru tha dad don gcig ste/ tshig gcig rnam par bsgoms na yang/ de dag thams cad bsgom par gyur.* This passage has been translated according to the textual references I could find, which all read, "If even a single word has been fully contemplated" (*tshig gcig rnam par bsgoms pa yis*). However, Garchen Rinpoche is confident that the correct wording is, "If even a single meaning has been fully contemplated" (*don gcig rnam par bsgoms pa yis*).

Chapter 7. Bringing Down Blessings Instructions

1. *dus las mi 'da' rdo rje'i dam tshig can.*
2. *dus las mi 'da' thugs rje'i dam tshig can.*

Chapter 8. Petition Instructions

1. *ngo bo bla ma chos sku sangs rgyas la/ rang bzhin longs sku zhi dang dam pa'i chos/ thugs rje sprul sku mkha' 'gro dge 'dun la/ byang chub ma 'thob bar du skyabs su mchi.*

Chapter 9. Feast Offering, Restoration, and Repelling Instructions

1. *tshogs gral gcig na dam tshig nyams pa'i mi gcig yod kyang/ de'i nyams grib kyis dam ldan brgya stong yod kyang sgrub pa'i 'bras bu cung zad kyang mi 'byin pa 'o ma rul ba thigs gcig gis ma rul ba zangs gang yang rul bar byed pa ltar.*
2. *rang lus bla ma yi dam dkyil 'khor la/ rtsa khams dpa' bo dpa' mo skor gyis bskor/ za btung tshogs kyi 'khor lo bskor ba yi/ dge bas 'gro kun he ru ka thob shog.*
3. *ston pa bla med sangs rgyas rin po che/ skyob pa bla med dam chos rin po che/ 'dren pa bla med dge 'dun rin po che/ skyabs gnas dkon mchog gsum la mchod pa 'bul.*
4. *do rje spyan gyis gsal bar hūṁ bsgoms te/ zos nas bla med byang chub mchog thob shog.*
5. Thogme Zangpo, *The Thirty-Seven Practices,* 38, verse 7.

6. Jigten Sumgön, *Prayers of Refuge, Bodhicitta and Dedication*, 13.
7. *yon tan chung la nga rgyal che.*
8. *snying rjes bsgral ba'i dam tshig ni/ gsad cig mnan pa ma yin te.*
9. *sems can rnams kyi bsam pa dang/ blo yi bye brag ji lta bar/ che chung thun mong theg pa yi/ chos kyi 'khor lo bskor du gsol.*
10. *gzigs shig mdzes ldan dam pa'i chos/ 'di la the tshom bya mi rung/ bram ze khyi dang gdol pa phag/ rang bzhin gcig tu dgongs te rol.*
11. *ah la la hoḥ/ bde gshegs chos la rin thang med/ 'dod chags dri ma dang bral bas/ gzung dang 'dzin pa rnam par spangs/ de bzhin nyid la gus pas 'dud.* Although there are many scriptural references with diverse wordings for this statement, this one reflects Lama Garchen Rinpoche's exact words.
12. *'dod chags zhen pa tshur ma blangs/ 'dod yon ltung ba phyir ma spang.*

Chapter 10. Taking Up Accomplishments Instructions

1. Chökyi Dragpa, "Protection and Repelling Practices of Mañjuśrī Yamāntaka," 19.
2. *chos kyi rtsa ba ma gcod sems kyi rtsa ba chod.*

Chapter 11. Practical Applications of the Instructions

1. *pha rgan mi la ras pa ngas/ res 'ga' nyal zhing nyal zhing sgom/ nyal zhing nyal zhing sgom tsa na/ gti mug 'od gsal du 'char ba'i gdams pa yod/ mi nga la yod de zhan la med/ kun kyang 'di ltar yod na dga' ba la/ pha rgan mi la ras pa ngas/ res 'ga' za zhing za zhing sgom/ za zhing za zhing sgom tsa na/ bza' btung tshogs 'khor du shes pa'i gdams ngag yod/ mi nga la yod de kun la med/ kun kyang 'di ltar yod na dga' ba la/ pha rgan mi la ras pa ngas/ res 'ga' 'gro zhing 'gro zhing sgom/ 'gro zhing 'gro zhing sgom tsa na/ 'gro 'dug bskor bar shes pa'i gdams ngag yod.*
2. Here, Rinpoche is referring to the Neck-Pouch Kīla Cycle (Phur pa mgul khug ma'i skor), a pure vision of Khenpo Jigme Phüntsog.
3. *rnam rtog rang sar grol na 'khor ba spang mi dgos.*
4. *blo chos su 'gro ba dang/ chos lam du 'gro ba dang/ lam 'khrul pa bsal ba dang/ 'khrul pa ye shes su 'char ba dang bzhi'o.*

Quoted and Referenced Texts

An Arrangement of the Empowerment for Accomplishing the Pure Field of Great Bliss According to the Sky Dharma (Namchö) Treasure, Gnam chos bde chen zhing sgrub kyi dbang 'grig chags su bkod pa

Aspiration for the Pure Field of Great Bliss, Rnam dag bde chen zhing gi smon lam

The Aspiration of Samantabhadra, Kun tu bzang po'i smon lam

A Collection of Liberation Narratives and Supplications of the Precious Kagyü Lineage, Bka' brgyud rin po che'i rnam thar gsol 'debs kyi skor

A Collection of Scriptures Necessary for the Protection and Repelling Practices from the Fiery Razor of Repelling of Mañjuśrī Yamāntaka, Lord of Life, 'Jam dpal Gshin rje tshe bdag yang zlog me'i spu gri'i srung zlog sgrub pa'i nyer mkho'i chos tshan phyogs bsgrigs

The Daily Practice of the Secret Attainment of the Unsurpassed Extremely Secret Vajrakīlaya called "The Essence of the Play of Concerned Activity" (translated by lamas of the Palyül lineage), *Rdo rje phur pa yang gsang bla med kyi gsang sgrub rgyun gyi phrin las rnam rol snying po*

Empowerment Guidance, Adorned by Spoken Instructions, on Devotion, the Life Force Yantra—*a Guru Yoga of the Profound Path, Lam zab bla ma'i rnal 'byor mos gus srog 'khor gyi dbang khrid zhal gdams kyis brgyan pa*

Essence of Display: A Regular Secret Accomplishment Liturgy of the Unsurpassed, Most Secret Vajrakīla (translated by Ari Kiev), *Rdo rje phur pa yang gsang bla med kyi gsang sgrub rgyun gyi phrin las rnam rol snying po*

The Excellent Path of Complete Liberation: An Activity Liturgy for the Approach and Accomplishment of Glorious Vajrasattva's Mind Siddhi, Dpal Rdo rje sems dpa' thugs kyi sgrub pa'i bsnyen sgrub phrin las kyi cho ga rnam grol lam bzang

The Exposition on the Great Accomplishment of Karuṇā Guhyasamaja from a Thousand Perspectives, Thugs rje Gsang 'dus kyi stong thun

The Exposition on the Great Accomplishment of Vajrakīla from a Thousand Perspectives, Rdo rje phur pa'i sgrub chen gyi stong thun

The Ganges: An Experiential Pith Instruction on Mahāmudrā, Phyag rgya chen po'i man ngag gangā ma, Mahāmudropadeśaṁ

Gongchig: The Single Intent, the Sacred Dharma, Dam chos dgongs pa gcig pa'i rtsa tshig rdo rje'i gsung brgya lnga bcu pa'i bsdus don

Great Treasury of Precious Termas, Rin chen gter mdzod chen mo

The Heart of Transcendent Wisdom Sutra, Shes rab kyi pha rol tu phyin pa'i snying po'i mdo, Prajñāpāramitāhṛdayasūtra

The Hundred Thousand Songs of Milarepa, Mi la ras pa'i mgur 'bum

The King of Aspirations for the Conduct of Samantabhadra, 'Phags pa bzang po spyod pa'i smon lam gyi rgyal po, Samantabhadracaryāpraṇidhānarāja

The King of Samādhis Sutra, Ting nge 'dzin gyi rgyal po'i mdo, Samādhirājasūtra

The Lotus King Tantra, Padma rgyal po'i rgyud, Padmorājatantra

Lotus Melody of Eighteen Perfections, Phun tshogs bco brgyad pad dbyangs

Maṇi Kabum, Ma ṇi bka' 'bum

The Neck-Pouch Kīla Cycle Sections Known as "The Commitment Deity: Sole Kīla of the Mind," Phur pa mgul khug ma'i cha shas thugs dam thugs kyi phur gcig

The Necklace of Sapphires: A Unified Arrangement of the Unsurpassed, Most Secret Vajrakīla Practice Manual with Required Supplements, Rdo rje phur pa yang gsang bla med kyi las byang la nye bar mkho ba'i zur 'debs phyogs gcig tu bsgrigs pa aindra nī la'i do shal

The Precious Treasure of Sakya Paṇḍita's Fine Explanations, Sa skya legs bshad rin po che'i gter

Precious Garland of the Supreme Path, Lam mchog rin chen phreng ba

The Supplication in Seven Chapters, Le'u bdun ma

The Supplication to Guru Rinpoche That Spontaneously Fulfills All Wishes, Bsam pa lhun grub ma

The Sutra of the Three Heaps, Phung po gsum pa'i mdo, Triskandhakasūtra

The Sutra on Emancipation, Thar mdo, Mokṣasūtra

Tantra of the Gathering of Sugatas of the Eight Sadhana Teachings, Bka' brgyad bde gshegs 'dus pa'i rgyud

The Thirty-Seven Practices of Bodhisattvas, Rgyal sras lag len so bdun ma

The Thorough Explanation of the Eight Sadhana Teachings, Bka' brgyad kyi rnam bshad

The Treasury of Experiential Pith Instructions, Man ngag mdzod

The Two Segments of the Hevajra Root Tantra, Dgyes pa rdo rje rtsa ba'i rgyud brtag pa gnyis po, Hevajramūlatantra

An Unelaborate Liturgical Arrangement of the Method for Accomplishing Vajrakīla, Rdo rje phur pa'i sgrub thabs spros med chog sgrig

The Union of Sun and Moon Tantra, Nyi zla kha sbyor gyi rgyud

The Way of the Bodhisattva, Byang chub sems dpa'i spyod pa la 'jug pa, Bodhisattvacaryāvatāra

Bibliography

Beer, Robert. *The Encyclopedia of Tibetan Symbols and Motifs*. Boston: Shambhala Publications, 1999.

Boord, Martin J., trans. *A Bolt of Lightning from the Blue: The Vast Commentary on Vajrakīla that Clearly Defines the Essential Points*. Berlin: Wandel Verlag, 2010.

Boord, Martin J. *The Cult of the Deity Vajrakīla According to the Texts of the Northern Treasures Tradition of Tibet (Byang-gter phur-ba)*. Tring, U.K.: The Institute of Buddhist Studies, 1993.

Dudjom Rinpoche, Jikdrel Yeshe Dorje. *The Nyingma School of Tibetan Buddhism: Its Fundamentals and History*. Translated and edited by Gyurme Dorje and Matthew Kapstein. Boston: Wisdom Publications, 1991.

Garchen Triptrül, Könchog Gyaltsen. *An Unelaborate Liturgical Arrangement of the Method for Accomplishing Vajrakīla*. Translated by Ari-ma. 8th ed. Gar Chöding Trust, 2012.

Gönpo Wangyal. *Chos kyi rnam grangs* [Enumerations of Dharma terms]. Chengdu: Si khron mi rigs dpe skrun khang, 1988.

Gyalse Thogme Zangpo. *The Thirty-Seven Practices of Bodhisattvas*. Translated by Ari-ma. 3rd ed. Gar Chöding Trust, 2005.

Jamgön Kongtrül Lodrö Thaye. "Rdo rje phur pa yang gsang bla med kyi gsang sgrub rgyun gyi phrin las rnam rol snying po [Essence of display: A regular secret accomplishment liturgy of the unsurpassed, most secret Vajrakīla]." In *Rgya chen bka' mdzod* [Treasury of vast buddha-words], vol. 11, 105–16. New Delhi: Shechen, 2002. BDRC: W23723

Jayarava, Dharmacārī. "The Hundred Syllable Vajrasattva Mantra." *Western Buddhist Review* 5 (October 2010): 1–13.

———. "Ye Dharmā Hetuprabhava: Causation." Visible Mantra: Buddhist Calligraphy. Last updated September 1, 2019. https://visiblemantra.org/dharma-hetuprabhava.html.

Jigme Phüntsog Jungne. "Phur pa mgul khug ma'i cha shas thugs dam thugs kyi phur gcig [The neck-pouch kīla cycle sections known as "The commitment deity: sole kīla of the mind"]." In *Chos rje dam pa yid bzhin nor bu 'jigs med phun tshogs 'byung gnas dpal bzang po'i gsung 'bum* [Collected works of the true Dharma lord, the wish-fulfilling jewel, excellent glory, Jigme Phüntsog Jungne], vol. 1, 282–90. Larung Gar, Sichuan, China: Bla rung sgar gyi par khang, 2002. BDRC: W23774

Jigten Sumgön. *The Song on Realizing Fivefold Mahāmudrā.* Translated by Ari-ma. Gar Chöding Trust, 2015.

Jigten Sumgön and Rigdzin Chokyi Dragpa. *Gongchig: The Single Intent, the Sacred Dharma with commentary entitled* The Lamp Dispelling the Darkness *by Rigdzin Chokyi Dragpa.* Translated by Markus Viehbeck, Khenchen Konchog Gyaltshen Rinpoche, and Khenpo Nyima Gyaltsen. Edited by Claudia Göbel. Munich: Otter Verlag, 2009.

Jigten Sumgön et al. *Abridged Prayers of Refuge, Bodhicitta and Dedication of the Glorious Drigung Kagyü.* Translated by Ari-ma. 5th ed. Gar Chöding Trust, 2013.

Khenchen Palden Sherab and Khenpo Tsewang Dongyal. *The Dark Red Amulet: Oral Instructions on the Practice of Vajrakilaya.* Translated by Samye Translation Group. Ithaca, NY: Snow Lion Publications, 2008.

Khenpo Namdrol. *The Practice of Vajrakilaya: Oral Teachings.* Translated by Sangye Khandro, Dorji Wangchuk, and David Germano. Ithaca, NY: Snow Lion Publications, 1999.

Mikyö Dorje, Ratna Lingpa, and Karma Chagme. "Rdo rje phur pa yang gsang bla med kyi las byang la nye bar mkho ba'i zur 'debs phyogs gcig tu bsgrigs pa aindra nī la'i do shal ces bya ba" [The necklace of sapphires: A unified arrangement of the unsurpassed, most secret Vajrakīla practice manual with required supplements]. In *Dpal spungs dpe rnying gsar bskrun las dkyil chog phyogs bsgrigs* [Arrangement of mandala rituals from the earlier and latter published texts of Palpung Monastery], vol. 4, 15–50. Upper Bhattu, Distt. Kangra, H.P., India: Dpal spungs gsung rab nyams gso khang, 2005. BDRC: W1KG4334

Paltrül Rinpoche, Orgyan Jigme Chökyi Wangpo. *Rdzogs pa chen po klong chen snying tig gi sngon 'gro'i khrid yig kun bzang bla ma'i zhal lung* [Words of the wholly excellent guru: Instructions in the preliminary practices of the great completion Longchen Nyingthig]. Delhi: Chos spyod dpar skrun khang, 2003. BDRC: W00KG04062

Rigdzin Chökyi Dragpa. "A Collection of Scriptures Necessary for the Protection and Repelling Practices from the Fiery Razor of Repelling of Mañjuśrī Yamāntaka, Lord of Life." Translated by Ari-ma. 8th ed. Unpublished manuscript, last modified August 11, 2016, Microsoft Word file.

Rigdzin Gödem. *The Aspiration of Samantabhadra*. Translated by Ari-ma. 7th ed. Gar Chöding Trust, 2011.

Shantideva. *The Way of the Bodhisattva*. Translated by Padmakara Translation Group. Boston: Shambhala Publications, 2006.

Tilopa. *The Ganges: An Experiential Pith Instruction on Mahāmudrā*. Translated by Ari-ma. 7th ed. Gar Chöding Trust, 2005.

Tsering Thakchoe Drungtso and Tsering Dolma Drungtso. *Tibetan-English Dictionary of Tibetan Medicine and Astrology*. 2nd rev. ed. Dharamsala, India: Drungtso Publications, 2005.

Zhang Yisun. *Bod rgya tshig mdzod chen mo* [The great Tibetan-Chinese dictionary]. 2nd ed. Beijing: Mi rigs dpe skrun khang, 1996.

Index

able force, 5, 8, 206, 272, 364
ablution, 214, 221
abyss of meditation, 25, 88, 91–98, 101, 372
Acala (Miyo/Miyowa), 178, 421n12
ācārya, 88
accomplishment(s), 42, 80, 82, 95, 125, 329
  of activities, 154, 319
  branch of, 254–55, 263
  charm of, 348, 354
  of common siddhis/common, 6, 76, 84, 129, 212, 296
  of deity/yidam, 4, 6, 80, 84, 133, 272
  of existence-vajrakīla, 315
  great (*see* great accomplishment)
  of kāyas and pure fields, 356
  mandala for, 310
  mantra (*see* accomplishment mantra/ kaṭaṅkaṭe)
  of mantra, 362
  and mantra strand, 224
  measure of, 252
  medicine, 217
  method of (sadhana), 4, 18, 26, 45, 54, 371
  mind, 3–4, 319
  of saṁbhogakāya, 123
  secret obstacles and, 96
  signs of, 6, 22, 80, 201, 354, 365
  substance(s), 130–31, 314, 354
  supports of/accomplishment-support, 291, 348
  taking up, 209, 284, 317, 347–354
  at time of death, 57–58
  of two purposes/objectives, 84, 139, 330
  of union of samsara and nirvana, 330
  of Vajrakīla, 209–10, 264
  See also four branches of approach and accomplishment; siddhi(s)
accomplishment mantra/kaṭaṅkaṭe, 238, 244, *247*, 257, 264, 267
  visualization for, 239–50
accomplishment retreat (drubpa), 54–55, 70–74, 236
  afflictions during, 323–25
  benefits/qualities of, 73, 203, 229, 355–56
  calm abiding and special insight in, 194–95
  Garchen Rinpoche's connection with, 15–17, 23
  great (*see* great accomplishment retreat [drubchen])
  hardships of, 71–72
  recollection of, 73–74
  secret (*see* secret accomplishment retreat [sangdrub])
  spontaneous understanding in, 45

accumulation(s), 121, 154, 190, 309-10, 339
through afflictions, 52, 77-78, 114
field of, 143, 146, 227
and gaṇacakra, 323, 327
of karma/karmic, 44, 120, 153, 200, 241
of mantras, 234, 252
of merit, 98, 276-77, 373
of merit and wisdom, 44, 249, 373
two (*see* two accumulations/ gatherings)
of wisdom, 277, 343, 373
action tantra (kriyatantra), 205, 213, 257
activities, 11, 21, 75, 100-101, 296
daily, 65, 92-93, 203, 345, 355-61
destructive (*see* destruction/ destructive activity)
of emanating and gathering, 262-63, 329
of enlightened action, 5, 8, 272
enriching, 10
and form kāyas, 139, 148, 166
four (*see* four activities/enlightened actions)
guardians/protectors and, 319-22
lower, 331, 335-36
magnetizing, 126, 294
and mantra, 12, 81-83, 239, 243
and material kīla, 125, 130, 291-92, 296
pacifying/peaceful, 10, 206
repelling, 342
of three sattvas, 196-97
worldly/samsaric, 54-55, 111, 279, 356
afflictions/negative emotions, 33, 38-40, 132, 208, 259
and abyss of meditation, 91, 93-97
accomplishment mantra and, 240, 243, 254
accomplishment retreats and, 70-71, 323-25
adventitious stains/confusion and, 5, 40, 51, 261, 269
antidote to/antidoting, 10, 132, 362-65
and autonomy, 19, 33, 39, 51-52, 68
bliss and, 135-36, 140, 250
bodhicitta and, 90, 115, 132, 208, 235
close approach and, 252
conduct and, 100
destructive activities and, 265-66
and disclosure, 159-60, 270
drawing in, 265, 321, 331-32
dualistic grasping and, 68, 330
empowerment and, 38-39, 212
five (*see* five afflictions/afflictive poisons)
as five wisdoms, 38, 112, 125, 212, 256, 333
four nails that pin life force and, 259, 261
great accomplishment and, 256
and hell realms, 43, 78
horse dance and, 345
karma and, 44, 118, 199, 336, 338, 359
kīla of bodhicitta and, 123, 125, 240, 243
kīla of primordial awareness-rigpa and, 104-14
liberation of, 19, 127-28, 198, 333-41
mantra and, 82, 233, 235, 254, 357, 360
māra of (*see under* māra)
māras/demons and, 134, 171-72, 233, 341-42
material kīla of signs and, 126-28
mindful awareness/mindfulness and, 203, 235, 273, 294, 359-60
offerings and, 161-63, 215-17, 315-16
pacification of, 198, 265
as path, 10
physical obscurations and, 231-32
primordial awareness and, 108, 115, 136, 140, 198, 261

purifying, 54, 267
recognizing/perceiving, 70–71, 132, 273, 349
repelling and, 341–42
self-appearances and, 78, 294
self-grasping/cherishing and, 140, 150, 199, 261, 341
single key point of three vows and, 19
six (*see* six afflictions)
six realms and, 282
six syllables and, 304, 332
unmitigated, 91, 160, 243, 359, 418n1
and view, 160
visualization of deity and, 171–74, 179–80, 190, 200
wrath of awareness/wisdom and, 112, 198–99, 349–50
See also five afflictions/afflictive poisons; five poisons; poisons; six afflictions; three poisons/poisonous afflictions
aggregate(s) (skandhas), 114–16, 69, 136, 163, 341
divine nature of, 60, 248, 261, 359
five (*see* five aggregates)
and five families, 211, 246–48
māra of (*see under* māra)
purity of, 35, 39, 115, 158, 162, 315
ripening into deity/illusory body, 73, 122–23
aggression, 109, 130, 141, 172, 266
and destructive activities/liberation, 265, 336
See also anger; aversion; five poisons; hatred; three poisons/poisonous afflictions
ĀḤ syllable, 163, 206, 304, 361
and blessing, 80, 224, 227–28
Akaniṣṭha, 17, 196, 347
Akṣobhya, 177
ālaya, 96, 167
altruism, 148, 254, 272
and self-grasping/self-cherishing, 93, 150–51, 157, 227
Amitābha, 364
Amitāyus, 364
Amoghasiddhi, 153, 177, 206, 208
amṛita (dütsi), 161–62, 178, 216–17, 321
Amṛitakuṇḍali. *See* Dütsi Khyilpa
anger, 52, 72, 90, 179, 339
and awareness/rigpa, 108, 349
and bodhisattva's samaya/vow, 6, 94, 325
See also aggression; aversion; five afflictions/afflictive poisons; hatred; three poisons/poisonous afflictions
animal realm, 38, 64, 128, 179, 282, 423n51
animals, 72, 280–81, 306, 344, 360
See also six classes of wayfarers/beings; three bad migrations/states; three lower realms
antidote, 113, 121, 228, 329, 340, 363
bodhicitta as, 34, 132, 157, 270
deity yoga as, 35, 55
offering as, 75–76, 213, 281
Vajrakīla practice as, 10, 94
appearance-emptiness, 82, 124, 163, 274, 276
all sights as, 98, 263
appearance-existence, 158–59, 161, 163, 169, 283
gathering in, 274
great accomplishment and, 255
as mandala of deity, 260, 333, 348
primordial purity and, 42
approach, 130–31, 310
branch of, 251–52, 257, 261
branch of close, 252–54, 257, 262
sudden, 63
visualization during, 226
See also approach and accomplishment

approach and accomplishment, 16, 83, 130, 224–50, 333
accomplishment retreats and, 73
consecration of implements and, 292, 294–95
Earlier System and, 44
and four nails, 259–263
mandalas of, 310–11
meaning/purpose of, 251–257, 317
See also four branches of approach and accomplishment
approach mantra, 15, 95, 220, 222, 252, 262
meaning of, 233
recitation of, 236–38
visualization for, 80, 224–30,
Arig Tengye, Mahāsiddha, 15
armor, 186, 298, 303
arrogant ones/arrogance, 127, 173, 294, 334
Āryadeva, 221
aspiration(s), 15, 76–77, 79, 118, 312
in accomplishment retreats, 229
of beings, 350
of buddhas, 10, 22–23
and dedication, 277
and gaṇapūja, 327
of harmdoers, 127
and ten strengths, 181–82
and white torma, 289–90
Aspiration for the Pure Field of Great Bliss, 43, 139
Aspiration of Samantabhadra, The, 40, 107, 176, 250, 353
and five wisdoms, 117, 148, 174
and primordial purity, 117, 268
aspiring faith, 76, 146, 148–49, 151
auspiciousness, prayer of, 277–283
autonomy, 19, 32–35, 64, 68, 284
awareness/rigpa and, 39, 100, 107, 108
deity yoga and, 199, 232
divine pride and, 46, 50–51, 202
love and compassion and, 51–52
Avalokita, 46, 52, 177, 280
avarice, 76–78, 162
See also six afflictions
aversion, 10, 13–14, 157, 173, 240
during accomplishment retreat, 323–24
bones as symbol of, 127, 320, 331, 350
as clarity-emptiness, 254
degeneration of seed essence and, 243
as dependency, 33
Dharma practice based on, 43, 156
drawing in and, 320, 331
dualistic grasping and, 68, 158, 160, 162, 241, 349
eightfold group of consciousness and, 167
gaṇacakra offerings and, 343
harmdoers/enemies/obstructors and, 127–28, 141, 158
hell realms and, 78, 282
inner offerings and, 161–62
karmic/afflictive winds and, 68
liberation and, 337
mantra and, 232, 235, 360, 368
māras and, 135, 171
material kīla of signs and, 130
and meditational abyss, 93
mirrorlike wisdom and, 108, 325, 349
samaya and, 325, 366–67
self-grasping and, 33, 261
sounds and, 82, 232, 235, 368
as Vajrasattva, 208
versus wrath, 199
See also aggression; anger; five afflictions/afflictive poisons; hatred; six afflictions; three poisons/poisonous afflictions
awareness, 55, 117, 198, 269, 306
abyss of meditation and, 92–94
accomplishment mantra and, 243–44, 250

afflictions and, 171, 200, 294, 359, 362-63
approach mantra and, 226, 230, 234-36
in bardo, 64
conduct and, 99-101
discriminating, 98, 108, 122, 147, 181, 244
gathering in and, 66-67
HŪṀ/seed syllable and, 190, 225, 371
kīla of (*see* kīla of primordial awareness-rigpa)
liberation and, 339
mantra recitation and, 361-62
māras and, 132-40, 171
mindful, 39, 70, 151, 203, 236
nail of changeless intent and, 260
nondual, 30n, 213, 216, 250, 325, 352
ten strengths and, 181
thoughts and, 71, 132, 115, 234, 260
visualization and, 175, 188, 190
See also awareness-wisdom/awareness-rigpa; primordial awareness; wisdom(s)
awareness-consort, 314
awareness-emptiness, 98, 254, 263
awareness-wisdom/awareness-rigpa, 104, 112-13, 136, 244, 373
disclosure and, 160
kīla of (*see* kīla of primordial awareness-rigpa)
liberating concepts/thoughts into, 108, 159, 338
lust and, 163, 243
and state of immortal knowledge holder, 268
transforming consciousness into, 361
See also primordial awareness; wisdom(s)
āyatanas. *See* sense fields
Ayurveda, 422n34
bardo, 57, 61, 69, 80, 171
consciousness, 68, 274
dream yoga and, 69-70
first, 41, 57
and māra of lord of death, 136-37
mental body in, 61, 133, 180
peaceful and wrathful deities in, 180, 280
propensities/imprints and, 47, 231, 250
realizing saṁbhogakāya in, 63, 123, 125, 134, 145, 359
second, 57, 64, 74, 145
sufferings of, 47, 69, 111, 133, 135
Bhagavan Buddha
causal and resultant vehicles and, 44
compassion and, 227
dedication and, 277
emanation as Guru Rinpoche, 10, 145
path of individual liberation and, 144
as personification of three kāyas, 273
on pride, 334
on sentient ones' nature, 38, 40, 277
on subduing mind, 193
See also Prince Siddhartha; Śākyamuni
bhikṣu, 18-19
bhūmis. *See* ten bhūmis (grounds); thirteen bhūmis of a vajra holder
bias, 41, 90, 118, 156, 216, 316
perverted views as, 43
birth(s)/rebirth, 33-34, 62-64, 68-70
bardo of becoming and, 171
buddha/mind's nature and, 136-37, 140, 270, 281
deity yoga and, 232
four modes of (*see* four modes of birth)
human, 34, 38, 63, 68, 251
immortal knowledge holder and, 268
liberation and, 128, 295, 335
of Lord Buddha, 121

birth(s)/rebirth (*continued*)
offering and, 77
refuge and, 151-52
in samsara/cyclic existence, 33, 106, 155, 173, 176, 270
secret sun and, 352
self-grasping and, 106, 270
in three higher realms, 33-34, 36, 51, 84, 154
in three lower realms/bad migrations, 33, 38, 64, 156
wisdom deities and, 209, 269-70
blessing(s), 25-26, 42, 84, 209, 374
of accomplishment retreats, 16, 23, 73, 203, 355-57
approach mantra and, 224, 226-29
in bardo, 61, 250
and benefiting beings, 369-70
of buddhas, 84, 88, 172, 255, 290, 420n8
dance and, 314, 318
of deity, 48, 52-53, 255, 356, 365
emanating and gathering and, 262-63
empowerment and, 206-8, 211, 307
of guru, 90, 356
lineage supplication and, 88, 90, 96-97
mantra as, 80
and mantra as siddhis, 79-80
of mantra's melody, 237-38
samādhi of total appearance and, 172
self-grasping and, 365
symbolic kīla of, 103, 352
taking up accomplishments and, 348, 350, 353-54
of Tibetan language, 26-27
blessing-practice lineage, 16-17, 23, 44, 92, 371
blessing-support(s), 297-98
bliss, 122-24, 136, 138-39, 328
accomplishment mantra and, 239-43, 248-50
bodhicitta and, 180
conduct and, 100
deity's blessing and, 356
dharmakāya and, 117, 138
and emptiness (*see* bliss-emptiness)
HŪṀ syllable and, 110
kīla of bodhicitta and, 130
māra of afflictions and, 135-36, 140
name of Khorlo Gyedebma and, 178
offering the charm and, 267
rakta offering and, 163
recitation of charm and, 222-23
of selflessness, 79, 251-52
skillful means and, 283
uncontaminated/inexhaustible, 135-36
bliss-emptiness, 124, 135, 239, 242, 253-54
wisdom of, 122, 128, 140
blue-black tetrahedron, 166, 168, 184, 304
bodhicitta, 31, 37, 54, 76, 315
accomplishment retreats and, 73
accomplishment visualization and, 239-40, 242-43, 248
as actual refuge, 151
afflictions and, 40, 90, 208
approach and accomplishment and, 252, 254-55, 257
approach mantra visualization and, 226-27
assurance/certainty of, 6-7, 203, 254
blessing-empowerment and, 211
body mandala and, 179-80
buddhahood/enlightenment and, 14, 36, 39, 47
buddha nature and, 51
dedication and, 277
deity as expression of, 5, 52, 60, 364, 367
fabricated, 148-49
facing generation and, 259

four immeasurables and, 154-57, 364
four nails and, 259-60
ground/foundation of, 6, 194
HŪṀ syllable and, 371
individual liberation and, 153
kīla of, 121-25, 128, 130-31, 138
kīla of immeasurable compassion and, 114-15
liberation and, 128, 332, 338
mantra and, 75, 77, 80, 235, 360
meaning of term, 282
melody and, 238
mind of deity and, 51, 202-3
offerings and, 215, 217, 289, 328, 342
peaceful and wrathful deities and, 280
preliminary practices and, 154
progressive stages of the path and, 53
samaya and, 195, 325
samsara and, 153, 315
scope of, 9, 75
self-appearances and, 79
self-grasping/-cherishing and, 34-35, 132, 150, 270-71
two types of (*see* two types of bodhicitta)
wisdom winds and, 68
bodhisattva(s), 90, 196, 279
grounds, 89, 138-40, 176-77, 353
Bodhisattva Vehicle, 19, 29, 36, 53, 92, 229
and afflictions, 349-50
distinction from Vajra Vehicle, 31-32
and four kīlas, 103
and six transcendent perfections, 43, 181
bodhisattva vows, 5-7, 19, 100, 325, 419n5
easy restoration of, 93-94
body/form, 43, 46, 116, 134-35, 151
accomplishment retreats and, 72-73, 357
approach mantra and, 224, 226-30
and causal basis for buddhahood, 5, 37
cherishing/clinging/grasping at, 47, 56, 60, 133-34, 232
clarity, purity, and stability and, 197, 200
of complete enjoyment (saṁbhogakāya), 278
as composite/aggregate, 69, 73, 115-16, 136, 151
death and, 68-69, 151, 231-32, 274
deity yoga/development and, 46-50, 54-63, 139, 154
and five nectars, 342
four māras and, 132-39
gross/ordinary, 46, 50, 56, 60, 133
of guru/master, 11-14, 39, 145
HŪṀ syllable and, 108-13, 172, 188, 362
human, 5, 37-38, 43, 122, 239
illusory, 123, 170
and inner Vajrakumāra, 325
kīla of bodhicitta and, 122-25
as king of divine forms, 5, 284
mandala (*see* body mandala)
as mandala of development stages, 296
mantra recitation and, 223, 236
maturation/ripening of, 39, 73
mental, 61, 133, 180
as microcosm of container/mandala, 59, 81, 167, 185, 204, 257
microorganisms and, 69, 81, 179, 223
and nail of samādhi, 261
as nirmāṇakāya, 125, 185, 228
OṀ syllable and, 163, 304
outer container as, 81, 167
pervaded by deities, 180, 248
pervaded by mind, 113
of practitioner, 12
propensities/imprints/obscurations and, 35, 56, 134, 231, 336, 367

body/form (*continued*)
rainbow, 122-23, 244
self-grasping and, 56, 136, 164, 281
seven dhātus/tissues and, 422n34
six constituents and, 37, 239
subtle, 115-16, 229, 243, 248
threefold sattva and, 195-96
three vajras and, 163, 304, 368
and visualized deity, 170-75
of wisdom being, 186
See also eightfold group of consciousness/eight consciousnesses; six sense faculties
body mandala, 178-80, 183, 221
and bliss/pleasure, 223, 248
deities of, 168, 186, 224, 229-30
border areas, 350
breath/breathing, 179, 302, 361-62
bringing down blessings, 309-18, 358
text, 401-2
buddha families, 177
Buddha family, 181
buddha-field(s), 75-77, 79, 139, 353
and five certainties, 196
guiding/leading beings to, 128, 332, 338
See also pure field(s)/pure realm(s)
Buddhaguhya, 18
buddhahood, 31-32, 56-58, 369-70
in bardo, 41, 74
bodhicitta and, 29, 36-37, 91, 147
buddha nature and, 90, 256, 281
cause/basis of, 37-38, 41, 47, 156, 256
compassion/love and, 120-21
existence-vajrakīla as, 210
four activities and, 256
as fruition of destructive activities, 141
mantric methods and, 47
nonduality and, 154, 312
as one's own purpose, 53
saṁbhogakāya pure realm/fields and, 139, 250
self-grasping and, 229
in a single lifetime, 7, 32, 35, 44, 47, 251
two accumulations and, 44, 277
two purposes and, 35
buddha nature (tathāgatagarbha), 38, 41, 44, 52, 275, 315
and adventitious stains, 54, 367
all beings endowed with, 126, 145, 251, 256, 333
as basis/cause of buddhahood, 5, 90, 156, 281
and deity, 51, 57, 175, 198, 201, 269
as emptiness, 145, 254, 259-60
and liberation, 127, 295, 331-32, 338-39
as luminosity/clarity, 109, 278
as mindful awareness/rigpa/mind, 21, 112, 172, 235
and nature/essence/condition of mind, 14, 136, 138, 269, 352
and primordial purity, 40, 94, 115, 117, 261, 278
singularity of, 9, 120, 241, 270, 317
See also tathāgatagarbha
buddha-word section (kama), 87, 89, 141

cakra(s), 115, 143, 178, 223, 248, 311
buddhas/deities in, 116, 169, 183, 186, 230, 267
four (*see* four cakras)
four-spoked, 169-71, 181
heart, 186
navel, 225
ten-spoked, 169, 171
See also channel(s): wheels/hubs
Cakrasaṁvara, 243, 246
calm abiding (śamatha), 34, 194-95, 230
candalī, 243, 302
canine maidens. *See* dog-faced/canine maids

causality, 150, 267, 295, 372
incontrovertibility of, 99-100, 365
causal Vehicle of Characteristics, 44
cause and effect/result, 149, 254, 279, 282
belief/faith/trust in, 149, 150, 272, 281
incontrovertibility of, 91, 93
and liberation, 128, 335
Chagme Rāga Asya, 24, 43, 97, 375
chamber of recitation, opening, 219-22, 258
channel(s), 94, 122-23, 125, 326, 362
and bliss/pleasure, 178, 223, 267, 328
central/main, 110, 245-46, 248
and kīla of bodhicitta, 128, 130, 332
and mandala deities, 223-24, 229-30, 246, 248-49
of subtle body, 115-16, 229, 248
wheels/hubs, 114-16, 170, 229-30, 249
and wind energies, 239-40, 243-44, 332
charm (dzap)
of accomplishments, 348, 354
offering of, 266-67
recitation of, 219-24, 248, 258
See also japa (dzap)
Chim, 89
Chime Dorje, Drubpön/Siddha, 6, 15
chö, 131
Choggyur Lingpa, 92
Chökyi Dragpa, Rigdzin, 191
Chökyi Wangchug, 92
circumambulation, 72, 83, 309, 314, 318, 357
clairvoyance, 6, 82, 140
clarity, 55, 186, 190, 192
aspect/factor, 117, 193, 272, 352-53
and awareness/buddha nature/rigpa, 106, 250, 278
and empty essence, 58, 112, 116, 166
and mantra recitation, 225, 236, 242
See also clarity, purity, and stability
clarity, purity, and stability, 197-203, 234, 280
clarity-emptiness, 112, 165, 254, 274-76, 326
See also union/unity: of clarity and emptiness
clear appearance, 54-55, 63, 65, 194, 262
in bardo/dream state, 61, 133-35
and mindfulness/mindful awareness, 92, 101, 218, 359
and practice with a partner, 123, 249-50
and purity, 232, 327, 355
See also clarity, purity, and stability
clinging, 167, 212-13, 343, 373
development stages and, 59-61, 67
māra of afflictions and, 135-36
to pleasure, 99-100, 137-38
to sexual pleasure, 240-41, 250
co-emergence (sahaja), 248
co-emergent ignorance, 40
co-emergent joy, 244
commitment. *See* samaya
commitment being (samayasattva), *x*, 183, 204, 208, 230, 310
and threefold sattva, 195-97
and wisdom deities, 210, 212-13
See also threefold sattva
compassion, 55, 148, 154-56, 240, 342
afflictions and, 51-52, 198, 363-64
approach mantra and, 224, 226-29
autonomy and, 34, 51-52
bodhisattva's vow and, 5, 7, 100
bringing down blessings and, 312, 315-18
conventional bodhicitta and, 90, 150, 152, 235
destructive activities/wrath and, 127, 130, 265-66, 333-39
as Dharma, 151
divine pride and, 202

compassion (*continued*)
for enemies, 152
four activities and, 264-66
gathering in and, 272, 275
guru and, 145, 366
as HŪṂ syllable, 371
invocation and, 207, 209, 211
kīla of bodhicitta and, 122-25
kīla of immeasurable compassion and, 114-21, 128-31
kīla of primordial awareness-rigpa and, 107-8, 232
lack of, 29, 101
as life force, 154, 192, 202, 254
loving, 5, 150, 272
mantra and, 78, 80, 240-41, 360
māra of afflictions and, 135
nail of changeless intent and, 259
as nirmāṇakāya, 166, 196, 303, 355
prayer of auspiciousness and, 278-79, 281-83
samādhi of total appearance and, 172
samaya/bond and, 75, 207, 223-24, 312, 366
self-grasping and, 84, 211, 281, 364-65, 373
selflessness and, 278
Small Vehicle individual and, 30
stage of accomplishment and, 254-55
sudden approach and, 63
taking up accomplishments and, 348, 351, 353-54
two purposes and, 52-53
ultimate/factual bodhicitta and, 7
vajra wing and, 174
water dragon (makara) and, 126, 300
white torma and, 288-89
wrathful deities and, 199
See also four immeasurables
completion stage/phase, 60, 65-70, 124, 168, 205
death phase of becoming and, 62
and gathering in, 271-76
See also development and completion
concentration being (samādhisattva), 60, *189*, 220, 224-25
visualization of, 188, 190-93, 196
See also threefold sattva
conch, 42, 178, 183
conduct, 7, 19, 128, 182, 357, 366
as life force, 97-101, 265, 372
of six transcendent perfections, 31, 53
See also ten strengths; view, meditation, and conduct
conduct tantra, 62, 65, 205, 257, 279
consciousness, 59, 62, 96, 133, 361
in bardo, 47, 68, 171, 274
and buddha nature, 269-70
dualistic, 186, 345
eightfold group of, *see* eightfold group of consciousness/eight consciousnesses
and liberation, 163, 295, 332-33, 338-39
and methods for accomplishing mastery, 109-10
as ordinary life force, 106, 111-12, 306, 330
at time of death, 68-69
unelaborated, 117, 125
versus primordial awareness, 106, 112, 198
See also five aggregates (skandhas); six constituents
consecration, 287-88, 321, 344
of material kīla, 291-307
of material mandala, 309-10
of offerings, 161-64
Consecration of the Material Kīla Mandala, 25, 291, 295, 297
text, 395-99
consort(s), 123-24, 170, 177, 240
body mandala and, 180

five nectars and, 342
gathering in and, 66, 275
Khorlo Gyedebma, 178, 233
kīla of bodhicitta and, 130
mandala deities and, 222
mantra strand and, 253
of regents, 314
visualization of, 193, 246
container, 81, 165, 217, 228, 220, 257
and five elements, 167, 256, 261
as macrocosm of one's body, 59, 81, 167, 257
world as, 38, 59, 163
See also container/vessel and contents
container/vessel and contents, 62, 66, 163, 256-57, 261
afflictions and, 161
as divine in nature, 94, 220
existence-vajrakīla and, 315
five elements and, 4, 94, 157-58
and gathering in, 274
grasping at, 64, 67, 161, 274, 368
as illusory phenomena, 59
as mandala of Vajrakīla/deity, 130, 185, 210, 274
nail/kīla of samādhi and, 261, 348
purity/pure perception of, 97, 115, 126, 251, 369, 419n5
as reflections of one's mind, 192, 260
as samsara and nirvana, 107
skandhas, dhātus, āyatanas and, 115-16
taking up accomplishments and, 353
contemplation, 118, 237, 307
contents, 59, 81, 168, 220, 257, 260
blessing of, 228
buddha nature of, 38, 256, 261
as torma, 217
See also container/vessel and contents
conventional bodhicitta, 29-30, 42, 90, 93, 99
as antidote to self-grasping/cherishing, 132, 150
emanating and gathering and, 235
fortress of view and, 90-91
kīla of immeasurable compassion and, 114, 119-20
seed essences and, 239-40
ultimate bodhicitta and, 7, 90, 260
white torma offering and, 289
See also fictional bodhicitta; two types of bodhicitta
criticism, 232
cyclic existence (samsara), 106, 147, 173, 241, 271, 330
as basis of Vajrakīla accomplishment, 210
birth(s) in, 33, 155, 176
and dualism, 242
faults of, 43

daily/personal practice, 16, 219, 357-58
ḍākiṇī(s), 12, 75, 122, 257, 284, 319
accomplishment mantra visualization and, 244, 246
and activities, 197, 296
gaṇacakra and, 342, 344
as guru's mind, 12, 145
See also Three Roots
Dalai Lama, 13, 280
ḍamaru, 355
dance, 98, 222-23, 267, 312, 328
in bringing down blessings, 314, 318
horse, 345
nine moods of (*see* nine moods of dance)
and recitation of charm, 248
while offering gaṇacakra residual, 344
Darchar, 97
death, 33, 52, 67, 136-37, 151
birth and, 140, 173, 270, 281, 352, 356
completion stage and, 62, 67
deity/development-stage yogas and, 231-32
discarding body at, 59, 137, 232

death (*continued*)
fear of, 112
and four mind-changing contemplations, 43
immortal knowledge holder and, 268
interruption of ignorance at, 41
lord of (*see* māra: of lord of death)
sufferings and, 68, 106, 132–33, 242
time of, 31, 58–59, 72, 231–32
deathlessness, 67, 112
dedication, 276–77, 312, 372–74
defilement(s), 31, 120, 171, 260, 367
adventitious, 40, 54, 120, 158
deity yoga, 45–58, 283–85, 366
clarity, purity, and stability in, 197, 199
death and, 231–32
friendship of yidam and, 11
fruition of, 210
grasping at body and, 60–61
inscription ritual and, 221
Jigten Sumgön on, 4–5
māra of aggregates and, 135
maturation of sādhaka and, 251
meaning of *yidam* and, 8
nine benefits of mantra and, 74, 78
petition and, 319
propensities/obscurations and, 35, 72–73
purification of mind and, 185
saṁbhogakāya and, 145, 194
three strengths and, 317
two accumulations and, 249
visualizing mantra strand and, 245–46
See also development stages
delusion(s), 33, 99, 156, 160, 357, 367
awareness-emptiness as, 254
destructive methods and, 295, 336
dualistic grasping/views as, 194, 333
inner offerings and, 217, 331
liberation offering and, 127–28
mantra and, 360
secret obstacles and, 94
self-grasping and, 33, 261
suffering of all beings and, 119
torma/mahābaliṅta as, 161, 163
See also five afflictions/afflictive poisons; ignorance; three poisons/poisonous afflictions
demigods, 306, 423n51
See also six classes of wayfarers/beings; six realms; three higher realms
demon(s)/demonic force(s), 47, 62, 288, 328, 330, 335
as afflictions, 341–42, 366–67
gods/deities and, 180, 202–3, 320, 367
harm from, 54
inner and outer, 233
liberation of, 339
māras and, 102, 131–32
taking form of, 337
desire(s), 76, 124, 135, 171, 250, 320
as bliss-wisdom, 130, 163
blood and, 162–63
diminishing, 327
human realm and, 282
melody of mantra and, 238
as primordial awareness, 350
rebirth and, 68
subtle, 343
See also five afflictions/afflictive poisons; lust; passion; six afflictions; three poisons/poisonous afflictions
desire realm, 162, 306
destruction/destructive activity, 10, 20, 126–28, 311, 340
Amoghasiddhi and, 177
approach/accomplishment mandalas and, 310–11
effigy yantra/liṅga and, 131
individual like a sandalwood tree and, 130
iron material and, 127
kīla of, 293–95

liberation and, 336-39
love and compassion and, 265-66
offering praise and, 218-19
ten grounds and, 333, 335
See also four activities/enlightened actions
Devanāgarī, 310n
development and completion, 65-66, 69-70, 336, 369
and attainment of buddhahood/three kāyas, 57, 122
union of, 49, 63-64, 81, 124, 276
development stages, 14, 60-67, 154, 192-94
of body mandala, 178-80
of concentration being, 188
of commitment being, 170-74
of Foremost Prince/material kila, 298-303
of immeasurable palace, 164-69, 184
individuals suited to, 59-60
and kīla of immeasurable compassion, 129-31
and māra of aggregates, 133, 135
and māra of lord of death, 137
as mudrā kīla, 347
and nail of samādhi, 261
and practice in daily life, 357, 361
and pure perception, 41-42, 232
and purification of grasping/ propensities, 49, 54, 57, 232
of surrounding mandala, 181-85
and visualization of approach mantra, 224-30
of wisdom being, 185-87
See also deity yoga
development through instantaneous surge, 62
devotion, 90, 251, 280, 312
and taking up accomplishments, 348, 351, 353-54
Devotion, the Life Force Yantra, 14
Dharma guardians, 12, 319-22
See also guardians/guards/guard maids/protectors
dharmakāya, 56, 124, 159, 174, 199, 268
and afflictions, 125
bliss of, 249
and bodhisattva grounds, 139
and completion stage, 66
and concentration being, 196
and first bardo, 41, 57
as five wisdoms, 147, 315
and gathering in, 271-76
and great bliss, 117, 138
as HŪṂ syllable, 14, 175
and Khorlo Gyedebma, 178
and kīla of primordial awareness-rigpa, 104, 112
and liberation on arising, 158
and mind of guru/buddhas/deity, 145, 347, 355
and prayer of auspiciousness, 277-78
and two objectives, 96-97
Vajrakīla as, 194
and wisdom being, 186
See also three kāyas
dharmasphere (dharmadhātu), 102-3, 112-13, 273, 318
and blue-black tetrahedron, 166
and gathering in, 274
Khorlo Gyedebma as, 218
and liberation, 163
planting kīla of primordial awareness-rigpa into, 129
as source of saṁbhogakāya/wisdom deities, 209, 348
wisdom, 148
See also sphere of phenomena/ dharmas
dharmatā, 18, 61, 82-83, 280
and body of deity, 172, 174
Dharmevajra, 102
See also Vajrapāṇi

dhātus. *See* elements
diligence, 34, 52, 71, 107, 147, 363
See also six transcendent perfections
diligent, lustful individual, 130
Dīptacakrā. *See* Khorlo Gyedebma
discerning/discriminating intelligence, 19, 32, 80, 188, 231, 365
and afflictions, 132, 134, 141
and attaining status of buddhas, 34, 51-52
and branch of accomplishment, 254
and compassion, 150
and deity yoga, 46, 185
and emancipation from samsara, 147
and exhaustion of self-grasping, 373
as means of subduing mind, 193
and name of deity, 233
and practice of mantric methods, 350
and special insight, 194
and unfit vessels, 43
and wisdom winds, 68
See also six transcendent perfections
disclosure/disclosing wrongs, 51, 158-60, 243, 268-71
dissolution, 67-68, 275
divine kīlas, 130-31
divine pride, 46, 50-51, 201-3, 226
and wearing material kīlas, 302
Yamāntaka liturgy on, 283
dog-faced/canine maids, 182-83, 321-22, 329
Dögyal (Ṭakkirāja), 179, 421n12
Dorje Chang. *See* Vajradhara
Dorje Namjom (Vajravidarana), 102
doubt(s), 22, 65, 108, 277, 369
about deities/deity yoga, 50-51, 185, 198, 269
dispelling/allaying, 287, 309
freedom from, 89-91, 317-18, 351
about insubstantiality of container and contents, 58-59, 69
and obliviousness to qualities of nirmāṇakāyas, 280
about pure appearances, 199-200
about pure fields and wisdom deities, 195-96
and refuge, 149-50, 152
about secret mantra practice, 263-64
drawing in, 320, 331-32, 337
dream(s), 66, 74, 95, 133, 202, 362
and daytime/waking appearances, 69-70, 231
and luminosity, 101, 357
and self-grasping, 111, 134
yoga, 67, 70
Drigung Dharmarāja, 41
Drigung Dharmasūrya, 184
Drigung Kagyü, 3, 15, 41, 184, 236
arrangement of Vajrakīla termas, 316
prayers of, 152, 277, 319
songs, 41-42
Drime Dorje, 92
drubchen. *See* great accomplishment; great accomplishment retreat
drubpa. *See* accomplishment retreat
Drugpa Künleg, 146
dualistic grasping, 4, 19, 68, 158, 172
and absence of luminosity, 279
and accomplishment mantra visualization, 240-42, 244, 250, 254
afflictions and, 266
and approach mantra visualization, 228
and bodhicitta, 315
clearing away, 56
and consecrating the offerings, 161-63
and deity yoga, 57
destruction of, 259
and disclosure, 160
and diverse appearances, 82
and fictional bodhicitta, 29n

freedom from, 91, 260, 277, 316, 325, 373
and HŪṂ/seed syllable, 113, 172, 326
as ignorance, 349
and kīla of primordial awareness-rigpa, 129
releasing, 276
at samsara and nirvana, 304
at self and other, 3, 278, 333, 372
and self-justifying compassion, 156
at sounds, 235
and three foes, 330
understanding, 41
and view, 216, 351
visualizing saṁbhogakāya mandala and, 204-5
and wisdom deities' compassion, 211
dualistic views/perceptions/concepts, 75, 101, 194, 213, 297, 345
and arising of samsara, 253
of clean and unclean, 343
and great purity, 355
and kīla of primordial awareness-rigpa, 103, 109, 111-14, 159
liberating oneself from, 333
of self and other, 41, 215, 244, 349
duality/dualism, 99, 114, 158, 177, 270, 372
and accomplishment mantra visualization, 241-42, 249, 253-54
and primordial awareness, 283, 349, 373
transcending/free of, 113, 219, 261, 312
Düdül Nüden, 92
Dütsi Khyilpa (Amṛitakuṇḍali), 178, 421n12
Dzamling Dorje Tsal, 92
dzogchen, 14, 89, 105, 110, 269, 359
and primordial purity, 40, 278
and rigpa, 103, 138
thögal, 200
view of, 13, 113
Earlier System (Nyingma), 42, 43-45, 89, 139, 418n11
and four branches of approach-accomplishment, 44, 205, 257
texts of, 58
treasures (terma) of, 25, 44, 87, 251
and view, meditation, and conduct, 25, 88
See also Nyingma
earth goddesses, 287-88, 290
earth-owning maidens/se, 183, 321
effigy yantra (liṅga), 131
See also liṅga
eight auspicious symbols, 262
eight charnel grounds, 167-68
eight common/great siddhis, 79, 140, 296, 329
eight consciousnesses. *See* eightfold group of consciousness
eight emancipations (aṣṭavimokṣa), 300, 423n2
eightfold charnel ground attire/charnel gear, 174, 322
eightfold group of consciousness/eight consciousnesses, 167, 204, 215
eight great/common siddhis, 79, 296, 329
See also eight qualities
eight herukas, 20, 174
eight knowledge holders (vidyādharas), 18, 20, 45, 88
eight mandalas of material kīla, 296
eight named "Glorious," 97
eight qualities, 140
See also eight great/common siddhis
Eight Sadhana Teachings, 15, 18, 20, 45
herukas of, 174
eighty-four thousand afflictions, 150
eighty-four thousand heaps of Dharma, 29, 271, 282
elementals, 288, 333, 360

elements (dhātus), 35, 115–16, 246–48, 359
  and purity, 158, 162, 335
  See also five elements; three seats
emanating/radiating and gathering, 35, 220, 242, 262–63, 329
  and accomplishment, 254–55
emanation(s), 8, 14, 75, 300
  and five elements, 179, 256–57, 261, 369
  of heruka's body, 183, 230, 369
  manifestation of, 68, 123–25
  and mantra, 75, 78, 223, 242
  and offerings, 214, 217–18, 262
empowerment(s), 19, 32, 130, 208
  as antidote to self-grasping, 228
  and attainment of buddhahood, 57–58
  and autonomy, 32, 35
  and blessings of deity, 211–12
  of co-emergence (sahaja), 248
  extensive, 184
  five (*see* five empowerments)
  of five wisdoms, 307, 316
  four (*see* four empowerments)
  and guru, 11–13
  of immortality/immortal life, 137
  invocation/invitation for, 208–11
  and purity of three seats, 117
  and reflexive awareness, 107, 129
  ripening/maturing, 37–39, 251
  and seeds of three kāyas, 122
  and strength of dharmasphere, 318
  and supplication, 329, 354
  supports for, 298, 303
  and taking up accomplishments, 347, 353
  Vajrakīla, 15, 18–19, 23
empowerment-blessing, 206–8, 211, 307
emptiness, 51, 172, 186, 193, 265, 277
  and afflictions, 108, 135, 140
  appearance(s)/sights and, 98, 263, 274, 276
  awareness and, 98, 263
  buddha nature as, 254, 318
  and conventional bodhicitta, 7, 29
  and development stages, 164–66, 169
  and duality/dualistic grasping, 241, 254
  and five elements, 256–57, 261
  and form/appearance of deity, 58, 164, 171–72, 174, 355
  and HŪṂ/seed syllable, 110, 171, 188, 326
  and kīla of bodhicitta, 121–25, 128
  and life force of deity, 8, 13, 15, 192, 201–2
  and mantra, 82, 98, 223, 232–33, 245
  and mind of guru, 12–13, 145
  and name of deity, 175–78
  and nature/condition of mind, 104–6, 112, 254, 269, 317
  as nonduality, 279
  and offerings, 163–64, 217
  and purity, 82, 115, 261, 368
  and skillful means, 283
  union of bliss and, 239, 242, 250, 253
  union of clarity and, 116, 198, 274–76, 352–53
  union of compassion and, 78, 119, 156, 202, 279, 297
  as view, 65–66, 269, 317
  and visualization, 66, 193, 263
empty essence, 194–96, 278, 303, 352
enemy in whom ten grounds are complete, 174, 294, 333, 335–38
enrichment/enriching activity, 10, 20–21, 265, 311, 340
  and gold material, 127, 181
  kīla of, 292–94
  See also four activities/enlightened actions
equanimity, 14, 95, 205, 343
  immeasurable, 121, 156, 265, 316, 321
  See also four immeasurables

equilibrium, 67
equipoise/meditative equipoise, 110
essence of dependent relations, 267, 271, 423n42
Essence of Display, 143
text, 381-91
Essence of the Play of Concerned Activity, The, 24
eternalism/permanence, 166, 269
ethical discipline, 31, 34, 51
See also six transcendent perfections
existence as vajra, 330, 348
existence-vajrakīla/existence-kīla, 129, 209-10, 315, 327, 348
Exposition on the Great Accomplishment of Karuṇā Guhyasamaja, The, 237
Exposition on the Great Accomplishment of Vajrakīla, The, 56
eye potion, 140

facing generation, 219-21, 230, 258-59, 315
See also three mandalas
factual bodhicitta, 7, 29, 90, 103, 114
See also two types of bodhicitta; ultimate bodhicitta
faculties (of practitioners), 9, 32, 36, 57, 340
highest, 63, 109, 184, 229, 311
lesser, 99
See also six sense faculties
faith, 76, 157, 207, 216, 255, 420n8
in bodhicitta, 51
and bringing down blessings, 314
in cause and effect, 272
in deity, 15-16, 155
and development-stage training, 60, 63
in five elements, 257
and magnetizing activities, 294
and purification of self-grasping, 84
and refuge, 144
and samaya, 224
and strength of one's intentions, 317-18
and taking up accomplishments, 348
in Three Jewels, 36, 254
See also three types of faith
falcon types/hosts (zasö), 102, 182, 218, 300, 329
feast offering, 323-28, 332-45
See also gaṇacakra/gaṇapūja
fictional bodhicitta, 7, 29, 90-91, 114
See also conventional bodhicitta; two types of bodhicitta
fifty-one mental arisings, 200
fire pūja, 81
five afflictions/afflictive poisons, 34, 108, 116, 204, 265, 341
as five father-buddhas, 208
and five wisdoms, 39, 112, 208, 212, 418n1
and wrathful deities, 198
See also five poisons
five aggregates (skandhas), 116, 341
five certainties, 184, 196, 204, 222
five desirables, 137-38, 167, 213, 218
and gaṇacakra, 326-27, 343, 345
five elements, 116, 161-63, 235, 287
dissolution of, 67-68
as divine emanations/ nirmāṇakāyas, 38, 94, 179, 221, 281, 369
as five mother-buddhas, 208, 212, 256, 261
pervaded by five families/deities, 4, 369
and protective spheres of Yamāntaka, 256-57
and rainbow light rays, 80, 165
five empowerments, 39
five families, 117, 173, 179, 211, 298, 318
aggregates and elements as, 246-48, 261

five families (*continued*)
buddhas/tathāgatas of, 116, 211, 274
and crown ornament, 173, 200, 208, 211
and empowerment, 207–8, 211, 307
and five elements, 369
and five fleshes/nectars, 342
and five prongs of vajra, 175
mother-consorts of, 157, 163, 212, 261
in upper knot of kīla, 299–300
of victorious ones, 102, 206, 261
five family lines, 173
five fleshes, 342–43
five kāyas, 174–75
five nectars, 342–43
five poisons, 333
See also five afflictions/afflictive poisons
five skandhas. *See* five aggregates
five-step development of manifest enlightenment, 62
five wisdoms, 117, 163, 204, 230, 259, 300
afflictions as, 34, 38–40, 112, 212, 256
and dharmakāya, 125, 315
empowerment of, 307, 316
and five kāyas, 174
and five poisons, 333
natural radiance/forms of, 254, 274
and vase nectar, 221
See also wisdom(s)
Foremost Prince, 219, 291, 295–302, 305, 306
mandala of, 221, 230
three perceptions of (*see* three perceptions of Foremost Prince/material kīla)
See also three mandalas
forsaking sentient ones, 93, 126
fortress of the view, 88–91, 101, 103, 164, 372
four activities/enlightened actions, 12, 18, 127, 140, 329–30
and bodhicitta/compassion, 11, 264–65
through emanating/radiating and gathering, 255, 369
and great accomplishment, 256
kīlas of the, 293
and mantra recitation, 12, 264
and material kīla(s), 127, 131, 181, 291–96
and material mandala, 310–11
and rainbow light, 158, 258
sadhanas of, 9
siddhi(s) of, 20, 81, 348
and syllables JAḤ HŪṂ VAṂ HOḤ, 233
four attributes of deity, 5–8
four branches of approach and accomplishment, 44, 121, 205, 251–52, 257
and four nails that pin life force, 259–63
See also approach and accomplishment
four cakras, 25, 244, 246, 248
four classes of tantra, 44, 62, 205, 257
four continents, 351
four dharmas of Gampopa, 370
four directions, 168–69, 181, 208, 300
four empowerments, 18–19
four extremes, 295
four families/family lines, 18, 181–82
four gatekeeping maids/female gatekeepers, 300, 301
four immeasurables, 121, 154–57, 172, 228
and bodhicitta/altruistic intent, 29, 129, 152, 370
and development stages, 194
and four female gatekeepers, 218–19, 300, 329
free of subject and object, 118–19, 265
and lower activities, 336
and syllables JAḤ HŪṂ VAṂ HOḤ, 210, 233, 321
and wrathful deities, 199
four joys, 244

four-kāya guru yoga, 14
four kīlas, 12, 103–31, 372
four māras, 102–3, 131–40, 178, 330
  and four kīlas, 103
  and seat of deity, 171–72
four mind-changing contemplations, 42–43, 118
four modes of birth, 62
four nails that pin life force, 259–63
four places, 18, 353–54
four princes, 169–70, 181, 184, 311
four quarters/directions, 169, 181, 208, 300
four root downfalls, 93
four-spoked cakra/wheel, 169–71, 181, 184
four-step vajra development, 62
fourteen mantric downfalls, 324
four tenet systems, 43
four types of development-stage yogas, 62
four types of knowledge holders, 139
four types of siddhi, 19–20
four types of transmission lineages, 18
four yogas of mahāmudrā, 122
frankincense, 298, 331

Gampopa, 87, 138, 370
gaṇacakra/gaṇapūja (feast offering), 323–28, 331–32, 343, 345
  liberation during, 128, 163, 296
  and offerings, 325, 342–45
  perceiving food and drink as, 81, 357
Ganges, The, 99, 137
Garchen/Gar Monastery, 6, 15, 336
Garchen Trinle Yongkhyab, 15
garland of human heads, 174, 200
gathering and reemergence (dudang), 276
gathering in, 67, 271–76, 312
Gathering of Sugatas of the Eight Sadhana Teachings, Tantra of the, 45, 236
Gelug, 331
generosity, 31, 34, 51, 75–78
  and gaṇacakra, 325, 344
  of white torma and smoke offerings, 287
  See also six transcendent perfections
gods, 62, 173, 239, 306, 359
  and demons, 179–80, 367
  and offering clouds of Samantabhadra, 214, 262
  and visualization of accomplishment mantra, 244, 249
  and visualization of approach mantra, 224, 229
  See also six classes of wayfarers/beings; three higher realms
golden libation, 288–90
Gongchig: The Single Intent, the Sacred Dharma, 63, 184
gradual types, 35–36
great accomplishment, 9, 81, 83, 263, 360
  branch of, 255–57
  See also four branches of approach and accomplishment
great accomplishment retreat (drubchen), 15, 296, 314, 336, 347
  mantra recitation in, 236–37, 422n29
  opening chamber of recitation in, 219–21
  physical mandala in, 309–11
  See also accomplishment retreat (drubpa)
Great Bliss, Supreme Means, 284
Great Treasury of Precious Termas, The, 25
Great Vehicle, 30, 93–94, 128, 196, 340
greed, 76–78
ground(s), 138–40, 176, 275, 295, 369
  of buddhas, 147, 244, 338–39, 351–53
  and paths, 89, 139, 177
  ten (*see* enemy in whom ten grounds are complete)

guardians/guards/guard maids/ protectors, 22, 102, 218, 300–301, 345
 and activities, 197
 of mandala, 182–84, 310, 328–29
 petition and, 319–22
 worldly, 149
guru(s), 11–15, 137, 201, 312
 and blessing, 48, 90, 356
 body, speech, and mind of, 145
 as born nirmāṇakāyas, 279
 and concentration being, 196
 and disciple(s), 19, 53, 93, 364–66
 and empowerment, 211–12
 of Garchen Rinpoche, 15–16, 60, 74, 134
 inner, 99–100, 260
 perverted views of/problems with, 43, 95
 prayers for longevity of, 364
 and refuge, 143–45, 319
 and samaya, 227
 See also Three Roots
Guru Padma. *See* Padmasambhava
Guru Rinpoche, 10, 42, 100, 203, 237, 314
 on accomplishment retreats, 73, 229
 on approach and accomplishment, 252–54, 256
 on deity yoga/development stages, 46, 50, 52, 192
 and Earlier System, 44–45, 87
 on mantra, 74, 84, 231
 mind accomplishment sadhana of, 3–4, 319
 on samaya taint in group retreat, 323
 and Vajrakīla transmission, 18–23, 88
 See also Lotus Born; Padmasambhava; Padma Thötreng Tsal; Śākyamitra; Vajra Thötreng Tsal
guru yoga, 11, 14
Gya Zhangtrom, 331
hatred, 43, 265–66, 302, 335, 339
 and inner offerings, 217, 315
 as mirror-like wisdom, 212
 See also aggression; anger; aversion; five afflictions/afflictive poisons; three poisons/poisonous afflictions
Hayagrīva (Tamdrin), 178, 345, 421n12
hearing
 intelligence arisen from, 237
 liberation through, 233
hearing lineage, 18, 122
Heart Sutra, 82
hell denizens, 128, 136, 306
 See also six classes of wayfarers/beings; three lower realms
hell realms, 43, 78–79, 162, 282, 423n51
 See also three bad migrations/states; three lower realms
heruka(s), 66, 89, 140–41, 175, 183
 charnel ground attire of, 174
 eight (*see* eight herukas)
 Karma (*see* Karma heruka)
 as sole hero, 295–96
 visualizing/imagining, 204, 248, 369
Hevajra Root Tantra, 31
Hinayāna. *See* Smaller Vehicle
homa (fire pūja), 81
homage, 151, 212–13, 233, 268, 357
horse dance. *See under* dance
human(s), 62–63, 251, 282, 306, 360
 beings, 30, 268, 287, 317, 320
 births and ethical discipline, 34
 body and microorganisms, 81, 179
 body and seeds of three kāyas, 122
 body and six constituents, 239–40
 body/form, 5, 31, 37–38, 43, 47
 connection/bond between deities and, 318, 327–29
 flesh, 342
 life, 71
 realm, 68, 70–71, 75, 148, 423n51

See also six classes of wayfarers/ beings; three higher realms
humility, 334
Hūṁkāra, 300, 301, 421n12
HŪṀ syllable/letter, 108–13, 143, 330, 358, 362
causal samādhi and, 171–72
and concentration being, 196
as dharmakāya, 175
as emptiness-rigpa, 164
exclaiming, 235
and gathering and reemergence, 275–76
and kīla consecration, 299
as life force, 225
meaning of, 233
as nature of bodhicitta, 371
and selflessness, 327
of varja mind, 304
and vajra recitation, 361–62
visualization of, 188–91, 193, 326, 371
visualization with accomplishment mantra, 245
visualization with approach mantra, 225–26
hundred families of peaceful and wrathful deities, 102, 116–17, 180, 230, 280
hundred-syllable mantra of Vajrasattva, 266–67, 271, 331, 422n41
Hundred Thousand Songs of Milarepa, The, 119, 250, 357

ignorance, 38, 40–41, 44, 71, 99
and afflictions, 159, 270
and arrogant ones, 333–35
and beings' harmful conduct, 6–7
and disclosure, 160
and dualistic grasping, 349
as flesh, 177, 320, 350
and kīla of primordial awareness-rigpa, 107
and name of deity, 175–77
and seed syllable, 188
and self-grasping/self-cherishing, 140, 151
and Vajrakumāra, 171, 173
and yawning, 235
See also delusion(s); five afflictions/ afflictive poisons; six afflictions; three poisons/poisonous afflictions
illness, 7, 33, 71, 100, 122, 242
and development stages, 50
and imprints/propensities, 133, 231–32
and inner obstacles, 94–97
and mantra, 81–82, 236, 264
pacification of, 265, 311
rumination on, 193
illusory body/form, 123, 133, 170, 196
immeasurable equanimity, 156, 316, 321
See also four immeasurables
immeasurable joy, 156, 233
See also four immeasurables
immeasurable love/loving-kindness, 121, 155–56, 202, 227–28
and Great Vehicle individual, 30
and purpose of all sentient ones, 373
See also four immeasurables
immeasurable/measureless compassion, 119–20, 156, 227, 255, 272
kīla of (*see* kīla of immeasurable/ measureless compassion)
and liberation, 336
material kīlas as manifestation of, 131
and selflessness, 278
See also four immeasurables
immeasurable palace, 58, 158, 301, 311, 337
Foremost Prince as, 302–3
and outer container, 220, 256–57
visualizing, 164–69, 183–84
impermanence, 43, 138, 168

implement(s), 131, 255, 301
as attributes of deity's mind, 174, 200
Foremost Prince as, 230
and kīla consecration, 291–304
and symbols, meanings, and signs, 123–24, 172
See also kīla(s); material kīla(s) (phurba)
incarceration pit, 127
indeterminate thoughts, 98–99
individual liberation, 29, 92, 96, 100, 128, 153
path, 31–32, 36, 53, 90, 144, 279
vows/precepts, 19, 93, 324, 419n5
and wrath of primordial awareness, 349–50
individual like sandalwood tree, 130
inscription ritual, 221
instruction(s), 14, 23, 221, 324, 367
on conduct, 97, 357
on deity yoga/development and completion, 60, 69
on dzogchen, 359
on gaṇacakra, 81, 345
of hearing lineage, 122
liberating, 39, 251
pith, 19, 129, 250, 285
to subdue mind, 157, 225
on Vajrakīla, 16, 19, 23
interdependent arising/interdependence, 125, 127, 324, 339

Jambhala, 364
Jambudvīpa, 148, 165, 325
Jamgön Kongtrül Lodrö Thaye, 24–25, 320, 375
and kīla consecration, 291
and lineage supplication, 87
and restoration, 328
japa (dzab), 219n
jealousy, 34, 116, 162, 265, 366–67
during accomplishment retreats, 323–24
and harmdoers/māras, 127, 171, 179
and sexual partners, 240–41, 243
See also five afflictions/afflictive poisons; five poisons; six afflictions
jewel wing, 174
Jigme Lingpa, 19, 100–101, 284–85
Jigme Phüntsog, Khenpo, 357, 425n2
Jigten Sumgön, 6, 14, 19, 273, 280, 282
on deity yoga/development stages, 4–5, 165, 284
on empowerment, 32
on extensive sādhanas, 184
guru yoga of, 11–12
on indeterminate thoughts, 99
on preliminaries, 154
on sudden types, 36
jñānasattva. *See* wisdom being
Jowo Atiśa, 280
Jowo statue, 146
joy(s), 8, 41, 77, 215, 354
four (*see* four joys)
immeasurable, 121, 156, 233, 265, 321
See also four immeasurables

Kagyü, 24, 87, 175, 331, 352
Drigung, 15, 152, 236, 277
Karma, 418n28
See also Drigung Kagyü
kalantaka bird, 130
kapāla, 131, 178
karma, 71, 176, 199, 260, 359, 365
and afflictions, 33, 44, 118, 132, 200, 336
and afflictive winds, 68
and aspirations, 15
and autonomy, 51–52
belief in, 90, 149
and bodhicitta, 185
and disclosure, 159, 270
individual, 120, 260
and liberation, 338–39
and propensities/habits/imprints, 5, 64, 66, 133, 231, 281

and repelling, 341-42
and samsara/samsaric appearances, 153, 241
Karma Chagme. *See* Chagme Rāga Asya
Karma family/family of enlightened activities, 153, 177, 181
Karma Gyurme Rinpoche, 418n28
Karma heruka, 154
Karmakīla, 152-53, 181
karmic causality, 150, 267, 295
incontrovertibility of, 99-100, 365
karmic imprints/habits/propensities, 10, 36, 47, 111, 165, 345
and bardo, 47, 180
body created by, 47, 336
destruction of, 110
and development stages, 54
and mantra, 232
purification of, 78, 326
and seed syllable, 190
and self-grasping, 152, 318
kaṭaṅkaṭe. *See* accomplishment mantra
kāyas, 124, 199
five (*see* five kāyas)
form (*see* rūpakāya [form bodies/kāyas])
and pure fields, 35, 56, 138, 353, 356
three (*see* three kāyas)
and wisdoms, 123-24, 200, 242
Khamsum/Khamsum Namgyal (Trailokyavijaya), 179, 421n12
khaṭvāṅga, 123, 173
Khön, 89
Khorlo Gyedebma (Dīptacakrā), 102, 178, 218, 233
and secret offering, 222-23, 246, 248
kīla(s), 301
of blessing, 103, 352
of compassionate emanation, 129
destructive, 294-95
divine, 130-31
enriching, 292-94
of the expanse, 104
four (*see* four kīlas)
of four activities, 291-92, 293
magnetizing, 294
natural, self-arisen, 347-48
of nonduality, 104
one hundred and eight (*see* one hundred and eight Kīlas)
pacifying, 292
of samādhi, 347-48
of wisdom, 104
See also implement(s); material kīla(s) (phurba)
Kīla Activity, 45, 88, 236
kīla of bodhicitta, 121-25, 130-31, 242
as conduct, 128
and liberation, 332
and māra of son of gods, 138
See also four kīlas
kīla of immeasurable/measureless compassion, 114-21, 129, 131
and māra of afflictions, 138
as meditation, 128
See also four kīlas
kīla of primordial awareness-rigpa/unfurled and pervasive primordial awareness, 21, 103-14, 130, 232, 304
afflictions and, 136, 159, 233, 273, 349
HŪṂ syllable and, 109-13
kīla of bodhicitta and, 123
māra of lord of death and, 112, 137, 330
name of deity and, 177
sky-like individual and, 129
as ultimate truth, 121
as view, 96, 128, 352
as wrathful wisdom, 350
See also four kīlas
kiṁkāra beings/men, 183, 295-96, 301, 321-22
kindness, 90, 295
King of Aspirations for the Conduct of Samantabhadra, The, 53, 118, 248

King of Samādhis Sūtra, The, 307
knowledge holders (vidyādharas), 18, 143, 264, 312, 348
 eight (*see* eight knowledge holders)
 four types (*see* four types of knowledge holders)
 with mastery of life/immortal, 20, 268
Könchog Tengye, 15
Kongpo, 22
Küntuzangpo (Samantabhadra), 89
 See also Samantabhadra

landholders/landholding spirits, 287-89
Lang, 97
Langlab Jangdor, 97
latencies, 71, 96, 336
Latter System (Sarma), 75, 87, 131, 166, 248, 418n11
 and four classes of tantra, 44, 205, 257
 mahāmudrā of, 89
Lekyi Wangmo, 89
Lharig Sigtrül Tülku. *See* Karma Gyurme Rinpoche
Lhasa, 146
Lho Nüden Dorje. *See* Nüden Dorje
liberation, 19, 36, 115, 163, 332-41
 on arising, 110, 158, 242
 and disclosure from view, 159-60
 through hearing, 233
 individual (*see* individual liberation)
 and kīla of immeasurable compassion, 119
 and malign tormas, 296, 337
 and material kīla, 128
 means/method(s) of, 39, 44, 128, 240, 257
 story (namthar), 4, 20, 88
 from suffering, 134
life force, 103, 109, 131, 147, 226, 306
 as bodhicitta/love/compassion, 52, 154, 254, 283
 four nails that pin (*see* four nails that pin life force)
 as HŪṂ/seed syllable, 188-90, 224-25, 245
 as self-grasping consciousness, 106, 111-12, 304, 306, 330
 as union of emptiness and compassion, 8, 13, 15, 192, 201-2
life force that is conduct, 88, 97-101, 265, 372
lightning, 109
lineage, 16, 18, 25, 122, 200, 242
 of blessing-practice, 16-17, 23, 44, 92, 371
 buddha-word, 87, 89, 141
 master(s), 88
 supplication, 24-26, 87-141, 358
 treasure, 22, 87, 92, 141
 Vajrakīla, 17-20, 97, 264
liṅga, 131, 331
 See also effigy yantra
liturgy/liturgical text, 15, 44, 184, 203
 of Mañjuśrī Yamāntaka, 119, 283
local deities/gods, 287-89
Longchen Rabjam, 83, 96, 367
longevity/long life, 80, 122, 229, 311, 364
lotsawa, 284
Lotus Born, 19, 96
 See also Guru Rinpoche; Padmasambhava; Padma Thötreng Tsal; Śākyamitra; Vajra Thötreng Tsal
Lotus King Tantra, 46
Lotus Melody of Eighteen Perfections, 41
love, 5-7, 9, 30, 76, 152
 and afflictions, 198, 240-41, 356, 363-64
 and approach and accomplishment, 251-55
 and bodhisattva's vow, 93-94, 100
 and buddha nature, 5, 120, 275

and conduct, 265
for deity, 47–49, 57, 64, 202, 364
and deity yoga/development stages, 78, 154, 164, 201, 282–84
and destructive activities/liberation, 266, 338–39
and emanating and gathering, 262
and four immeasurables, 154–56
of guru, 13–14, 144–45, 366
and kīla of immeasurable compassion, 119
and offering(s), 76, 216
and purification/destruction of self-grasping, 55, 84, 120, 228, 281, 365
and purification of obscurations, 78
and purposes/objectives of self and others, 52–53, 227
and samaya, 207, 223–24, 312–14, 317
and samaya among sādhakas, 325, 366
and sangha, 151
and seed essence, 122, 240–43
and selflessness, 251, 278
as sign of accomplishment, 79–80, 354
and six transcendent perfections, 34, 51–52
and white torma, 289
and wrath, 130
loving-kindness, 5, 29, 52–53, 240, 282
blessings of, 353
and dedication, 277, 372–73
as deity's life force, 202
and destructive/liberating activities, 333, 336, 339
Dharma as cultivation of, 151
and emanating and gathering, 235
and HŪṂ syllable, 371
immeasurable (*see* immeasurable loving-kindness)
and samaya, 223–24, 325
and six transcendent perfections, 34
See also four immeasurables
lucid faith, 76, 146, 148, 150
luminosity, 109, 278–79, 351, 357
of deep sleep, 67, 101
luminosity-emptiness, 186, 188
lust, 108, 130, 173, 240, 243–44
as inner offering, 127, 161–63, 217, 315, 331
nature of, 240, 254
and practices of channels and winds, 122, 125
See also desire; five afflictions/afflictive poisons; passion; three poisons/poisonous afflictions

Ma, 97
Madhyamaka, 89, 113
magnetization/magnetizing activity, 20–21, 126, 233, 265, 340
and copper material kīla, 127, 181, 293–94
and kīla consecration, 306
torma of, 311
See also four activities/enlightened actions
Mahābala (Tobchen), 300, 301, 421n12
See also Tobchen
mahāmudrā, 19–20, 89, 159, 192, 216
four yogas of (*see* four yogas of mahāmudrā)
and guru, 13–14
and kīla of primordial awareness-rigpa, 96, 103–6, 112–13
method for seeing, 235
and nail of changeless intent, 259
and nail of essence mantra, 262
and secret obstacles, 94, 96
and two objectives, 96–97
Mahāyāna. *See* Great Vehicle
mahāyoga, 45, 87
makara. *See* water dragon
māla, 12, 252, 262, 297–98

māla (*continued*)
and strand/cord, 120, 151, 270
used as blessing-support, 297, 347, 353
malign torma, 296, 336-37
mandala(s), 58, 72, 81, 169, 203-5
appearance-existence as, 210, 260, 333, 348
and bliss, 223, 248, 267
bodhicitta and, 122, 124
body, 178-81, 186
and completion stage/gathering in, 66-67, 273-75
confidence in presence of, 170
container and contents as, 130, 210
deities, 102-3
eight (*see* eight mandalas of material kīla)
and Eight Sadhana Teachings, 45
elaborate/extensive, 24n, 166, 169
of enlightened activities, 45
established through four kīlas, 128-29
facing, 258-59
and implement, 296-302
and mantra, 224, 229-30, 356
material/physical, 299, 309-12, 314, 318, 358
offerings to, 81, 161, 325-26, 328, 342
and opening chamber of recitation, 219-22, 258
outer, 168, 421n12
planet Earth as, 66, 185, 204
as reflection of mind, 190, 192
of self-generation, 203-5, 219
sentient ones as divine hosts of, 255, 257
surrounding, 181-84
as tetrahedron, 166
three (*see* three mandalas)
of wisdom deities, 203-5
Maṇi Kabum, 65
Mañjuśrī, 112
Mañjuśrī Yamāntaka, 24-26, 42, 256
destructive activities of, 265
Garchen Rinpoche and, 16
Gya Zhangtrom and, 331
liturgy/practice manual of, 54, 119, 283-84, 306, 352
and Master Yangga, 365
as method for realizing mahāmudrā, 112
Sign-Based Praise of Mañjuśrī Yamāntaka, 218
three samādhis and, 171
See also Yamāntaka
mantra(s), 37, 81, 95, 140, 362, 368
accomplishment (*see* accomplishment mantra)
approach (*see* approach mantra)
as blessing, 80
and branches of approach and accomplishment, 251-57
and charm, 219n
and close approach, 262
in daily life, 356-65
as deity, 12, 74-75
and destructive/lower activities, 265, 336
as dharmatā, 82-83
as dispelling obscurations, 78-79
as enlightened activities, 81-82
for kīla consecration, 292, 298
and liberation, 332, 337-38
and melody, 236-38, 355-56, 359
nine benefits of (*see* nine benefits of mantra)
as offering, 75-78, 248, 297, 345
purifying imprints/propensities/obscurations, 57, 232, 367
quintessence, 190-91, 196, 245, 361
and radiating/emanating and gathering, 220, 242, 262-63
recollection of, 356-57
retaining, 292

secret (*see* secret mantra)
and self-resounding nāda, 245
self-resounding/self-arisen sound of, 248-49, 253, 256, 368
as siddhis, 79-80
when sleeping, 73-74
sounds as, 98, 234-35, 256, 263, 368
strand (*see* mantra strand/garland)
at time of death, 232
transforming sounds/speech into, 55, 115, 360
as wish-fulfilling jewel, 83
mantra recitation(s), 48, 55, 151, 222, 234-38
at all times, 361
approach and accomplishment and, 252-56
audio recording of, 359-60
benefits of, 74-84
for consecrating four kīlas, 292-94
and ḍākiṇī, 12
during daily activities, 203, 361-62
meditation methods during, 230-32
as meditation on misery, 363
and nail of essence mantra, 261-62
numbers of, 234-35, 252
as offering, 297, 345
and offering the charm, 266-67
prayer wheel as substitute for, 83
and purifying propensities/obscurations of speech, 54, 57, 232, 367
with samādhi/ultimate bodhicitta, 223, 240
signs of accomplishment from, 264
mantra strand/garland, 77, 79, 83-84, 258-59
and accomplishment mantra, 239-48
and approach mantra, 224-27, 231
and nail of essence mantra, 261-63
and stages of approach and accomplishment, 252-55
māra(s), 103, 131-40, 161-62, 341
of afflictions, 125
of aggregates, 26, 125, 338
four (*see* four māras)
of lord of death, 112, 330
of son of the gods, 71
māra-subduing queen. *See* Yeshe Tsogyal
Māra-Subduing Secret Mantra Sanctuary, 25, 328
text, 406-8
Marpa, 87
Mase Sengge, 15
mastery, 105-14, 140, 241-42, 268, 332
material kīla(s) (phurba), 130-31, 230, 295-302, 305
as accomplishment-support, 291, 347
eight mandalas of (*see* eight mandalas of material kīla)
and mandala of Foremost Prince, 221
and mandala of ten wrathful ones, 168
in material mandala, 181, 310
See also implement(s); kīla(s); material kīla of signs
material kīla of signs, 125-30, 133, 168, 221, 230
and liberation, 332, 338
See also four kīlas; material kīla(s) (phurba)
material/physical mandala, 204, 299, 309-12, 358
and four activities' material kīlas, 181
as meditation support, 309, 347
meaning(s). *See* symbols, meanings, and signs
medicine(s), 16, 126, 162, 238, 243, 342
of accomplishment (mendrub), 217
meditation, 67, 69, 110, 156, 171, 216
abyss of, 91-97
in accomplishment retreat, 70, 73, 355

meditation (*continued*)
and certainty, 318
diligence in, 107
and heart visualization, 185–88
on HŪṂ/seed syllable, 175, 188–94, 225, 326, 371
and mandala of samādhi, 128
and mantra, 234–39, 257–58, 360–63
methods during approach mantra, 230–32
and nail of intent, 263
and nail of samādhi, 261
and purification of afflictions, 267
support(s), 168, 297, 309, 338, 348, 358
ultimate bodhicitta as, 132
and victorious ones' blessings, 206
See also view, meditation, and conduct
meditative absorption, 31, 34, 67, 156, 423n2
See also six transcendent perfections
Melodious, Māra-Destroying Vajra Song, 87
text, 377–80
melody, 25, 223, 348
and mantra, 234, 236–38, 356, 359–60
merit, 98, 200, 310–11, 350, 369
accumulation/reaping of, 249, 360
and bodhicitta, 31, 148, 180
and buddhahood, 44, 215
dedication of, 276–77, 372–74
enrichment of, 292–94, 311
and gaṇacakra, 323, 327, 342
and group retreats, 73, 324
and offerings, 76–78
See also two accumulations/gatherings
messenger-guardians/messengers, 321
microorganisms, 69, 81, 179
Milarepa, 4, 57, 81, 95, 170, 419n10
appearance inside yak horn, 191
and compassion, 119
and daily conduct, 357
and hearing lineage, 122
and māra of lord of death, 136
and preciousness of human body, 239
on view/awareness/rigpa, 107–8, 112, 114, 250, 259, 352
on view, meditation, and conduct, 101
mindful awareness, 83, 137, 151, 172, 203, 362
and abyss of meditation, 92–94
and conduct, 100–1
and kīla of bodhicitta, 243
and kīla of primordial awareness-rigpa, 104–5, 107–8
and mantra recitation, 234–36
and transformation of afflictions, 39, 70, 198, 243, 294, 359
mind lineage of victorious ones, 18
miracles, 20, 22, 82, 140
Miyowa/Miyo (Acala), 178, 421n12
mountain-like individual, 129
Mount Meru, 61, 163, 173, 207, 228, 345
mudrā(s), 207–8, 307, 310, 312, 348
as deities, 329
and offerings, 214, 288
and system that is conduct, 97–98
mudrā kīla, 347
Münsel, Khenpo, 74, 134–35

nāda, 223, 245
Nāgārjuna, 159
nail of activities of emanating and gathering, 262–63, 329
nail of changeless intent/of view, 259–61, 263
nail of essence mantra, 261–62
nail of samādhi, 261
Namgyal (Vijaya), 178, 421n12
Nanam, 89
Nāropa, 87, 107
Six Yogas of, 122
navel, 110, 178, 193, 225, 302, 361–62

Necklace of Sapphires, The, 15
Neck-Pouch Kīla Cycle, The, 425n2
nectar pills, 217
New Treasure Traditions (Tersar), 3, 177
Ngülchu/Gyalse Thogme Zangpo, 33, 266
Niguma, 107
nihilism, 166, 269
Nīldaṇḍa. *See* Yug-ngön
nine benefits of mantra, 74-84
nine moods of dance, 186
nine sadhana sections, 45
nine successive vehicles, 45, 173
nirmāṇakāya(s), 79, 125, 242, 268, 297, 319
  all sentient ones as, 279
  and bardo, 57, 68
  born and created, 279-81
  and compassion, 166, 303, 355
  and deity's form, 173-74, 185, 196
  emergence of, 73, 97, 123-25, 139, 272
  and enlightened activities, 8, 148, 166
  as five elements, 38, 179, 281
  and guru, 12, 14, 145
  seed of, 122, 228
  See also three kāyas
nonduality, 104, 177, 244, 325, 355, 374
  of bliss and emptiness, 128
  of deity and sādhaka, 83, 193
  meaning of, 275
  and offerings, 217-218
  as primordial awareness/view/emptiness, 91, 113, 135, 279
  realization of, 177, 211, 242, 250
  of samsara and nirvana, 156, 315
  of self and other, 100, 113, 154, 192, 194
nonhumans, 53, 287, 344, 360
Nub, 97
Nüden Dorje, 3, 319
Nuru, Ācārya, 97
Nyag, 97
Nyangral Nyima Özer, 236
Nyingma, 25, 44, 418n28
  See also Earlier System

obscuration(s), 79, 185, 231-32, 315-16
  of afflictions, 259, 270
  cleared away by practice, 54, 72-73, 225, 336, 354
  of harmdoers, 127-28
  and illness, 82
  to knowable things, 259
  of laziness, 71
  mental, 65, 76, 231-32, 354
  and misdeeds, 294
  physical, 50, 231
  purification of/dispelling, 36, 78, 84
  of sentient ones/six classes, 53, 84, 172, 176, 255
observer, 359
obstacles, 6, 76, 94-96, 320
  as abyss of meditation, 92, 94, 96-98
  dispelling/eliminating/repelling, 177, 229, 287, 311
  Guru Rinpoche and, 20, 96
obstructors/obstructive forces, 140, 152, 303-4, 321, 329
  afflictions/obscurations of, 127, 140-41, 338
  arisen from grasping/afflictions, 132
  destructive/lower activities for, 130-31, 296, 335-37
  drawing in, 331
  harm from, 54
  inner, 234
  liberation of, 295, 338-39
  proffering of, 340-41
  ultimate nonexistence of, 158
  See also māra(s)
Odren, 97
offering(s), 53, 81, 128, 172, 213-18
  of charm, 222, 266-67
  clouds of Samantabhadra, 214, 262
  consecrating, 161-64

offering(s) (*continued*)
and freedom from self-grasping, 281
and gaṇacakra, 134, 325–27, 342–45
through mantra recitation, 223, 297
and material mandala, 309–10
perception of mantra as, 75–78
in petition, 321
and radiating/emanating of light rays, 226, 254–55
and restoration, 328–29
to sangha, 229
secret, 222, 248–49, 345
to torma, 337–38
torma, 320
and turning prayer wheel, 83–84
vastness of, 315–16
white torma, 287–90
OṀ syllable, 163, 304, 321, 361–62
in invocation, 205–6,
and kīla consecration, 304, 306
and visualization of approach mantra, 80, 224, 227–28
one hundred and eight Kīlas, 295
oral instructions of hearing lineage, 122
oral/reading transmission (lung), 15, 23, 27
ornaments, 50, 58, 123–24, 172–74, 200
Ösal Dorje, 366
outflows/leakage, 138, 240, 242–43

pacification/pacifying activity, 21, 198, 265, 292, 293, 311
and silver material, 127, 181
See also four activities/enlightened actions
Padma family, 181
Padmakīla, 181
Padma Lingpa, 92
Padmasambhava, 19–20, 145, 375
See also Guru Rinpoche; Lotus Born; Padma Thötreng Tsal; Śākyamitra; Vajra Thötreng Tsal
Padma Thötreng Tsal, 321
See also Guru Rinpoche; Lotus Born; Padmasambhava; Śākyamitra; Vajra Thötreng Tsal
pain, 50, 71, 153, 156, 241, 365
and mantra, 81–82
and self-cherishing imprints/propensities, 47, 111, 133
and view, 92, 100
Paltrül Rinpoche, 420n8
Palyül, 24
paṇḍita, 221, 285
passion, 93, 176, 243, 248, 359–60
and autonomy, 33–34
difficulty of liberating, 135
and freedom from grasping, 343
See also desire; five afflictions/afflictive poisons; lust; three poisons/poisonous afflictions
patience, 14, 52, 80, 151, 156, 282
and assurance of bodhicitta, 7
for enemies, 90
See also six transcendent perfections
peaceful deities, 198–99, 280, 292, 334
See also hundred families of peaceful and wrathful deities
peaceful means/method(s), 126, 295, 334–35, 338
permanence, 269
personal deity, 15
perverted view(s)/attitudes/understanding, 14, 43, 199, 280, 334
petition, 212, 319–22
text, 403–4
PHAṬ syllable, 110, 233
phenomena, 64–66, 82, 99, 166, 176
composite/compounded, 138, 165, 167–68
grasping at/fixation on, 260–61, 356
of hell realm, 43, 162
illusory, transient nature of, 59, 70, 134, 274–75, 325

purity of, 39, 164, 257, 278, 368-69
and samādhi of suchness, 172
and self-appearances, 78-79
sphere of (dharmadhātu), 57, 114
See also six outer sense objects
phowa, 338
planet Earth, 69, 168
as mandala, 66, 185, 204
pleasure, 33, 123, 239-44, 248-50
clinging to, 99-100
and māra of afflictions, 135
and māra of son of the gods, 71, 132, 137-40
perceived as gaṇacakra, 326, 343, 345
and secret offering, 222-23, 328
and view, 92, 100
poison(s), 162, 338
five (*see* five poisons)
three (*see* three poisons/poisonous afflictions)
See also afflictions/negative emotions
poison hat of Zhangtrom, 331
post-attainment, 110, 112
Prabhahasti, 18, 88-89
practice manual/liturgy/sadhana, 87n, 169, 184, 358
concise, 23-24, 167
extensive, 109, 143, 153, 172, 183, 326
of Mañjuśrī Yamāntaka, 54, 171, 283-84, 306, 352
of Ratna Lingpa, 23-24
recitation of, 236, 422n29
See also liturgy/liturgical text
praise(s), 153, 197, 201, 267, 322, 333
attachment to, 232, 368
of mandala deities, 212, 218-19
of Mañjuśrī Yamāntaka, 284
in subsequent rites, 268, 357
prajñāpāramitā literature, 107
prayer of auspiciousness, 277-83
prayer wheel, 83-84, 190
Precious Garland of the Supreme Path, 138
Precious Treasure of Sakya Paṇḍita's Fine Explanations, The, 46
preliminaries/preliminary practices (ngöndro), 42-43, 154
pretas, 62, 78, 138, 162, 306, 423n51
bulbous ones, 288
See also six classes of wayfarers/beings; three lower realms
pride, 157, 171, 294, 333-34
See also divine pride; five afflictions/afflictive poisons; five poisons; six afflictions
primordial awareness, 174, 257, 268, 317, 370
accomplishment mantra and, 239-44, 248
afflictions as, 19, 108, 115, 171, 261, 418n1
consciousness and, 106, 112, 198
disclosure and, 159-60
divine pride and, 283-84
empowerment and, 208, 212
as essence of mind/buddha nature, 37, 107, 112, 269-70
gathering in and, 275
kīla of (*see* kīla of primordial awareness-rigpa/unfurled and pervasive primordial awareness)
kīla of bodhicitta and, 122-24
liberation and, 338
māra of afflictions and, 140
nail of samādhi and, 261
as nonduality, 113
rakta offering and, 162-63
recollection of purity and, 198, 200, 261
secret sun of, 284, 317, 350-53
ten transcendent perfections and, 181-82
two accumulations and, 277, 373

primordial awareness (*continued*)
view and, 103, 136, 284
wisdom being and, 186
wrathful, 348-50
See also awareness; awareness-wisdom/awareness-rigpa; wisdom
primordial purity, 40-41, 117, 138, 278, 368
princes, 169-70, 184, 248, 311, 329
of four families, 181-82
Prince Siddhartha, 121
See also Bhagavan Buddha; Śākyamuni
prison, 134, 332
proffering, 332, 340
propensities/imprints,
of embodiment,
prostration(s), 83, 213
protective sphere(s), 158, 168, 184, 256
pure field(s)/pure realm(s), 79, 139, 195-96, 223
accomplishing deity and mantra in, 74
attainment of buddhahood in, 250
and bodhicitta/compassion, 279, 282, 325
causes for birth in, 310
human realm/this world as, 148, 165
kāyas and, 35, 56, 138, 356
and liberation, 332, 339
and mandala of wisdom deities, 358
mastery of, 140, 241
offerings and, 215, 262
saṁbhogakāyas and, 274, 278
See also buddha-field(s)
pure perception, 39-43, 115, 232, 367-69
and conduct, 97
and development stages/deity's appearance, 62, 125, 253, 348, 359
and fortress of view, 91
of guru, 145
and mantric vows, 419n5
material mandala as support for, 309-10
sealing with view, 175
as secret autonomy, 35
purity, 39-41, 82, 117, 162, 309
and buddha nature, 40, 327, 367
of container and contents, 39, 107, 115, 157, 261, 348
and development stages, 41, 215, 261
and dreamlike nature of phenomena, 325
and eightfold group of consciousness, 167
as emptiness, 115, 261
establishing mind in, 355
of gaṇacakra offerings, 343
and kīla consecration, 297
and kīla of samādhi, 348
and love and compassion, 115
and mantra recitation, 238
of phenomena, 39, 164, 368-69
primordial, 117, 138, 159, 278, 368-69
recollection of, 50, 198, 201
as rigpa, 138
threefold (*see* threefold purity)
See also clarity, purity, and stability

Queen of Great Bliss. *See* Yeshe Tsogyal

Rāga Asya. *See* Chagme Rāga Asya
rainbow(s)/five-colored lights, 58, 82, 91, 148, 196, 248
body, 122-23, 244
and completion, 168, 273
deities appearing/vanishing like, 48-49, 59, 66, 197-98
and emanating and gathering, 254-55, 262
and form/body of deity, 133, 137, 185, 194-95, 232
and illusory body, 170

and immeasurable palace, 158, 165, 169, 257
and mantra recitation, 223
reflections, 138, 147-48, 168, 170, 200
and saṁbhogakāya, 73, 75, 194, 202, 272-74
spheres/bubbles, 198-99, 248
rakta/blood, 163, 174, 298, 422n34
and inner offerings, 161-62, 216-17, 321
Ratna family, 181, 207, 292
Ratnakīla, 181
Ratna Lingpa, 15, 22-24, 153, 316, 375
Ratnasambhava, 10
Ratön, 92
receptacle girls, 288
recitation of the charm, 219-24, 248, 258
refuge(s), 43, 118, 280, 317-19
and bodhicitta, 39, 143-57
object(s)/source(s) of, 12, 143-46, 326
vow of, 8, 52, 350
regent(s), 11, 17, 314, 347
rejoicing, 156
renunciation, 128
of worldly activities, 55
repelling, 341-42
text, 410-12
tormas, 296, 336
request to remain, 271
restoration, 267, 328-30
text, 406-8
of vows, 93-94
retinue(s), 182, 297, 341
beings/sentient ones appearing as, 205, 256
certain, 196
as self-radiance of principal deity, 170, 183
Rigdzin Gödem, 92
rigpa, 104-14, 136, 138, 166, 303
being beyond birth and death, 137, 268
and development stages, 172
and disclosure, 159-60
and kīla of nonduality, 104
mastery of, 103, 105-9, 111-14, 268
reflexive, 107
and seed syllable, 164, 175, 196
and vajra mind, 368
See also kīla of primordial awareness-rigpa/unfurled and pervasive primordial awareness
Rinchen Palzang, 92
Rinchen Phüntsog, 236
Rinchen Zangpo, 418n11
Rinzang, 97
ritual, 25, 32, 97-98, 184, 296
Rogchal, 97
Rongzom, 89
rūpakāya (form bodies/kāyas) 97, 124-25, 148

sadhana(s), 3-4, 9, 26, 54, 184
abbreviated, 8-9, 24, 184
and blessing-practice lineage, 371-72
of Earlier System, 44, 251
and four nails, 259
for individuals of varying faculties, 186
mind accomplishment, 3-4, 206, 319
practice where Dharma has not been heard, 287
sections, nine (*see* nine sadhana sections)
Teachings, Eight (*see* Eight Sadhana Teachings)
of Vajrakīla (*see* Vajrakīla sādhanas/practice manuals)
wrathful, 130
See also accomplishment(s): method of (sadhana)
sadhana class of mahāyoga, 87
Sakya, 18, 166
Śākyamitra, 18
See also Guru Rinpoche; Lotus Born; Padmasambhava; Padma Thötreng Tsal; Vajra Thötreng Tsal

Śākyamuni, 10, 56, 146, 423n51
See also Bhagavan Buddha; Prince Siddhartha
Sakya Paṇḍita, 31, 46, 334
samādhi, 84, 124, 128, 131, 190, 357
kīla of, 347–48
and mantra recitation, 80, 223, 231, 238, 261
nail of, 261
and nail of essence mantra, 262
three (*see* three samādhis)
three-step (*see* three-step samādhi development)
of total appearance, 172
Samantabhadra, 136, 139, 175, 250, 352
offering clouds of, 213–15, 262
See also Küntuzangpo
samaya (damtsig; commitment), 8, 19, 216, 227, 321, 329
and bodhicitta/loving-kindness, 95, 195, 223–24
and bringing down blessings, 312, 314, 316–18
and gaṇacakra remainder, 344
and invocation, 207, 210
maintaining/preserving, 366–67
restoring/repairing, 324–25, 327–28
taint, 323–25
of three vajras, 368
samayasattva. *See* commitment being
Samayatārā, 178, 208
saṁbhogakāya(s), 39, 123–24, 199, 204–5
in bardo, 57, 63, 125, 134, 145, 359
and bringing down blessings, 309–15
buddha-fields/pure realms, 139, 165, 250, 358
as clarity factor/nature of clarity, 196, 272, 278, 303, 355
and dharmakāya/dharmasphere/space, 194, 209, 272–74
of five certainties, 184, 196, 204, 222
and guru, 12, 14, 145
and mantra/speech/wind energies, 74–75, 122, 228
symbols of, 166, 174
See also three kāyas
samsara, 41, 100, 153, 253, 315, 367
impure appearances of, 167
karmic habits/propensities of, 56, 152
and liberating activities, 332–33
liberation/freedom/emancipation from, 126, 147, 153, 241, 296, 300
overcoming/undermining, 233, 244, 254
samsara and nirvana, 59, 91, 259, 304, 353, 372
dividing line between, 52, 106, 244
and existence-vajrakīla/existence as vajra, 210, 315, 330
inseparability/nonduality/union of, 113, 156, 158, 276, 332
mind as root/creator of, 11, 176, 260
purity of, 107, 277–78
single ground/basis of, 259–60, 278
sangdrub. *See* secret accomplishment retreat
Sanggye Lingpa, 22, 24, 92, 375
Sanggye Tendzin, Lama, 15
sangha, 151, 203, 229, 319, 326
guru/virtuous friend as, 11, 14, 144
Śāntideva, 266
Sarma. *See* Latter System
scripture and reasoning, 89, 101, 113
Se, Chag, and Dung, 182–83, 218
seat(s), 20, 39, 181, 256, 284–85
awareness capturing/holding its own, 138, 359
of/for deity/deities, 171, 210, 311
of É, 303–4, 307
lotus, 165, 171, 311
offering, 210, 288, 321
three (*see* three seats)

secret accomplishment retreat (sangdrub), 15-16, 71, 268, 353, 356
  dance in, 314
  focused on self-generation, 204, 219, 258-59
  fulfillment of, 185
  kīla consecration in, 297
  texts for, 23, 169, 375-416
  three isolations in, 55
  three perceptions in, 303-4
  use of mantra recording in, 359-60
  visualizing elaborate/other mandalas in, 169, 220-21
secret accomplishment text(s), 169, 296, 375-416
secret mantra, 91, 145, 202, 287, 349
  abyss of meditation and, 94-97
  approach and accomplishment, 251-57
  approach mantra and, 233
  autonomy and, 34-35
  and basis of mind, 284-85
  and body mandala, 179-80
  calm abiding with support in, 194
  continuous cultivation of deity yoga in, 361
  deities visualized with consorts in, 177-78
  diversity of methods in, 193, 362
  Earlier System of (*see* Earlier System)
  empowerment and, 31-32, 37-39, 57, 122
  equanimity according to, 156
  gaṇacakra, 323-28, 332-41, 342-45
  guru and, 11, 13, 145
  and increase of bodhicitta, 53, 239
  intent/perspective of, 250, 281
  Latter System of (*see* Latter System)
  life force of conduct and, 100
  pure perception and, 278, 325, 348, 367-69
  purity of container and contents in, 115, 261
  qualities and results of practice of, 263-64
  samaya(s)/vows, 19, 94, 325
  secrecy of, 39-43
  sudden types and, 35-36
  suitable vessels for, 37
  teachings as daybreak of Vajrarākṣasa, 350
  ten transcendent perfections and, 181-82
  Three Roots and, 145
  unfit vessels for, 42-43
  visualization of mantra strand in, 239-49
  yogic practices of, 239-40
  See also Vajra Vehicle (Vajrayāna)
seed essence(s), 121-25, 239-48
seed syllable(s), 66, 188-91, 195, 261-63
  of five families, 207
  gathering awareness into, 225
  mandala of, 296
  and material kīla, 299
  properties of, 188
  rainfall of, 227
  of six realms, 306
  visualization methods, 175, 194, 225-26, 362, 371
  as weapon, 108-11, 172
self, 33, 60, 109, 115, 202, 251
  apprehending/belief in a, 111, 240
  and co-emergent ignorance, 40
  exhaustion of, 373
  fabricating a, 270, 318
  freedom from/lack of, 79, 111-12, 188, 270, 373
  notion/sense of a, 33, 57, 325
  as root of all suffering, 373
self-appearances, 78-79, 168-69, 294
self-cherishing, 5, 133, 150-51, 153, 282
self-empowerment, 211
self-generation, 180, 203-5, 219-20, 230
  See also three mandalas

self-grasping, 13, 51–52, 93, 269–72
adventitious/circumstantial, 120, 153, 259, 261, 269, 315
and afflictions, 140–41, 150, 256, 362–65
antidote to, 34–35, 281
as cause of cyclic existence, 33
and empowerment, 211, 228
exhaustion of, 204
and HŪṂ syllable, 108–10
and impure perception, 42, 117, 199
and liberation, 127–28
as life force, 111–12, 330
and love and compassion/bodhicitta, 120, 201–2, 281, 373
and mantra, 80
and māra of the lord of death, 136
and maturation, 251
and offering, 281, 326–27
purification/liberation of, 84, 275
and recollection of deity, 57, 61, 74, 164, 326
and repelling, 341
and torma offering, 217
selflessness, 7, 79, 81–82, 108–9
and compassion/love, 251–52, 264, 278
sense fields (āyatanas), 35, 60, 158, 315, 359, 423n2
and kīla of immeasurable compassion, 114–17
and offerings, 162
ripening through liberation, 335
sentient one(s)/being(s)
adventitious defilement/temporary ignorance of, 38, 45, 259, 261, 281
difference between buddhas and, 9, 201
as divine hosts/inhabitants of mandala, 210, 255, 257, 274
downfall of forsaking, 93, 126
drawing in afflictions of, 331–32
harm from, 6, 80, 331
methods that suit dispositions of, 340
offering afflictions of, 161–64, 217, 315–16, 320
as principal of mandala, 185
and refuge in field of accumulation, 146
as retinue of principal deity, 256
respect for, 151
and seed syllables of six classes, 304, 306, 332
transformation into buddhas (emergence from), 39–40, 56–57, 146
Seven-Line Supplication, 134, 314
seven outer/daily offerings, 214, 321
seven tissues (dhātus), 422n34
Shübu, 89
siddha, 4, 88, 191, 284
siddhi(s), 20–21, 209, 307, 327, 329
of body, speech, and mind, 262
common, 6, 65, 81–82, 140, 212
of deity, 80, 155
eight common (*see* eight common siddhis)
and emanating and gathering, 263
of four activities, 20, 81, 348
four types of (*see* four types of siddhi)
of mahāmudrā, 20, 96
mantra as, 79–80, 83
and material mandala, 310
obstacles and, 95–96
and offerings, 213
supreme and common, 11, 129, 310, 320–21, 355
supreme/uncommon, 65, 79, 83, 229, 321
and taking up accomplishments, 347
See also accomplishment(s)
sights, 234
as appearance-emptiness, 98, 263
sign(s), 3, 48–49, 145, 203, 334
of accomplishment, 80, 96, 264, 330, 354, 365

of bodhicitta, 209
of boredom, 237
of civility, 287
of conjoining mind and winds, 362
of deity accomplishment, 202
of deity's blessings, 354, 356
of deity's body/appearance 123, 172–73
of dualistic grasping, 212
of empowerment, 209
of good fortune, 37
of great love, 344
of ignorance, 297
of mind's inner accomplishment, 124
of siddhi of deity, 80
See also symbols, meanings, and signs
Sign-Based Praise of Mañjuśrī Yamāntaka, 218
sign lineage of knowledge holders, 18
Śīlamañju, 88–89
single form of deity/sole hero, 177, 295–96
single key point of three vows, 19
single taste, 113
six afflictions, 162, 270, 304–6, 330, 363
self-grasping and, 52
six causes, 161–62, 345
six classes of wayfarers/beings, 128, 148, 162
birth in, 62, 68, 270
kīla of immeasurable compassion and, 118–20
mantra as dispelling obscurations and, 78–79
and six afflictions, 270
syllables of, 304
teachers of, 75
See also six realms
six constituents, 37, 239
six munis, 279, 423n51
six outer sense objects, 116
six realms, 110–11, 173, 176, 270, 282
and afflictions, 162–63, 304, 332, 345, 363
blocking birth in, 62, 270
emanations/nirmāṇakāyas in, 8, 75, 223, 279
See also six classes of wayfarers/beings
six seeds, 304
six sense faculties, 116
six sufferings, 363
six transcendent perfections, 31, 121, 181–82, 329, 363
and altruism/Bodhisattva Vehicle, 34, 51–53
signs of, 172, 200, 302
Six Yogas of Nāropa, 122
skandhas. *See* aggregates
skillful means, 77, 249–50, 299, 309
and altruistic mind/compassion, 150, 174, 283
of development stages, 194, 336, 369
Sky Dharma (Namchö) Treasure, 207, 421n23
sky-like individual, 129
sleep, 66–69, 71–74, 357, 362
luminosity of (*see under* luminosity)
waking from, 57, 64, 69–70, 74
Smaller Vehicle (Hinayāna), 30, 67, 340
smoke, 287, 298
sneezing, 236
So, 97
sole hero Kīla, 295–96
Song on Realizing Fivefold Mahāmudrā, The, 4–5, 284
Songtsen Gampo, 65, 418n11
sorcery, 140, 336
Sosaling Charnel Ground, 18
sound(s), 55, 82–83, 111, 232
attachment to/grasping at, 213–14, 235, 368
imprints/propensities related to, 35, 54, 367

sound(s) (*continued*)
as mantra, 98, 234-35, 253, 256, 263
of mantra, 74, 223, 245, 249, 356, 360
of melody, 237-38
sovereigns/sovereign maidens, 182-83, 321-22
special insight (vipaśyanā), 34, 194-95, 230
speech, 35, 83, 101, 151, 296, 353
blessings of, 80, 224, 227-28, 255
and consecrating the offerings, 163-64
divisive, 99
of guru, 11-14, 144-45
and mantra, 54-55, 115, 223, 232, 234
and saṁbhogakāya, 97, 124, 145, 228
transformation into deity's speech, 39, 57, 73, 357
vajra, 304, 368
sphere of phenomena/dharmas, 57, 114, 175, 195, 208, 251
strength of, 277, 317-18
See also dharmasphere (dharmadhātu)
spirits, 341, 287-88
evil/harmful/harmdoing, 100, 311, 321, 345
opportunistic, 265, 320, 331
stability, 197-203, 234, 280
of mind, 190, 253-54
and shape of wrathful tormas, 166
See also clarity, purity, and stability
statue(s), 48, 146, 271
as created nirmāṇakāyas, 280-81
subsequent rites, 51, 268-71, 357
substances, 130-31, 243, 297, 337-38
offering, 161-63, 214, 217, 328
smeared (*see* three smeared substances)
subtle body, 115-16, 229, 243, 248
sudden approach/method, 60, 63, 80-81, 257-58, 276
and entire mandala/visualization, 169, 183, 193
and opening chamber of recitation, 220-21
sudden types, 35-36
Śuddhodana, 56
suffering(s), 78, 82, 99-100, 332
and afflictions, 33, 68, 114, 179, 270, 304
antidote to/antidoting, 121, 365
in bardo, 47, 69, 111, 133, 135
body and, 46-47
causes of, 10, 30, 106
and compassion, 118-19, 156
and four māras, 131-39, 171, 330
grasping at, 363, 365
illusory nature of, 5, 118, 365
liberating beings from, 37, 39, 143, 151
and refuge, 143-44, 148
ripening through lower activities, 336-39
and self-cherishing/self-grasping, 33, 78, 117, 150, 157, 281
of three lower realms, 40, 53, 367
Sukhacakra, 18-19
Sukhāvatī, 207, 339
supplication, 206, 252, 307, 330, 332, 351
to achieve a particular purpose, 364
to receive empowerment, 353-54
Supplication in Seven Chapters, The, 96
Supplication to Guru Rinpoche That Spontaneously Fulfills All Wishes, The, 150
Sutra of the Three Heaps, The, 277
Sutra on Emancipation, The, 30, 67
Sutra System, 102, 144
swift-footedness, 140
symbol(s), 123-24, 166, 201, 303
See also eight auspicious symbols; symbols, meanings, and signs
symbolic kīla of blessing, 103, 352
symbols, meanings, and signs, 123, 172, 200, 242, 302, 369

taking up accomplishments, 209, 284, 317, 347-354
text, 415-16
Ṭakkirāja. *See* Dögyal
Tamdrin. *See* Hayagrīva
Tārā, 48, 52, 56, 95, 363-64
tathāgatagarbha, 21, 123, 137, 151, 176, 211
See also buddha nature
taxes, 76-77
ten accoutrements, 174
ten bhūmis (grounds), 182, 196
ten characteristics of spontaneously produced great bliss, 138
ten directions, 173, 205-7, 224-25, 268, 357
and offering clouds, 214, 262
of outer mandala, 168
and radiating and gathering, 220, 255
ten-spoked cakra/wheel/sphere, 169, 180-81, 184
ten strengths, 102, 181-82, 218, 329
ten transcendent perfections, 50, 181-82, 218, 328-29
ten virtues, 328-29
ten wrathful couples/pairs, 102, 230, 328-29, 341, 421n12
and bliss, 180
in material kīla, 300
as self-radiance of principal, 170
in ten-spoked cakra/sphere, 169, 181, 184
Tenzin Chökyi Gyaltsen, 316
Terdag Lingpa, 97
terma, 21-22, 24, 44, 87
See also treasures
thangka, 27, 58, 208, 218, 271, 280
thirteen aspects of peaceful attire, 198
thirteen bhūmis of a vajra holder, 198
Thirty-Seven Practices of Bodhisattvas, 31, 59, 100, 105, 216, 266
and abyss of meditation, 93
and accomplishment retreats, 54-56
and liberation, 332
and patience, 7, 14
and self-grasping, 33-34, 132
thirty-six sections of Vajrakīla tantras, 21
thögal, 200
Thorough Explanation of the Eight Sādhana Teachings, The, 56
thoughts, 55, 112, 132, 249, 338, 357
as awareness, 98, 235, 263
and dualistic grasping, 241
Jigten Sumgön on, 98-99, 282
mantra and, 82, 262-63, 233-34, 360
mindful awareness/rigpa and, 101, 104, 114, 159, 198, 273
as nirmāṇakāya, 242
recognition/liberation on arising, 68, 70, 108, 158, 260, 367
secret obstacles of, 94-95
and seed syllable, 109-11, 164, 188, 326
and stages of development, 59, 65
three bad migrations/states, 38, 176, 179
See also three lower realms
three doors, 35, 144, 146, 151, 234, 251
three features of ultimate fruition, 196
three foes, 330
threefold perceptual sphere, 164
threefold purity, 374
threefold sattva, 195-97
See also three sattvas
three freshly flayed garments, 174
three higher realms, 31, 51-52, 128, 154, 176
and autonomy, 33-34
three incessant things, 84
three inner offerings, 216-17
three isolations, 55
Three Jewels, 8, 12, 77, 144-45, 326
faith in, 36, 146-152, 254, 319
three junctures (at time of death), 67

three kāyas, 39, 124, 273, 319, 331, 355
arising from and dissolving into one another, 272
as fruition, 144
and guru, 12
innate presence in body, 122
qualities of, 147, 353
in sentient ones, 228, 278
subsumed in dharmakāya, 175
symbolized by deity's three faces, 172–73
symbolized by tetrahedron, 166, 169
and three blades of kīla, 302
and twofold purpose, 35
and Vajrakīla practice, 125
See also dharmakāya; nirmāṇakāya(s); saṁbhogakāya(s)
three limitless kalpas, 44, 215
three lower realms, 33, 40, 52, 111, 128, 367
See also three bad migrations/states
three mandalas, 230, 299, 304, 306, 353
three perceptions of Foremost Prince/ material kīla, 299, 303–4
three periods of the day, 101
three places, 80, 206, 227–28, 304, 306
three planes, 206, 210, 212, 300, 304, 330
three poisons/poisonous afflictions, 40, 126, 163, 217, 331–32
and inner meaning of outer signs, 123, 173, 303
three realms, 41, 43, 67, 75, 304, 331
Three Roots, 144, 224, 227, 319–20, 331
blessings of, 88, 365
faith in, 146
guru as embodiment of, 11–12, 145
offering to, 326
three samādhis, 171
three sattvas, 195–97
See also threefold sattva
three seats, 114–16, 315
three secrets, 251
three smeared substances, 174
three spheres, 12, 217, 332
three-step samādhi development, 62
three strengths, 277, 317–18
three successive paths, 19, 31–32, 143, 350
three times, 153, 268, 276–77, 357, 372
three types of faith, 146–151, 206
three vajras, 163, 304, 368
three vehicles, 92, 239
three vows, 19
throwing star, 169, 331
Tibet, 3–4, 20, 44–45, 87
accomplishment retreats in, 236–37, 354, 422n29
Garchen Rinpoche and, 16–17, 72
Tibetan language, 21
reciting in, 26–27, 269, 287
Tibetan medicine, 422n34
Tilopa, 87, 137
time/age of dregs, 10, 42, 83, 145
Tobchen (Mahābala), 178, 421n12
See also Mahābala
torma, 163, 166, 217, 320, 344–45
drawing harmdoers/afflictions into, 265, 320–21, 331–32
inner offering of, 161, 216, 321
and liberation, 163, 338–39
main, 302, 311, *313*
and material mandala, 311
of Vajrakīla, *313*
weaponized/malign, 127, 296, 336–38
white, 287–90
Trailokyavijaya. *See* Khamsum/ Khamsum Namgyal
transcendent perfections
six (*see* six transcendent perfections)
ten (*see* ten transcendent perfections)
transparency, 104, 106
treasure (terma) section, 87

treasure revealer(s), 3, 22, 87, 236, 319, 331
treasures, 18, 21-22, 42, 44
of Earlier System, 25, 87, 251, 288
lineage of, 92, 141
See also New Treasure Traditions (Tersar); terma
Treasury of Experiential Pith Instructions, The, 96, 367
Trinle Yongkhyab, 15
Tri Ralpachen, 418n11
Trisong Detsen, 418n11
trusting faith, 146, 150
Tsangnyön Heruka, 419n10
twelve kīla guard maids/protectresses, 183, 218, 300, 301
twenty-four wrathfuls, 181-82
twenty-one crosses of É, 310-11
two accumulations/gatherings, 276-77, 343, 372-73
two Kīla family lines, 295
two kinds of ignorance, 40-41
two purposes/objectives of self and others, 12, 53, 129, 153, 256, 263
accomplished together, 84, 139-40, 147, 227, 373
buddhahood/enlightenment and, 35, 330
and mantra, 83, 227, 243
and three kāyas, 96-97
two truths, 121
two types of bodhicitta, 12, 29, 90, 98, 147, 239
and deity yoga, 235
Vajrakumāra couple as, 124

ultimate bodhicitta, 29, 37, 132, 235, 240, 260
See also factual bodhicitta; two types of bodhicitta
understanding, experience, and realization, 70-71
Unelaborate Liturgical Arrangement of the Method for Accomplishing Vajrakīla, An, 23-24, 87n
Union of Sun and Moon Tantra, The, 46
union/unity
of appearance and emptiness, 82, 124, 274, 276
of awareness and emptiness, 254
of bliss and emptiness, 124, 254
of calm abiding and special insight, 230
of clarity and emptiness, 104, 106, 116, 254, 352-53
of compassion and emptiness/rigpa, 78, 124-25, 192, 232, 265
connate, 213, 215
of development and completion, 49, 63-64, 81, 124, 276
of dharmakāya and saṁbhogakāya, 196
of father-mother couple/consorts/deities, 66, 123-24, 214, 241
of kāyas and wisdoms, 123-24, 200, 242
of method and wisdom, 174
pleasures of, 223, 248
of samsara and nirvana, 210, 276, 330
of sound and emptiness, 232
of ultimate and conventional, 168
See also nonduality

vajra(s), 13, 117, 173, 186, 244
channel wheels, 114, 116
of concentration being, 185, 188-91, 196, 224-25
diamond-like quality of, 176-77
existence as, 330, 348
meaning of, 175-77, 233
three (*see* three vajras)
wrathful, 109, 172
wrathfuls, 126
vajra body, 122, 304, 368

Vajradhara (Dorje Chang), 174–75, 196, 284, 317, 352
as fundamental disposition/essence of mind, 37, 250
ground of, 275
and lineage, 87, 89
vajra eye, 326
Vajra family, 102, 175, 181
Vajrakīla sādhanas/practice manuals, 23–24, 143, 172, 291, 347
composed by Jigme Phüntsog, 357
elaborate mandala visualization in, 166, 169
elaborate retinue described in, 182–83
enjoyment of offerings according to, 326
Gathering of Sugatas of the Eight Sadhana Teachings, Tantra of, 236
Guru Rinpoche and, 20–22
material kīlas described in, 291–92
Necklace of Sapphires, The, 15
praise in, 153, 219
special methods in, 109–11, 219
three mandalas in, 230
Yeshe Tsogyal and, 20–22
Vajrakīla tantras, 19–21, 45, 141, 197, 338
Vajrakumāra (Vajra Youth), 102, 171, 220, 353
and approach mantra, 233
and awareness/buddha nature, 51, 111–12, 132, 175, 269
body/form of, 172–74, 303
invocation/invitation of, 205–12, 255
and kīla of primordial awareness-rigpa, 273
and mandala deities, 180–81, 183
as manifestation of bodhicitta, 124
name of, 175–77, 351–52
outer, inner, and secret, 325
and refuge visualization, 143–44
and Vajrakīla transmission, 17–18
See also Vajra Youth
vajra master, 12–13, 79, 354–57
attaining ground of, 275
and gaṇacakra offerings, 343–44
vajra mind, 176, 304, 368
Vajrapāṇi, 87, 102, 175, 297
See also Dharmevajra
Vajrarākṣasa (Adamantine Carnivore), 164, 177, 213, 217, 350
vajra recitation, 361–62
Vajrasattva, 102, 154, 175, 177, 206, 208
mantra of, 266–67, 271, 331, 422n41
and peaceful activities, 10, 206
vajra siblings, 324, 356, 367
vajra song, 273
vajra speech, 304, 368
Vajra Thötreng Tsal, 88–89
See also Guru Rinpoche; Lotus Born; Padmasambhava; Padma Thötreng Tsal; Śākyamitra
Vajravārāhī, 179
Vajra Vehicle (Vajrayāna), 44, 194, 239–40
and antidoting obstacles, 94–97
and empowerment, 31–32, 57
secrecy of, 39–43
teachings of, 37, 145, 350
See also Vehicle(s): Mantric
Vajravidarana. *See* Dorje Namjom
vajra wing(s), 174, 181
Vajra Youth (Vajrakumāra), 171, 177, 208, 314
and drawing in, 320, 331
praise of, 218, 268
and recitation of charm, 222–24, 248
and taking up accomplishments, 348, 352
See also Vajrakumāra
vase generation, 219, 221
Vehicle(s), 19, 29, 31–32, 92–94, 128
Bodhisattva, 36, 53, 103, 229, 349–50
Causal, 44, 93, 128
Fruition/resultant, 44, 94

Great/Greater (Mahāyāna), 30, 67, 196
Mantric, 39, 57, 103, 239-40, 350
resultant, 44
Small/Smaller (Hinayāna), 30, 67
successive, nine (*see* nine successive vehicles)
three (*see* three vehicles)
See also Vajra Vehicle (Vajrayāna)
verse translations, 25-27
victorious ones, 173, 177, 200, 206, 261, 300
mind lineage of, 18
subsumed in Vajrakumāra, 102
vidyādharas. *See* knowledge holders
view(s), 12, 198, 202, 249, 345, 368
and afflictions, 125, 136, 243
and appearances, 216, 273
and arising of mandala, 158
assurance/certainty/freedom from doubt about, 90-91, 101, 128, 317-18, 351
completion stage and, 66, 271-76
and disclosure, 159-60
dualistic, 75, 194, 213, 244, 370
fortress of, 89-91, 164, 372
and gaṇacakra, 325-27
introduction to, 13, 135, 279
and kīla of primordial awareness-rigpa, 103-14, 128
and liberation, 332-33
and mantra recitation, 226, 230, 234, 262-63
and māra of lord of death, 140
nail of, 259
perverted, 43, 199, 280
and purity, 65, 278, 348
sealing with, 175, 192-93
secret accomplishment and, 296
of special insight, 34
See also view, meditation, and conduct
view, meditation, and conduct, 4, 25, 88-101, 128, 131
Vijaya. *See* Namgyal
Vimalamitra, 88-89
vinaya, 19, 93, 131, 236, 331
vīras (heroes), 244, 246, 257, 326, 342, 344
and offering clouds, 214
seed essences as, 122
virtue(s), 44, 83, 99, 213, 370
and bodhicitta, 31, 151, 154
dedication of, 276-77, 372-74
and motivation, 37, 276
sealing with view/emptiness, 192, 277
ten (*see* ten virtues)
visualization, 14-15, 65-66, 164
of accomplishment mantra, 224-30
of approach mantra, 239-50
for beginners, 59-62, 371
and bodhicitta, 6, 154, 194
of body mandala, 178-80
as calm abiding with support, 194-95
of concentration being, 188-93, 196, 261-62
for consecration of material kīla, 298-99
in daily activities, 357-58
of deity/commitment being, 131, 133, 170-75
for drawing in, 332
of facing generation, 258-59
of field of accumulation, 143
gathering in, 273-75
of immeasurable palace, 164-69
like beehive broken open, 256
like king's envoys, 254-55
like moon with garland of stars, 252
like sparkler's circle, 253
of mandala, 204, 206
of mandala inhabitants, 181-85
and mantra recitation, 75, 231, 262
of offerings, 213-18

visualization (*continued*)
of other mandalas, 219-22
point of, 46, 365
and purification/destruction of grasping, 49, 55, 64-65, 74
of seed syllable, 108-11, 326, 358, 371
for taking up accomplishments, 353
of wisdom being, 185-88
vow(s)/precepts, 419n5
of bodhisattva, 5-7, 19, 93-94, 100, 325
of individual liberation, 19, 93, 324
of refuge, 8, 52, 350
of secret mantra, 19, 94
vowels and consonants, 266

water dragon (makara), 126, 300, 301
Way of the Bodhisattva, The, 266
wheel of existence, 176-77
White Tārā, 364
white torma offering
instructions, 287-90
text, 393-94
winds/wind energies, 68, 82, 94, 110, 231, 236
and accomplishment mantra, 239-40, 248
and candalī, 302
karmic, 68-69, 126, 232
and kīla of bodhicitta, 122-23, 125, 128, 130, 332
outflows of, 138, 243
and rainbow body, 244
and secret offerings, 328
as seed of saṁbhogakāya, 122
and seed syllable, 188, 225, 362
wisdom(s), 68, 107, 147-48, 199, 337
accumulation of, 277, 343, 373
activity-accomplishing, 147
of bliss-emptiness, 122, 128, 140
dharmasphere, 147
of equality, 147
five (*see* five wisdoms)
flames, 167-68, 174, 184, 199
individually discriminating, 108, 122, 147, 244
mirrorlike, 108, 147, 212, 325, 349
nondual, 29, 67, 145, 263, 276, 330
omniscient/knowing, 5, 147-48, 272, 337
secret sun of, 284, 317, 351-53
wrathful, 348, 350
See also awareness; awareness-wisdom/awareness-rigpa; primordial awareness; two accumulations/gatherings
wisdom being (jñānasattva), 186-88, 195-97, 207, 225
See also threefold sattva
wisdom deity/deities, 39, 196, 203-13, 227, 315
accomplishing, 295-96
and approach, 251
blessings of, 226-27, 348, 369
drawn into principal deity, 271
of facing generation, 258-59
inviting into material mandala, 309-10, 312, 317-18
invoking and merging with, 197, 206-9, 228, 255
and mantra, 75, 226-27
offerings to, 163, 217, 327, 342
pervading sphere of dharmas, 195, 272
and sealing visualization with view, 192
and taking up accomplishments, 347
and worldly appearances, 320
word empowerment, 19
wrath, 102-3, 130, 199, 349
wisdom-wrath, 105, 111-12, 306, 327, 330
wrathful(s)/wrathful ones, 123-24, 198-200, 242, 306
couples, 168-69, 180-82, 248
as material kīla, 299-302

seat of, 116
ten (*see* ten wrathfuls)
tiny, 124, 256–57, 298, 303
wrathful deities, 112, 199
and flame heaps, 112, 173–74, 198–99, 349
See also hundred families of peaceful and wrathful deities
wrathful methods, 126

X marks/cross-hatched markings, 310

Yamāntaka (Shinje She), 186, 421n12
See also Mañjuśrī Yamāntaka
Yangga, Master, 365–66
Yangleshö, 20, 96
yantra/protective circle, 158
yawning, 235–36
yellow hat of Gelug lineage, 331
Yeshe Tsogyal, 18, 20–22, 52, 203, 375
cave at Gar Monastery, 15
as māra-subduing queen, 88
as Queen of Great Bliss, 88–89
yidam, 8, 54, 75, 196, 317
accomplishment of, 6, 354
approach and accomplishment of, 251–57
in bardo/at time of death, 64, 145, 232
and benefiting others, 364
and bodhicitta/altruistic intent, 51–52, 202
establishing beings as, 227, 342
existence as mandala of, 330
and existence-vajrakīla, 315
fleeting appearances of, 197–98, 202
friendship of, 11, 282
never forgetting, 48, 202, 354
perceiving future parents as, 62
supplicating, 364
visualizing/clear appearance of, 170, 248–49, 358–59
See also Three Roots
yoga(s), 94, 343
of candalī, 243, 302
of channels and wind energies, 121–25, 128–30, 239–40
of completion, 60, 62, 65–70, 122
deity (*see* deity yoga)
of development stages, 62, 125, 133, 191, 194, 232
dream (*see* dream yoga)
guru (*see* guru yoga)
of mahāmudrā (*see* four yogas of mahāmudrā)
of Nāropa (*see* Six Yogas of Nāropa)
in reliance on a partner, 121–25, 239, 241, 246, 248–49
yoga tantra, 62–63, 65–66, 205, 257
highest, 161, 217
unsurpassed, 157, 205, 219–22, 257–58
Yug-ngön (Nīlaṇḍa), 178, 421n12

Zahor, 18
zasö, 181–82, 218, 300, 301
See also falcon types/hosts (zasö)
Zur, 97

About the Author

Born in Eastern Tibet in 1937, Kyabje Garchen Rinpoche of the Drigung Kagyü lineage came of age during the final years of Tibetan sovereignty. When his three-year retreat was close to completion, imminent invasion by the Communist Chinese disrupted some of the trainings. Against the wishes of his lamas, Rinpoche transitioned from solitary retreat to a life as a guerrilla fighter for two years in the harsh mountain terrain. It was during this period that he was offered an escape route for safe passage to India, which he declined, remaining in the mountains with his comrades. Eventually, he was captured and sent to a labor camp. During the twenty years of his imprisonment, he became a disciple of Kathog Khenpo Münsel Rinpoche. Due to the love and samaya shared among his fellow prisoners—some of the greatest Vajra Vehicle masters of the twentieth century—the labor camp became his training ground and, eventually, a pure realm.

Finally, in 1980 the political prisoners who had survived were set free into a changed world. Garchen Rinpoche returned to the Nangchen area to rebuild his monastery. At a time when others were afraid to propagate Dharma teachings publicly, Rinpoche was the first to resume offering vows of refuge ordination to any and all who requested them—even at the cost of his life. He worked tirelessly to reestablish the monastic sangha and ritual practices that had long been interrupted.

Having received travel permission from government authorities in 1993, Rinpoche visited Nepal and India, which eventually led him to the United States, where he settled in 1999. Thereafter, he toured extensively, establishing Dharma centers throughout North America, Europe, and Asia while also building temples, housing for monks and nuns, schools, and medical facilities in eastern Tibet. He retired from touring in 2019 and currently resides in Chino Valley, Arizona.